D 37955   KALB, BEN   AND
            ANDERSON, JOHN GOTTBERG

SOUTHERN CALIFORNIA

917·94   9·50

INSIGHT GUIDES
IN THE SAME SERIES

ASIA	ISBN ASIA	ISBN USA, CANADA	ISBN BRITISH ISLES	ISBN AUSTRALIA, NEW ZEALAND
Bali	9971-925-62-1	013-056200-9	0245-54119-5	0-7018-1852-2
Burma	9971-925-71-0	013-090902-5	0245-54021-0	0-7018-1861-1
Hong Kong	9971-925-69-9	013-394635-5	0245-54019-9	0-7018-1860-3
Indonesia	9971-925-43-5	013-457391-9	0245-54129-2	0-7018-1836-0
Java	9971-925-63-X	013-509976-5	0245-54118-7	0-7018-1853-0
Korea	9971-925-66-4	013-516641-1	0245-54016-4	0-7018-1859-X
Malaysia	9971-925-64-8	013-547992-4	0245-54121-7	0-7018-1855-7
Nepal	9971-925-70-2	013-611038-X	0245-54020-2	0-7018-1863-8
Philippines	9971-925-65-6	013-662197-X	0245-54017-2	0-7018-1857-3
Singapore	9971-925-73-7	013-810710-0	0245-54120-9	0-7018-1854-9
Sri Lanka	9971-925-75-3	013-839944-1	0245-54025-3	0-7018-1866-2
Taiwan	9971-925-77-X	013-882192-5	0245-54128-4	0-7018-1867-0
Thailand	9971-925-67-2	013-912600-7	0245-54117-9	0-7018-1856-5
AMERICAS				
American Southwest	9971-925-47-8	013-029521-3	0245-54176-4	0-7018-1872-7
Florida	9971-925-72-9	013-322412-0	0245-54022-9	0-7018-1862-X
Jamaica	9971-925-76-1		0245-54024-5	0-7018-1865-4
Mexico	9971-925-74-5	013-579524-9	0245-54023-7	0-7018-1864-6
New England	9971-925-50-8	013-612854-8	0245-54175-6	0-7018-1837-9
Northern California	9971-925-45-1	013-623562-X	0245-54173-X	0-7018-1869-7
Southern California	9971-925-46-X	013-823600-3	0245-54174-8	0-7018-1870-0
PACIFIC				
Hawaii	9971-925-68-0	013-384651-2	0245-54018-0	0-7018-1858-1
New Zealand	9971-925-49-4	013-621111-9	0245-54177-2	0-7018-1871-9
GRAND TOURS				
Australia	9971-925-48-6	013-291832-3	0245-54184-5	0-7018-1868-9
Western Europe	9971-925-52-4	013-053828-0	0245-54186-1	0-7018-1838-7

southern california

Edited by Ben Kalb and John Gottberg Anderson
Photographed by Bret Reed Lundberg
Directed and Designed by Hans Johannes Hoefer

APA PRODUCTIONS
PRENTICE-HALL   HARRAP   LANSDOWNE

THE INSIGHT GUIDES SERIES RECEIVED SPECIAL AWARDS FOR EXCELLENCE FROM THE PACIFIC AREA TRAVEL ASSOCIATION IN 1980 AND 1982.

SOUTHERN CALIFORNIA
First Edition Published by:
© APA PRODUCTIONS (HK) LTD, 1984
All rights reserved ISBN 9971-925-46-X
Printed in Singapore by Singapore National Printers Pte Ltd.

| U.S. and Canadian Edition: PRENTICE-HALL INC. ISBN 013-823600-3 | British Isles edition: HARRAP LTD. ISBN 0245-54174-8 | Australia and New Zealand edition: LANSDOWNE PRESS ISBN 0-7018-1870-0 |

Photographs and text are also available for further use at special library rates from the Apa Photo Agency, Singapore, P.O. Box 219, Killiney Road Post Office, Singapore 9123.

APA PRODUCTIONS
Publisher and Managing Director: Hans Johannes Hoefer
Executive Director Marketing: Yvan Van Outrive
Financial Controller: Henry Lee
Administrative Manager: Alice Ng
Managing Editor: John Gottberg Anderson
Assistant Editor: Vivien Loo
Production Coordinator: Nancy Yap

Contributing Editors
Ravindralal Anthonis, Jon Carroll, Virginia Hopkins, Jay Itzkowitz, Phil Jarratt, Tracy Johnston, Ben Kalb, Wilhelm Klein, Saul Lockhart, Sylvia Mayuga, Gordon McLauchlan, Kal Müller, Eric M. Oey, Daniel P. Reid, Stuart Ridsdale, Kim Robinson, Ronn Ronck, Rolf Steinberg, Desmond Tate, Lisa Van Gruisen, Made Wijaya.

Contributing Writers
Edward Abbey, Ruth Armstrong, T. Terence Barrow, F. Lisa Beebe, Bruce Berger, Dor Bahadur Bista, Clinton V. Black, Star Black, Frena Bloomfield, John Borthwick, Roger Boschman, Tom Brosnahan, Linda Carlock, Jerry Carroll, Tom Chaffin, Nedra Chung, Tom Cole, Orman Day, Kunda Dixit, Richard Erdöes, Guillermo García-Oropeza, Ted Giannoulas, Barbara Gloudon, Harka Gurung, Sharifah Hamzah, Willard A. Hanna, Elizabeth Hawley, Sir Edmund Hillary, Tony Hillerman, Jerry Hopkins, Peter Hutton, Michael King, Michele Kort, Thomas Lucey, Leonard Lueras, Michael E. Macmillan, Derek Maitland, Buddy Mays, Craig McGregor, Reinhold Messner, Julie Michaels, Barbara Mintz, John Nichols, M.R. Priya Rangsit, Al Read, Elizabeth V. Reyes, Victor Stafford Reid, Harry Rolnick, E.R. Sarachchandra, Uli Schmetzer, Ilsa Sharp, Norman Sibley, Leslie Marmon Silko, Peter Spiro, Harold Stephens, Keith Stevens, Michael Stone, Colin Taylor, Deanna L. Thompson, Randy Udall, James Wade, Mallika Wanigasundara, William Warren, Cynthia Wee, Tony Wheeler, Linda White, H. Taft Wireback, Alfred A. Yuson, Paul Zach.

Contributing Photographers
Carole Allen, Roland Ammon, Ping Amranand, Walter D. Andreae, Ray Cranbourne, Rennie Ellis, Alain Evrard, Ricardo Ferro, Lee Foster, Manfred Gottschalk, Allen Grazer, Werner Hahn, Dallas and John Heaton, Brent Hesselyn, Dennis Lane, Max Lawrence, Bud Lee, Philip Little, R. Ian Lloyd, Bret Reed Lundberg, Kal Müller, Ronni Pinsler, Günter Pfannmüller, G.P. Reichelt, Dan Rocovits, David Ryan, Frank Salmoiraghi, Thomas Schöllhammer, Blair Seitz, David Stahl, Tom Tidball, Paul Van Riel, Joseph F. Viesti, Paul Von Stroheim, Rolf Verres, Bill Wassman, Jan Whiting, Rendo Yap.

Apa's editors direct the creation of all new titles and revisions of existing titles. In most cases, a project editor is assigned the task of coordinating a team of writers in his or her assigned geographical region, editing their work for publication, and supervising the selection of stock photography and historical materials.

While contributions to Insight Guides are very welcome, the publisher cannot assume responsibility for the care and return of unsolicited manuscripts or photographs. Return postage and/or a self-addressed envelope must accompany unsolicited material if it is to be returned. In no event shall any writer or photographer subject the publisher to any claim for holding fees or damage charges on unsolicited material. Please address all editorial contributions to the Managing Editor, Apa Productions, P.O. Box 219, Killiney Road Post Office, Singapore 9123.

MARKETING, SALES AND ADVERTISING
Insight Guides are available through the international book trade in 30 countries around the world as single copies or as complete collectors sets at dis-

counts. Visit your nearest bookshop. Should any of the Insight Guides listed below be unavailable or out of stock, please refer to the ISBN numbers when ordering through the bookshop or direct through these distributors.

Distributors:
Australia and New Zealand: Lansdowne Press, 176 South Creek Road, Dee Why, N.S.W. 2099, AUSTRALIA. **Benelux:** Uitgeverij Cambium, Maliebaan 113, 3581 CJ Utrecht, The Netherlands. **Denmark:** Copenhagen Book Centre Aps, Roskildeveji 338, DK-2630 Tastrup, Denmark. **France:** Librairie Armand Colin, 103 Boulevard St. Michel, 75005 Paris, France. **Germany:** GEO Center Vertrieb, Neumarkterstrasse 18, 8000 Munich 80, West Germany. **Hawaii:** Pacific Trade Group Inc., P.O. Box 1227, Kailua, Oahu, Hawaii 96734, U.S.A. **Hong Kong:** Far East Media Ltd., Vita Tower, 7th Floor, Block B, 29 Wong Chuk Hang Road, Hong Kong. **India and Nepal:** India Book Distributors, 107/108 Arcadia Building, 195 Narima Point, Bombay-400-021, India. **Indonesia:** N.V. Indoprom Company (Indonesia) Ltd., Arthaloka Building, 14th floor, 2 Jalan Jendral Sudirman, Jakarta Pusat, Indonesia. **Jamaica:** Kingston Publishers, 1-A Norwood Avenue, Kingston 5, Jamaica. **Japan:** Charles E. Tuttle Co. Inc., 2-6 Suido 1-Chome, Bunkyo-ku, Tokyo, Japan. **Korea:** Korea Britannica Corporation, C.P.O. Box 690, Seoul 100, Korea. **Mexico:** Distribuidora Britannica S.A., Rio Volga 93, Col Cuauhtemoc, 06500 Mexico 5 D.F., Mexico. **Pakistan:** Liberty Book Stall, Inverarity Road, Karachi 03, Pakistan. **Philippines:** Print Diffusion Pacific Inc., 2135-C Pasong Tamo Street, Makati, Manila, Philippines. **Singapore and Malaysia:** MPH Distributors (S) Pte Ltd., 51 Lorong 3, Geylang #05-09, Singapore 1438. **Sri Lanka:** K.V.G. de Silva & Sons (Colombo) Ltd., 415 Galle Road, Colombo 4, Sri Lanka. **Spain:** Altair, Riera Alta 8, Barcelona 1, Spain. **Sweden:** Esselte Kartcentrum, Vasagatan 16, S-111 20 Stockholm, Sweden. **Taiwan:** Caves Books Ltd., 107 Chungshan N. Road, Sec. 2, Taipei, Taiwan, Republic of China. **Thailand:** The Bookseller Co. Ltd., 67/2 Soi Tonson, Nang Linchi Road, Bangkok 10120, Thailand. **United Kingdom:** Harrap Ltd., 19-23 Ludgate Hill, London EC4M 7PD, England, United Kingdom. **Mainland United States and Canada:** Prentice-Hall Inc., Englewood Cliffs, New Jersey 07632, U.S.A.

German editions: Nelles Verlag GmbH, Schleissheimerstrasse 3716, 8000 Munich 45, West Germany. Distributor: Geo Centre, Vertrieb, Neumarkterstrasse 18, 8000 Munich 80, West Germany. **French editions:** Less Editions Errance, 11 rue de l'Arsenal, 75004 Paris, France. Distributor: Librairie Armand Colin, 103 Boulevard St. Michael, 75005 Paris, France.

Advertising and Special Sales Representatives
Advertising carried in Insight Guides gives readers direct access to quality merchandise and travel-related services. These advertisements are inserted in the Guide in Brief section of each book. Advertisers are requested to contact their nearest representatives, listed below.
Special sales, for promotional and educational purposes within the international travel industry, are also available. The advertising representatives listed here also handle special sales. Alternatively, interested parties can contact marketing director Yvan Van Outrive directly at Apa Productions, P.O. Box 219, Killiney Road Post Office, Singapore 9123.

Asia and Australia: Martin Clinch & Associates Ltd., 20th floor, Queen's Centre, 58-64 Queen's Road East, Hong Kong. Telephone: 5-273525. Telex: 76041 MCAL HX. **Japan:** Media House Ltd., R. 212 Azabu Heights, 1-5-10 Roppongi, Minato-ku, Tokyo 106, Japan. Telephone: (03) 585-9571. Telex: 28208. **Europe:** Publicitas, 12 Avenue des Toises, 1002 Lausanne, Switzerland. Telephone: (021) 207111. Telex: 24986 PDG CH.

United States: Sfw-Pri International Inc., 1560 Broadway, New York, N.Y. 10036, U.S.A. Telephone: (212) 575-9292. Telex: 422260. **Hawaii:** The Brogden Group, 635 Pamaele Street, Kailua, Oahu, Hawaii 96734, U.S.A.

APA PHOTO AGENCY PTE LTD
General Manager: Sylvia Muttom
The Apa Photo Agency represents the work of photographers for publication rights. More than 150,000 original color transparencies are in the agency's picture files, including Southeast Asia's most complete photographic collection. All works are rented for commercial, cultural or educational purposes. Agency stock is given first consideration in choosing photography for Insight Guides.

CARTOGRAPHY
To complement **Insight Guides** and bring readers a more complete package of travel information, Apa Productions — in cooperation with cartographer Gunter Nelles of Munich, West Germany — has begun publication of a series of detailed maps on selected travel destinations. Initial maps cover Asian countries and cities:

INDONESIA   MALAYSIA   NEPAL   PHILIPPINES   SRI LANKA   THAILAND

As the city of Los Angeles was making final preparations for the 1984 Olympic Games, Apa Productions was putting the finishing touches on the latest in its series of internationally acclaimed travel books — *Insight Guide: Southern California.*

The Asia-based publishing house had released two previous titles on North America, *Florida* (1982) and *Mexico* (1983). Both were warmly received by readers and critics alike. But California was regarded as the crucial step in establishing *Insight Guides* in the awareness of the American traveling public.

Lundberg

Kalb

In fact, the state was so awesome in its scope that it seemed to be *two* steps. Twin volumes on *Southern California* and *Northern California* evolved simultaneously, structured around the urban focuses of Los Angeles

Anderson

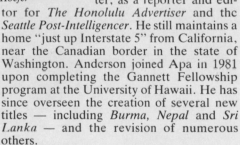

Hoefer

and San Francisco with their diversity of people and surrounding landscapes.

A 30-strong team of resident writers, editors and photographers, headed by native sons **Bret Reed Lundberg** and **Ben Kalb**, took charge of the project in Southern California. Lundberg coordinated photography and graphics for all of California from his Orange County studio, while Kalb orchestrated and edited some two dozen wordsmiths — including the famed San Diego "Chicken," **Ted Giannoulas** — from his Santa Monica office. Giving behind-the-scenes direction to the project were Apa Productions managing editor **John Gottberg Anderson** and founder-publisher **Hans Johannes Hoefer.**

Hoefer established Apa Productions in the Southeast Asian island nation of Singapore in 1970. A graduate of printing, book production, design and photography studies in Krefeld, West Germany, he is a disciple of the Bauhaus tradition of graphic arts. Under his creative direction, the *Insight Guides* series has won worldwide recognition for its sensitive cultural portrayals of leading travel destinations.

Hoefer had his eyes on California since he first visited the state in the mid Seventies.

But it wasn't until the Eighties, with the resounding success of his guide to *Hawaii,* that he was able to look seriously across the Pacific. He assigned Anderson to organize and supervise Apa's California project teams. The project was finalized in January 1984, when Lundberg joined Hoefer and Anderson in Singapore for the final photo selection and design phases.

Anderson knew California well, having traveled extensively in that state while a student at the University of Oregon and, later, as a reporter and editor for *The Honolulu Advertiser* and the *Seattle Post-Intelligencer.* He still maintains a home "just up Interstate 5" from California, near the Canadian border in the state of Washington. Anderson joined Apa in 1981 upon completing the Gannett Fellowship program at the University of Hawaii. He has since overseen the creation of several new titles — including *Burma, Nepal* and *Sri Lanka* — and the revision of numerous others.

Lundberg operates a thriving photography business based in Newport Beach, California. In addition to his commercial work, Lundberg handles assignment work for photojournalistic markets worldwide. He has been published in more than 80 books, magazines and newspapers in over 20 countries, and his credits include *National Geographic, Time, Der Spiegel, Paris Match, The New York Times* and the *San Francisco Examiner.*

Kalb, who grew up in Sherman Oaks in the San Fernando Valley, is the former editor of *Incentive Travel* and *Racquetball Illustrated* magazines. A former writer for *The Honolulu Advertiser,* he cut himself a successful free-lance career, contributing to *The New York Times, Sport, Us* magazine and other publications. He currently is embarking on a television career, producing regular segments for *PM Magazine* on Los Angeles TV.

Kalb's staff includes some of the outstanding free-lance writers in Southern California. The opening chapter on "California Geography" was the combined effort of **Roberta Wax** and **Kathleen Neumeyer.** Wax, whose coverage of regional geology comprises the bulk of the section, is a former United Press International reporter. A native Angeleno, her free-lance credits include *The Los Angeles Times*, the L.A. *Daily News, Sunday Magazine*, and *Consumer's Digest.* Neumeyer, who wrote about the area's propensity for natural disasters, is another former UPI writer who currently is a contributing editor to *Los Angeles Magazine* and a correspondent to the *Baltimore Sun*, *The Times* of London and *The Economist*, a British newsweekly.

Joan Talmage Weiss, who penned the lengthy section on Southern California history, is a veteran travel writer and instructor of English at California State University, Fullerton, and Orange Coast Community College. She is the author of five books, two Public Broadcasting System television documentaries, and a wide range of articles in such publications as *Oceans* magazine, *Off Duty*, *The Los Angeles Times*, the *San Francisco Chronicle* and the *Chicago Tribune.*

The work of three different writers comprises this book's "Californians" section. **Eddie Rivera** ("Hispanics") is the author and director of a nationally syndicated radio comedy program called *Topanga Plaza: A California Girl.* His words have appeared in such diverse publications as *The Los Angeles Times*, *Inside Sports* and *Crawdaddy* magazine. **Jeri L. Love** ("Blacks") is a staff writer for KFWB radio, an all-news affiliate

Shindler

Tipping

of NBC in Hollywood, and a former writer and photographer for the Wave Newspapers, a weekly suburban chain. **Karen Huie** ("Asians") is a free-lance writer, playwright, actress and stage photographer whose print credits include *The Los Angeles Times*, *The New York Times* and *Jade* magazine. She has acted in such television programs as *The Jeffersons* and *Cagney and Lacy.*

Numerous writers were commissioned to

capture the varied moods of sprawling Los Angeles County. The author of the introductory piece and essay on "Downtown L.A." was **William Franklin**, a columnist for *Focal Point* magazine. Formerly editor of *The Hollywood Reporter*, one of the city's two major entertainment industry trade papers, he is a frequent free-lance contributor to *Los Angeles Magazine* and *The Los Angeles Reader.*

Wax

Neumeyer

Weiss

Rivera

Love

Huie

Jones

Day

Burgess

Margy Rochlin ("Hollywood") grew up and still resides in Hollywood. She is a regular contributor to *Los Angeles Magazine*, *Women's Sports* and *The Los Angeles Reader.* The sidebar ("An Unusual Side of Hollywood") was excerpted from **Ken Schessler's** *This Is Hollywood: An Unusual Movieland Guide* (copyright 1984, Ken Schessler Productions, P.O. Box 99, La Verne, CA). Schessler, an ex-newspaperman, is now a self-publishing consultant.

Wolff

Charles Warn ("Beverly Hills and the West Side") is a media consultant who specializes in entertainment accounts and political campaigns. **Jeff Spurrier** ("South Bay") is a free-lance writer who contributes to *Los Angeles Magazine*, *The Los Angeles Reader* and various music journals. **J. Frank Farrar** ("San Gabriel") is a staff writer for the *San Gabriel Valley Daily Tribune* and a lifelong resident of that valley.

Merrill Shindler ("San Fernando") is the *Los Angeles Herald-Examiner* restaurant critic, the *Los Angeles Magazine* film critic, and head writer for the American Top 40 radio program. Formerly the music editor of *Rolling Stone* magazine, his work has appeared in *Playboy*, *People*, *Us*, *New West* and other periodicals.

The book's Orange County expert is **Orman Day**, a staff writer for *The Register*, Orange County's leading daily newspaper. An incurable traveler who has visited

'Chicken'

Franklin

Schessler

Warn

Farrar

Grant

Morrow

Lustman

Vivian

48 countries and all 50 states, Day was well qualified to write about Disneyland: as a youth, he once worked at the park as a Christmas tree that played holiday carols with handbells.

Moore

Larry Burgess, who wrote on the "Inland Empire," is widely recognized as a leading authority on the history of the Riverside — San Bernardino area. Since 1972 the archivist and head of special collections at the A.K. Smiley Public Library in Redlands, he is the author of five books, numerous magazine articles, and a regular history column for *Inland Empire* magazine.

San Diego coverage was divided among three writers. **Glenn Grant**, who presented the city and the excursion to Baja California, is a free-lance writer and publicist who has written for *The Los Angeles Times*, *New West* magazine and *California Business*. A Southern California native, he has worked extensively in the travel industry. **Thomas J. Morrow**, who wrote on San Diego County, is a free-lance travel writer and marketing communications specialist who has written for the *San Diego Union* and the *Palm Springs Desert Sun*. Morrow publishes his own monthly travel newsletter, *Travel of ToMorrow*, circulated throughout the American West.

Ted Giannoulas ("A Bird's Eye View of San Diego") is one of the best-known characters in the United States. Clad in his colorful fowl feathers as The Fabulous San Diego Chicken, Giannoulas — a migrant to Southern California from the Canadian province of Ontario — travels to sporting events throughout North America to promote teams and activities. He was a journalism major in college.

Santa Catalina and the other offshore islands were covered by **Lewis Lustman**, a bank vice-president by vocation, a writer by avocation. Lustman's work has been published in *Los Angeles Magazine*, *The Los Angeles Times* and other periodicals. A semi-professional musician, Lustman played lead guitar in the L.A. production of the rock opera *Tommy*.

One of this book's most prolific writers was **Michele Kort**, who not only wrote about the "Central Coast" but also penned the 1984 Olympic supplement. Los Angeles-born and bred, Kort is a free-lance writer whose work has appeared in such diverse publications as *Ms.*, *Mother Jones*, *Women's Sports*, *Los Angeles Magazine*, *The Los Angeles Times* and *The Los Angeles Reader*.

Peter F. Tittl, who covered the San Joaquin valley, is a staff writer for *The Bakersfield California*. He has also written for *American Film* magazine and *California* magazine. Tittl travels all over the state of California writing a "Tripping by the Tankful" series for his newspaper.

Two journalists wrote on the California desert. **Mark Jones** ("North L.A. County" and "Death Valley and the Mojave") is a

Continued on page 328

TABLE OF CONTENTS

TABLE OF CONTENTS

WELCOME TO SOUTHERN CALIFORNIA

"Go West, young man!"

That was editor Horace Greeley's advice to an opportunistic American nation more than 130 years ago. His words encouraged ambitious men and women to follow the Gold Rush to the Pacific frontier, across high mountains and vast deserts to a land of sunshine and expectation.

How surprised Greeley would be to set foot in California today, were he alive.

Today, one out of every eight Americans is a Californian. Hostile desert landscapes have been turned into veritable gardens of Eden producing vegetables and fruit to feed a nation. Isolated beaches and foreboding mountains have become recreational paradises. A tiny Spanish mission has become one of the great cities of the world, Los Angeles. And one small district of the Los Angeles basin has become the focus of a world dreaming of glitter and glamour — Hollywood, jaded capital of a gargantuan motion-picture industry that was only science fiction in the mid 19th Century.

Southern California has paid a price for this incredible success story, of course. In fact, when many Americans think of Los Angeles, they think of just two words: "smog" and "freeways." There is no doubt that the polluted skies exist, locked into the basin by ocean breezes blowing industrial contaminants against the city's constraining mountain walls. There is also no question about L.A.'s love affair with the automobile; tangled traffic jams are a fact of life in this sprawling city.

But these annoyances are minor compared to the fascination of the L.A. lifestyle. Its mélange of cults and cultures is mind-boggling: Whites and Blacks, Hispanics and Asians, gays and punks, Valley Girls and low-riders, latter-day hippies and future-day businessmen, down-and-out vagrants and up-and-coming intellectuals, *nouveau riche* and ghetto poor. Health spas and fitness clubs alternate blocks with fast-food restaurants. Beverly Hills mansions are just a short drive from eclectic surfing beaches.

The contrasts continue outside of the Los Angeles basin. Mount Whitney, at 14,494 feet (4,418 meters) the tallest peak in the continental United States, is only 60 miles (97 kilometers) away from the lowest point on earth — Death Valley, 282 feet (86 meters) below sea level.

Remnants of two-century-old Spanish influence run deep along the central California coast in Franciscan missions restored from San Diego to San Luis Obispo. Visitors can feast their eyes on this heritage, then scamper off to Disneyland to say hello to the world's favorite mouse, Mickey. The Universal Studios *Glamourtrain* offers tours of special-effects sets and an understanding of props and costuming in the movie industry. The *Queen Mary* in Long Beach and the original London Bridge, now spanning a channel of Lake Havasu, bring tears to the eyes of nostalgic British visitors. In one desert weekend, it is possible to camp in the "Grand Canyon of the West," explore a mysterious castle, scale a dormant volcano, then wave at wealthy celebrities on a Palm Springs golf course.

In the mid 19th Century, hordes thronged to California in search of gold and opportunity. In the late 20th Century, people from all over the world are still coming. The seductive lure of Southern California has lost none of its magic.

CALIFORNIA GEOGRAPHY: FAULTS AND ALL

California, with all your faults, we love you still ... only you don't stay still long enough.
— *Romeo Martel, earthquake engineer*

For years, doomsayers have been predicting "The Big One," the massive earthquake that will once and for all send California slipping and sliding into the Pacific Ocean. There is a long-standing joke that says smart Californians are investing in beachfront property — in Nevada.

Earthquakes, indeed, have played a major role in creating this state and are still a geological force to be reckoned with. Southern California's constant flux makes the area extremely interesting to geologists.

The shaking and quaking occur because the region straddles two plates of land that scrape against each other. The suture that separates the Pacific and North American plates is the infamous San Andreas Fault, a 650-mile (1,046-kilometer) earthquake zone that has been trembling for about 65 million years. The land on the west side of the fault strains northward, while the land on the east side moves ever south. Because San Francisco is east of the fault, and Los Angeles is west, the two cities actually move closer with every slip of the fault — about two inches (five centimeters) a year.

The last major movements of the San Andreas Fault in Southern California were in July 1855 and January 1857. They collapsed nearly every building standing in the L.A. area, and probably measured around 8.3 on the open-ended Richter scale. A similar quake today would cause far greater devastation, obviously, because of the dense population. Yet everyone agrees that another big quake is due. Movement is expected on an average of every 160 years, so city and state officials are gearing up now for the likelihood of the greatest natural disaster ever experienced in the United States.

The 1906 San Francisco earthquake was the biggest since 1857. There was great devastation in 1933, when a quake centered in Long Beach killed 120 people and caused $41 million damage, and in 1971, when a San

Fernando Valley quake took 64 lives and caused more than $1 billion damage.

There was a scare in the Seventies, when geologists discovered that land close to the fault, in the desert area of Palmdale northeast of L.A., was rising. As land has been known to rise significantly before a major quake, this phenomenon was seen as ominous. But more recent studies have shown that the so-called "Palmdale Bulge" is not bulging quite as much as was first believed.

Fire, Ice, Water and Wind

While earthquakes have been a major force in folding and forming the land, Southern California is truly the creation of all of nature's elements — fire, ice, water and wind. Volcanoes helped built up the land; glaciers molded it. Water carved it and the wind etched its character. It is a land of great geological ranges and contrasts. More than 500 soil samples, representing most of the world's soil groups, can be found in Southern California.

High mountain peaks and low desert valleys are within unusually close proximity. For example, Mount Whitney in the Sierra Nevada range at 14,494 feet (4,418 meters) is the tallest peak in the contiguous United States, yet it's only 60 miles (97 km) away from the lowest point on earth, Death Valley, at 282 feet (86 meters) below sea level. This is within a state that is 780 miles (1,255 km) long and from 150 to 350 miles (241 to 563 km) wide.

In geological years, California is still a baby. The coastline, where volcanoes continued to belch out smoke and lava until only 15 to 20 million years ago, is in a period of emergence. Because of this uplifting, there are only a few navigable rivers or inland estuaries, unlike America's East Coast. The only natural harbor in Southern California is in San Diego. Los Angeles is man-made. San Francisco and Humboldt in the north have the only other natural harbors in the state. This uplifting also leaves a coastline that is often rugged. Bartolomeo Ferrelo, who arrived at California's shores with Juan Cabrillo's expedition of 1542-43, described mountains "that rise to the sky, and against which the sea beats and which appear as if they would fall on the ships."

One anomaly about the California coastline is its direction. Most people think of the

Preceding pages: L.A. reflections; Southern California surf; Death Valley crossing; Sierra Nevada panorama from Mount Whitney; Los Angeles freeways; a Laguna Beach stroll. Left, the granite ridge of Mount Whitney.

shoreline as running north and south. But there is really an eastward bent, which means Los Angeles is actually east of Reno, Nevada, and San Diego is on a line with the Oregon-Idaho state border.

'Ring of Fire'

About 130 million years ago, the land that is now California lay beneath the water, part of the "ring of fire" that created the Pacific Basin. Four out of every five earthquakes in the world occur in this ring. To the east of the ocean was North America, to the west was Cascadia. Debris washed down from these shores to form layer upon layer of sedimentary rock, building up the land. But there were also weak spots — faults — in

Nicholas Islands, which lie offshore between Los Angeles and San Diego, were formed in basically the same way about 20 million years ago from the Peninsular Ranges.

Still farther south, deep convective currents within the earth spread the sea floor out in the area that is now the Gulf of California. This earth movement — only a few million years ago — ripped Baja California away from mainland Mexico, creating the gulf. Since the Salton Sea near San Diego is an extension of that gulf, some geologists believe the process many continue and San Diego may someday be separated from Arizona by a strip of sea.

Glaciers played a major role in shaping the Sierra Nevada about 3 million years ago. The huge ice sheets were active as recently

this new crust, and the evolving land strained in different directions.

The quakes and volcanoes folded and molded the newly formed land into two great mountain ranges — the longer Coast Range that runs the length of the state and the higher Sierra Nevada to the east.

It wasn't so long ago geologically that the group of islands off the Southern California coast was a peninsula. Anacapa, Santa Cruz, Santa Rosa and San Miguel, where Portuguese explorer Juan Cabrillo is supposedly buried, are now known as the Channel Islands; but they were once extensions of the Santa Monica Mountains and called the Cabrillo Peninsula.

San Clemente, Santa Barbara and the San

as 10,000 years ago, and there are still some small ice pockets in the higher elevations. During the Ice Age, some of the glaciers were 40 miles (64 km) long and thousands of feet thick.

When the great sheets of polar ice melted in North America, raising the level of the ocean, salt water was sent coursing through the Coastal Range, carving out deep canyons and beautiful valleys. Millions of years ago, the desolate Mojave Desert had rustling meadows and life-giving streams. A

Left, the lowest point on earth, seen from Dante's View, Death Valley. Center, aftermath of the 1983 Coalinga earthquake. Right, firemen fight 1980 Panorama blaze.

14

600-foot (183-meter) deep lake once existed where Death Valley is today and mountain peaks were made islands in the flood.

As the air warmed, the water started to evaporate. The mountains of the Coastal Range and Sierra Nevada kept ocean moisture away from the soon-to-be desert.

A large portion of South California is given over to two deserts — the high desert, or Mojave, and the low desert, or Colorado. Ancient volcanoes formed much of the higher planes of the Mojave Desert, which at 25,000 square miles (64,750 sq km) is larger than Rhode Island, Massachusetts, Connecticut and New Jersey combined. The Mojave was covered by the sea at least twice, and many dry lake beds exist there. Hot lava streams once flowed into the saline lakes of

of about six feet (1.8 meters) a year, making some volcanic knobs into islands.

The Los Angeles Basin

Another locale forged by the forces of volcanoes and ocean was the Los Angeles Basin. Volcanic activity helped build up the basin, which once was under water. The basin became filled with mud, sand and other debris until it rose above sea level. Folds and fault lines still riddle the area, which is so young in geological terms that the beautiful hills of Palos Verdes were islands in the ocean only 1 million years ago.

Because of the abundant sea life and the constant layering of the soil, the basin is rich in oil. Some of this oil has been known to

the Mojave, forming borax, a mineral that is prized as a cleanser.

Some of these dry lakes have developed into *playas*, utterly flat natural basins. One-half inch of rain can cover many square miles of a *playa*; a good wind can blow all the water from one end of the *playa* to the other. Even a minor indentation, such as a tire track, can upset the balance of nature in this flat land.

The lower desert, formed by the collapse of the rear slope of the Coastal Range, is younger geologically than the Mojave. One interesting feature of the lower desert is the Salton Sea. Its water surface elevation is now about 232 feet (71 meters) below sea level, but the water is evaporating at a rate

bubble to the surface, forming sticky pools of asphalt, or tar. These have left a treasure trove of fossils for scientists. The best legacy is found at Rancho La Brea, about 10 miles (16 km) west of downtown Los Angeles. In the midst of bustling, commercial Wilshire Boulevard, the La Brea Tar Pits offer a window to the prehistoric world.

The tar pits were formed about 12,000 years ago by layers of soil that built up into sedimentary formations. Eventually, heat and pressure sent oil oozing through cracks in this sediment. As the water began to dry up, the oil turned into sticky asphalt, imprisoning animals which had come to drink or prey on those already stuck. The bones of all these animals were eventually covered by asphalt. Water brought more sediment, causing a buildup. All this was bad for the animals, but good for scientists, who have dug up more than 1 million fossils representing 4,000 mammals and 126 types of birds. Among the fossils discovered were the bones of a 25 to 30-year-old woman, dubbed "La Brea Woman," in 1914. Carbon dating indicated the woman died about 9,000 years ago, apparently killed by a blow to the head. It seems the streets weren't safe then, either.

The topography of the land plays a distinct role in two of Southern California's least desirable feature — the smog that becomes trapped by mountains in the Los Angeles basin, and the hot, dry and dangerous Santa Ana winds that fan flames and spread any fires in their wake.

The Santa Anas begin with a change in the barometric pressure that sends great masses of air across the mountains from the desert, racing through the canyons to the sea. Compression heats the wind, which then sucks away any moisture in the air. Some people say the arid winds can drive one crazy. Mystery writer Raymond Chandler, in his short story *Red Wind*, talks of "those hot, dry Santa Anas that come down through the mountain passes and curl your hair and make your nerves jump and your skin itch. On nights like that every booze party ends in a fight. Meek little wives feel the edge of the carving knife and study their husbands' necks. Anything can happen."

The Cycle of Disaster

The cyclical pattern to disasters in Southern California follows the changing of the seasons, and one disaster has a cause-and-effect relationship with the next. Hillsides denuded by late autumn brush fires slide away under the onslaught of heavy winter rains, while the same bountiful rainfall promotes lush growth of new vegetation in the spring. During the long hot days of summer, when it rarely rains, the new grasses and brush dry out to tinder, fuel for fall's fires. And the cycle begins again.

As writer Richard Reeves once pointed out: "God never really intended for some seven million people to live in this arid basin, and every few years he demonstrates why not."

The winter and spring of 1982-83 may have been the most severe ever experienced in California. The state was pummeled by snow in the higher elevations, more than 30 inches (762 mm) of rain at lower levels, high surf and even tornadoes, combining to leave most of California an official disaster area.

The storms began on Nov. 9, 1982, with unusual tornado-like winds. Heavy rains continued sporadically through the Christmas holidays and into January. A high-pressure ridge which normally protects Southern California from Pacific storms had broken down, and by Feb. 1, 1983, the weatherman was reporting storms backed up across the ocean all the way to Japan, with every one aiming for Los Angeles. By the end of March, 30 beachfront homes had tumbled into the sea, and more than $500 million in damage had been done. Some beaches were completely washed away.

More beachfront homes were destroyed a few months later when gigantic waves propelled by tropical storms slammed into Southern California's coastline houses, crashing through windows and tearing off decks.

Brush Fires

Los Angeles is surrounded by dense brushland and some near-wilderness areas, such as the slopes of the Santa Monica Mountains, which cut through the city separating the Los Angeles Basin from the San Fernando Valley. Most brush fires occur in unpopulated areas and destroy only grasses, trees, chaparral and valuable watershed, but homes sometimes go up in smoke.

Once a fire begins, it is likely to char many hundreds or even thousands of acres before it can be contained. Forty acres (16 hectares) of burning brush releases as much energy as the atomic bomb dropped on Hiroshima in 1945.

One of L.A.'s worst fires occurred in 1961, when 496 homes in the exclusive suburb of Bel Air were destroyed along with thousands of acres of land. Two weeks later, the rains came and kept coming. Ironically, during the 3½ years prior to the Bel Air blaze, the rainfall at the Bel Air Hotel measured only 19 inches (483 mm); but in the six months afterward, 27½ inches (700 mm) fell, and many who survived the fire were not as lucky with mud.

In November 1980, three separate fires in Southern California devoured 114,200 acres (46,200 hectares) and destroyed 383 homes, mainly in the San Bernardino National Forest. And in October 1982, four fires burned 38,000 acres (15,300 hectares) and razed 185 homes, most of them at Malibu.

Wind and water for eons have carved the beaches and headlands of the central California coastline along State Highway 1.

par Norblin d'après Choris

Lith. de Langlumé, r. de l'Abbaye N.4

de Californie.

THE SIMPLE LIFE OF THE INDIANS

The first *homo sapiens* to be seduced by Southern California's sun-kissed climate were the Indians who had come from Asia along the Bering Strait. When they left home, they knew they were looking for better living conditions, but none among them could have foreseen the splendors that became known as California.

They settled along the Pacific Coast, the Colorado River and the inland mountain foothills. Here nature took care of them and they prospered. The Mediterranean climate and fertile soil turned any seed into a flourishing plant. Once settled, they breathed a long, collective sigh. Their tiring journey was over. They were home. Soon there were many tens of thousands of Indians in California.

Deerskins and Shamans

California Indians were a simple people. Their houses matched the climate — igloo-shaped abodes made of reed provided breezy shelter in summer; deerskins placed over the roofs protected the occupants during the rainy season; and when it got cool, an open fire was built in the homes, each of which had a hole in the roof through which the smoke was allowed to rise. Easily whipped together in a few hours, these makeshift houses were burned when they became infested with insects and dust. New units were built nearby to replace them.

On sunny days, the men usually went about naked except for ornaments such as necklaces, earrings, bracelets and anklets. So did the children. In cold weather, however, they wore robes of yellow cedar bark or of crudely tanned pelts, and rain capes in downpours. Some groups practiced tattooing. The womenfolk wore two-piece aprons of deerskins or reeds.

Not exactly nomads, the Juanenos and Gabrielinos Indians, who got their names from the Spanish missions that later absorbed them, lived in *rancherias*, small settlements of 120 people or less. The scattered tribes spoke more than two dozen tongues, but they overcame this communications snag by developing sign language for use during bartering sessions.

Their religious practices had much to do with the forces of nature: the cycle of the seasons, the annual renewal of spring, the coming of the acorn crop, the personal

crises of birth, puberty, marriage and death. Under the power of shamans, rites involved fasting and in some instances the use of psychedelic drugs. Shamans served as tribal physicians. Believing that illnesses were caused by some malevolent element in nature, they used incantations to draw out evil spirits. These early homeopaths treated the ill with powders made from weeds, berries and roots.

Their "sweat house" became a dominant feature of every village. Men would gather around a fire to induce perspiration in the

dry heat, then make a headlong leap into cold water. Ironically, this hygienic ritual became a death trap in mission days when stricken Indians gathered to recover from measles, smallpox and syphilis.

Although early Indians kept no records, since they had no alphabet, desert tribes used sand paintings to depict the meaning of life. One such painting shows the visible world peopled with friendly and hostile creatures under the stars. The Cahuilla Indians left behind many rock paintings.

Artist Louis Shorey's sketches depicted early California Indian life. Preceding pages, mission Indians gambling. Above, seafarers paddle a handcrafted canoe.

The Chumash tribe, living in what is now Santa Barbara, were adept fishermen who used seashell hooks, basket traps, nets and even vegetable poisons. The agile ocean tribe even caught fish with their bare hands. So many tons of shellfish were eaten over the centuries that mounds of discarded shells accumulated to a depth of 20 feet.

Acorn mush was their staple food. The women gathered nuts in the fall, pounded them to meal in stone mortars, then leached the meal in hot water to remove the poisonous tannic acid.

distinguishing feature of canoes made by Indians in this region was the emphasis on symmetry, neatness of finish, and frequent decoration of the surfaces with relief carving and painting. All of this was achieved with limited tools, the principal ones being chisels, curved knives, abrasive stones, wedges and sharkskin.

The Chumash in particular were expert boat builders. One of their vessels, preserved today at the Santa Barbara Country Courthouse, has been rated one of the finest in the New World.

Among the crafts left by the Indians, basket-making and canoe-making were the two most outstanding. Baskets held an utilitarian function in cooking, storing and carrying. Twined basketry — made from long, flexible splints split from spruce roots — was made with great skill. Waterproof, tightly woven baskets were made for cooking, especially for boiling acorn flour. The Pomo weavers made baby carriers; treasure baskets in which to store valuables large and small; snug and caplike rainhats worn only by the women; gambling trays and even asphalt-lined water bottles.

Canoe-making was facilitated by the natural endowment of easily worked timbers, especially the red cedar and the redwood. A

This lifestyle of Southern California Indians lasted and prospered for 10,000 years. Then the White man came and bewildered these simple people. The Indians began to acquire manufactured articles such as guns, metal utensils, axes, knives, blankets and cloth. This inevitably led to a decline of the native arts and crafts. With the coming of the immigrant wagons and the encroachment of White settlements, warfare became a unifying force. Tribes that had formerly been hostile to one another often united against the intruders. But in the end they were overwhelmed. The culture of the Indians was radically changed. They had survived regular earthquakes and droughts, but the White man proved too strong for them.

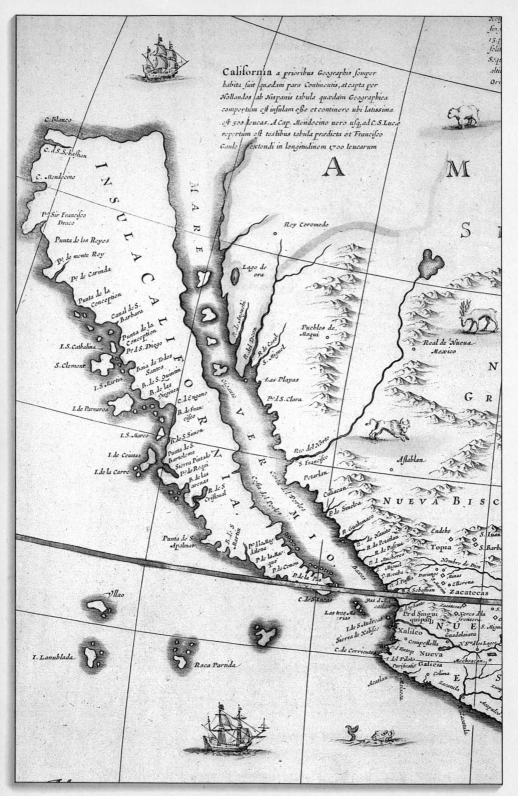

California a prioribus Geographis semper
habita fuit quædam pars Continentis, at capta per
Hollandos sab Hispanis tabula quædam Geographica
compertum est insulam esse et continere ubi latissima
est 500 leucas. A Cap. Mendocino uero usq; ad C.S. Lucæ
repertum est testibus tabula prædicta et Francisco
Gaule extendi in longitudinem 1700 leucarum

C. Blanco
C. d. S. Sebastian
C. Mendocino

INSULA CALIFORNIA

P. de Sir Francisco
Draco
Punta de los Reyes
P. de monte Rey
P. de Carinda
Punta de la
Conception
Canal de S.
Barbara
Punta de la
Conception
I. S. Cathalina
S. Clement
I. S. Martin
I. de Putratos
I. S. Marco
I. de Ceintas
I. de la Carre
Punta de S.
Bartolome
Sierra Pintado
P. de Regui
R. de las
arenas
R. de S.
Cristobal
R. de S.
Martin
Punta de S.
Apalmar

Baia de Todos
Santos
B. de S. Quintin
B. de las
Virgines
C. d. Engano
R. de Fran-
cisco
R. de S. Simon

P. de Natas
dalena
P. de las Mar-
que
P. de Cenos
P. de la Paz

MARE VERMIO

Rio del Norte

Rey Coromedo

Lago de
oro

R. de Aleguchi
R. del Doran
R. del Coral
S. Miguel

Las Playas
P. d. S. Clara

Pueblos de
Moqui

Real de Nueva
Mexico

S. Francisco
P. Tarlan
Culiacan
P. de Sineloa
R. Guachmaco
R. de Nauto
R. de Petatlan
R. de Poslua
R. Muchevez
R. Miguel
R. Horaba
R. Paltla
R. Sebastian

Astablan

N

GR

NUEVA BISC

Endehe
Topia

S. Inau
S. Barba

Nombre de Dios
Durango
Sunas
Ellerena
Zacatecas

C. de S. Lucas
Las tres ma-
rias
I. de S. Andreas
Sierra de Xalisco
C. de Corrientes

Mas. d. Ma
catlan

Zacatecas
P. d Singui
quipas;
Xalilco
Compostella
d. Hinoro
Acatlan
Xeres d la
frontera
Guadalaiana
N S. d. los Lagos
Mechoacan
Colima
Zacatula

NUES

NUEVA
Galicia

E

S

Yllao

I. Lanublada

Roca Partida

ARRIVAL OF THE EUROPEANS

"Know then, that on the right hand of the Indies, there is an island called California, very close to the side of the Terrestrial Paradise, and it was peopled by black women, without any men among them, for they lived in the fashion of Amazons. They were of strong and hardy bodies, of ardent courage and great force. Their island was the strongest in all the world, with its steep cliffs and rocky shores. Their arms were all of gold, and so was the harness of the wild beasts which they tamed and rode. For, on the whole island, there was no metal but gold. They lived in caves, wrought out of the rock with much labor. They had many ships with which they sailed out to other countries to obtain booty.

"In this island, called California, there were many griffins, on account of the great ruggedness of the country and its infinite host of wild beasts, such as much were seen in any other part of the world ... and their Queen was called Calafia."

— from a translation of Las Sergas de Esplandian *by Garcia Rodriguez Ordonex de Montaivo, circa 1510.*

Incredibly, this fictional account was believed by explorers who were swept into a realm of fantasy beyond their home seas. Calafia, of course, was never found; but some claim they can hear her singing in the La Brea Tar Pits late at night.

Twenty-five years after this legend was written, Hernando Cortés, the Spaniard who conquered Mexico, sailed up the west coast of North America. Stumbling upon a "peninsula" which stretched down between the sea and a gulf, he believed he'd found the fabled island. Accordingly, he named it "California."

But the discovery of the state of California is officially credited to Juan Rodriguez Cabrillo, Portuguese commander of two Spanish caravels. Virtually nothing is known of his early life. According to what can be pieced together from the various accounts of his California explorations, he is thought to have embarked from the Mexican port of Navidad on or about June 27, 1542. He explored most of the coast of what is now the

state of California, entering San Diego Harbor on Sept. 28 and labeling it "enclosed and very good."

In 1602, Sebastian Vizcaíno arrived, searching for suitable ports of call for his Manila galleon on its annual return to the Philippines. Vizcaíno gave lasting names to several California sites, such as San Clemente Island, San Diego and Santa Catalina Island. Of more importance was his glowing report on the virtues of the California coast that urged Spain to colonize California.

Another name which lingered was "Nova (New) Albion" coined by Sir Francis Drake, the greatest of the English seamen of the Elizabethan age. As his *Golden Hind* nosed its way up north, after an exploration of the South American waters, it anchored at the site of modern San Francisco. He went ashore and claimed the land in the name of Queen Elizabeth I, the financial supporter of his expedition. However, just where Drake landed is an issue of much controversy. Giving credence to the notion that Drake didn't land at San Francisco, but at Santa Barbara, is the recent discovery of 13 cannon and five cast-iron guns near the latter city. These weapons are believed to have come from Drake's ship. If true, this could cause four centuries years of California history to be rewritten.

Despite these early explorations, California was left very much to the primitive Indians. The actual occupation of the land by Spain began only in 1769 with the Portolá expedition. The final springboard was provided by the Russians who were fast expanding their territory. Rather than let the Russians gain a foothold, King Charles III of Spain was pressured to colonize the country rapidly.

Over the centuries, Spain had developed standard methods for settling a new territory. Where there was hostility from the natives, the sword swiftly cleared the way. Once they had been conquered, their missionary victors brought the benefits of Christianity to the "heathens." This strategy had been successfully used in Mexico. In areas where the natives were peace-loving, the missionaries led the way, accompanied by a small group of soldiers for protection. The second approach was selected for settling California.

Gaspar de Portolá and his party traveled north through what are now the coastal com-

Early European explorers believed California to be an island. This map was drawn by Dutchman Joannes Jansson in 1638.

munities. With them was Franciscan friar Junípero Serra whose later missionary work here was to earn him the title "Apostle of California."

Long before the establishment of the Franciscan Order, the Jesuits — in cooperation with Spanish authorities — had begun in 1697 to organize a chain of missions in Baja California, modern Mexico. These missions thrived and expanded for the first two-thirds of the 18th Century. But the Jesuits were expelled from all of Spain's American colonies in 1767 on the grounds that their emphasis on papal supremacy ran counter of that of the King, who maintained that absolute authority belonged to the crown. With the relinquishment of the Jesuit Order, the stage was somewhat set for the entry of the Franciscans (also known as "greyfriars" because of the color of their religious habits).

March of the Missions

Chosen to lead the California movement, Father Serra set up the Mission San Diego de Alcala, the first within the state. A native of Majorca, Spain, Father Serra's statue stands today in the rotunda in Washington, D.C. He suffered a leg injury during his first month in Mexico which was to plague him for the rest of his life. But his missionary zeal was not to be quelled. Standing a mere 5 feet 2 inches (one meter 57 centimeters), Serra eventually covered thousands of miles on foot and helped establish a series of missions which were to bind Upper (*Alta*) California into one province.

From San Diego, Portolá and Serra continued northward toward Monterey Bay. They had to, first, locate the great harbors of California that were glowingly described by Vizcaino in his report 167 years earlier; and secondly, they were to establish a series of mission settlements. Between 1769 and 1823, 21 missions were strung along the coast of California like a string of pearls around a beautiful woman's neck.

At first Portolá and Serra worked well together. Later, however, it became a power struggle. While Portolá answered only to the Crown of Spain, God-driven Father Serra had the advice of a "higher, more spiritual authority." Despite this conflict, Serra founded the first six missions — San Diego (1769), San Carlos (1770), San Antonio and San Gabriel (1771), San Luis Obispo (1772) and San Francisco (1776) — and set in motion plans to build the seventh at San Juan Capistrano.

On arrival there in 1775, Serra was just about to break ground when an Indian uprising at the San Diego mission stopped his plans. Hastily, the traveling priests buried the bells, left the cross and headed back with their accompanying soldiers to assist at San Diego. To their horror, they discovered that a Franciscan, the only martyr of the Order, had been killed. This incident led them to delay their expansion plans.

A year later, the undaunted father returned to San Juan Capistrano with two priests and 11 soldiers to officially break ground. He conducted services within the walls of "Serra's church," since enlarged. While the mission at San Juan Capistrano is not the oldest, "Serra's Church" is considered the oldest structure of a mission still standing, having survived the 1812 earthquake which shook and destroyed most of

the mission settlements. It's also remembered as the only church building in which its founder celebrated Mass.

As these missions became established, each of them gradually grew into a community where all activities and commerce were centered. Each became self-sufficient, as it was meant to be, with its own blacksmith shop, cannery, wine press and warehouses. Priests served as teachers in religious matters and in manual arts. Indians, who had never seen horses or cattle before,

Left, Father Junípero Serra in a late 18th Century portrait. Right, the interior of Mission San Michel Archangel looks much the same today as when it was built.

were trained to be cowboys. Sewing and cooking were taught to the women.

At first, the Indians resisted conversion. Yet it wasn't long before the last of their tribal customs was swept aside, replaced by a new and bizarre lifestyle which left the natives bewildered. Some *padres* learned the tribal tongues and used them in celebrating Mass. Later generations owe their knowledge of Indian culture to the few priests who took pains to record the intricacies of the Indians' languages and customs in several volumes of journals.

The self-reliant Indians were seduced into mission life by free and generous offers of food, colored beads, bright cloth and trinkets. But once baptized, they developed "a strange lethargy and inaction."

munities. They evoke to the minds of residents and tourists alike a unique California history of Indians and White man, of war and power, and of priests and heathens. Each mission still holds its own unique feature. The uncanny punctuality of the return of swallows to San Juan Capistrano on Saint Joseph's Day (March 19) marks the annual *Fiesta de Las Golondrinas* (Feast of the Swallows). The San Gabriel Mission has six bells which have rung over the countryside for over half a century. The mission at Santa Barbara (also called the Queen of the Missions) boasts a white classic facade which reflects in a tranquil fountain. The Riverside mission marks the site where the first orange tree was planted in Southern California. The candle-dipper found in the San Miguel mis-

White man's diseases, such as measles and chickenpox, killed thousands; hundreds more fell ill with venereal diseases. Their trusted "sweat houses" proved impotent against raging viruses.

As deaths increased, the Indians developed a mortal fear of mission life and its dreaded diseases, which eventually killed half the Indian population.

But the *padres* sallied forth to persuade thousands of Indians to accept the benevolent despotism of the mission system. Under their prodding, often backed by the threat of punishment, Indian labor developed the missions into a successful operation.

Today, peppering the coastline and the inland area are ruins of these mission com-

sion consists of a circular metal bar holding dozens of tappers upon which the wax is layered by repeated dippings.

Detractors of the mission system condemn it as one which promoted outright slavery under the disguise of piety. The missions thrust a totally new, but not necessarily improved, way of living down the throats of the native Indians without giving adequate adjustment time. Extreme skeptics blame the saints for the ultimate destruction of California's Indian population.

There were others who point out, however, that slavery was an accepted colonial institution of the 18th Century, and that it persisted in the United States for three decades after the missions were secularized.

FROM RANCHOS TO STATEHOOD

After three whole centuries of Spanish rule, Mexico broke away in 1821 and declared itself a republic on Sept. 27. At about this time, secularization of the missions was sought by Spanish-Mexican settlers known as the *Californios*. Mexico City, beset by revolutionary turmoil, could only send a few governors and some ragtag soldiers north. The proud Franciscans refused allegiance to the revolutionary regime in Mexico, so they left the missions to return home to Spain.

Thus, 8 million acres of mission land were fragmented into 800 privately owned ranch-

The Secularization Acts

In 1834 Governor Figueroa issued the first of the Secularization Acts, which in theory gave lay administrators and Indian neophytes the right to ownership of the missions and their property. In practice, however, these acts were badly snubbed; secularization drove the Indians out into the world of poverty and helplessness. Like other slaves, they were psychologically ill-prepared to cope with freedom. Some returned to the hills, others indentured them-

es with some governors handing out land like after-dinner mints. Sold for as little as 23 cents per acre, the mission ranches were parcelled out to political favorites by the Mexican government. Orange orchards were cleared for firewood and herds were given to private hands. Even the influence of Hispanic Catholicism sank to a low ebb. Almost overnight, the "string of pearls" was transformed into a patchwork quilt of ranches.

Soldiers who had finished their time in the army often stayed on in California rather than return to Spain or Mexico. Under Mexican law, a *ranchero* could ask for as many as 50,000 acres (20,200 hectares). Indian slave labor became part of the plunder as did orange trees and grape vines.

selves as ranch hands or turned to drinking or gambling in the pueblos.

Quickly life changed to that of a frontier cattle range. Cattle raising in this part of the world made few demands on its owners. With no line fences to patrol and repair on the open range, and no need for vigilance because of branded stock, the *vaquero* had little work to pass his days. So he practiced feats of horsemanship to prove his masculinity and to impress the *señoritas*. His sports were violent, including calf branding, wild-

Left, a North Hollywood mural depicts the transition of California to Mexican sovereignty. Right, an 1842 portrait of Richard Dana, author of *Two Years Before the Mast*.

horse roundups, bear hunts, cock and bull-fights. His entertainment included dances like the Spanish *fandango* and the Western waltz. His fiestas were fabulous; the host was generally bedecked in gold-braided clothes, dripping with silver.

The climate and the land were on the *rancheros'* side. Crops and game waxed plentiful. There were quail and hawks, eagles and turkey vultures, and the lordly California condor circled gracefully over the plains of tall mustard and wild grasses. Wildlife — badgers, coyotes, "jackass" rabbits and, in

the mountains, grizzly bears, deer, gray wolves, mountain lions and wildcats — was in great supply. The weather remained temperate except for the occasional hot, dry, gale-force wind the Indians called "wind of the evil spirits." The Spaniards called them *santanas*, a name which has become corrupted to Santa Ana winds today.

Of course, an occasional earthquake rumbled down the San Andreas Fault. The *rancheros* spent their energy rebuilding damaged *haciendas*, made from red-tile roofing set on white-painted adobe brick walls, but let the missions fall into ruins. Restoration of the missions has only begun this century since they were declared to be historical landmarks.

Author Richard Henry Dana, who came to California in 1835 to find his health at sea, called the *Californios* "an idle, thriftless people." Many *rancheros* made visits to the larger pueblos such as San Diego and brought syphilis back with them. Ranchos were lost during frequent visits to El Pueblo de Los Angeles' infamous "Nigger Valley," a cesspool of gambling and prostitution.

In his novel *Two Years Before the Mast*, Dana told of how cattle hides were thrown off the cliffs at Dana Point to the waiting ships below. These hides and tallow in 500-pound (227-kilogram) bags were the basic units of barter. The tanned hides skinned from three-year-old steers became rugs, blankets, curtains, sandals, chaps and even saddles. Rawhides were twisted into *reatas* (used for roping cattle) or were used to lash timbers togeether. Edible meat which did not hit the pot immediately was sun-dried as beef jerky or pickled for barter with trading ships. Curiously, milk was considered unhealthful and was never drunk. All fat became rendered into tallow; what wasn't traded was processed into candles and soap.

The Yankee trading ships which survived the precarious Straits of Magellan often stayed an entire year, working up and down the coast. They carried miniature department stores on board: gleaming copperware, framed mirrors, Irish linen, silk stockings, silver candlesticks, cashmere shawls and mahogany furniture. For many of the native-born, these were their first amenities of the civilized world.

A genteel contraband soon developed. To reduce import taxes, ships worked in pairs to transfer cargo from one to the other on the open seas. The partially emptied ship would then make port and submit to Customs inspection. With duties paid, it would rejoin its consort and reverse the transfer. Sometimes the Yankee traders unloaded cargoes in lonely coves and these were eventually smuggled ashore. Both sides fared well: the Yankee traders sailed south with full holds and the *rancheros* displayed their new finery with yet another fiesta.

The Mexican War

Official Washington soon became aware of this land of milk and honey on the Pacific coast. President Andrew Jackson sent an emissary to Mexico City in the 1830s to buy

California for $500,000. The plan failed. When James K. Polk took office in 1845 he pledged to acquire California by any means. He felt pressured by the English financial interests which plotted to exchange $26 million of defaulted Mexican bonds for the rich land of California.

Incidents along the Rio Grande river erupted into war between the United States and Mexico in 1846. That summer Captain John C. Frémont pursued Governor Pio Pico from his Los Angeles home south to San Juan Capistrano but Pico escaped to Mexico. Later, Fremont and his forces occupied Los Angeles for the U.S. government.

The bloodiest battle on California soil took place in the Valley of San Pasqual, near Escondido. The Army of the West, com-

manded by General Stephen W. Kearney, fought a brief battle during which 18 Americans were killed.

Kearney's aide-de-camp was U.S. naval officer Robert F. Stockton. Together they had to skirmish with Mexican-Californians at Paso de Bartolo on the San Gabriel River. The *Californios*, however, soon capitulated and California's participation in the Mexican War ended with the Treaty of Cahuenga.

The Treaty of Guadalupe Hidalgo, which came into force on July 4 (U.S. Independence Day), 1848, ended the Mexican War. By this treaty, California became a territory of the United States of America. Through fierce negotiation, San Diego was saved from being on the south side of the Mexico-California boundary.

The crudely designed Bear Flag (now the California flag) was replaced by the Stars and Stripes at Monterey in 1846. In 1850 the Bear Republic became the 31st state of the union.

Life on the *ranchos* flowed on with little change. Washington, D.C., was even further away from Southern California than Mexico City, so communication by land was slow. The *rancheros* had to depend on the Yankee trading ships. Cattle was still king. But a new word crept into the news — gold.

The Gold Rush

Gold was discovered in Placeritas Canyon, north of Mission San Fenando, in 1842. Francisco Lopez, rounding up stray horses, stopped to rest beneath an oak tree. He opened his knife to uproot some wild onions, and their roots came out attached to something bright in the sun — a nugget of gold.

Six years later, gold was discovered at Sutter's Mill near Sacramento in Northern California. Word spread to Easterners and the stampede began. What had been a single file of men trekking through the Sierras to California now became a torrent of gold-dazzled prospectors.

Rather than the solitary trapper, entire parties in covered wagons made their way west. When they encountered the sheer cliffs of the Sierra Nevada, they winched up the wagons or took them apart and lowered them down precipices. Hundreds of Blacks came to the gold region and worked as independent miners, sometimes earning enough from the diggings to buy freedom for their families. Other immigrants died en route in Death Valley; the name stuck. Ironically, more money was made by merchants supplying gold diggers than by the prospectors themselves.

The Pueblo de Los Angeles was still a sleepy, dirt-street town. The Gold Rush brought about the town's first population explosion which inevitably generated business for the *rancheros*. The country of gold saw a beef boom, true to the money-make-money concept. Undesirables created a booming, roisterous town; street killings and lynching became daily events. A time of change exploded its force upon the land.

Left, portrait of Gold Rush-era Chinese immigrant in traditional garb. Right, poster entices New Englanders to join the migration to California following the Civil War.

CALIFORNIA.

EMIGRATION TO
CALIFORNIA !

Do you want to go to California? If so, go and join the Company who intend going out the middle of March, or 1st of April next, under the charge of the California Emigration Society, in a first-rate Clipper Ship. The Society agreeing to find places for all those who wish it upon their arrival in San Francisco. The voyage will probably be made in a few months.— Price of passage will be in the vicinity of

ONE HUNDRED DOLLARS !
CHILDREN IN PROPORTION.

A number of families have already engaged passage. A suitable Female Nurse has been provided, who will take charge of Young Ladies and Children. Good Physicians, both male and female go in the Ship. It is hoped a large number of females will go, as Females are getting almost as good wages as males.

FEMALE NURSES get 25 dollars per week and board. SCHOOL TEACHERS 100 dollars per month. GARDNERS 60 dollars per month and board. LABORERS 4 to 5 dollars per day. BRICKLAYERS 6 dollars per day. HOUSEKEEPERS 40 dollars per month. FARMERS 5 dollars per day. SHOEMAKERS 4 dollars per day. Men and Women COOKS 40 to 60 dollars per month and board. MINERS are making from 3 to 12 dollars per day. FEMALE SERVANTS 30 to 50 dollars per month and board. Washing 3 dollars per dozen. MASONS 6 dollars per day. CARPENTERS 5 dollars per day. ENGINEERS 100 dollars per month, and as the quartz Crushing Mills are getting into operation all through the country, Engineers are very scarce. BLACKSMITHS 90 and 100 dollars per month and board.

The above prices are copied from late papers printed in San Francisco, which can be seen at my office. Having views of some 30 Cities throughout the State of California, I shall be happy to see all who will call at the office of the Society, 28 JOY'S BUILDING, WASH— INGTON ST., BOSTON, and examine them. Parties residing out of the City, by enclosing a stamp and sending to the office, will receive a circular giving all the particulars of the voyage.

As Agents are wanted in every town and city of the New England States, Postmasters or Merchants acting as such will be allowed a certain commission on every person they get to join the Company. Good reference required. For further particulars correspond or call at the

SOCIETY'S OFFICE,
28 Joy's Building, Washington St., Boston, Mass.

RAILWAYS, ORANGES AND THE LAND BOOM

The lure of gold turned to tarnished tinsel by 1854 and the state slumped into a depression. Unemployed miners gravitated to the cities, businesses that had catered to them failed, and over-committed banks closed.

Gradually the army of fortune hunters dispersed. Many returned home. Some chased golden dreams in other states and a few enlisted in expeditions to Mexico. But thousands remained and carried on businesses they had founded during the Gold Rush.

among the Latinos. Five years earlier, vigilantes had driven 10,000 Sonorans out of the southern mines, forcing them to take the long trail back to northern Mexico.

Resentment of Anglo domination spread. The young bandits had the support of the Spanish-Mexican community. In a 14-year period, Wells Fargo stages were stripped of nearly $400,000 in 313 holdups. Stage robberies continued until the railroads took over the transportation of gold and valuables, but these too were robbed.

Politically, California lived in a limbo.

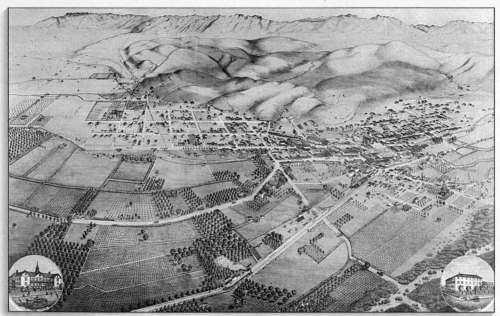

Somehow, through depressions, natural disasters and five wars, more than 150 of these firms survived. A few even gained world fame, such as Levi Strauss and Wells Fargo, which started as an express service in 1852 but later branched out into banking and still later covered the West with a network of stagecoach lines.

But these successes were the exceptions. California was in a depression. Depressions almost always bred crime; bandits were around every bend of Southern California's highway. Some foreigners were believed to have been forced into crime by the "Greaser Law" (the term used in the text of the law) of 1855. The law, levying a $20 a month tax on foreigners, stirred anti-*gringo* sentiment

Courts were either classified as "American-Mexican" or "Military-Civil," with a good degree of vigilante justice thrown in. As usual, the first group to be persecuted was the Indians. Their numbers dropped from 100,000 in 1852 to 53,000 three years later, and their tribal lands were again snatched from them.

Anglo natives also lost out. A major blow struck with the Congressional decision to review all Mexican land claims and titles. In 1852 a special tribunal to hear land cases was

Left, the City of Los Angeles depicted in an 1871 lithograph. Right, workers in a late 19th Century fruit-packing house in the San Gabriel Valley pose for posterity.

set up, and it took five years to process the enormous mass of litigation. The court reviewed 800 cases and ruled favorably for 500 original landowners. Proof of title had to be shown by the owners, who also had to prove they had actually received and used the land. Claims were hard to document because the original grants had been casually defined by ephemeral boundaries. Oak trees had died; streams had changed courses; piles of rocks had been moved. Records were often too vague to stand in court. This translated into a bitter irony. Trespassers with the gall to

Collis Huntington and Mark Hopkins) were at first neither well-known nor wealthy. As individuals, all four were strong-willed and stubborn. As a team they were unbeatable. They decided to join forces to build the railroad. But they needed a great deal of money. For each mile of construction, Congress allotted the Central Pacific 12,800 acres (5,180 hectares) of public land and a cash bonus of $18,000 that soared to $48,000 for mountain construction. Hard-working Chinese laborers were imported to clear the right of way and to lay the track. By 1869 the

dispute claims often won in court.

By that time, there existed a great imbalance in population between Northern and Southern California. Perhaps due largely to the abundance of water resources in the north, its southernmost town of San Luis Obispo was already a metropolis of 35,000 while Los Angeles had only 1,600 or so. As late as 1865, Los Angeles was still off the main mail route, and had just one newspaper and no banks. Railroads considered the town so unpromising that they demanded a heavy subsidy before entering. But the only answer to the area's strangling isolation was that same coast-to-coast rail service.

Typical of all rags-to-riches tales, the "Big Four" (Leland Stanford, Charles Crocker,

rails of the transcontinental railroad were completed and joined in an historic ceremony north of Salt Lake City.

Rail Power

Once their line was in operation, the Big Four rail magnates became power brokers. By withholding or granting economic concessions, they controlled the fate of towns, cities and even agricultural regions. Such power led to abuses and corruption and bred public ill-will for two generations. But it also gave the state the adrenalin it needed to grow.

The transcontinental rail line ("Uncle Sam's Waistband") started a construction boom, crisscrossing the state with tracks and opening up new areas to farming and commerce. The Central Pacific (later renamed the Southern Pacific) brought feeder lines to Los Angeles in 1876, then to San Diego, and lastly to Santa Barbara, linking these cities to the East.

California's dependence on the iron horse became more and more obvious during the 1880s, when a stampede of immigrants poured into Southern California. Simultaneously, steamships began scheduled runs to the Hawaiian Islands and to the Orient. San Pedro established a customhouse where foreign goods could be unloaded without having to be transshipped with heavy fees from San Francisco. Eagerly, San Diego and Santa Barbara drew up blueprints to expand their harbors also.

Orange Orbs

The thousands who jammed the trains destined for Los Angeles during the 1880s did not come here by chance. They knew why they had come — to seek out the golden avalanche of orange orchards. One photograph issued by the Chamber of Commerce was enough to convince the Easterners that these orchards existed in abundance in the Golden State, so they lost no time in coming. The photo showed an indelible image of snow-capped peaks, waving palms, and golden orbs amid dark-green leaves.

Sometime between 1873 and 1875, two or three orange trees were sent from the Department of Agriculture, Washington, D.C., to Eliza and Luther Tibbetts in Riverside. The young trees had been budded from a seedless orange whose origin was Bahia, Brazil. The Tibbetts planted the trees, little knowing that a decade later navel oranges would alter the agricultural, economic and social patterns of the area. The Washington navel orange, as the seedless and sweet fruit was officially known, became (in the words of Charles F. Lummis) "not only a fruit but a romance."

Durable enough to survive long-distance shipping, this citrus fruit hit its prime by 1889 when more than 13,000 acres (5,260 hectares) of land in the six southern countries were devoted to its cultivation. Growers formed a marketing cooperative, the California Fruit Growers Exchange, famed for its ubiquitous trademark, Sunkist.

In a mere 18 months, Horace Greeley's "Go West, young man" philosophy became a reality and families carved up the landscape into city lots. Many boom towns took root. Others vanished into thin air while

hundreds of speculators lost fortunes in paper profits. Soon the population soared to equal that of the north.

This vast semitropical, often desert-like land reached its potential. Thousands of acres of good farmland sold by the railroads at low prices were planted with wheat, oranges, grapes, cotton, tea, tobacco and coffee. Irrigation converted vast tracts of this arid waste to fertile land bearing fruit and field crops. Agricultural colleges introduced techniques of erosion control, planting, irrigation, harvesting and processing. Machines brought by the railroads chugged their way through the fields, furrowing, weeding and picking. Agriculture, boosted by rail transportation, became the backbone of Southern California.

Word of this prosperity reached the East. It drew the curious and the convinced. Part of the hype came because of flamboyant railroad posters extolling California as "the cornucopia of the world" with "room for millions of immigrants and 43,795,000 acres of government lands untaken, railroad and private land for a million farmers, a climate for health and wealth without cyclones or blizzards."

Grand hotels such as the Del Coronado, Del Monte, Raymond and Arlington advertised their "mud baths, mineral waters and special treatments." Pasadena held its first Tournament of Roses on January 1, 1889, using horse-drawn floats and chariots. An ostrich farm (now Glendale) also attracted residents and tourists alike.

The land bandwagon rolled on. Brass bands, street processions, free excursions and lunches, lotteries and balloon ascensions promoted land. Developers of Coronado Island promised lot buyers one year's free supply of water and a monthly allotment of street railway and ferry boat tickets.

Lots in Los Angeles leaped from $500 in 1886 to $5,000 the next year. The value of nearby ranchlands increased by 1,500 percent in the same period. San Diego climbed from $600,000 assessed value to nearly $15 million. Santa Barbara County doubled in population.

In addition to fancy hotels, private colleges and universities such as Pomona College, La Verne College, Occidental College, Whittier College, University of Redlands and the California Institute of Technology in Pasadena, all owed their origin to the land boom.

A turn-of-the-20th Century advertisement in a national magazine extols the virtues of Southern California to potential tourists.

32

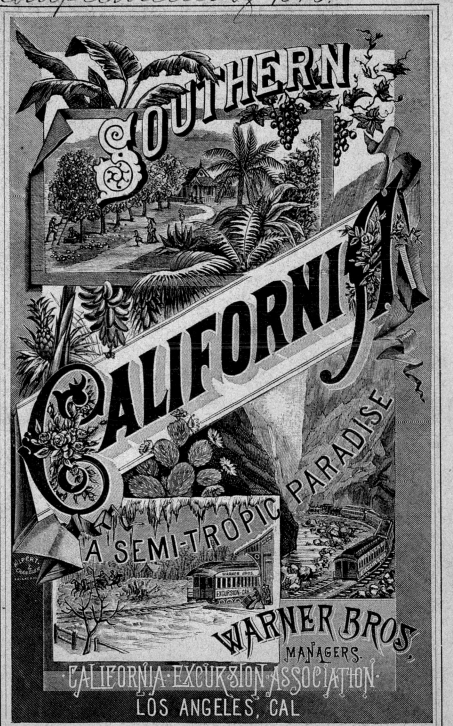

SOUTHERN CALIFORNIA

A SEMI-TROPIC PARADISE

WARNER BROS, MANAGERS.

CALIFORNIA EXCURSION ASSOCIATION

LOS ANGELES, CAL

CALIFORNIA COMES OF AGE

The 20th Century brought about more radical changes within the state. Southern California mushroomed from an agricultural community to an industrial complex, being spurred by the discovery of oil.

Edward L. Doheny's discovery of oil in 1892 in what is now the Westlake Park area made Los Angeles aware it was sitting on a fat reservoir of wealth. The "Salt Lake Field" in southwestern Los Angeles was developed, followed by fields in Huntington Beach, Santa Fe Springs and Signal Hill. Oil derricks sprouted from the hills to the sea.

The air age, which began in 1883 when the country's first glider flight took off near San Diego, was here to stay. In 1905 a balloon had landed on the grounds of the Raymond Hotel near Pasadena. In January 1910 the first Aviation Meet was held at Dominguez Field, now Dominguez Hills in the South Bay. Louis Paulhan, the genius of the air, earned $50,000 for appearing.

Glenn Martin assembled his first plane in an abandoned church in Santa Ana. Three years later, he flew a hydroplane to Santa Catalina Island. In 1916 the Lockheed

Even Venice, constructed with canals rather than streets and sporting gondolas like its Italian counterpart, became an oil city. Fresno struck oil in 1899 and began steady oil refining as well as producing cotton, alfalfa, potatoes and fruit.

Skyward Development

Previously handicapped by lack of coal, the traditional industrial fuel, the Southland could offer fuel oil and, later, electric power as clean and cheap substitutes. Ample land lay waiting for factories to be set up. The tragic earthquake and fire of 1906 in San Francisco moved even more businesses to the south.

Brothers introduced their now-famous planes in Santa Barbara and four years later planes were launched by Donald W. Douglas, who pieced together his first transport in a shack behind a Santa Monica barbershop.

The two world wars plunged the aircraft industry into a spasm of activity. The U.S. military gave large orders, thus creating heavy employment in the area. Even today, the National Aeronautics and Space Administration uses the Jet Propulsion Lab at the

Preceding pages: the 20th Century brought prosperity and a new carefree lifestyle. Left, a 1908 postcard pictured the new oil industry. Right, cast and crew held their breaths on an underwater film set of the 1920s.

California Institute of Technology and support services at Edwards Air Force Base.

Another boost to the economy arrived with the prolific motorcar. City folks migrated to the suburbs, inspiring one jokester to describe the Los Angeles area as "eighteen suburbs in search of a city." L.A. became the first major city in the world to mature after the arrival of the automobile. Mobility shaped its character as the Two-Cylinder Tourist Car chugged to life in 1904.

More efficient rails promoted recreation. The Pacific Electric Railway, started in 1902

beach houses on the water's edge as did the Pavilion at Newport Bay. Boats took visitors to Catalina Island where they climbed the hill to look down on sparkling Avalon Bay. Even a Lion Farm (in El Monte) and an Alligator Farm (in Buena Park) were opened for tourists. In 1915, the International Exposition in San Diego began capitalizing on the newly opened Panama Canal. In 1932, Los Angeles hosted the Olympics in its newly constructed Coliseum.

Yet it was the film industry that shot Los Angeles to fame, and unwittingly, it was Le-

by Henry E. Huntington, helped make Los Angeles a place of interest. With its headquarters in the city, the rail offered four delightful trips: The Old Mission Trolley Trip, the Triangle Trolley Trip, the 62-degree Cogwheel Mount Low Trip and the Balloon Route Trolley, which took riders through the Morocco Junction village (now known as Beverly Hills) for $1.

Horse-drawn trolleys on tracks still climbed the city hills in some areas because farm areas held out against progress. But, as with computers of today, new technology soon won out.

Meanwhile, each summer lured Easterners to the sun, surf and sand of Southern California. Santa Monica offered wooden

land Stanford who helped with its beginnings. In 1878 he had wagered $25,000 that a galloping horse would at some time have all its four hooves off the ground. With a set of 24 cameras tripped a fraction of a second apart as the horse ran by, a photographer proved Stanford right. He collected his money and this film sequence became film history.

The Movie Industry

With its origins in the five-cent peep show, the movie industry began in 1908. Everyone clamored for "flickers" and that brought in an influx of self-made producers from the East to crank out one-reel Westerns and comedies. Filmmakers took advantage of the mild Californian weather for outdoor shooting. A special bonus was the geographical diversity of Southern California — mountains, deserts and ocean were all within a day's drive, duplicating the entire world's scenery.

But for years directors could only shoot outdoors due to a lack of sophisticated photographic equipment. Even indoor scenes were shot outdoors in strong sunlight. The fields around Hollywood became filled with standing sets; an Arabic false front supplied the set for Douglas Fairbanks' *Thief of Bagdad*. From 1926, the Pickford-Fairbanks Studio immortalized such luminaries as actor Charlie Chaplin and directors D.W. Griffith and Cecil B. de Mille. Comedy became king. Mack Senett's Keystone Kop comedies sent the whole nation rolling in the aisles.

Before long, studios sprang up in Culver City and Universal City as well as Hollywood. The latter name, particularly, had by now become synonymous with the word "movies."

Silent movies accompanied by organ music gave way to the "talkies." Hundreds of movie houses sprang up. If a movie wasn't doing good box-office business, dishes were given away. Instant fortunes came to stars, directors and producers. Novelists earned more from film rights than for the original novel published. Studios started instant fads, and shaped tastes and ideas the world over.

The Watery War

Although the movies molded latter-day Southern California, without water it would have dried up. Since water that originated in the north had to supply the thirsty south, the state soon became divided into the "haves" and the "have-nots." Before 1913 Los Angeles depended on the Los Angeles River and local wells. The first settlers built a ditch, the *Zanja Madre*, to bring water to their fields. They also dug artesian wells.

Casting about for new sources of water to sustain the city's relentless growth, William Mulholland, water-bureau superintendent, explored the Owens Valley about 250 miles (400 km) northeast of Los Angeles. His bold plan was to construct a long aqueduct carrying melted snow from the southern slopes of the Sierra Nevada to Los Angeles faucets.

In 1907 citizens had voted for two bond issues providing $24.5 million to build it. On its completion on Nov. 5, 1913, the Los Angeles Aqueduct water gates opened. Some 30,000 Angelenos gathered near San Fernando to watch the first mountain waters cascading down the open aqueduct at the rate of 26 million gallons (98 million liters) a day. The 233-mile (375-km) aqueduct has been supplemented by a conduit and today supplies 525 million gallons (nearly 2 billion liters) of water a day. All firmly believed this supply would take care of Southern California's thirst forever. They were wrong.

Residents at the spigot end of the pipeline in northern Los Angeles were furious to find their bond money had only brought water to the outskirts, and they had to spend more to bring it to the city's mains. Angry Owens Valley activists dynamited the pipeline in 1923, cutting off water to 1 million Angelenos. However, the line was eventually repaired and Los Angeles got its water. Hostility and frustration mounted on both sides. There was talk about dividing the state into north and south. Neither side pushed this idea to fruition, yet rivalry and hard feelings persist today.

More water from the Parker Dam on the Arizona border arrived in 1941, but it cost the city a staggering $200 million. Electric power came mostly from Hoover Dam on the Colorado River about 206 miles (330 km) away.

With water and electricity, communities bloomed. Visalia began raising wheat and sugar beets. The Imperial Valley flourished with citrus groves, date plantations and produce. At present, more than 3,000 miles (4,800 km) of canals serve 500,000 cultivated acres (about 200,000 hectares) and a dozen major cities.

Even as water problems slowed to a trickle, the flood of newcomers to Southern California continued at a frightening rate. The Great Depression of 1929 led to still another wave — Dust Bowl farmers from Oklahoma, Arkansas, Missouri and northern Texas. Some 365,000 limped westward in caravans of overloaded autombiles — a hard journey captured brilliantly in John Steinbeck's *The Grapes of Wrath*. Three generations of a single family ate, slept and lived in a car for months.

As the Dust Bowlers congregated in miserable shanty towns in the hot valleys, they became the most exploited of the poor. Also deprived were the Mexican laborers, called "wet backs" because so many of them swam across rivers to gain illegal access to the United States. Politicians did little to protect their cheap "stoop labor."

The automobile ushered in a new era of personal transportation, as depicted in this 1930s photo of an L.A. family on vacation.

Modern Southern California

Although California is famous for sand and surf, oranges and what's known as the "good life," it was the "bad life" that played a major role in developing California in the latter half of this century. Much of the $100 billion the federal government pumped into the state between 1940 and 1970 went to a defense industry that thrived during World Wars I and II, the Korean conflict, the Cold War and the Vietnam War.

Granted, a good chunk of that enormous sum went into highways, housing, education, agriculture and social welfare programs, all of which contributed to the population jump of 13 million during these 30 years. But the war certainly played a dominant role in building today's Golden State.

When World War II broke out in 1941, the federal government doled out $83 million in contracts to the California Institute of Technology (Cal Tech) alone. War jobs were generated everywhere. Even though 750,000 Californians left for stints in the service, the number of wage earners in California during the first half of the Forties increased by nearly a million.

The war dollars raining down from Washington were gathered in a great bulk by Henry J. Kaiser, the man who took on the steel monopoly of the northeast and built warships. He built so many ships that Kaiser was nicknamed "Sir Launchalot."

While Kaiser kept the navy float, factories owned by Lockheed and North American kept Uncle Sam flying by producing twice as many planes as President Roosevelt had called for in 1940.

As war industries boomed, personal liberties and family life suffered. Sons, young fathers and husbands were drafted by the Selective Service

While creating many hardships, of which ration books are a reminder, the world wars also brought new industry to Southern California.

System. There was rationing of gasoline, tires, sugar and meat, which created a thriving black market.

Pre-judices flared. Despite songs about "Rosie the Riveter," women were not welcomed in the shipyards. Unions stayed adamantly unsympathetic toward Blacks, as did the Armed Forces. In Los Angeles, rioting soldiers and sailors attacked Mexican "zoot-suiters," so-named because of the bizarre cut of their clothing.

Yet the greatest injustice fell upon the Japanese. Their affinity with the soil had led them to control 90 percent of the truck farms around Los Angeles, to maintain a fishing colony at San Pedro harbor, and to raise most of the commercial flowers. But Japan's sneak attack on Pearl Harbor in 1941 brought paranoia to the California coast. Rumors spread that Japanese submarines lay poised just off the coast ready to attack Santa Barbara. A collective finger was pointed at the 112,000 Californian Japanese, who were suspected to be the enemy.

President Roosevelt signed Executive Order 9006 and the roundup began. About 71,000 of these "potential enemies" were American-born Japanese, supposedly entitled to the same protection America gives other citizens. Yet most of them lost their property and were forced to spend from two to three years behind barbed wire in relocation camps such as the converted Santa Anita racetrack in Arcadia and the Manzanar on U.S. Highway 395 in the high desert. At the end of the war they found their property sold for taxes or storage fees and their enclaves overrun. In 1952 the California Supreme Court declared the Alien Land Act, intended to discourage land ownership by Orientals, unconstitutional. After years of litigation, about 26,000 claimants were reimbursed for their losses at about one-third of claimed valuation. About 85 percent of the Japanese Americans had been farmers, but with their land gone, they became gardeners or went into businesses and professions. Eventually, they gained the respect of a society that had unjustly humiliated them.

After the war, factory workers stayed on

to create another land boom. Cracker-box housing uprooted citrus groves and new schools and freeways were built to service the newcomers. The $1.75 million Feather River project brought more water into Southern California.

Riots and Social Reform

Politically, many big names emerged out of California: Earl Warren, Chief Justice of the U.S. Supreme Court; Presidents Richard Nixon and Ronald Reagan; and Governors Edmund G. Brown and Jerry Brown.

Blacks in Los Angeles had multiplied ten-fold and were fed up with discriminatory employment and "unwritten" housing restrictions. On one desperately hot summer

evening in 1965 the palm-shaded ghetto of Watts exploded. For six days the inner city of Los Angeles boiled until the National Guard restored order.

In the late Sixties, students were outraged by the draft law and by the unpopular war in Vietnam. Protests erupted into riots that damaged property and caused mass arrests.

The state's problems were just beginning. While Ronald Reagan was governor, the long-distance busing of schoolchildren to achieve racial balance in schools infuriated Blacks and Whites. Militant Black Muslims demonstrated and two members of the Black Panthers organization died on the UCLA campus in demonstrations over the Black Studies program.

After the violence subsided, social reforms came by "working within the system." The first Black lieutenant governor was Marvyn Dymally. March Fong Eu, a woman of Chinese ancestry, became Secretary of State. Thomas Bradley became the first Black mayor of Los Angeles. Cesar Chavez, a Mexican-American, organized the farm workers in the upper agricultural valleys.

Smog, Smoke and Spills

Then Californians stopped concentrating on themselves and started looking at the environment which had long been exploited by many. There had been generations of abuse. Smog, created when the natural inversion layer in the Los Angeles basin traps industrial pollution and the exhaust fumes of the millions of automobiles on the miles of freeways, contributed to the quick decline of the citrus groves and damaged other crops. Despite legislation, studies and controls, smog still hovers over the basin especially in the summer months, and it's not likely to change soon.

Despite severe traffic problems, smog, oil spills and noise pollution from expanding airports, California became the largest state in population in the United States in 1963.

Los Angeles city today has about 3 million residents; the population of L.A. County is about 7½ million. That figure is expected to rise to 10 million by the year 2000.

A shifting but strong economy supports this boom. From 1910 into the 1950s, L.A. County led the United States in agricultural production. Freeways and urban development ate up 31,000 acres of orange groves between 1950 and 1965, but manufacturing (especially aerospace and electronics equipment) and petroleum industries took up the slack, today accounting for nearly 1 million jobs.

Developers still pit their wits and legal expertise against the environmentalists. Yet these "eco-freaks" now have a vocal constituency. The Sierra Club plays caretaker of the wilderness; the Coastal Commission reviews all construction near the coastline; and all plans for major construction must be preceded by a federal environmental impact report. Nuclear power plants at San Onofre and Mount Diablo (near San Francisco) also have strict legal controls. New voices are not only speaking; they are being heard.

Left, screen legend Marilyn Monroe, who typified the Hollywood image until her death in 1962. Right, President Ronald Reagan relaxes on his ranch near Santa Barbara.

42

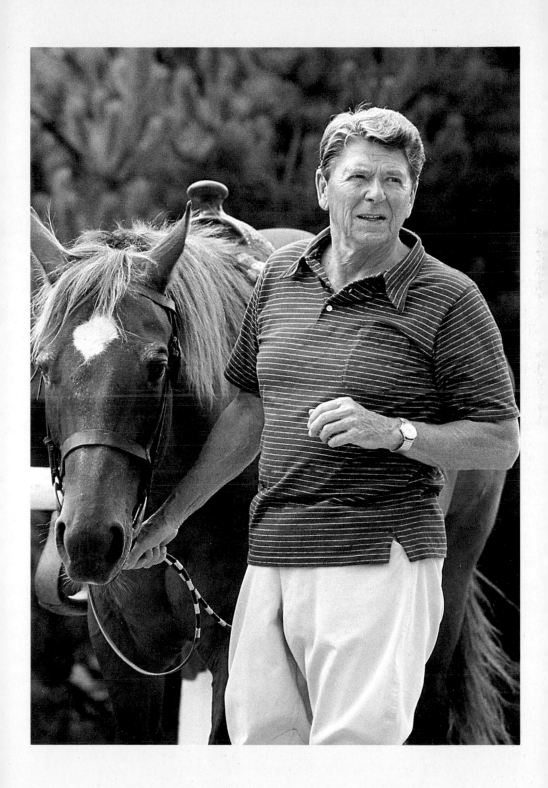

CALIFORNIANS

Southern Californians are a truly multifarious breed. Among the 16 million people who make their home in this southwesternmost corner of the United States are men, women and children of virtually every ethnic and cultural extraction, and every lifestyle persuasion, to be found on the North American continent. There are Whites and Blacks, Hispanics and Asians; "possibility-thinking" Christians and orthodox Jews, Buddhists in meditation and Scientologists in auditing; movie stars and desert recluses, pin-striped businessmen and blue-jeaned farmers, pink-haired punk rockers and a handful of native Indians fighting for their very existence as a race.

Certainly, not all of these widely diverse people — perhaps not even 10 percent of them — are deserving of the universal stereotype that Southern Californians are narcissistic worshippers of sun, self and automobile. But there is probably some validity to this assessment. Los Angeles, more than any other city on earth, depends upon the automobile to tie one end of the sprawling metropolis to the other. Rush-hour traffic jams are so much a fact of life that lifelong commitments are known to have developed from chance meetings between the occupants of immobilized vehicles. More relationships start in the myriad health clubs: "working out" is considered prerequisite to successful socializing in some circles.

The preoccupation with body beautiful has a historical foundation in the film industry, which made Hollywood the glamour capital of the world almost before anyone knew where it was. Hollywood was responsible for attracting many of Southern California's multitude of newcomers. Even today, "transplants" far outnumber native-born Californians.

Not coincidentally, members of California's three largest cultural minorities — Hispanics, Blacks and Asians — have contributed as much to the building of this society as their White counterparts. The following pages will take a closer look at these three groups.

Hispanics, comprising some 3.2 million from San Diego to San Luis Obispo, are overwhelmingly Mexican in ancestry. They are the living legacy of California's Spanish heritage, and their language and traditions still reign supreme in many parts of L.A. and elsewhere in Southern California.

Blacks, among the pioneers of the region, number about 1.2 million. One of their number, Thomas Bradley, currently is serving his third consecutive four-year term as Mayor of Los Angeles.

Adding their diverse cultures to the racial mix are the energetic Asians, including Chinese, Japanese, Koreans, Thais and Vietnamese. Ancestors of the Chinese labored in the Gold Rush and on the transcontinental railroad, while the Japanese, as early 20th Century horticulturalists, turned the Imperial Valley from desert to farmland.

Southern California is full of fantasy and dreams. For many, it is a place where dreams are fulfilled.

HISPANICS

Trends, both fashionable and sociological, seem to begin in Southern California, then slowly fade like the sun at the end of each weary day.

Yet there is one influence that defies any notion of trendiness, one so deeply ingrained it is felt in nearly every aspect of Southern California living, from eating to shopping, travel to communication. That is the influence of the Hispanic culture.

The terms "Hispanic" and "Latino" are somewhat interchangeable. They are used to describe those residents whose bloodlines run the gamut from the original Spanish aristocracy of the early 1700s to the Mestizos, the mixed-blood offspring of Spaniards and Indians. These terms also include the numerous legal and illegal immigrants from Mexico and Central America who have fled to Southern California to escape economic hardships and/or political upheavals in their home countries.

It is estimated there are more than 3.2 million Hispanics from San Diego to San Luis Obispo. By far the largest ethnic division is the Mexican Americans, sometimes called Chicanos. In fact, only one city in the world has a larger Mexican population than Los Angeles — Mexico City.

To understand the depth of influence of the Spanish-Mexican-Indian cultures of modern-day Southern California, one must go back to the 18th Century. In 1769, when the Spanish began to set up their string of missions and towns, they also began forcing their language, culture and architecture, not to mention their Catholic religion, on the indigenous Indian population. This influence has remained strong in the region.

L.A.'s Mexicans Today

Today, Spanish is heard almost as frequently as English all over Southern California. It is the *lingua franca* in many areas, particularly East Los Angeles, where the second generation of Mexican Americans has settled in great numbers.

There exists a kind of peaceful coexistence between the Mexican and Anglo (non-

Preceding pages: summer sun worshippers crowd Huntington Beach; downtown festival goers at City Hall; California blonde. Left, father and son peddle Mexican nationalism. Right, students at East L.A. College.

Hispanic White) cultures. While history has shown this to be less than sturdy at times, Los Angeles has created a unique and nearly perfect blending of the two.

One gets a sense of the ethnic flavor of Los Angeles immediately. Streets and boulevards carry the names of the original settling families — Pico, Alvarado, Sepulveda, Figueroa (the longest continuous municipal street in America) and Cahuenga, to name a few. In fact, few areas of Southern California are free of the Mexican influence. From the posh shopping areas of Beverly Hills' Rodeo Drive, to the Jewish enclave of L.A.'s Fairfax district where kosher *burritos* are sold, one need not travel too far in any direction to feel the touch of Mexico.

Tradition plays a major role in the lifestyle of the Latino in Southern California. In East L.A., where relatively little attempt is made to assimilate the Anglo world, neighborhoods have the appearance of Mexican villages with large, church-going, exclusively Spanish-speaking families, tightly knit and law-abiding. It is in families such as these where children grow up learning the legends and folklore of their culture.

One tale (and one that likely has other versions in other cultures) is about the White

Lady, *La Llorona*. Legend has it that a poor Mexican woman turned to prostitution to lift herself out of poverty. Whenever her activities led to her delivering a child, the new baby was drowned in a nearby river. After many years of this, the woman was confronted by a representative of heaven. She would not be allowed to darken the pearly gates, she was told, until she found her doomed offspring. To this day, she is traveling through the night in search of her children. She is said to frequent "lovers lanes" — a fact not lost on the teenagers to whom the tale is directed.

There are other traditions a bit less frightening. In December, the faithful gather at the old church on Olvera Street, where the city of Los Angeles was founded, for the

San Diego County and its eastern neighbor, Imperial County, are largely agricultural, and consequently have large populations of migrant farm laborers. Not all of these workers enter the United States through legal channels. For this reason, the 300,000-plus Hispanics in the border region remain relatively docile politically while maintaining a strong profile culturally. San Diego is filled with shops and stores, catering to non-English speaking clientele, that are more than ready to exchange American dollars for Mexican pesos. Meanwhile, at the border, thousands of workers commute to jobs in the United States each day and return to the mother country, Mexico, at night.

There is one Southern California Hispanic custom that falls into the category of sociolo-

pre-Christmas *Las Posadas* festival. This eight-night candlelight procession commemorates the trek of Joseph and Mary to find lodging before the birth of Jesus. Despite its historical significance, Olvera Street — a gaudy tourist trap most of the year — finds relevance for Latinos only one other time a year, for the Blessing of the Animals ceremony.

In Santa Barbara, natives celebrate Fiesta Days each August with a parade and a fair. The holiday recalls the Spanish establishment of the lovely Mission Santa Barbara. Curiously, the only people wearing the colorful and dashing outfits of the Spanish *dons* are the wealthy residents of nearby Hope Ranch and Montecito.

gical phenomenon. It is a curious hybrid of the Latin macho instinct mixed with a taste of the American dream.

The Low-riders

The purveyors of this lifestyle are the "low-riders," so called because of the gaudy low-slung vehicles which they drive back and forth down the streets at night. They usually call themselves *pachucos* or *cholos*. Whatever the name, it refers to a style that had its

Left, traditional Mexican dancing during an Olvera Street fiesta. Right, a downtown Los Angeles cinema is one of many catering to Spanish-speaking clientele.

beginnings in the Forties among the children of the second generation of Mexican American settlers.

The first generation remained largely within the boundaries of their ethnic community. The second generation was lured away, according to historian Carey Williams, to shopping, beaches and Hollywood glamour. "It was this generation of Mexicans that first came to the general notice and attention of the Anglo," wrote Williams in his book, *North From Mexico*.

A hostile feeling developed between the ethnic groups. As if to emphasize the distinction, the *pachucos* adopted a kind of uniform derived from military and jail uniforms, both familiar to their brethren. This uniform consisted of crisply starched shirts,

Anglo soldiers — even though thousands of young Mexican American men had been drafted or enlisted for the U.S. war effort. The hostility culminated in early June 1943 when mobs of soldiers ran relatively unchecked through East Los Angeles, beating and stripping any young dark-skinned male they came across, Mexican, "zoot-suiter" or not. It was an unprecedented attack which most local Anglo citizens and newspapers seemed to endorse. It certainly was the low point of Anglo-Mexican relations in Southern California.

Although he has never represented more than a small proportion of the Mexican American population, the low-rider of the Forties lives to this day. He is fueled by an odd mixture of gang loyalty and the search

buttoned all the way to the neck, and equally starched khaki pants. To add flair, they wore wide-shouldered coats and wide-brimmed hats, usually topped with a long feather. Completing the ensemble was a long chain suspended from the belt and allowed to drag low, nearly below the knees. This they swung jauntily when they "walked that walk," an exaggerated feet-apart swagger.

Pachuco women wore tight skirts, beehive hair-dos (the better to hide deadly razors, so the rumor went) and high-heeled shoes. As a group, these men and women were called "zoot-suiters," a term used with pride by *pachucos* and with disdain by Anglos.

During the years of World War II, "zoot-suiters" were regarded as unpatriotic by

for the perfect car. In a curious adaptation of the Angeleno's marked affection for things automotive, the low-rider has taken it a step further. Along Whittier Boulevard in East Los Angeles and other main streets in Southern California on Friday and Saturday nights, the low-riders can be seen cruising in their sparkling, dazzling four-wheeled creations.

The phenomenon has roots as far back as the days of the conquistadors, who rode into towns and villages in their battle-and-dress finery. It is unfortunate that the violent tradition of the conquistadors has also come along for the ride.

Most Chicanos are unassuming and unpretentious — quiet, hard-working people. The predominantly young low-riders have more visibility, but should never be considered representative of Mexican Americans as a group.

Hispanics have distinguished themselves in many facets of life in Southern California. Los Angeles boasts a Latina as its deputy mayor, the highest ranking Hispanic woman in municipal office in America. Grace Montanez Davis was born and raised in Lincoln Heights, a Mexican American community just up the street from City Hall. She acts both as a troubleshooter and liaison for the Hispanic community, a job she pursues quietly with a minimum of fanfare.

Though the potential political impact of the Mexican American community in Southern California is tremendous (Hispanics con-

stitute 19 percent of all registered voters in California), there has been a distinct and disappointing lack of leadership in their history. The single outstanding leader of Latinos in Southern California has been United Farm Workers of America president Cesar Chavez. Chavez gained fame during the early Seventies for leading boycotts of non-union lettuce and grapes, and for the substantial gains he made possible for the predominantly Hispanic farm laborers of California's San Joaquin and Imperial valleys.

In the early Seventies, attempts were made to mobilize the Hispanic vote. A political party, *La Raza Unida* ("The United People"), was even formed. But as with much of the rhetoric of the late Sixties and

early Seventies, the party — though it still exists — has lost much of its thunder. In keeping with a long tradition, most Mexican Americans in Southern California vote a strict Democratic Party ticket. Theirs is a generally liberal working-class electorate.

While moving slowly to establish themselves as political heavyweights, triumphs have come much sooner and with more regularity for Latinos in the fields of music and sports in Southern California.

In the late Fifties, a junior high school student from the dingy suburb of Pacoima riveted a country just discovering a curious music called rock 'n' roll. Richie Valens (born Richard Valenzuela), who would later die in a tragic plane crash that also killed Buddy Holly and J.P. "Big Bopper" Richardson, had three giant hits: *Donna, Let's Go* and the venerable *La Bamba*, to this day a Mexican party staple.

Valens began a tradition of Latin rock 'n' rollers that hit a zenith in the mid Sixties. Then, four boys from East Los Angeles with the curious moniker of Cannibal and the Headhunters toured America with The Beatles. In Los Angeles these days, the tradition has been revived by several groups, most notably Los Lobos, who combine traditional Mexican ballads and *corridos* (folk songs) with a decidedly American beat.

In sports, the triumphs are many. Boxing and baseball lead the way. For some inexplicable reason, Southern California has produced more than its share of sturdy and fiesty boxing champions who display their skills in a screaming-mad sweatbox known as the Olympic Auditorium several nights a week. Among the local champions have been Carlos Palomino, former world welterweight champion, and Bobby Chacon, former featherweight king.

As for sports, every baseball fan in America is familiar with the exploits of Los Angeles Dodger pitcher Fernando Valenzuela. He burst onto the national scene in late 1980 with a terrific display of pitching fireworks, followed by media cannons. Although Valenzuela is a Mexican citizen and not a Mexican American, he galvanized the Hispanic community as no one else had ever done. When he beat the New York Yankees in a gritty World Series performance in 1981, mothers cried. There was Latino blood in every curveball he threw, and every Chicano felt it.

Left, a "low rider" proudly shows off his wheels. Right, a Central American beauty, in festive dress for the L.A. Street Scene Parade, waves to spectators.

BLACKS

They came as settlers, among the first inhabitants of the City of Angels. They came as explorers, forging new paths through America's Western frontiers. They came as slaves, bearing the brands of Southern chains, carrying the vestiges of second-class citizenship. They came as free men and women in the quest for a better life in the place hailed by some as the Black Mecca.

In Southern California, Black men and women planted the seeds of new life and hope, seeking refuge from the terrors of slavery and discrimination. Today, nearly 1.2 million Blacks — 60 percent of California's Black population, and nearly 10 percent of the total population of Southern California — make their homes in this half of the state. One of them, Thomas Bradley, currently is serving his third term as mayor of Los Angeles. (He was elected in 1973 to the highest post in the third largest U.S. city.)

Perhaps that is fitting, for the history of Blacks in Southern California is a political history. It is imbedded with stories of struggles for recognition as equals under the laws of the state, and as equals in the eyes of other men. It is a story of a people who overcame baptism by fire to survive and prosper.

The Early Days

A census taken by Spain in 1790 identified 18 percent of California's population as being of African descent. Blacks as well as Mulattoes (descendants of Blacks, who intermarried with native Indians and Spaniards) played a major role in the expansion of the Spanish empire into the New World. Members of expeditions which explored the American Southwest, they set up missions, towns and forts. They comprised more than half of the founding families of Los Angeles in 1781. What is now the affluent city of Beverly Hills was once *Rancho Rodeo de Las Aguas*, owned by Maria Rita Valdez whose Black grandparents were among L.A.'s founders. The San Fernando Valley was owned by Francisco Reyes, another Black, who sold the area in the 1790s and

Left, Los Angeles Mayor Tom Bradley poses in his office in Dodger blue. Right, fashion-conscious Black woman corn-rolls her hair at an outdoor festival.

became mayor of Los Angeles.

The Mulatto Pico family included high-ranking military officials, large estate holders and two governors. Pio Pico, born at the Mission San Gabriel, was the state's governor in 1832 and from 1845 to 1846. He was succeeded by his brother, Andres, as one of two provisional governors during a Southern California revolt against the United States' annexation of the state. Pico Boulevard in Los Angeles is named in honor of the Pico family.

In the wake of the U.S. victory over Mex-

ico, the growing Black population became the object of debate: Should Blacks be prohibited from migrating to California, either as free men or as slaves? In the early 1850s, the new state passed the Fugitive Slave Act which declared that all escaped slaves or slaves who were brought into the state and freed prior to California's statehood, were fugitives and could be arrested.

At the time, the aim of the legislation was to frighten Blacks into leaving the state. To a limited extent, the measure worked. Blacks migrated, albeit in small numbers, to Canada, Mexico and Central America. To combat this sort of institutionalized discrimination, the remaining Blacks tended to form more close-knit relationships and set up their own ethnic communities in several cities.

The Visionary Col. Allensworth

The goal of some Black Californians was to live in communities free of enforced segregation. Lt. Col. Allen Allensworth attempted to make that dream a reality.

Allensworth, born a slave, was a retired Union Army chaplain who had achieved the highest rank ever conferred, up to that time, on a Black. He joined the western migration and settled in the Los Angeles area for awhile shortly before the turn of the 20th Century. But Allensworth, citing inferior living conditions for Blacks, wanted more for himself and his people. Along with four

stunted the growth of the small Black enclave. Today, only a handful of families live there.

But the history and the tradition still thrive. In 1976, the state of California dedicated the Colonel Allensworth State Historic Park, where the commitment made by the city's founder and his followers is remembered annually at October rededication ceremonies.

Living Outside of L.A.

The Black community presence in small cities outside the Los Angeles basin dates to before the turn of the 20th Century. Santa Barbara's Black roots, in fact, have been traced to the late 18th Century. According

others, he formed the California Colony and Home Promotion Association. They purchased 20 acres (eight hectares) of land in Tulare County, about 170 (272 kilometers) miles north of Los Angeles.

The community of Allensworth sprang to life in August 1908. In the *Tulare* (County) *Register*, the purpose of the town was outlined:

... in order to enable black people to live on an equity with whites and to encourage industry and thrift in the race.

The town soon spread to 80 acres (32 hectares) of homes, streets, several stores, a livery stable, a train station and other public buildings. But the untimely death of Allensworth, the man, in an accident in 1914

to historian William Mason, history curator for the Los Angeles County Museum of Natural History, the oceanside city's famous Black or Mulatto residents included Juan Ibarra of Mazatlán, Lieutenant Commander at Santa Barbara in the 1830s, and Luis Quintero, a Los Angeles founder who migrated to Santa Barbara to be closer to other members of his family. Blacks and Mulattoes probably made up as much as 19 percent of Santa Barbara's population in 1785.

The African Society, founded in San Ber-

Left, gospel singers; religion is historically important to the Black community. Right, Jackie Robinson, first Black to play major league baseball, is immortalized on stamps.

58

nardino in the late 1890s, induced Southern relatives of Black settlers to come West. Their efforts doubled San Bernardino's Black population in six months. Sleeping-car porters, rail workers, waiters and cooks on the Southern Pacific line spread the word about unoccupied land and financial opportunities in Southern California to Blacks who lived in other parts of the country. Pockets of Blacks in many areas today — including Riverside, Redlands, Victorville, Goleta, Oxnard, Ventura, Calexico, Brawley, Pasadena and Santa Monica — owe their settlement here to the railroad men.

San Diego's oldest Black churches — Bethel African Methodist Episcopal, Mt. Zion Baptist and Second Baptist — today

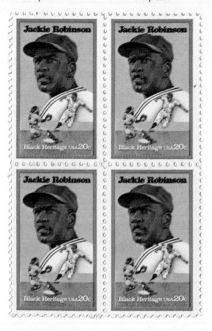

remain major anchors of the community. San Diego has also chosen to name streets after two of its most famous Black residents — Nathaniel Harrison, who was the county's first permanent Black resident, and America Newton, one of the area's earliest Black women settlers.

Black Los Angeles

Before the 1880s, the Black population in Los Angeles was minute. But the land boom of that period contributed to a tenfold growth.

The Black community of the 1880s settled around the area that is today known as Little Tokyo, the center of Japanese American culture in downtown L.A. It was there that

Black businesses and social institutions were born, including the First African Methodist Episcopal Church and Second Baptist Church. The Alvine House, later known as the Ohio House, was the first Black hotel in the city. There was also the Liberia Restaurant, J.B. Loving's Hayfeed Store and Benjamin Talbot's Wagon Shop. After 1900, Blacks moved southward along Central Avenue, the hub of commercial activity for Blacks. As the community grew around it, the business district thrived. The Progressive Business League listed 186 Black businesses along Central Avenue in 1919.

Perhaps the most prominent Black newspaper of that time was *The California Eagle*, first edited by John Neimore and later by John and Charlotta Bass. *The Eagle*, as per the tradition of the Black press, was both a source of information and an advocate of justice. Under the Basses' direction, *The Eagle* battled for equal rights in housing, fought against the Ku Klux Klan, campaigned for fair treatment ("Don't Spend Your Money Where You Can't Work"), supported organized labor, and heralded the heroes of the day. The current Black community newspapers — the *Los Angeles Sentinel*, founded in the Thirties, and *The Wave Newspapers*, established as a chain of weeklies in the Sixties — picked up the ball with the demise of *The Eagle*.

Anglos (non-Hispanic Whites) dubbed the Central Avenue district as "the West Coast's answer to Harlem," the famed New York City Black community. In many ways, it was. Central Avenue bustled with stores, barber shops, beauty parlors, drugstores, restaurants, nightclubs and theaters. There was a sense of community there, a spirit that overcame the obstacles which still existed on the "outside."

In the heart of the district was the Dunbar Hotel (previously the Sommerville Hotel). Located at 43rd Street and Central Avenue, the Dunbar was the only place in Los Angeles where visiting Blacks could stay. White hotels would not accommodate them. The likes of Lena Horne, Cab Calloway, Louis Armstrong, Joe Louis and Duke Ellington all graced its hallowed halls. Today, the Dunbar is the object of a restoration project: it is being turned into a museum.

California's restrictive housing covenants perhaps had the greatest impact on the shape of Los Angeles' Black community. These clauses in housing deeds prohibited occupancy by non-Caucasians. Not until 1948 — with the success of Henry and Anna Laws' Supreme Court battle for housing rights — was this practice finally ended.

While no one section of Los Angeles' modern Black community has filled the void left by the decline of Central Avenue when the Black population moved further west, the Crenshaw district is the closest in character to a hub of Black economic life. On the west side of Crenshaw Boulevard is one of the most affluent Black communities in the nation, Baldwin Hills. On the east side reside middle to lower-income Blacks. Bounded by the Santa Monica Freeway on the north and Slauson Avenue on the south, the Crenshaw district is undergoing renovation.

Perhaps the Black community was most affected by the cultural gap left by Central Avenue's decline. Many individuals tried to compensate. Nick and Edna Stewart, products of vaudeville (and he of early Black television programs), opened the Ebony Showcase Theatre, now on Washington Boulevard, in 1951. The Stewarts have since been credited with bolstering the careers of many Black television and film actors. Marla's Memory Lane, possibly L.A.'s oldest jazz club, is located on Martin Luther King Junior Boulevard; it was purchased by actress Marla Gibbs in the late 1970s. For decades, however, classic jazz artists caught in the turbulence of the commercial market have played there for appreciative fans. The Crenshaw District is also the home of Brockman Gallery, one of the city's oldest Black-owned art galleries; and the home for the Western States Black Research Center, which houses the largest privately owned collection of Black memorabilia in the Western United States.

Explosive Watts

Few people outside of Southern California had ever heard of the Watts district until it etched its name in flames onto the pages of American history books. The "Watts Riot" of 1965 was a message of frustration and anger that rudely jarred the rest of the nation into facing the problems of America's Black ghettos.

Watts was incorporated in 1907. Separate from Los Angeles, it was a city where Blacks existed on an "island" surrounded by Anglo communities. For the most part, the city was heterogenous until World War II. Although Watts abandoned its municipality in 1926 and was annexed by the city of Los Angeles, it never lost its community identity.

By 1946, two-thirds of Watts' population was Black. Three housing projects, built earlier in the decade for Black war-industry workers, were home to nearly everyone.

Although poverty was not the rule of thumb in Watts, many sections were paralyzed by disillusionment, unemployment and frustration. The situation was a time bomb waiting to explode. Even city officials recognized the problem as early as 1947.

It did explode in 1965. Violence and balls of flames poured through what had become Los Angeles' amalgamated Black community. Today, the scars of the riot remain. "Charcoal Alley," a section of 103rd Street (once the commercial district of Watts), is filled with empty boarded-up buildings and vacant lots. But many of the same problems which triggered the 1965 uprising still exist today.

Organizations, community facilities and activities sprang up in the wake of the "Watts Riot." The Watts Health Foundation, the Watts Chamber of Commerce, the Economic Development Corporation, the Watts Labor Community Action Committee, the Watts Towers Art Center and the annual Watts Festival have all contributed to improving the quality of life in the community and have attempted to give the area a positive image.

The impact of Blacks as an ethnic force in Southern California has been largely unheralded. Yet the race has made lasting contributions in the areas of government and politics, music, culture and the arts, films, science and athletics.

In addition to Mayor Bradley, many native-born or bred Southern California Blacks have become well-known around the nation and the world. They include botanist George Washington Carver, actor Charles Muse, jazz musician Charles Mingus, composer William Grant Still and baseball player Jackie Robinson.

To much of America, Los Angeles Blacks may be most prominent in the field of sports. Since 1965, for example, four winners of the Heisman Trophy as the year's best college football player have been Black men from the University of Southern California. Best known was O.J. Simpson, a professional superstar and now a budding actor. The championship Los Angeles Lakers basketball team is dominated by Blacks.

In the Olympic year of 1984, a number of potential gold medalists are Southern California Blacks, including hurdler Edwin Moses and sprinter Evelyn Ashford. It would be fitting for them to bring medals home — at home.

The streetwise look of a youth contrasts with the vision of optimism projected by Hispanic and Black Christians in a Watts mural.

ASIANS

At a video arcade across the street from a city college, hoards of Asians gather to try their hands at their favorite games. Dressed in blue jeans, tennis shoes and polo shirts, their dark hair and Southern California suntans give them an appearance of sameness.

Individually, they may be quite different. They may have different ethnic heritages and even speak different languages. But they've all come here for the same purpose — to try their best and, learning from each other, to win at their chosen games.

Whether the game is Pac Man or life itself, the Asians' behavior is typical of first, second, third or even fourth-generation immigrants from the Orient. Chinese, Japanese, Korean, Thai and Indochinese Americans comprise well over 10 percent of California's total population, far more than any other state with the exception of Hawaii. Group cooperation is a characteristic of all these people, and it has helped them to succeed royally in their difficult adaptation to American society.

The Chinese

Asian immigration to the United States began in the 1850s. Then, the last words heard by Chinese families as their men boarded ships bound for California were: "You can pick gold from the streets of America!"

That was not literally true, of course. But the Gold Rush did uproot several thousand Chinese from Canton in Southern China, where economic strife had afflicted the masses.

In America, the diligence of the Chinese was regarded as a threat to the livelihood of the California miners. High tariffs were imposed on the newcomers through the Foreign Miners' Tax of 1852. When gold started to get scarce around 1860, the Chinese sojourners found themselves in desperate circumstances. In 1863, the transcontinental railroad employed many Chinese laborers; but when it was completed in 1869, they were out of work again. The building of a wagon road near Newhall lured the laborers south, and by 1870, Los Angeles had a

Chinese community of 1720 persons.

Predominantly farmers in China, these immigrants' abilities were fruitfully adapted to mining, harvesting, railroad building, cooking and cleaning, as well as farming. Generally, the Chinese settled close to their occupational sites. As a result, where there were railroad tracks, there were Chinese.

The character of early Chinese immigrants still lingers in the Southern Pacific railyard just north of where the Chinese first settled in Los Angeles. Formerly called "Nigger Alley," its site was a block south of the

Plaza. In the Garnier buildings, near Macy and Los Angeles streets, basement walls were broken out to create catacombs where wares were sold and where prohibited gambling was a way of life.

The intention to get rich quickly and return home to China made the early Chinese society in America a male-dominated one. Chinese women were exclusive commodities. One beautiful young woman, sold into prostitution and smuggled into the United States, became the love object of two powerful men in 1871. Outside the Garnier buildings, the right to her ownership was to be decided by bullets. A deputy died in an attempt to stop the duel, and a young boy also was killed. Days later, a mob of 500

Sights at a Japanese festival in downtown L.A.'s Little Tokyo: left, a kimono-clad traditional dancer; right, a contemporary presentation of Oriental art.

63

Calfornians showed their outrage by chasing down 19 innocent Chinese and hanging them from a tree. That infamous tree stood for many more years, but today it has given way to an on-ramp for the Hollywood Freeway.

Despite incidents like this in Los Angeles and the tearing down of "Nigger Alley" in 1891, the Chinese community continued to grow. The basic shape of Chinatown had been determined, with Alameda, Apablasa, Marchessault and Los Angeles streets its main thoroughfares. By the turn of the century, the Chinese population in L.A. was about 2,000. By 1910, there were at least 15 Chinese restaurants and 17 produce companies.

During the Twenties, some Chinese began moving to the City Market area on San Pe-

just two blocks east of New Chinatown. Chinese peddled their wares from shop houses, and rickshaws were a unique way of getting around. Mysteriously, China City was burned down by arsonists in 1949.

Since 1967, Monterey Park and Alhambra have attracted a large population of Chinese, especially new arrivals from Hong Kong and Taiwan. Although there are no formally established Chinatowns in these cities, their main shopping thoroughfares are of heavily Chinese influence. In Monterey Park, this district is on Garvey Avenue between Atlantic Boulevard and Garfield Avenue; and in Alhambra, it is between the San Bernardino Freeway and Valley Boulevard.

Los Angeles Chinatown today teems with activity to accommodate its growing popula-

dro Street and 9th Avenue. There they sold wholesale produce and opened shops and restaurants. Today, this area is still a small Chinatown.

The Chinese were not restricted to Los Angeles. Jobs in Riverside's orange and citrus groves drew many Chinese, although they left when the jobs dried up. They moved as far east as San Bernardino and south to San Diego, though no formal Chinatowns developed there.

To make way for the building of Union Station in 1933, half of L.A. Chinatown east of Alameda Street was obliterated. Flourishing on North Broadway, New Chinatown had its gala opening in 1938. In 1939, China City opened on North Spring Street,

tion. Novelty shops, law offices, grocery stores, movie theaters, jewelry shops and restaurants line its streets, with pedestrian traffic painting a lively scene. Dressed in a printed polyester pantsuit, a Chinese grandmother minds her grandchildren while shopping in the live poultry market. A young Chinese American girl with dyed patches of green, orange and pink hair, clad in a tight black leather outfit, rushes into Madame Wong's to hear a New Wave band. Sitting on benches in the arcade, retired men look up

Left, tastes of the Far East light up the night sky in Chinatown. Right, most of today's third-generation Asian Americans have assimilated well into California society.

from their Chinese language newspapers to argue the details of an ancient legend. These are everyday scenes in Chinatown.

The Japanese

The mass migration of the Japanese at the turn of the century also brought laborers and farmers to America. Refused the right to own land, the Japanese created special means of earning their livelihoods. Japanese gardeners have sculpted the Southern California landscape, for example. The shrubs at Disneyland — trimmed to resemble rhinoceroses, tigers and other animals — are the work of Japanese gardeners.

As native-born Americans, the children of Japanese immigrants did have the right to

with the Chinese settlement, this Japanese community stayed put, only shifting slightly east or south to accommodate its growth.

But the life which the Japanese knew in America dramatically changed on Dec. 7, 1941. The sneak air attack on Pearl Harbor was followed by the dictates of Executive Order 9066. Persons of Japanese ancestry had to vacate their homes for "protective" stays at internment camps throughout the United States. Lives were uprooted. Long, hard efforts by the Japanese to cultivate their farmlands went uncompensated in the scramble to sell their property. Gathered in churches and meeting halls, the evacuees huddled with their belongings, parted with friends, and cried because they couldn't understand why this was happening. Three

own land. However, the land offered to them was largely desert wasteland. Determined to make better lives for themselves, they turned deserts such as the Imperial Valley into fertile farmlands. Their skill contributed to the flourishing agriculture and flowering beauty of Southern California, integrating the Japanese into American society.

During the Twenties, the Japanese began to establish an area near 1st and Central streets in Los Angeles. It became known as Little Tokyo. Shops sold fresh produce and wares. Japanese delicacies competed with Chinese. In its early years, Little Tokyo was packed with pool halls where Japanese men spent much of their idle time. In contrast

to four years of internment — supposedly "proof" of their allegiance to the United States — left second-generation Japanese Americans (*nisei*) traumatized.

The experience made new impressions on the *nisei*. At the end of World War II, many recoiled in shame. In an effort to see that such an event could never recur, the *nisei* tried to sever links between their children (*sansei*, or third generation) and their Japanese heritage.

The *sansei* grew up largely unaware of the specifics of how their parents spent the war years. They assimilated well into the American community. They spoke little or no Japanese; many never even studied Japanese culture. It wasn't until the late

Seventies, with the issue of reparations for interned Japanese Americans, that *sansei* were seized by a desire to understand this unpleasant chapter in Japanese American history.

The evacuation of the Japanese and the Japanese Americans left Little Tokyo bare. During these years, Blacks moved in. But the district's characteristics changed little. The end of the war in 1945 brought the Japanese right back to Little Tokyo. This time, however, the Japanese had little capital. Some continued to live in Little Tokyo, but others moved to Torrance, Carson, Gardena and Monterey Park.

Today, Little Tokyo is an ever-expanding community with a changing face. The New Otani Hotel is impressive with its addition of

Weller Court, a shopping complex. Older buildings have been torn down to erect tall office fixtures. On 3rd and San Pedro streets is the $1 million Japanese American Cultural and Community Center. In May 1983, its new 800-seat Japan America Theater was christened with a production by the Grand Kabuki Company from Japan. Among the most visible Asians in Southern California today is Thomas Noguchi, the controversial Los Angeles County coroner.

Other Asians

Although Chinese had been in America for more than a century and Japanese for over half that, Koreans were not well represented in the United States until after the Korean War of the early Fifties.

Intermarriage with servicemen and dissatisfaction with the change in Korean government brought many Koreans to America. Unlike their agriculturally oriented Chinese and Japanese counterparts, they were mainly business people. They established restaurants, martial-arts schools (*Tae Kwan Do*), travel agencies and driving schools, to name a few.

Olympic Boulevard, between Hoover and Western avenues, is today a bustling Korean community. The Korean alphabet is displayed alongside English translations on pagoda-style structures. In September, a traditional parade celebrates the harvest and brightens Olympic Boulevard.

As newly arrived immigrants who are still faced with language problems and unfamiliarity with American culture, Koreans tend to stay in their own society. This includes Korean-language newspapers, television stations, a cultural center and business associations. All of these things reinforce the feeling of home comforts.

Similar in circumstances, the Indochinese people — Vietnamese, Cambodians, Lao and Hmong — migrated *en masse* in 1975 following the Vietnam War. Many ethnic Chinese were forced out of Vietnam by the communist takeover. The price of evacuating was high; the refugees who escaped to America were chiefly upper-middle class. This is one of the prime factors differentiating Vietnamese immigrants from most others in America. Entering Southern California by the thousands, they disturbed the ethnic balance of Orange County, Anaheim and Long Beach, all heavily White. Their presence and customs have not always been well received by their neighbors.

Nor have those of the Thais, who began moving to America at about the same time. The beautiful Wat Thai Buddhist Temple in Panorama City is gaining attention with its big celebrations, much to the dismay of many nearby American neighbors. Since their migration to California, Thais generally have inhabited the Hollywood area, where their restaurants have thrived.

Other large Southeast Asian communities can be found adjacent to Chinatown (Vietnamese), in Garden Grove (Vietnamese) and in Wilmington (Filipino).

Left, Vietnamese refugees display memories of their family's escape from Indochina. Right, Asian businessmen represent an important link between philosophies of East and West.

PLACES

Southern California is Hollywood and Disneyland, Sea World and Knott's Berry Farm, Universal Studios and the San Diego Zoo. Glitter, glamour, Donald Duck, performing whales, roller coasters, movie stars, koalas: such images come readily to mind at the mention of these place names. Here are "Fantasy Island" and the "Love Boat," Beverly Hills and the fabulous Hearst Castle. Here are Howard Hughes' bizarre *Spruce Goose* and the opulent J. Paul Getty Museum at Malibu.

But Southern California is also San Juan Capistrano and Santa Catalina, Palm Springs and Bakersfield, Death Valley and the Rose Bowl. Rough and rugged terrain challenges backpackers to turn off the roads and vanish into looming woods, leaving civilization behind. There are desert areas sprinkled with cacti, Indian dwellings built before Europeans surmised a "New World," snow-capped mountains, valleys drowned in wildflowers and wildlife, parks, lakes and canyons.

Most of all, Southern California is Los Angeles, the sprawling, smoggy metropolis straddling the notorious San Andreas Fault. Wedged between the rolling Pacific surf and the arid Mojave Desert, it has maintained much of its old Spanish flavor while becoming a cosmopolitan 20th Century entertainment capital. In downtown L.A., the ambience is informal and intimate. Stroll through the narrow alleyways off Olvera Street; listen to the echoes of the past within museum walls; shop for Mexican and Japanese crafts; kick off your shoes and feel the track on which Olympic heroes sprint to international fame.

In the following pages, marginal maps will show you which region you are in, while smaller marks will identify your specific location.

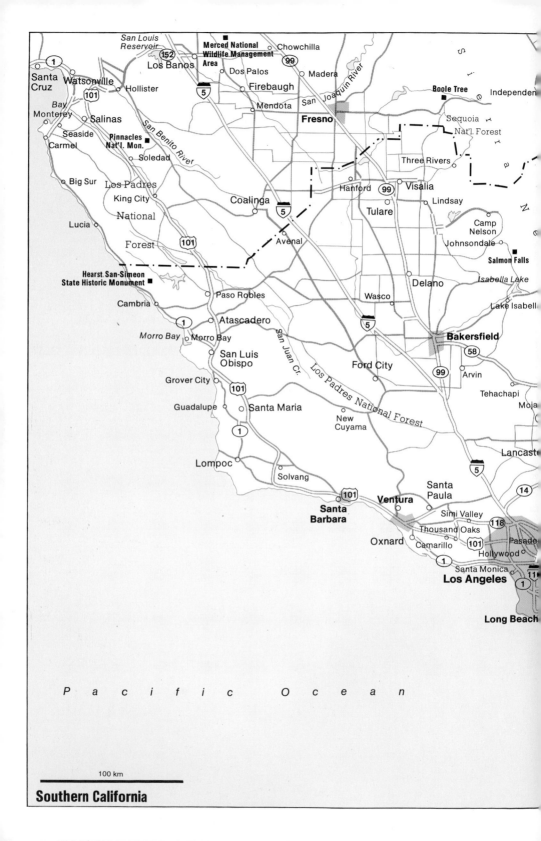

Southern California

100 km

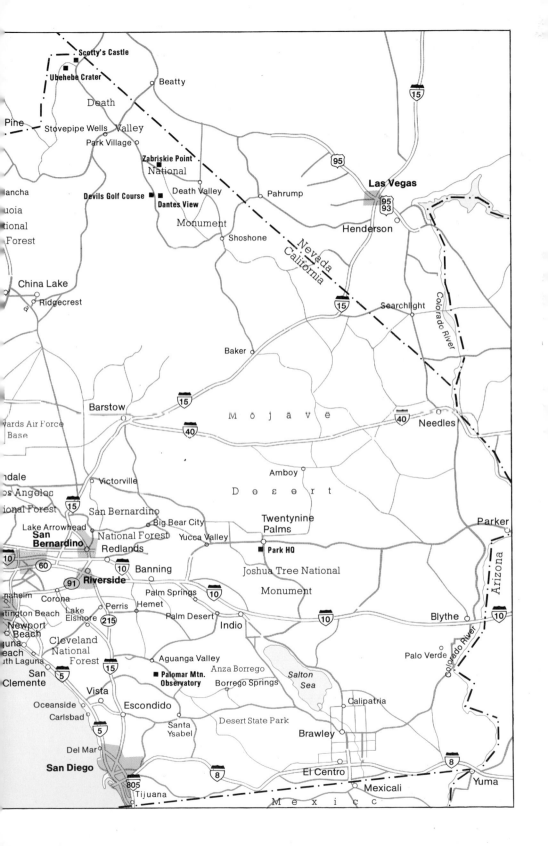

LOS ANGELES: CITY OF THE ANGELS

Los Angeles is hypnotically seductive. Graceful, gravity-defying palm trees sway next to rippling aquamarine pools. Perfect bronzed bodies recline under the hushed midday sun in exotic beach areas. Sleek automobiles with sunroofs open dodge in and out of traffic at sunset.

The images play on, perpetuated by the very L.A. residents who created them. Los Angeles has digested its own astounding mythology and embraced its own narcissistic reflection to the point that there is no longer a dividing line between the factual L.A. and the fantastical one.

Non-Southern Californians often hold a very different image of Los Angeles — that of a concrete, smog-breathing monster city. In fact, visitors complain about the technicolor air far more vociferously than L.A. residents themselves. In the past two decades, Angelenos (as the residents are known) have taken major steps to reduce the amount of smog in their air. Had they not done so, they might have had to match their clothes to the polluted hues of the sky.

There are very few other cities in the world which have been so thoroughly shaped by itinerant dream-makers. The alluring appeal of the golden city poised on the edge of the Pacific, ripe for new beginnings, has enticed thousands from every corner of America. Consequently, this unique city is just beginning to carve its own traditions.

Heart Like a Wheel

One tradition near and dear to the Angeleno's heart guzzles gas and is air-conditioned. There is no doubt that Los Angeles is consumed by its affair with the automobile.

Most of America's major urban centers had their boundaries rigidly set before the internal combustion engine belched to life. But L.A. was and is geographically amorphous, constantly evolving along an undisturbed, seemingly endless, Pacific coastline. Other American cities patterned themselves after Europe's "walking cities"; L.A.

embraced the automobile and felt no confines.

Thanks to Henry Ford and the assembly-line process, the City of the Angels quickly became the City of the Automobile. Los Angeles became a kaleidoscopically uneven patchwork of suburban areas, linked casually together under the vague concept of "Greater L.A." To many, Los Angeles seemed to say: "Have your cake and eat it, too." Here was the centrality and glamour of a sophisticated metropolis coupled with the treasured tranquility of country living.

But what started out decades ago as a carefree, flirtatious affair with the passenger car soon careened into a full-blown relationship with a lifetime commitment. The automobile has united the city to the point where distances are measured not in miles but in estimated driving time.

The downside of Los Angeles' sense of absolute mobility and freeway freedom is that drivers spend an inordinate part of each working day behind the wheel, often combating bumper-to-bumper bottlenecks on one of the country's busiest freeway systems.

Preceding pages, L.A. glitter from Griffith Park observatory. Left, rush hour on the Hollywood Freeway. right, actress Debra Wakeham.

Although for years local politicians have promised a metropolitan rail system, plans for a subway are still on the drawing board as the city's movers and shakers argue about proposed pathways and possible final destinations. If the politics are ironed out, it might be completed in the 1990s.

One wonders whether L.A. residents would use such a system. No one has yet come up with a viable plan to convince locals to abandon their cars for the pleasures of a community underground rail system. Even a concentrated effort at using a car-pool system proved futile.

The California Look

It is hardly surprising that all of these hours of freeway frustration have exploded into an obsession with health spas, gymnasiums and aerobic centers. As if to compensate for the stressful hours spent nervously inhaling exhaust fumes, residents of the city have flocked to sweat emporiums in nearly every part of the suburban basin. Whether it be pumping iron or just luxuriating in a heated jacuzzi, residents have found a new social institution for the inimitable L.A. lifestyle.

Of course, Los Angeles' passion for all things physical is hardly new. Thanks to the city's semi-tropical climate, residents always have been able to exhibit a maximum of skin nearly year-round. Local fashion designers have cooperated, creating the *California Look*, which revolves around the concepts that assets shouldn't be hidden. They should be flaunted.

Not only are health spas the new cathedrals of the physically inclined, the workout spots have eclipsed the infamous singles bars as gathering places to finalize new fast-lane contacts. Cosexual aerobic classes and whirlpool dips have ushered a whole new, slightly sweaty vocabulary into L.A.'s dating lexicon. In the Seventies, the cliché opener was: "So what's your sign?" In the Eighties, at least in Los Angeles, it is clearly: "So where do you work out?"

In the heady, palm-festooned atmosphere that so readily fostered an appreciation for pet rocks, terrariums and macramé, few are surprised by this latest fad. National trends have a way of sprouting up first in Southern California, and health spas are just the newest

Realization of the California dream.

in a long list of popular L.A.-born diversions to infect the rest of America.

Celluloid Idols

Los Angeles' infatuation with the physical is historically rooted. Ever since D.W. Griffith pointed a primitive camera at his stable of aspiring starlets, Hollywood's film efforts have celebrated seductive physicality. With these colossal silver-screen projections, L.A. presented celluloid idols with uncanny regularity. Hollywood's sexuality became a passion (many would argue an obsession) for most of Los Angeles.

L.A. is a company town — or more accurately, an industry town. Movie and television shows are "The Industry's" products, with the studios that make them dotting the suburban landscape like the steel furnaces of the Northeast. The city of Los Angeles is kept in a perpetual state of show-biz dazzle, with film crews continually invading local neighborhoods like renegade battalions on frequent military maneuvers.

Few would dispute that Los Angeles is the world's film capital. No wonder, then, that great talents from around the globe have gravitated to L.A. and made a remarkable difference in the quality of the city's life. During the past 60 years, some of the century's greatest writers, directors and artists have fashioned one of the most electric, unpredictable, creative cities around. They have produced milestones in the film industry while contributing to the artistic evolution of the region.

Los Angeles today continues to grow, flexing its creative muscles in the music and video industries, and in the process once again influencing aesthetic choices around the world.

Los Angeles is a mesmerizing study in diverse, mutually appreciative lifestyles. From the relaxed beach scene where local surfers spend unhurried days paddling for the ultimate ride, to the city's bustling commercial centers where the business-oriented anxiously negotiate for the ultimate deal, L.A. fosters a climate of limitless possibilities for nearly everyone.

As Los Angeles grows, its astoundingly diverse ethnic populations expand as well, assisting in the creation of a richly textured cultural environment.

eft, keeping shape with ane Fonda at er workout udio. Right "he Look."

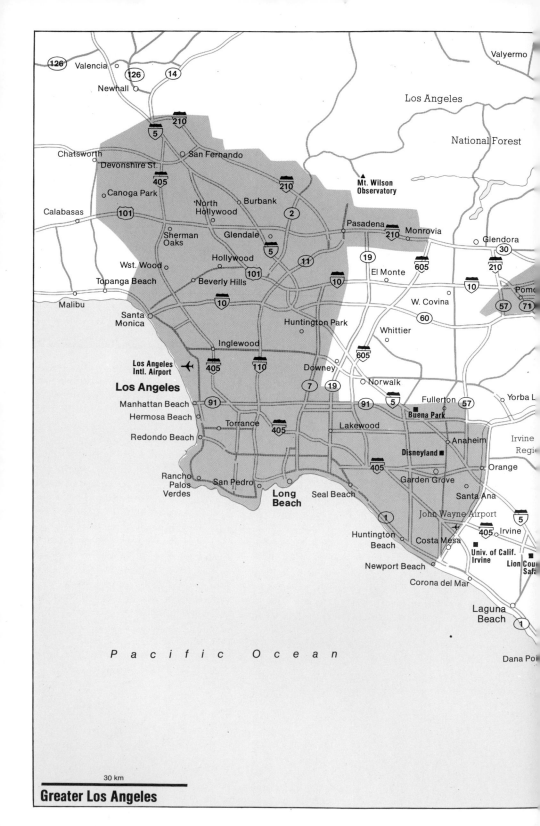

Greater Los Angeles

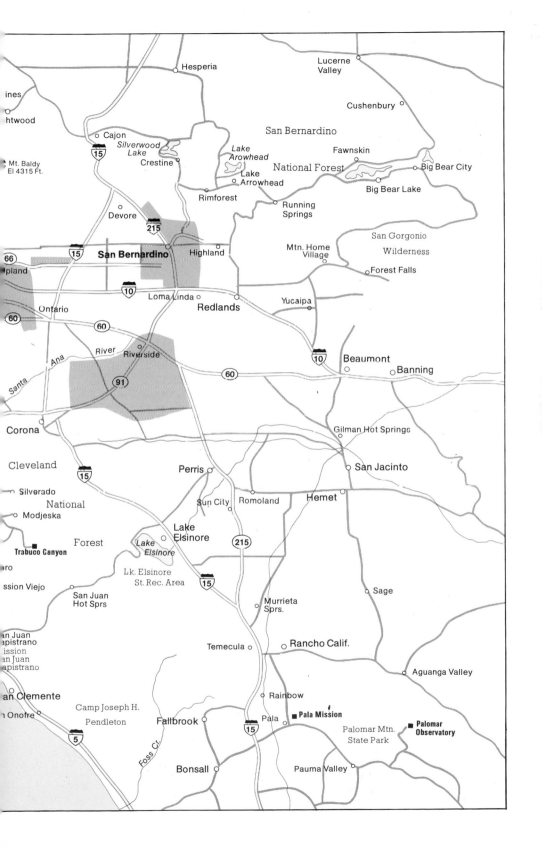

DOWNTOWN L.A.. THE CITY WITHIN

Downtown Los Angeles is often dismissed as the antithesis of Southern California's endless line of suburbs, the forgotten wasteland dedicated to rail-riding tramps and Bible-thumping fanatics. But beyond the grim facade lies a vital, widly, diverse city-within-a-city, sporting hidden cultural treasures and historic meanings not always visible to the hurried traveler.

The City of the Angels has replaced Ellis Island as the most heavily burdened immigrant entry point in the United States, and the weighted cultural baggage of the newly arrived is usually dumped first at the heart of L.A.'s downtown urban core. Street life is animated and sometimes illuminating as dozens of different languages reverberate along the busy sidewalks, crowded with throngs bent on survival. The air is thick with the competing aromas of hundreds of fledgling ethnic cafes and luncheonettes specializing in regional cookery, all vying for the attention of the casual passer-by as well as the curious visitor.

Los Angeles' downtown, in fact, is currently undergoing a renaissance of sorts, emerging with a reenergized spirit of entrepreneurship and a sense of the creative. With all the possibilities of transforming itself into another stylish Soho, new art galleries and fashionable cafes are opening their doors to an enthusiastic public anxious to embrace the arts. Abandoned warehouses and industrial spaces are rapidly metamorphosing into imaginative living spaces, inhabited by the new tribe of urban pioneers — artists, scholars and musicians ready to experiment with new concepts of contemporary urban living.

Historic Olvera Street

The casual visitor may not immediately grasp the fascinating cultural history, the diverse ethnic building blocks, upon which Los Angeles was so securely founded more than 200 years ago. The city's overwhelmingly Spanish beginnings are nowhere more evident than along festive, artily manicured **Olvera Street** in the heart of bustling

Afternoon colors on the downtown L skyline.

downtown near Sunset Boulevard and Main Street. The cobblestone walkway celebrates the first actual settlement in Los Angeles. Some of the curious architectural feats along the animated avenue date back to the 18th Century, while others are merely replicas of pre-existing structures.

Olvera Street is a combination of the picturesquely ethnic and the outrageously contrived. A casual stroll down this historical street, restored as a Mexican marketplace in 1930, is rarely dull. Vendors hawking everything from hand-painted *piñatas* to velvet paintings designed to glow in the dark are tirelessly enthusiastic about their wares, and several Mexican restaurants offer homemade *tortillas* and margaritas.

Of particular historical note along the avenue is the **Avila Adobe,** 14 Olvera St., the oldest (1818) residential dwelling in Los Angeles. And just a few steps away stands one of L.A.'s first brick houses, **La Casa Pelanconi,** 33–35 Olvera St.

Olvera Street opens onto a quiet, shady plaza where the **Church of Nuestra Senora la Reina de Los Angeles** (Old Plaza Church) has hosted religious services since 1822. Currently undergoing restoration, the nearby **Pico House** (built by former governor Pio Pico) and the **Merced Theater** (the city's first) are expected to reopen as soon as funds become available to finish the work. This 44-acre (18-hectare) historical area, best known as **El Pueblo de los Angeles State Historic Park,** is also the site of the city's oldest firehouse. **Firehouse No. 1,** now a museum of antique firefighting equipment, is open to the public year-round.

The Asian Connection

Although Spain and Mexico have undoubtedly influenced the evolution of Los Angeles more than any other single regional force, pioneering Japanese and Chinese settlers have left their marks for well over a century. Los Angeles' **Chinatown,** just north of Sunset Boulevard on North Broadway, is a microscopic version of its counterpart in San Francisco. But the community's restaurants offer some of the finest Chinese cuisine on the West Coast. Small curio and other tourist-oriented shops dot the area. **The Friendly Shop,**

Underground shopping at the Hyatt Regency's Broadway Plaza.

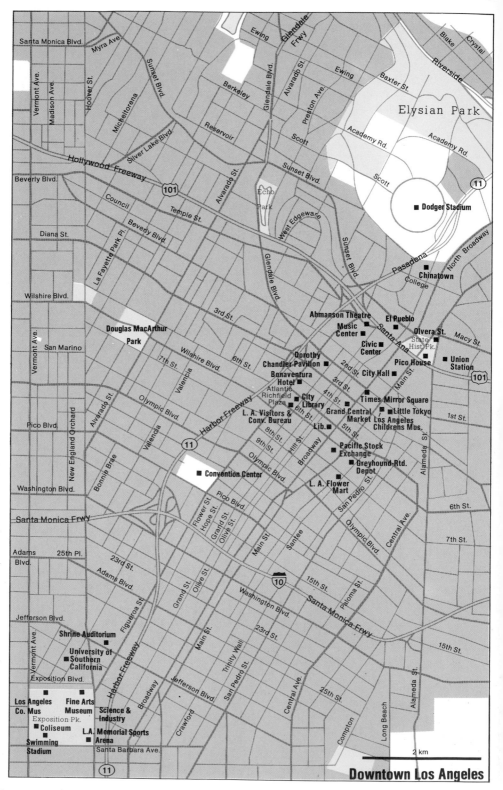

Downtown Los Angeles

an odd retail outlet directed by businessmen from mainland China, is of special note.

Also situated in the heart of downtown L.A. is **Little Tokyo,** a spotlessly manicured area just south of Olvera Street between 1st and 3rd streets. It is chockablock with little pastry shops, *sushi* piano bars, punk nightclubs and toy stores featuring the latest in Japanese robot technology.

Those who prefer soft-shell *tacos* to *sashimi* and *shabu-shabu* can have the edge taken off their hunger at the **Grand Central Market,** 3rd and Hill streets. The open-air bustle of this international food emporium is entertaining as well as taste-tempting. For sale are hundreds of exotic foods, sparklingly fresh produce and scrumptiously prepared gourmet treats.

Early risers and late-night revelers are also amused by the scurrying activity of the **Los Angeles Flower Market,** one of the largest of its kind in the United States. The market unfolds in the wee dawn hours along Wall Street near 8th Street. Florists and insomniacs haggle over the latest shipment of gladiolus; many of the floral outlets cater to the retail buyer at wholesale prices.

Dignity and Culture

Los Angeles' **Civic Center** provides the downtown area with a much-needed touch of quiet dignity. It centers around the classically drafted 28-story **City Hall** (2nd Street near Temple and Spring streets), dedicated in 1928 at a cost of nearly $5 million. The observation deck on the 27th floor of City Hall offers a relatively unobstructed view of downtown L.A.

Crowning the Civic Center is the much-touted **Music Center,** 135 N. Grand Ave., home base for the Los Angeles Philharmonic Orchestra and the Civic Light Opera. Three separate theaters are nestled within the complex, offering year-round productions which run the gamut from touring Broadway musicals to the experimental.

The Society for the Preservation of the Variety Arts recently unveiled an important new contribution to the downtown theater scene, the **Variety Arts Theater**. The midnight Comedy Lounge of this handsomely refurbished theater at 940 S. Figueroa St. has also become a fashionable "in" spot for late-

night locals who like their stand-up comedy raucous and unpredictable.

Those who prefer unstaged drama can drop in on the visitors' gallery of the **Pacific Stock Exchange,** 618 S. Spring St. Frenzied buying and selling goes on 7 a.m. to 1:30 p.m. Monday through Friday. Tours can also be arranged at Western America's largest daily newspaper, the **Los Angeles Times,** housed in a huge complex at 1st and Spring streets.

While downtown Los Angeles is not especially renowned for higher achievements in architectural arts, it does have several intriguing examples of man's attempt to deal with his everchanging Southern California environment. The **Bradbury Building,** 304 S. Broadway, was designed in 1893 by novice draftsman George Wyman after consulting a Ouija board. An undistinguished facade masks a remarkable interior laced with delicate ironwork, birdcage elevators and Mexican floor tiles.

The **Union Passenger Station,** 800 N. Alameda St., signaled the final chapter in the history of monumental rail terminals in the United States when it was completed in 1939. The oft-photo-

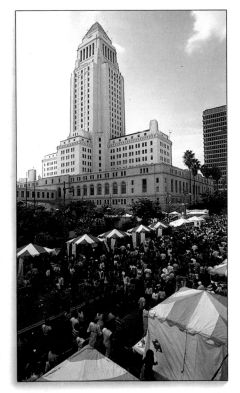

City Hall looms over festivities of the annual L.A. Street Scene.

graphed station was designed by John and Donald Parkinson in an unmistakable and highly dramatic style described as "monumental Moorish."

The futuristic **Westin Bonaventure Hotel** strikes out at downtown Los Angeles as a courageous if solitary reminder that the 21st Century is rapidly approaching. This dramatic architectural statement, made by John Portman, incorporates 35 acres (14 hectares) of waterfalls and ponds in the lobby area alone! The glass-enclosed exterior elevators shoot unforgettably skyward to offer an exquisite vantage point from the hotel's 35th floor. Located at 404 S. Figueroa St., the hotel makes 1,474 rooms available to well-fixed patrons.

The twin-tower 52-storey **Atlantic Richfield Plaza,** 6th and Figueroa streets, is a huge office complex capping an underground shopping mall. The headquarters of the **Greater Los Angeles Visitor and Convention Bureau** can be found on Plaza Level B.

Exposition Park

A short distance south of these architectural behemoths on Figueroa

Street is **Exposition Park.** Site of the 1932 Olympic games, it has become a focus of the city's cultural and recreational pursuits. Indeed, the main venues of the 1984 Olympics are the sports facilities found here — the **Los Angeles Memorial Coliseum** and the **Los Angeles Sports Arena.** Several professional and collegiate teams play football, basketball and other sports here the better part of the year.

The park also encompasses picnic areas and a carefully tended rose garden with 190 varieties in seven acres. But its pride are its two fine museums. The **Los Angeles County Museum of Natural History** is one of the finest institutions of its kind in the world. Its exhibits focus on the evolution of plant and animal life, including the development of man's civilizations, and on the history of California from the 16th to 20th centuries. Situated next door to the Coliseum, it is often packed with hordes of adolescent schoolkids on their first field trip. Nevertheless, it merits a visit.

Just steps from the Museum of Natural History is the state-operated **California Museum of Science and Industry.** Exhibits underscore achievements in the sciences, including health, aviation, space technology, mathematics, communications, agriculture and industrial design. The "hands-on" series of inventive displays encourages the educational process and helps break the tedium found in many more conventional museums.

There are other fine museums at the **University of Southern California** (USC), just across Exposition Boulevard from the park. Founded in 1880, the university has more than 24,000 students on its 150-acre (61-hectare) campus. The **Fisher Gallery** has an outstanding permanent exhibit of 16th and 17th Century Flemish and Dutch paintings, while the **Hancock Memorial Museum,** housed in an 1890 mansion, includes items from the palace of former Mexican Emperor Maximilian.

The rich ethnic and religious diversity of cosmopolitan Los Angeles has helped nurture museums which focus on unique groups or interests. The **Skirball Museum,** located on the grounds of the **Hebrew Union College** (32nd and Hoover streets), houses a vast collection of Judaic art and artifacts. Old Testament archaeology and anthropological material from the Negev desert.

Left, Little Tokyo capitalizes on the latest culinary fad. Right, the Westin Bonaventure Hotel.

88

The Dunbar Hotel, America's first hotel built and designed by the Blacks to fulfill the early needs of the Black community, has recently been converted into the **Dunbar Museum of Black Culture and History.** The long civil-rights battle of Black Americans is meticulously captured in this hotel, which has been designated a historic landmark. It is located at 4233 S. Central Ave.

In the unpredictable melange of Los Angeles, kids also get their very own museum — christened, appropriately enough, the **Los Angeles Children's Museum.** It is located in the heart of downtown at 310 N. Main St. A kaleidoscope of exhibits appealing to youngsters is on hand here, including scientific models which serve as a basic introduction to urban planning.

Quiet Escapes

Numerous neighborhoods and recreational sites within easy reach of downtown Los Angeles expand the visitor's appreciation of the central city. A short distance north are **Silverlake** and **Echo Park** — hilly, wooded residential districts of meticulously cared-for older homes. In recent years, a bohemian influx has helped transform this sector into one of the most colorful in Southern California.

Boating enthusiasts can float away the afternoon at **MacArthur Park** on West Sixth Street, probably the most picturesque of the downtown area's palm-dotted green spots. The park offers more than affordable summer boat rentals. An undiluted vision of Los Angeles' varied population, from the most fortunate to the most downtrodden, congregates here. Sunday afternoons are especially lively with local musicians improvising on makeshift instruments to the delight of onlookers.

One of the most rustic recreational parks in Los Angeles is **Elysian Park,** dramatically overlooking the downtown Civic Center and the suburban sprawl of the San Gabriel Valley. The 575-acre (233-hectare) park is an unusual hybrid of unabridged wilderness and cultivated picnic areas. It includes a 10-acre grove of carefully labeled trees and a variety of nature trails. **Dodger Stadium,** home of the Los Angeles Dodgers baseball team, traditionally among the National League's leaders, is perched high up in

Left, the ever-bustling Central Market. Right, Watts Towers.

Elysian Park. Every Dodger game attracts thousands of enthusiastic fans during baseball season, extending from April to October.

Students of religious architecture can visit the **Cathedral of St. Sophia** (1324 S. Normandie Ave.); it has an austere Greek Orthodox facade but a beautiful interior of marble, travertine, crystal and stained glass. The **Wilshire Boulevard Temple** (at South Hobart Street) was L.A.'s first Jewish temple. Close neighbors at West Adams Boulevard and Figueroa Street are **St. John's Cathedral** (Episcopal), a replica of an 11th Century Italian church; and **St. Vincent de Paul Church** (Catholic), a survivor from Spanish colonial days.

For a truly illuminating vision of the lifestyle of the Hispanic people of East Los Angeles, visitors should visit **Plaza de la Raza,** formerly known as Lincoln Park. Located just three miles (five km) from the Civic Center at 3501 Valley Blvd., its recreational facilities include a performing arts center and museum focusing on California's ever-growing Chicano population.

Undoubtedly, Los Angeles attracts its share of creative iconoclasts. One of those eccentrics, Italian immigrant Simon Rodia, helped redefine primitive art. Rodia labored in his back yard for nearly 35 years to build a monument to his personal artistic vision. Using odd bits of tile and glass, the professional tile-setter sculpted the internationally celebrated **Watts Towers.** They have stood at 1765 E. 107th St. in the economically depressed area of Watts since completion in 1954.

While some Los Angeles eccentrics prefer to build dizzying monuments to themselves, others opt to congregate in one of the most peculiar communities in all of California. Fifteen miles (24 km) from the Civic Center, the tiny incorporated city of **Gardena** has sanctioned the operation of six gambling emporiums where draw poker, low ball and pan are permitted 24 hours a day. The high rollers in Gardena's decidedly-less-than-posh casinos range from the amused tourist to the clearly desperate. The atmosphere tends toward funereal, the cocktail waitresses are surly, and most faces are ghoulishly pale.

Of course, building a city in the desert is a high-stakes gamble itself. In Los Angeles, it succeeded grandly.

Macarthur Park

HOLLYWOOD: THE WAY WE WERE

You can take Hollywood for granted like I did, or you can dismiss it with the contempt we reserve for things that we don't understand. It can be understood, too, but only dimly and in flashes.
— *F. Scott Fitzgerald*, The Last Tycoon *(1939)*

Hollywood is a part of Los Angeles that visitors would no sooner bypass than they would Disneyland or the long strand of Southern California beaches. Newcomers journey to Hollywood Boulevard by rental car or tour bus or urge their friends to take them there. They expect to catch a glimpse of Robert Redford or Paul Newman, or at the very least, to peer into the smoked windows of a limousine and try to guess zo sidewalk.

The reality is a rude awakening. Instead of limos, they find Chevys painted wild metallic-flake colors, outfitted with dangling chi-chi balls, fake fur on the dashboards and hydraulic lifts to make the cars bounce. The closest thing to a movie star are the names embedded in bronze on the district's smudged terrazzo side-walk.

Instead of stars, they find grizzled, flabby-bellied bikers; crazies muttering to themselves as they push their worldly goods down the streets in wire shopping carts; and sullen Mohawked punks thudding along in unlaced Doc Martens and with kick-butt gleams in their eyes. They see lean and mean Marines, pathetic junkies, pimps toting two-ton ghetto blasters, bunny-jacketed prostitutes in hot pants, and too-young ragged runaways. Visitors see everything but the glamour they anticipated.

Gone With the Wind

To have contempt (as Fitzgerald warned) because the city cannot fulfill one's fantasies would be an unfortunate mistake. In many cases, like Frederick's of Hollywood's impressive deco facade, Hollywood's glitter is merely covered by a gaudy coat of paint. It only takes a little information and imagination to see what the town once was.

Originally called the Cahuenga Valley, Hollywood was renamed by its developers, Mr. and Mrs. Horace H. Wilcox. In typical Hollywood fashion, people argue either that Mrs. Wilcox borrowed the name of a friend's suburban Chicago home, or that Junípero Serra once said the Mass of the Holy Wood nearby.

A farmland for citrus, watermelon, bell peppers and other produce, the tiny community of 700 was incorporated in 1903, and continued in pastoral harmony until the Horsely brothers leased an abandoned bar on the corner of Gower Avenue and Sunset Boulevard to shoot movies. Film studios flooded the area. The clever industry doyens saw the powerful draw of the growing film center by the early Twenties, and launched a city development program to cash in on the lure.

Today the census count shows that more than 50,000 Latinos (Hispanics), Asians and Blacks live in Hollywood, and more than 40,000 Armenians arrived in the 1970s from the Soviet Union. Mental patients routinely ask when released from institutions to be sent to Hollywood. Vagrants and teenage runaways converge there for the same reason. Regardless of Hollywood's tawdry physical form, in the hearts and minds of people it remains a symbol of renewed chance and opportunity.

Every year on the late November weekend following Thanksgiving, for example, the Hollywood Christmas Parade weaves down Sunset Boulevard and up Hollywood Boulevard in a preholiday evening display of glitter and glamour. Hundreds of spectators begin parking on the sidewalks early in the morning to be assured of seeing the celebrities, floats and marching bands pass near them.

Stardust Memories

The first thing one notices while walking down Hollywood Boulevard past the T-shirt shops, pizza joints and crummy boutiques is that lots of people are staring at their feet. This isn't because (unlike New York's Times Square) it's dangerous for a person to make eye contact.

It's simply that the **Walk of Fame,** which forms a 1½-mile crisscross down the boulevard from Gower to Sycamore streets, and down Vine Street from Sunset Boulevard to Yucca Street, is hard

Hollywood hype captured on cotton.

to ignore. The 1,760-plus pink-and-charcoal speckled terrazzo stars feature the names of celebrities from the music, film, art direction and fashion industries. To be immortalized with a star, one must first be nominated and approved by a special committee, then must pay a $3,000 installation fee. Approximately one star a month is dedicated, so it's estimated there are still 50 more years of stars before the spots run out.

Another place where visitors stumble over one another is the infamous courtyard at **Mann's Chinese Theater** (6925 Hollywood Blvd.). It's "the thing to do" to stick one's stiletto heels in the points left by the shoes of Marilyn Monroe and 160 other stars. Legend claims the tradition began when Norma Talmadge wandered into wet cement during the opening-night premiere of Cecil B. deMille's *King of Kings* on May 18, 1927. Not true: owner Sid Grauman skidded into the goo himself. Knowing a good deal when he saw it, he promptly invited Talmadge, Douglas Fairbanks and Mary Pickford to do likewise.

The **Egyptian Theater,** also owned by Sid Grauman, was built to resemble the Temple of Thebes in order to capitalize on the Egyptian rage caused by the discovery of King Tutankhamen's tomb. Opened on Oct. 18, 1922, with Fairbanks starring in *Robin Hood,* the ornate theater entryway was lined with wafting potted palms and usherettes in Cleopatra drag. Since then, the theater has fallen into unfortunate decline.

All in the Family

One house unmarred by the times is the **Janes Residence** (6541 Hollywood Blvd.) a Queen Anne-style Victorian with a mossy, turreted roof, tropical banana trees and an overgrown spooky appeal. The Janes sisters, Carrie, Grace and Mabel, moved with their parents and brother in 1904 to Prospect Avenue (as the boulevard was then called) from Aurora, Illinois. To capitalize on the growing entertainment community, Mary Ruth Janes and her daughters opened a school for show-biz kids. Carrie was the last resident; she moved to a convalescent home in 1982. Still visible from the sidewalk is Janes' Auto Service, a tiny Spanish colonial-style gas station covered with day-glow blue

Cast membe[r] roars over script on set of 1920s comedy.

paint. It is currently being renovated by the Hollywood Revitalization Program.

Another landmark recently saved was the 1923-vintage **Hollywood Sign.** First erected to attract attention to a real-estate development on the side of Mount Lee, the 50-foot (16½-meter) high sign, illuminated by more than 4,000 light bulbs, originally spelled "Hollywoodland." In the early Thirties, a blonde starlet named Peg Entwhistle, despondent over the decision by RKO Studios not to renew her contract, told her uncle she was going out for a pack of cigarettes. Instead, she climbed to the top of the "H" and jumped to her death. Over the years, the sign fell into a state of tattered disrepair. In 1978, the Hollywood Chamber of Commerce and several celebrities raised $243,000 and rebuilt the sign.

Frederick's of Hollywood (6608 Hollywood Blvd.) is known by even the most sexually naive due to its expansive mail-order service. The zigzag modern exterior has been covered by Frederick's ridiculous purple-and-pink trademark colors. Inside, the gold-and-silver deco sales area features a smorgasbord of erogenous articles such as edible panties, peek-a-boo housedresses and any other trashy accessory one's libido might conjure up.

Except for the four markers dedicated to the Apollo XI astronauts, the intersection of **Hollywood and Vine** is perplexingly drab. Just up the street, though, is the **Capitol Records** building (1750 Vine Ave.), designed by composer Johnny Mercer and singer Nat "King" Cole to resemble a stack of 45s topped with a symbolic phonograph needle.

The Pantages (6233 Hollywood Blvd.), opened in 1929, is still one of L.A.'s thriving legitimate theaters. Owned by Alexander Pantages, a Greek theater magnate, and designed by B. Marcus Priteen, the Academy Awards were held there for 11 consecutive years.

Guess Who's Coming to Dinner?

The Hollywood area was home to many literati. Among those who ate and drank at **Musso and Frank's Grill** (6663-67 Hollywood Blvd.) were Ernest Hemingway, Dorothy Parker and William Faulkner. They also stopped by the **Brown Derby** (1620–28 Vine St.). The Hollywood atmosphere inspired locations and characters that could be found in the pages of many novels — particularly the Hollywood detective stories. Raymond Chandler used the **Montecito** (6650 Franklin Ave.) as a model for *Chateau Bercy* and *Little Sister*. The **High Tower** (at the north end of Hightower Avenue) was used as Jules Amthor's house in *Farewell, My Lovely* and later as the home of Elliott Gould's Phillip Marlowe in Robert Altman's film *The Long Goodbye*. Geiger's pornographic bookstore from *The Big Sleep* was actually the **Book Treasury** (6707 Hollywood Blvd.). Marlowe's Cahuenga Building, formerly the beaux-arts Guaranty Building where gossip columnist Hedda Hopper had her office for many years, is now the **Bank of America** (6331 Hollywood Blvd.).

The **Hollywood Bowl** (2301 Highland Ave.) is above Hollywood Boulevard, just south of the Hollywood Freeway (U.S. Route 101). This huge outdoor amphiteater seats 17,000 in its 116-acre (47-hectare) park. Since 1923, the Bowl has hosted "Symphonies Under the Stars" from July to September. It is also

Concrete
memories
at Mann's
Chinese
Theater.

THE UNUSUAL SIDE OF HOLLYWOOD

The House Where Marilyn Monroe Died — On the morning of Aug 5, 1962, actress Marilyn Monroe was found dead in the bedroom of her home at 12305 Fifth Helena Dr. in Brentwood (between San Vicente and Sunset boulevards, west of Bundy Drive). Her nude body was found lying face-down on her bed, following the ingestion of 47 sleeping pills. Although numerous reports have come out that she was murdered, her death was officially ruled a suicide.

The "Mommie Dearest" House — Actress Joan Crawford bought the home at 426 N. Bristol Dr. (off Sunset Boulevard) in Brentwood before she married actor Douglas Fairbanks Jr. in 1929. At one time, in the Forties, Crawford removed the bathtubs from the house, saying it was "unsanitary to sit in one's bathwater." In 1978, her daughter Christina wrote her *Mommie Dearest* book tracing a life filled with "alcoholism, abuse and terror."

Not So Funny Deaths — Comedian Freddy Prinze, who co-starred in the television show *Chico and the Man*, shot himself in 1977 at the age of 22 at an apartment located at 865–75 Comstock St. (near Wilshire and Beverly Glen boulevards) in Westwood. Prinze's idol was comedian Lenny Bruce, who died at the age of 41, at his home at 8825 Hollywood Blvd., in 1966 after injecting himself with morphine. Prinze often told friends he was the reincarnation of Bruce and many times visited the house where Bruce had died.

Hollywood's Most Bizarre Suicide — Albert Dekker, who appeared in several horror movies and was best known for his role as *Dr. Cyclops*, killed himself in 1968 at his apartment at 1731 N. Normandie in Hollywood. Dekker, who also was elected to the California State Assembly, was found in his bathroom hanging by his neck at the end of a rope that was tied to a shower curtain rod. The rope was also tied around both his legs and one of his arms, and two hypodermic needles were stuck in his body. Police ruled the death a suicide, although they could find "no information why he wanted to take his own life."

Marilyn and Joe's Honeymoon Home — When actress Marilyn Monroe married baseball star Joe DiMaggio in 1954, they settled down at 508 N. Palm Dr. in Beverly Hills. The house is next door to the last home of actress Jean Harlow (512 N. Palm Dr.). Monroe and DiMaggio met on a blind date at the Villa Nova restaurant, 9015 Sunset Blvd. The restaurant is now called the Rainbow Bar and Grill.

Janis Joplin's Final Night — Rock singer Janis ("Pearl") Joplin died of a heroin-morphine overdose in 1970 in a room that was part of the old Landmark Hotel, 7047 Franklin St. in Hollywood. She was 27. She had earlier set aside $2,500 for her own wake. The Grateful Dead provided music for more than 200 guests who had invitations that read: "Drinks are on Pearl."

Chateau Marmont Hotel, site of many a Hollywood intrigue.

popular for its spectacular presentation of Tchaikovsky's "1812 Overture" on the Fourth of July, to the accompaniment of a brilliant fireworks display and a real cannon-blast finale. In the exclusive reserved section up front, there is an inevitable "battle of the box lunches" in which upper-class folk compete to see who can bring the most absurdly elaborate picnic. There is ample parking at the Bowl, but much uphill trudging to the seats, so flat shoes are in order.

In the Heat of the Night

The best-known part of the district of **West Hollywood** covers Sunset Boulevard from Crescent Heights Boulevard to Doheny Drive. It is internationally famous as the **Sunset Strip.** In its heyday, the Strip was the location of steamy nightclubs such as the Mocambo, the Trocadero and Ciro's. (The latter, now occupied by **The Comedy Store,** is the only structure of the three still standing.) During the 1960s, other clubs took names like The Daisy, The Trip and Pandora's Box, making the Strip a headquarters for the so-called

Santa Claus "flies" down Hollywood Boulevard in the annual Christmas Parade.

"Love Generation."

The only two venues to have survived since the Sixties in name and substance are **The Troubador** (9081 Santa Monica Blvd.) and **Gazzari's** (9039 Sunset Blvd.), and both now cater to a leather-and-stud heavy-metal crowd. Forlornly decrepit is the hollow **Whisky a Go Go** (8901 Sunset Blvd.). **The Roxy** (9009 Sunset Blvd.) upholds the musical tradition by booking a wide mix of rock, soul, blues, country-western and new wave bands. Across the parking lot is **The Rainbow Bar and Grill** (9015 Sunset Blvd.). Once the Villa Nova restaurant, where Joe Di Maggio and Marilyn Monroe had their first blind date, the place is now a watering hole for young fringe music-industry types with too-tight jeans and pineapple haircuts.

Laurel Canyon was one of Los Angeles' first developed canyons. In the 1920s it became a retreat for movie stars. Later, in the Sixties, it was home to rock stars Joni Mitchell, David Crosby and Jim Morrison. Near the junction of Laurel Canyon Boulevard and Lookout Mountain Road are the ruins of magician Harry Houdini's once-lavish

California retreat. Across the street is the charred skeleton of a log cabin which once belonged to singing cowboy Tom Mix. It was occupied briefly by avant-garde rock composer Frank Zappa and his family.

Near the foot of Laurel Canyon, on Sunset Boulevard, is a replica of a Norman-French castle, the **Chateau Marmont Hotel.** Built in 1927, the hotel has continued to uphold the tradition of catering to the stars. Greta Garbo lived there, as did Howard Hughes, who had the peculiar habit of leaning out of his suite window to ogle girls by the poolside with binoculars. In recent years, Robert De Niro, Tony Randall, Bianca Jagger and rock singer Sting of The Police have stayed there. The Chateau Marmont was also, sadly, the site of comedian John Belushi's fatal drug overdose.

Divine Madness

From Doheny to La Brea avenues, **Melrose Avenue** is the mother of invention. Though its fashion boutiques cater to all tastes, its current "in" styles are the punk look, Fifties retro and Sixties mod. The entire street is worth checking out, as are many of its pedestrians' hairdos — dreadlocks, multi-colored layers and rolled spikes that radiate straight out from the skull. Currently the stores feature a melange of avant-thrift garb, pre-packaged "new wave," and oddball knickknacks. The rent is high and so is the turnover. One never knows what one will find on Melrose Avenue on a Saturday afternoon.

On the other hand, the **Fairfax District,** a 2½-block area just below Melrose, is steeped in religious tradition. On any afternoon except the Sabbath, Yugoslav, Russian and Israeli immigrants mingle with an equally large population of furry-hatted, curly-sideburned Orthodox Jews. The neighborhood is made up of delicatessens, bakeries, ethnic grocery stores and *falafel* stands. The din of customers haggling with proprietors is often deafening. Visitors should not plan on driving in Fairfax for two reasons. First, the street is so dense with shops that there is no need to do so. Second, Fairfax residents tend to pilot their large American cars down the district's narrow byways with a legendary reckless abandon.

One fixture in the neighborhood is **Canter's Delicatessen** (419 S. Fairfax Ave.). Because Los Angeles shuts down fairly early and Canter's is open 24 hours, the place is perpetually jumping with employees from nearby CBS Television City, and after 2 a.m. with an eye-bulging array of energetic punksters and unemployed comedians. Canter's has a deli counter and bakery, always open, plus a wonderfully dark ragtag bar, The Kibbitz Room, which features a glowing seascape mural along one wall fronted by a surplus of pink bakery boxes. Above all, Canter's is known for its terminally cranky waitresses, whose dispositions range from truculent to psychotic.

The other indelible institution in Fairfax is **Al's Newsstand** (370 N. Fairfax Ave.), open from 6 a.m. to midnight. Owner Al Brooks dispenses periodicals from Europe, international newspapers, a surprisingly open-minded section of fan magazines, music magazines and tabloids, and many of the free local papers.

Farmer's Market, in the nearby **Wilshire District,** opened in 1924 as a marketing cooperative for local farm-

Peek-a-boo at Frederick of Hollywood

ers. Now it is a popular stopping point for tour buses whose passengers want to take advantage of the 160 different stalls offering food, souvenirs, coffee, cheese, meats and produce, not to mention the market's location next door to **CBS Television City.** Despite the heavy tourist traffic, locals plow daily through the sea of plaid Bermuda shorts and snapping Nikons to make their way to the popular cappucino bar and nearby doughnut stand at the southwest corner of Farmers Market, near DuPars Coffee Shop. A meeting ground for caffeine hungry photographers, actors, artists and literary types, this way station offers the best and cheapest espresso in town, dispensed by a squeaky-voiced proprietress named June.

The Last Detail

Wilshire Boulevard is the district's cultural center. Within one block are three of Los Angeles' most respected museums. The **La Brea Tar Pits** and **George C. Page Museum** — centered around a black, bubbling morass that frequently entraps paper cups and occasionally snares a misdirected bird —

often cause unknowing visitors to scratch their heads. But these benign-looking pits have been a part of L.A. for a long time. In 1906, paleontologists discovered that this "black gunk" contains the largest collection of Pleistocene fossils ever found in one place. Within the museum, exhibitions and dioramas chart the history and evolution of the prehistoric mammals.

The **Los Angeles County Art Museum** (5905 Wilshire Blvd.) is located directly adjacent to the tar pits. Divided into three sections, it contains the Hammer Gallery, where contemporary exhibitions are staged; the Leo S. Bing Theater, where cultural films are shown and an art rental library offers its services; and the Ahmanson Gallery, with the museum's permanent collection.

Just across the street is the **Craft and Folk Art Museum** (5814 Wilshire Blvd.). In the 1960s, the walls of Edith Wiley's restaurant, The Egg and the Eye, were cluttered with inspirational folk art. In 1973, Wiley turned her upstairs into a non-profit museum and dedicated it to studying, preserving and exhibiting contemporary and ancient folk art from around the world.

Blue Whale" acific esign Center owers behind lelrose istrict outiques.

BEVERLY HILLS & THE WEST SIDE

The dream of stardom is the essence of the west side of Los Angeles. It's in the air, as real as smog.

Visitors can almost reach out and grasp their fantasies while driving down the streets of Beverly Hills. It seems as though everyone who lives here is a star, with a star's car and a star's mansion. There are movie stars, television stars, sports stars, news stars, hairstylist stars, real-estate stars, even used-car-salesmen stars.

In fact, the spirit of this part of Los Angeles makes aspiring stars out of everyone. People who are already stars want badly to become bigger and brighter stars. The TV star wants to be a movie star. The soap opera star wants to be a prime-time star. The tourist wants to touch any of them.

Wealth and Fame

The heart of this dream of stardom is **Beverly Hills**. Located midway between downtown Los Angeles and the Pacific Ocean on less than six square miles (15 square kilometers) of gently sloping land, the City of Beverly Hills is world renowned as the place which the rich and famous — 34,000 of them — call home.

The average home in Beverly Hills is a palatial estate, complete with swimming pool, tennis court and lush manicured greenery. It doesn't come cheap. Real-estate prices have leaped so high in recent years that million-dollar homes are commonplace.

Shops, consequently, cater to the demands of wealth — fashion and luxury. On **Rodeo Drive**, the focus of Beverly Hills commerce, merchants showcase the most outrageous extravagances and everything that is truly trendy. A $500,000 necklace is sold next to $25 keycases. Famous faces dart in and out of elegant stores like Gucci, Van Cleef, Arpels and Bijan. Some stores even provide valet parking.

The development of Beverly Hills as a celebrity estate parallels the development of Southern California's motion-picture industry. Douglas Fairbanks and Mary Pickford started the opulence

Preceding pages, Saturday night road show in Westwood Below, a Beverly Hills residence.

in 1919 when they commissioned architect Wallace Neff to remodel a pre-existing hunting lodge to create for them a white colonial manor, **Pickfair**. The site of some of the most memorable parties in show business history in the decades since, Pickfair (1143 Summit Dr.) is still a gathering spot for international celebrities.

The current owner is a sports entrepreneur, Dr. Jerry Buss. He was just a real-estate baron until he bought the pro basketball Los Angeles Lakers, the pro hockey L.A. Kings, and The Forum — home arena to both teams — in the 1970s. When he added the historic Pickfair to his personal holdings, he became an even bigger media darling.

A Pink Palace and Polo

Another astounding home from a similar era is the **Greystone Park Mansion** at 905 Loma Vista Dr. This 55-room manor, with a spectacular view of Los Angeles city, was built in 1923 by oilman Edward L. Doheny on 18½ landscaped acres (7½ hectares). The grounds feature balustraded terraces, fountains and ponds. The mansion is

not open to the public, but visitors are free to roam around the grounds.

The area which now comprises the City of Beverly Hills began as a Spanish land grant known as *El Rancho Rodeo de las Aguas*, "Ranch of the Circling Waters." Until the early 1900s, the land produced wheat, cattle, oil, wool and beans. But in 1906, Burton E. Green of Beverly Farms, Massachusetts, bought the land and supervised a subdivision of gently curving streets lined with trees.

With the construction in 1912 of the pink **Beverly Hills Hotel** on Sunset Boulevard, a community focus was established on what for generations had been 12 acres of bean field. By the fall of 1913, public sentiment for incorporation mandated city status for Beverly Hills. The population was then 500.

Movie producers, directors, actors, writers and technicians migrated to the enclave to be near the hypnotic silver screen. On Sunday afternoons, many of them played their favorite game — polo — then gathered at the Beverly Hills Hotel to see and be seen. The **Polo Lounge** survives today as a legacy of that glamorous time. Warm embraces and table-hopping are a part of a regular ritual there. But it isn't true that all Polo people are close personal friends. The mood in the lounge is more akin to that of feeding time in a shark tank.

Porcelains and Oscars

A far more subdued atmosphere prevails at the **Francis E. Fowler, Jr., Foundation Museum**, 9215 Wilshire Blvd. This small museum specializes in European and American decorative arts. It features extensive collections of 15th to 18th Century silver, paperweights, carved ivory and Russian porcelains.

Enthusiasts of progressive architecture will find one of Frank Lloyd Wright's final works at 328 N. Rodeo Dr. Wright designed the **Anderton Court**, an office building which features angles and ramps that make the place seem as if it's coming apart at the seams.

At the corner of Beverly Drive and Olympic Boulevard, a bronze spiral of film stands as a monument to stars of the Twenties who fought the annexation of Beverly Hills by the City of Los Angeles. Among the celebrities who rallied to the cause were Pickford and Fairbanks, Will Rogers, Rudolph Valentino, Harold Lloyd and Tom Mix.

Those who carry an undying fascination for the film industry can visit the research library of the **Academy of Motion Picture Arts and Sciences** on Wilshire Boulevard. These are the people who hand out the Oscars every spring. Every so often, the Academy gives public tours or sponsors lectures related to the movies.

Star Gazing

For the visitor who cannot resist doing some star-snooping, maps of stars' homes are sold everywhere for a few dollars. Up-to-date maps may be more expensive. It is good to remember that these maps are intended only to give directions, and are not licenses to trespass. High fences, angry dobermans and unsmiling security guards — all of which are seen more often than stars — exist for one reason: privacy.

Nearly as many stars live in lush **Bel Air,** directly adjoining Beverly Hills north of Sunset Boulevard, as in Beverly Hills itself. On **Carolwood Drive**, for

Comfort in a plush Bel-Air home.

instance, are the homes of Burt Reynolds, Barbra Streisand, Gregory Peck and Rod Stewart, as well as the former home of Elvis Presley. Not far away are the homes of Johnny Carson, Jerry Lewis and Tom Jones. A good place for a break between rounds of not-seeing stars is the **Bel Air Hotel** on Stone Canyon Road. It offers an idyllic retreat from the madding crowd amidst gliding swans and purple bougainvillea.

On the other side of Beverly Hills, south of Santa Monica Boulevard, is **Century City**. This community developed on the old backlot of Twentieth Century-Fox Pictures. Among its highlights are the **Schubert Theater**, the **ABC Entertainment Center** complex, **Century City Shopping Center** and the **Century Plaza Hotel**, where Ronald Reagan stays when he's in town.

In the arcade between the high-rise office buildings and the hotel, a 55-minute, multi-screen show about the Golden Days of Hollywood is presented. It is called **The Hollywood Experience**. Nearby is **The Road Show**, which displays such legendary automobiles as the Stutz, Clenet, Auburn, Sceptre, Maserati and Lamborghini.

Westwood Village

West of Beverly Hills is **Westwood Village**, which has the most intense concentration of first-run movie theaters in the world. Thousands of shoppers and movie-goers jam the streets *on foot*, a rarity for car-crazy Los Angeles. Just behind the AVCO theaters on Wilshire Boulevard is the **Westwood Memorial Cemetery**, final resting place for screen legends like Marilyn Monroe and Natalie Wood whose names once graced the marquees of these very theaters.

An undeveloped ranch until the 1920s, Westwood was purchased by the Janss Investment Corporation which turned it into a Mediterranean-style shopping village. It began to thrive in 1929 when the **University of California at Los Angeles** (UCLA) opened for classes in Westwood. It is now a cultural hub, packed with numerous stores and restaurants.

The UCLA campus consists of more than 85 buildings in a variety of architectural styles, surrounded by 411 acres (167 hectares) of serene, prime Westwood real estate. Enrollment is more than 32,000. A relaxing stroll

nal resting
ace of a
creen legend.

MARILYN MONROE
1926 — 1962

105

around campus can include stops at the **Franklin D. Murphy Sculpture Gardens**, the **Frederick S. Wight Art Gallery**, and the **Mathias Botanical Gardens** — 8½ acres (3½ hectares) of woodsy canyon designed specifically as a sheltered environment.

A word of caution: on Friday and Saturday nights, Westwood experiences the kind of street crunch more often associated with rush hour in Manhattan. Most of the bodies are those of teenagers and university students going to the movies. In Los Angeles, the litmus test for any new film is how well it succeeds in Westwood.

Brentwood, westward of Westwood, is the home of many young singles and upwardly mobile professionals. Its main street is **San Vicente Boulevard**, an artery lined with quaint boutiques. The joggers who seem to take over this stretch at dawn and dusk each day will give way during the 1984 Olympic Games to the world's best marathon runners.

Sunset Boulevard leads through Brentwood to **Pacific Palisades.** Between 1924 and his death in 1935, American cowboy humorist Will Rogers lived in a ranch house located on a 187-acre (76-hectare) estate at 14235 Sunset Blvd. Now it is a **State Historic Park** dedicated to Rogers' memory.

Until his election as U.S. President, Pacific Palisades was also the home of Ronald Reagan. Among its current famous residents are movie-industry VIPs Steven Spielberg and Sylvester Stallone.

Seaside Santa Monica

Adjacent **Santa Monica** is the center of a Southern California beach lifestyle envied the world over. The ocean breeze is refreshing, the sun warm, and the attitude laid-back. Not everyone is here on vacation; it just seems that way.

And why not? Santa Monica offers three miles (five km) of sandy beach for swimming, fishing and boating. **Santa Monica Pier's** 75-year-old carousel with 56 prancing horses was featured in the movie classic, *The Sting.* Even though the pier is undergoing repairs following severe winter storms, it remains colorful. Four major boulevards — Wilshire, Santa Monica, Olympic and Pico — lead in its direction.

Beverly Hills Hotel, home of the Polo Lounge.

In 1769, Gaspar de Portolá claimed for Spain the area now known as Santa Monica. Legend says the town received its name from Father Juan Crespi, who was reminded by gentle spring waters of the tears shed by the good Sta. Monica when her wayward son, later to be known as St. Augustine, embraced Christianity.

Santa Monica began to be developed as a seaside resort community in 1875. For many years it was a sleepy suburb, a full day's bumpy stagecoach ride from downtown L.A. The character of the town changed dramatically in 1966 when the Santa Monica Freeway opened and reduced the commuting distance to downtown to less than 30 minutes. An influx of new residents ended the quieter era.

Today, many of Santa Monica's new "immigrants" can be found on **Main Street** in the **Ocean Park** area south of the pier. This has become a unique seaside shopping and dining area.

The Roller-skating Capital

If, as author Tom Wolfe has written, Southern California is the great cultural laboratory of America, then **Venice** is the home of advanced research. The fads of this bohemian beachside community seem to sweep the nation. Roller skating is the most recent manifestation: visitors must be on their quick-stepping toes to dodge skaters on **Ocean Front Walk**.

Main Street provides the approach to Venice from Santa Monica, dead-ending at the Venice Post Office. The tall, gull-like **sculpture** in the center of the traffic circle here is dedicated to freedom. Indeed, Venice's inhabitants do their eclectic best to adapt their lifestyles to this concept.

Tobacco magnate Abbot Kinney developed Venice in 1905 as a tribute to the great Italian city of the same name. In doing so, he hoped to inspire a cultural renaissance in the United States. His city plan included 16 miles (26 km) of canals with gondolas to ferry visitors from place to place. But by 1929, the community had paved over most of the waterways. Those that remain are filthy.

Today, however, Venice has its Italians. It also has many other Europeans, along with Blacks, Asians, Central

Americans, Brazilians, Australians, Hare Krishnas, Mormons, Jews, burnt-out beach bums, wealthy movie directors, and every other form of humanity doing its own thing.

In recent decades, Venice has established its fame as a free-spirited stop on the young vagabond's circuit. In the Fifties, it ranked with New York's Greenwich Village and San Francisco's North Beach as a home for the beatniks. In the Sixties, rock music took over: Venice spawned Jim Morrison's influential Doors and other groups.

Now, a visitor can partake of an ocean-side lunch at the **Sidewalk Cafe** and watch the passing parade of bowling-ball jugglers, mimes, magicians, folk singers, Elvis Presley impersonators, unicyclists, Muscle Beach weightlifters, pretty girls in string bikinis, roller skaters and skateboarders. It's never dull. Street vendors push T-shirts, electronic gadgets, sunglasses, posters, prints, hats, watches, postcards, paisley pullovers and leopard-skin leotards. It seems as though everything and anything is for sale. Occasionally, there's even a good value.

Just south of Venice is **Marina del Rey**, the largest man-made small-craft harbor on earth. The harbor holds more than 10,000 private pleasure craft, all of them belonging to devotees of sailing or deep-sea fishing. Sailors being among the world's great pleasure seekers, there is also a heavy concentration of singles bars in the vicinity of the marina.

From the **Fisherman's Village**, visitors can tour the harbour on the *Marina Belle*, a replica of a Mississippi riverboat. The cruise affords passengers a glimpse of some of the world's most spectacular yachts cruising in and out of the marina channel.

Marina del Rey was once a large duck marsh. The only remaining vestige of the former life is the **Bird Sanctuary** between Washington Boulevard and Admiralty Way.

Majestic Malibu

At the north end of Los Angeles' west side, north even of Pacific Palisades, is the chic area of **Malibu**. This isolated beach resort has a long history as L.A.'s "last frontier," a place of tranquility overlooking the majestic Pacific.

Left would-be sailors catch the ocean breeze at Venice Beach, right, rolls to a disco beat.

Although the Malibu region was once occupied by Chumash Indians — skeletal remains of whom are still regularly recovered here — its modern history began in 1887. In that year, a wealthy Easterner named Frederick H. Rindge bought the entire area. He spent the rest of his life trying to keep others out. His widow continued that effort, so that it wasn't until 1928 that California's state government finally was permitted to build a highway on a right-of-way through the Rindge ranch. Soon after, Mrs. Rindge was forced to sell off some of her beachfront property. The development of Malibu had begun.

Certainly, Malibu's wild surf and secluded beaches are its big attraction. The private **Malibu Beach Colony,** for instance, is home to some of the motion-picture industry's biggest stars. It isn't surprising, therefore, that some of the beach "cottages" are as expensive as Beverly Hills estates.

Malibu is also the home of the highly touted **J. Paul Getty Museum.** Since 1974, one of the world's greatest private art collections has been displayed free to the public within the Getty villa, a detailed replica of the Villa del Papyri

at Herculaneum in the old Roman Empire. (The original villa, destroyed by a 79 A.D. eruption of Mount Vesuvius, was owned by Julius Caesar's father-in-law.) Mosaics, frescoes and Romanesque landscaping attempt to recapture a Mediterranean setting.

The art collection is set in several galleries connected through an atrium courtyard. There is a superb collection of Greek and Roman antiquities, a section on European paintings from the Renaissance through the baroque period, and many items from the French decorative arts.

When oil billionaire Getty commissioned architects Langdon and Wilson and consultant Norman Neuerburg to design and construct his museum, he directed that the spirit of 1st Century A.D. Rome be recreated in order to properly showcase his treasured acquisitions. Many thousands of appreciative art lovers believe the museum has done just that in the 10 years since it opened.

There's one hitch: visitors can't just drop by the Getty Museum. They must call in advance for a parking reservation. It could only happen in L.A.'s west side.

.eft, lazy fternoon in Marina del Rey. Right, ctress Pia Zadora at her Malibu ungalow.

SOUTH BAY: BLUE SKIES, BLUE WATER

When an area is host to the world's third-busiest airport; when it includes a city called the aerospace center of the world; when one of its biggest attractions is the aviation industry's albatross; it's obvious that its heart is in the clouds rather than on *terra firma.*

Such is the case of Los Angeles' South Bay region. Stretching from **Los Angeles International Airport** (LAX) to Long Beach, home of the bizarre *Spruce Goose,* the South Bay looks to the sky. But it never forgets Southern California's sworn oath of providing great beach towns and loads of sun.

Before the visitor — if he jets into L.A., that is — can enjoy the salt air at beach communities like Manhattan Beach or the quiet life of the Palos Verdes Peninsula, he must trudge through LAX. No mean feat, this.

Runaway Runways

LAX's statistics are mind-boggling. More than 32 million passengers a year pass through the airport; there is parking for 20,000 vehicles; the 3,500-acre (1,416-hectare) site handles nearly half a million landings and takeoffs annually and 750,000 tons of air cargo. Seventy-eight different airlines and cargo companies use the airport.

And now a three-year, $700 million expansion and improvement project is nearly complete. It includes a new five-story international terminal, a new domestic terminal, new cargo facilities and expanded parking areas. The new terminal space represents a doubling of the pre-existing space. That will make life much easier for the hordes of passengers expected to come for the 1984 L.A. Olympics.

Los Angeles International Airport was built in 1928 when the city leased a square mile of land in a field of lima beans, wheat and barley from the Bennett Rancho for a planned municipal airport. In those days, the airport was known as Mines Field and the single runway was a mere 2,000 feet (610 meters) of oiled ground. Immediately after the lease was signed, construction began on two 100-foot-square hangars,

neither of which would accommodate a modern medium-sized airplane.

Next to the airport is the City of **El Segundo**, which bills itself as "the aerospace center of the world." In 1911, when five representatives of Standard Oil Company came to a deserted melon patch overlooking the rolling sand dunes that stretched down to the Pacific Ocean, El Segundo didn't exist, except as a potential site for a future oil refinery. That refinery was to be the second in Southern California — hence the name El Segundo, "The Second."

Standard Oil thought the site was perfect: close to the beach where tankers could tie up easily and load their product, and near a growing population center where the workers could live. A tent city was hastily constructed and men from all over the West headed for El Segundo.

The arrival of the airport just outside the city limits boosted employment, as many of the pioneering aviation firms decided to base companies in El Segundo. Today aerospace, computers and electronics are the major industries.

It's not just jobs and travel that bring people to South Bay. Located in **In-**

glewood, slightly east of the airport, is **The Forum,** L.A.'s most prestigious sports-entertainment complex.

Situated at the corner of Manchester Boulevard and Prairie Avenue, The Forum was first conceived by sports-entertainment mogul Jack Kent Cooke in 1965. Despite the concerns of skeptics, Cooke went ahead and built the multi-purpose all-weather arena in 15 months, mainly for his pro basketball Lakers and pro hockey Kings.

The Forum, a.k.a. "The House That Jack Built," was copied after the Roman Forum but on a much grander scale. With a circumference of nearly 1,400 feet (about 425 meters), voiced by a $100,000 sound system and standing 87 feet (26½ meters) from playing floor to ceiling, the 18,000-seat Forum hosts a wide variety of attractions. Besides the Lakers and Kings, members of the audience can also see rodeos, ice-skating troupes, political gatherings, World Team Tennis, championship boxing, indoor soccer, horse shows, indoor track meets and rock concerts.

"Playing the Forum" has become synonymous in popular music circles with having made it to the top. David Bowie, Neil Diamond, Bob Dylan, Billy Joel, Willie Nelson, Linda Ronstadt, Bruce Springsteen and The Police have all played The Forum, to name a few.

Next to The Forum is **Hollywood Park,** a 350-acre (142-hectare) horse-racing venue with room for 34,000 spectators and parking for 31,000 cars. The park is one of Southern California's most beautiful, with lagoons, tropical landscaping and a large screen which provides stop-action look at close finishes and backstretch positions. Thoroughbred racing lasts from late April to mid-July while harness racing takes place from August to December.

Catch a Wave

Heading south from the airport area, one passes through the communities of **Manhattan Beach, Hermosa Beach** and **Redondo Beach** — the prototypes of the California lifestyle that was popularized by the "Surf Sound" of the Sixties.

While the Beach Boys hailed originally from nearby **Hawthorne,** Manhattan Beach was the band's spiritual home. Throughout the Sixties, the South Bay beach towns presented a combination of

Surf punks, Redondo Beach.

upper-class elegance and fun in the sun. The stately **Kings Harbor** in Redondo Beach was Southern California's premier private marina until San Pedro Harbor was built.

Nowadays the surfers in the South Bay follow a different sort of music — new wave. Radical new contingents of "surf punks" and "surf nazis" vie for waves, and the cry of "locals only" is heard frequently during the hot, crowded summer.

While the South Bay has made a name for itself in local music for its beach punk bands, there is still room for milder music forms. The local jazz spots, **The Lighthouse** (Hermosa Beach) and **Concerts by the Sea** (Redondo Beach), are two of the area's oldest and best established venues for hearing top-notch jazz and blues.

Heading southwest on Hawthorne Boulevard, one leaves behind the jumbled mess of Los Angeles and enters the **Palos Verdes Peninsula,** a 26.3-square-mile (68-sq-km) section of land that features many of L.A.'s most attractive homes.

Palos Verdes means "green trees" in Spanish and is the home of four sepa-rate municipalities: Palos Verdes Estates, Rolling Hills, Rolling Hills Estates and Rancho Palos Verdes. While the names may differ, the mood of all four is strikingly similar.

Entering the Palos Verdes Peninsula is like taking a trip back in time to a period in Southern California history when the streets were safe for walking, when neighborhoods were quiet and shaded by tall trees. The biggest problem facing most home owners was trying to decide if the back yard should be converted into a swimming pool or a horse stable for the kids.

Because the peninsula is in the path of many ocean breezes, it has the cleanest and coolest air in L.A. Thus it is an area that demands outdoor activity. There are four 18-hole golf courses (one is private), several public tennis courts, more than 60 miles (97 km) of maintained horse riding trails that wind through canyons and over hillsides, and several excellent fishing and diving access points.

While Palos Verdes stands as a symbol of upper-middle-class living for many, it is the beauty of the area which leaves a lasting impression. To fully

Rugged cliffs of the Palos Verdes Peninsula.

appreciate this aspect of the Peninsula, one should make a trip to the **Wayfarer's Chapel.**

The Wayfarer's Chapel (5755 Palos Verdes Dr. S.) was conceived by Elizabeth Schellenberg in the late Twenties. Mrs. Schellenberg was a member of the Swedenborgian Church and had a dream of building a chapel on a hillside overlooking the ocean where travelers could rest and meditate on the grandeur of the area's natural beauty. The chapel, a simple construction of glass, redwood beams and Palos Verdes stone, was designed by Lloyd Wright, son of the famous architect Frank Lloyd Wright. From inside its glass walls, one may rest protected from the elements with (in Wright's words) "a sense of outer as well as inner space."

Following the completion of the chapel in 1951, work began on building a tower, visitor's center and a colonnade. **The Wayfarer Tower,** topped by a lighted cross that is visible from far out at sea, is called "God's Candle" by sailors passing through the Catalina Channel.

Because of its history and beauty, the Wayfarer's Chapel has become a much-sought-after marriage facility, and wedding dates are booked many months in advance.

Marineland and Its Whales

Close by the chapel is the Palos Verdes attraction that draws more visitors than any other in the Peninsula. **Marineland,** which recently celebrated its 30th anniversary, is unlike any other Los Angeles-area amusement park. Its low-key approach to family entertainment and the incredible natural beauty of the surroundings make it a real treat for visitors.

Situated just south of the historic **Point Vicente Lighthouse,** Marineland sits 150 feet (46 meters) above the Pacific and offers a spectacular view of the ocean and Santa Catalina Island. During the annual migration of the gray whales (December through March), spectators enjoy more than 100 sightings a day of the giant mammals breaching and spouting just offshore. Closer to land is **Sea Lion Point** where Southern California's only beachside rookery of sea lions is situated.

Of course, the main attraction of

Visitors take the plunge a Marineland' Baja Reef swim-throug aquarium.

Marineland is not wild marine life but rather the 4,000 different mammals and fish that inhabit the park's various tanks. Part aquarium and part sea circus, Marineland specializes in teaching about sea life in an entertaining way.

Over the years the park has helped to advance marine studies on several fronts. It was the first to train a whale in captivity and the first to prove that dolphins have sonar capabilities. It is the home of Orky, a seven-ton killer whale, the largest animal in captivity; Bubbles, the world's oldest and largest pilot whale; and the only pair of killer whales and walruses in any aquarium.

While the various circus-type shows are the most popular features — there is a Sea Lion Show, a dolphin show and a killer whale show — the newest attraction, the **Baja Reef,** offers a really unique experience. The Reef is a "swim-through" aquarium which invites any visitor over four feet (122 cm) tall and weighing more than 70 pounds (32 kg) to take a dip. It holds more than 1,000 different fish and sharks (not dangerous) commonly found in the warm waters off the Baja Peninsula. Included in the 85-yard (78-meter), horseshoe-shaped facility are leopard sharks, garibaldi (California's state fish) sheepshead and numerous other brightly colored fish.

Also of particular interest is the dolphin community pool where visitors may don aquatic earphones and listen to the whistles and clicks that compose the mammal's language. The pool allows one to get within touching distance of mankind's closest marine relative. The dolphins prove to be just as curious about humans as humans are about them. They roll on their sides and stare up at the faces looking down at them, swimming close to the sides of the tank in long, slow, graceful movements. For years, Southern California surfers have held a strong affection for dolphins because of their friendliness and their ability to drive away sharks.

One word of caution: because of its exposed location, Marineland can be chilly on winter days. Visitors should take along sweater or coat if the day is overcast.

Point Fermin to L.A. Harbor

Yachties compete off Long Beach.

As one heads south from Marineland, the reality of Southern California's growth quickly intrudes. Point Fermin is the last chance to sample the beauty of the coastline. Here at the 37-acre (15-hectare) **Point Fermin Park,** one may stop for a brief visit to the extensive tidepools of the **Marine Life Refuge** or just take in the magnificent vistas that overlook the harbor and the ocean. There is a wonderful old lighthouse here, built in 1874, that unfortunately is not open to the public. But it's still a good vantage point for spotting migrating whales. Further along the drive south is the **Cabrillo Beach Marine Museum** (3700 Stephen White Dr. S.) where one of the world's largest seashell collections is housed. It is not as spectacular as Marineland but is certainly educational.

Almost as commanding as the ocean is **Los Angeles Harbor,** one of the world's largest man-made ports. The 28 miles (45 km) of waterfront facilities provide berths for thousands of pleasure boats and service over 4,000 larger container ships annually. When the original port landing was built in 1835, **San Pedro Bay** was only two feet deep in many places. Most ocean-going vessels, therefore, had to anchor off shore. In

the 1850s, Phineas Banning used a simple dredge to deepen the port to 16 feet (five meters). The present depth is 51 feet (15½ meters).

Before arriving at the industrial side of the harbor, one comes to the **22nd Street Landing,** a dock area that caters mainly to sport-fishing boats. Here one may buy crabs for as little as $2 apiece and crack them dockside while watching the boats unload their catches of halibut, tuna, perch, cod, mackerel, yellowtail and bass. For a more active role, visitors can buy space on one of the 18 private boats that take out fishermen for quarter, half-day or all-day cruises. Tackle may be rented and bait is provided by the boat.

Further into the port is **Ports O' Call Village,** the first of three ersatz "villages" that are little more than glorified malls. Ports O' Call, like its relatives to the south, Londontowne and Shoreline Village, provides shopping and dining but little else. Its Disneyland-like atmosphere is an attempt at recreating a mid 19th Century port town.

The one exception to Ports O' Call's consumer appeal is **Buccaneer Cruises,** which features four different ships and a variety of cruises. There are two paddleboats (the *Show Boat* and the *Princess*) and two high-masted sailing ships (the square-rigged barque *Buccaneer Queen* and the topsail schooner *The Swift.*) The cruises range from leisurely harbor tours to sunset dinner cruises, trips to Santa Catalina Island and whale-watching voyages.

Just before crossing the 6,500-foot (1,980-meter) long **Vincent Thomas Bridge** — a 185-foot (56-meter) high suspension bridge which connects San Pedro with **Terminal Island** — the **Los Angeles Maritime Museum** is located in the old Port of L.A. ferry building at Berth 84. The museum has a splendid collection of model ships (including a 16-foot scale model of the *Titanic*) and offers one of the best viewing spots to watch the harbor activity.

Once one crosses onto Terminal Island, two of Long Beach's most prominent tourist attractions are close by: the *Queen Mary* and the *Spruce Goose.*

Royalty and Reclusion

Ever since the **Queen Mary** arrived at her permanent berth in Long Beach, Howard Hug *Spruce Goos*

the ship has been a question in the minds of local officials and residents. For years the 81,000-ton vessel was seen as a white elephant by city fathers, whose revenues were puny compared to maintenance costs that exceeded $2 million a year. "Let's turn the *Queen Mary* into razor blades," some suggested, only half-jokingly. Others proposed a floating poker parlor.

Then, like the cavalry coming over the hill to rescue the settlers from hostile Indians, the Wrather Corporation, operator of the Disneyland Hotel, stepped in and leased the boat from the city. The company immediately began a $12 million facelift that finally returned the ship to her former glory. With the massive refurbishing and the opening of the *Spruce Goose* next door, the crowds began to come in droves and the *Queen Mary* was spared the ignominy of making a final voyage to the scrap heap.

A tour of the *Queen Mary* — which crossed the Atlantic Ocean 1,001 times — includes stops in the hospital, beauty salon, gymnasium, Observation Lounge and Grand Salon, where a band plays music of the Thirties, Forties and Fifties nightly. Staterooms are available for overnight guests. Adjacent to the ship is the theme-oriented **Londontowne** shopping village.

The **Spruce Goose** is located in the Howard Hughes Flying Boat Expo right next door. The 400,000-ton craft — which is made of birch, not spruce at all — made only one flight. On Nov. 1, 1947, its designer, millionaire recluse Howard Hughes, took the plane for a one-mile flight at a height of 70 feet (21 meters) over the harbor waters to silence government critics who complained that it was a $25-million boondoggle. After its brief flying career, the *Hercules* (as Hughes had named the craft) was sequestered in a temperature-controlled hanger for 36 years. Its original purpose — to be a mammoth troop-carrying plane capable of transporting 750 soldiers and two tanks — was quickly forgotten.

Only on a tour of the plane, which has drawn large weekend crowds since it opened in early 1983, does one begin to absorb the craft's bizarre statistics. It has eight propeller-driven engines, is taller than an eight-story building, and has a wingspan of more than 300 feet (91 meters). Equally as fascinating are

Shoreline Village and Marina, adjacent to downtown Long Beach.

the various slide shows and photos that offer details about the life of its eccentric inventor.

'Iowa-by-the-Sea'

Unfortunately for the City of **Long Beach,** its reputation for years has been anything but fascinating. The city recently changed its motto from "The Friendly City" to "Long Beach: A City Alive." That's certainly better than its previous image of being "Dullsville by the Drink," "Sinking City" (a reference to a problem of subsidence in the Fitties), or "Iowa-by-the-Sea" (for its popularity with transplanted Midwesterners during the Second World War).

When the Spanish explorer Juan Cabrillo first sailed into San Pedro Bay in 1542, he could barely make out the shoreline because of smoke from fires set by local Indians hunting for rabbits. Consequently he named the area *Bahia de los Fumos* ("Bay of Smokes"), hardly a title to promote immigration.

Long Beach was overshadowed by its northern neighbor, Los Angeles until 1911 when the first docks were built.

Goo

The discovery of oil at **Signal Hill** in 1921 set off a massive building boom. But in 1933 a tremendous earthquake leveled sections of the city, killing 57 people and causing $41 million in damage. The arrival of World War II prompted the construction of the world's largest drydock, and the opening of the Douglas Aircraft plant encouraged workers to head for the harbor instead of L.A.

During the Seventies, about the only thing that Long Beach had to boast about was the (formerly) dilapidated *Queen Mary*. It was known as a city full of "old oil wells, old buildings and old people." But this decade has seen a renewed surge of building and a new sense of civic pride. Population has passed 360,000, making it the fifth largest city in California.

Helping to boost the city's image is the recent completion of the **Hyatt Long Beach Hotel,** on the edge of the city's tidelands area (where the world's largest tideland oil reserves exist). The 16-story building has a strikingly modern design and includes a quarter-mile boardwalk that effectively links the ocean with the downtown area.

Close by is the new **Shoreline Village,** a mock-Victorian "village" which is the focal point for a $27-million marina providing berths for more than 1,700 pleasure boats.

But history doesn't live only in the mock village. Despite its reputation as a place of no culture and little history, Long Beach does possess some fascinating samples of California's past. In the Drake Park Historical District, one of Long Beach's oldest residential neighborhoods, is the **Bembridge House.** This is the city's only perfectly preserved example of a Queen Anne mansion. Well maintained since its construction at the turn of the century, the Bembridge has beveled Tiffany windows, turrets and some beautifully intricate scrollwork.

Pre-dating the Bembridge by a century are the remnants of **Rancho Los Alamitos.** The adobe core of this Spanish-era ranch was built in 1806 and represents the oldest adobe structure still standing in Los Angeles County. Located at the southern end of Long Beach (6400 E. Bixby Hill Road), the Rancho — and its neighbor **Rancho Los Cerritos** (1844) — offers a variety of exhibits depicting the life of early California settlers.

Left, Formula One driver dons helmet for start of Long Beach Grand Prix. Right, bikinied beauty struts her stuff for contest judges and audience.

SAN GABRIEL: ROSES AND SMOG

For many people, there's only one day a year to be in **Pasadena,** and that's the first one.

Every New Year's Day, the spectacular **Tournament of Roses** parade steals the national limelight for a few short but memorable hours. Televised throughout the United States, the parade has become as much a part of the holiday tradition as party hats and noisemakers on New Year's Eve. In 1990, in fact, it will celebrate its 100th anniversary.

But from January 2 onward, Pasadena and the **San Gabriel Valley** in which it is located clearly play third fiddle to a pair of more famous valleys, the San Fernando to the west and Death Valley to the northeast.

Two decades ago, one of the most popular duos in California and America, Jan and Dean, used to sing about "The Little Old Lady From Pasadena" who couldn't "keep her foot off the accelerator." They never explained why. But were the truth to be told, she probably couldn't wait to get out of the San Gabriel Valley.

That doesn't mean to imply that the Valley lacks virtues. In fact, this basin of suburbia — lying just to the east of downtown Los Angeles — is within an hour's drive of desert, mountains, beaches and Hollywood glitter, making it a great base of operations for Southern California visitors. Wedged between the towering **San Gabriel Mountains** and the less conspicuous **Puente and Chino hills,** it is surrounded by four major routes (the Long Beach, Foothill, Pomona and Orange freeways) and bisected by two more (the San Bernardino and San Gabriel freeways).

But San Gabriel's biggest drawback is its infamous smog. During the summer, second and third-degree smog alerts are commonplace. Toxic fumes and smoke filter into the Valley, stack up against the highlands, and create an "abracadabra effect": they make the San Gabriel Mountains vanish before one's very (watery) eyes.

Historical Treasures

Nevertheless, the San Gabriel Valley is a pleasant place to visit on relatively smog-free days. There are numerous attractions of historical, cultural and recreational interest in and around the valley and abutting mountains. One just needs to know where to look.

The first major settlement in the San Gabriel Valley grew around the **Mission San Gabriel Arcangel,** founded in 1771. The fourth of the 21 Franciscan missions in California, it was an agricultural center controlling thousands of acres and some 40,000 head of cattle, sheep, hogs and horses at the peak of its power in 1830. Today, visitors can see the original altar with six wooden statues from Mexico, a belltower restored following an 1812 earthquake, and a series of 18th Century Indian paintings. The mission, open daily except major religious holidays, is located at 537 W. Mission Dr. at the corner of Junipero Serra Drive in **San Gabriel** city.

The first party of overland settlers from the East arrived in the Valley in 1841. John Rowland and William Workman came with their wives, bought a 48,710-acre (19,713-hectare) expanse from the Mexican government for about $1,000, and settled in the southern part of the Valley. Their houses, the **Rowland House** and the **Workman Adobe,** have been restored and are located in the town of **Industry.** Alongside the Workman home on East Don Julian Road is **La Casa Nueva,** a Spanish-style mansion built between 1919 and 1923 by Workman's grandson, Walter Temple. There are hourly tours every afternoon but Mondays.

The coming of the railroad in the 1880s brought the first real rush of population to the area. The Valley offered settlers proximity to the growing city of Los Angeles without the attendant congestion. The same is relatively true now, although lack of congestion now means having a large back yard or patio.

Oasis Amid the Asphalt

Nearly all of the 35-plus cities and communities that make up the San Gabriel Valley claim a few unique characteristics. But to the untrained eye, it is difficult to discern where one ends and the next begins. Apart from the road signs designating city boundaries, the changes are subtle — a short break in street lighting, a change in housing density, new forms of graffiti, or a shift

Patriotic entry floats through the Tournament of Roses Parade.

in the models of old cars parked along the street. (The '64 Mercedes of **South Pasadena** give way to the '69 Volkswagens of **Arcadia** and the '56 Chevys of **El Monte**.)

Smack in the middle of this tangled web of asphalt, apartments and single-family dwellings lies one of the few true oases of the Valley, the **Los Angeles State and County Arboretum** on North Baldwin Avenue in Arcadia. A 127-acre (51-hectare) sanctuary and test site for flora, it features more than 30,000 plants, including 5,000 different species and the exotic Lasca Lagoon, whose name comes from the park's acronym. The arboretum has been used as a film setting for various TV commercials as well as *Fantasy Island* and *Roots*. The site also contains the 1839 **Hugh Reid Adobe**, the 1885 **Queen Anne Cottage and Coach Barn**, and the 1889 **Santa Fe Railroad Depot**.

The arboretum's sister facility is the **Descanso Gardens** in **La Canada**. Its specialties include roses, begonias, 100,000 camellias and *bonsai* shrubbery. Other garden reserves include the **Rancho Santa Ana Botanical Garden**, 1500 N. Claremont Ave., **Claremont**;

and the 130-acre (53-hectare) botanical garden at the **Huntington Library and Art Gallery**, 1151 Oxford Road in **San Marino**.

The Huntington Library houses one of mankind's greatest collections of rare books and manuscripts. They belonged to the late Henry E. Huntington, mastermind of the Pacific Electric Railway, whose "Big Red Cars" connected the San Gabriel Valley with Los Angeles proper in the first half of the century. Among the more famous items are a Gutenberg Bible and Benjamin Franklin's autobiography in his own handwriting. The gallery contains fine tapestries, sculpture, furniture, and paintings, among them Thomas Gainsborough's "Blue Boy" and Gilbert Stuart's famed portrait of George Washington.

Pasadena Peculiarities

Another impressive display of a local multimillionaire's artistic eclecticism is the **Norton Simon Museum**, 411 W. Colorado Blvd., Pasadena. Originally the Pasadena Museum of Modern Art, it was rescued from financial ruin in 1974 by Simon, who has since expanded

San Gabriel Mountain panorama from Mount Wilson.

(some say distorted) its original focus to include tapestries, sculptures and paintings (including Renoir, Van Gogh and Monet) from the early Renaissance period through the 20th Century.

Pasadena is home to numerous other cultural institutions. They include the **Pacific Asia Museum** 47 N. Los Robles Ave., which purports to be the only Southern California museum specializing in the arts of Asia and the Pacific. **Kidspace,** 390 S. El Molino Ave., encourages children up to age 12 to make their own scientific and technological discoveries. A "hands-on" concept is applied to play participation in various vocational roles, communication networks and education through Gutsie, a human anatomy cutaway model.

Bigger kids make their own discoveries at the **California Institute of Technology,** 1201 E. California Blvd. Cal Tech is a key research center for seismology and space engineering. Its **Jet Propulsion Laboratory** served as the monitoring headquarters for the Voyager I and II satellites. Regrettably, the JPL does not offer public tours on any regular basis. Cal Tech, which has had 14 Nobel laureates among its staff and a

research assistant named Albert Einstein, caters its tours only for prospective students.

Those students weren't around at the turn of the 20th Century, when Pasadena was best known for its elegant homes. Many of those lushly landscaped estates are now deteriorating or giving way to mammoth office condominiums. One of the best remaining examples of this recent past is the **Gamble House,** 4 Westmoreland Place. This 1908 wooden home was designed by architects Henry and Charles Greene. Another fine home is the **Tournament House,** 391 S. Orange Grove Blvd., former home of chewing-gum magnate William Wrigley. It was donated to the Tournament of Roses Association.

The Tournament of Roses

For all these attractions, it is still the New Year's Day extravaganza that packs in the visitors from Los Angeles, the rest of California, and many parts of the globe. Each year, in fact, hordes of masochistic onlookers begin setting up camp as early as 72 hours before parade time to be assured of a prime viewing

First down and 10 to go in the Rose Bowl, Pasadena.

spot. It's no wonder that some of the best-selling items along the parade route are T-shirts emblazoned with the slogan: "I Survived New Year's Eve in Pasadena."

Following the parade, the mobile flower garden of 60 floats is routed to a nearby park, where entries remain on display for two days before withering away to their polyvinyl-coated steel and chicken wire frames.

The parade precedes the longest-running of all America's collegiate football championship shows: the **Rose Bowl.** Since 1923 (the eighth contest), two outstanding gridiron teams have lined up against each other on New Year's Day in Pasadena's 104,699-seat Rose Bowl stadium at **Brookside Park.** For many years, the game has pitted the champions of the West Coast's Pac-10 Conference and the Great Lakes region's Big 10 Conference.

There are two other important seasonal events in Pasadena. For the two weeks preceding the Rose Parade, a stretch of Santa Rosa Avenue in adjacent **Altadena** turns brilliantly festive with the illumination of **Christmas Tree Lane.** And several weeks earlier, the **Doo-Dah Parade** makes its editorial rebuttal to the Tournament of Roses. Entries in this entertaining procession have included a California Bank synchronized briefcase unit, the Toro Toro Toro lawnmowing marching group, and a dentists' variable speed drill team.

The Feeling Is Parimutuel

There are other festivities in the Valley. The **Los Angeles County Fair** — the largest county fair in America — is held from mid September to early October every year at the fairgrounds in **Pomona.** First held in 1922, it was originally slated to be the Pomona Valley Fair until its backers learned the L.A. County title was still up for grabs. Along with standard carnival fare of thrill rides, game booths and cotton candy amid dusty surroundings, the L.A. County Fair features a cross-section of cultural performing groups, agricultural contests and shows, a vast smorgasbord of international foods, and parimutuel horse racing on most days.

For horse racing the rest of the year, **Santa Anita Race Track,** 285 W. Huntington Dr., Arcadia, is open from early

Left, campaigning for votes at the Doo Dah Parade. Right high-speed amusement at the L.A. County Fair.

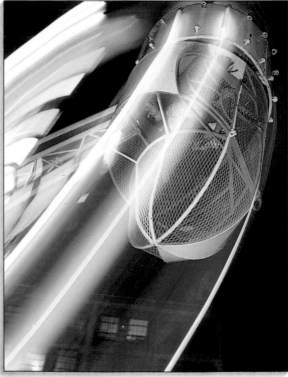

October to mid November and again from Dec. 26 to late April. This is the track where the starting gate, electrical timing and the photo finish were first introduced. Morning workouts (7:30 to 9.30 a.m.) are open to the public every race day. The season's big event is the $500,000 Santa Anita Handicap, the pioneer of big-stakes handicap races.

A different kind of horse show is presented at the **Kellogg Arena** of **California State Polytechnic University, Pomona.** At 2 p.m. on the first Sunday of each month during the school year (October to July), the school's Arabian Horse Center stages a show of horsemanship techniques, usually involving between 10 and 15 of its 80 horses.

Pomona lies at the eastern edge of the San Gabriel Valley. Just north of it is **San Dimas,** where lies the **Frank G. Bonelli Regional Park.** This is a fully developed reservoir for swimming, fishing and water skiing. In 1983, it added a water-slide theme park called **Raging Waters** to its grounds. It's located at 150 E. Puddingstone Dr.

Two memorial parks in the Valley — **Forest Lawn** in **Covina Hills** and **Rose Hills** in **Whittier** — offer works of artis-

tic and natural beauty. Forest Lawn, 21300 Via Verde Dr., displays three marble sculptures (David, Venus de Milo and St. George) and two huge mosaics. One is a reproduction of Michelangelo's work in the Vatican's Sistine Chapel. The other, called "The Life of Christ," is a 172-foot (53-meter) long, 34-foot (10-meter) high depiction with 26 scenes. Rose Hills, 3900 S. Workman Mill Road, features a 3½-acre Pageant of Roses garden that includes 2,000 climbing rose bushes, lakes, bridges and a Japanese Garden.

Nixon: Prettier in Whittier

Whittier is probably still best known to most Americans as the hometown of former President Richard Nixon. Though Orange County claims two sites important to Nixon's personal history — his birthplace at Yorba Linda and his "Western White House" at San Clemente — the Whittier Chamber of Commerce goes a step further by providing a map entitled "President Nixon: Points of Interest." A drive around the city, however, indicates that not much interest has been shown in preserving

Scorching the turf at Santa Anita.

the landmarks. The old Nixon family store has been replaced by a service station and the apartment where Nixon resided while running for Congress in 1946 has been leveled for a senior citizens center.

One site that Whittier has partially restored and preserved is the **Pio Pico Casa State Historic Park,** 6003 S. Pioneer Blvd. The *hacienda* of the last governor of California under Mexican rule, it contains period furnishings.

Not far from Whittier, at 301 S. Euclid St., the **La Habra Children's Museum** features a nature walk, a live bee observatory, styrofoam building blocks and a model-train village.

Whittier Narrows Recreation and Nature Center, 1000 N. Durfee Ave., is a 277-acre (112-hectare) wildlife and plant sanctuary that includes a lake, bicycle and equestrian trails, a golf course, and rifle, skeet and archery ranges. The odd thing is that it's actually located in **South El Monte.**

Better golfers will rave about the **Industry Hills and Sheraton Resort** course, 111 S. Azusa Ave., Industry. There are two championship courses here — the Dwight D. Eisenhower and

the Babe Zaharias. Neither is designed for the Sunday hacker looking to get through the round with just one ball.

Six separate snow-skiing resorts are located along the northern and eastern slopes of the San Gabriel range. The most highly regarded by keen skiers are **Mount Baldy,** with four chairlifts and a summit elevation of 8,600 feet (2,632

The San Gabriel Mountains

Visitors are welcome at the **Mount Wilson Observatory,** perhaps the most famous landmark of the San Gabriel Mountains. A photo gallery, museum and viewing room relate the story of the Hooker 100-inch reflecting telescope (the first of its kind) and the discoveries it has made. Those include the realization that there is more than one galaxy, and a gauging of the true extent of the Milky Way Galaxy.

The San Gabriel range, stretching in name from the Antelope Valley Freeway east to Interstate 15, forms the basis for the 693,454 acres (280,637 hectares) of wilderness and nature that comprise the **Angeles National Forest.** The mountains hold a virtual gold mine of recreational opportunities.

meters), and the **Holiday Hill-Mountain High** complex at **Wrightwood,** which offers night skiing. Others include **Ski Sunrise** at Wrightwood, **Mount Waterman** at La Canada and **Kratka Ridge,** also at La Canada. Several of the areas have snow-making equipment, allowing them to extend their seasons from December to April.

More than 36,000 acres (14,500 hectares) in the heart of the Angeles National Forest have been set aside as the **San Gabriel Valley Wilderness.** Special permits are required to enter this area. Surrounding the wilderness area is an interlocking network of trails that can take hikers up, around, over and through every kind of terrain, from Mount Wilson to Mount Waterman, past **Crystal Lake,** and to the summit of **Mount San Antonio** ("Old Baldy"), the highest point in the range at 10,064 feet (3,067 meters).

Near the southeast corner of the wilderness area is an off-road recreational vehicle area (at the north end of San Gabriel Reservoir on State Highway 39). Hundreds of RV drivers regularly engage in a free-for-all frolic through the riverbeds.

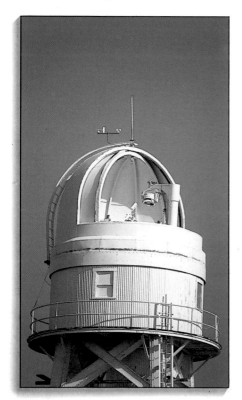

Left, Mount Wilson observatory Right, winter bliss at Mount Baldy

SAN FERNANDO: THE VALLEY SCENE

According to the 1980 census, some 1.3 million people live in the San Fernando Valley — or as it is better known to those who live in Los Angeles, *The* Valley. If The Valley were a city unto itself, it would be the sixth largest in the United States, surpassed only by New York, Chicago, Los Angeles, Philadelphia and Houston.

On one level, of course, The Valley is a place that conforms to certain physical parameters. It runs, loosely, from the Ventura County line on the west, to the San Gabriel Mountains on the east and north, to the Santa Monica Mountains on the south. But The Valley isn't so much a geographical area as it is a state of mind. It has been the butt of 1,000 Johnny Carson jokes and numerous other disparaging remarks. To paraphrase the classic line from *Love Story*, "Living in The Valley means always having to say you're sorry."

In truth, the San Fernando Valley is a very good place to live. Shopping is abundant and easy, parking is convenient (something the rest of Los Angeles has trouble claiming), and broad freeways make much of The Valley readily accessible — even though traffic jams at rush hours are among the worst in Southern California. Downtown L.A. can be reached from most parts of The Valley in less than 30 minutes. Yet The Valley also has places where orange groves still prosper, where people ride horses down shaded lanes, and where corn stalks grow tall in the summer sun.

'Valle de los Encinos'

In a way, there is still much of what Father Juan Crespi called "a very pleasant and spacious valley" when he first climbed over **Sepulveda Pass** in 1769. He named the area "Valle de Santa Catalina de Bononia de los Encinos." The only part of the original name that survived has been given to the town of **Encino**, the Spanish word for "oak."

For its first century or so, the San Fernando Valley lived a life of its own north of Los Angeles. The San Fernando mission was established in 1796 and finished in 1806. Around the mission,

huge ranchos sprang up — El Encino, El Escorpion, San Rafael and La Providencia. At first, the semi-arid Valley was used for pasture. But the Francisans brought more than religion to California. They also brought the technology that would first turn the Valley into lush farmland and later into the single largest suburb in America.

The Valley remained essentially rural until the 1870s, when the great ranchos were sliced up like pies by men whose names (Isaac Lankershim and I.N. Van Nuys) later were given to the grand boulevards of the area. With the coming of the railroad in 1874, the California land speculation boom swept over The Valley in what would be the first of many waves. Towns such as **Burbank, Glendale, Reseda, Chatsworth** and **Pacoima** sprang up.

The railroads paid the way, and wages, of dozens of Eastern writers to come to California and publicize the good life. One journalist, Charles Nordhoff, wrote a book called *California: For Health, Pleasure and Residence*. In it, he said: "The cost of living is today less in California by a third than in any eastern state." To that sort of hype, the railroad added incredible incentives to the land boomers. At first, the fare from Kansas City to Los Angeles was $125; but it quickly dropped to a mere $15, and for a very brief time to only $1. California and the San Fernando Valley were touted as the Promised Land. And it cost only 10 thin dimes to get there.

The boom was short-lived, though, and the Valley boom went bust for approximately the next three decades.

What happened next is an event which historian Morrow Mayo has called "The Rape of the Owens Valley." By 1900, the population of Los Angeles had shot over 100,000, and the city had to make a choice between stopping its growth or finding a way to get more water. Fred Eaton, an engineer and former mayor, hatched a plan to build an aqueduct that would direct the melting snows of the Sierra Nevada to the Owens River some 250 miles (400 km) north of Los Angeles. He sold the idea to William Mulholland, the city's water chief, and Mulholland put a $24.5 million price tag on the project.

"Titanic Project to Give City a River" announced *The Los Angeles Times* in July 1905. Two months later, voters passed a $1.5 million bond issue to buy

It's "like so bitchin', fer sure," to be a Valley Girl.

Owens Valley land, including that owned by Eaton, the scheme's mastermind. Work began on the "Panama Canal of the West" in 1907 after another bond issue, for $23 million, was passed.

Although many entrepreneurs got rich in behind-the-scenes dealings, the project ultimately worked. On Nov. 5, 1913, about 40,000 Angelenos turned out to witness the Owens River water cascading into a San Fernando Valley reservoir. "There it is," said Mulholland. "Take it."

L.A.'s Bedroom

By then, the City of Los Angeles had annexed the San Fernando Valley, adding a staggering 177 square miles (458 sq km) to the 107 square miles (277 sq km) which already made up this burgeoning megalopolis. At the time, there was only one policeman in the whole Valley — making it, very possibly, the world's largest beat.

In the years that followed, The Valley became a major center for the motion picture and television industries. Companies such as Universal, Warner Bros. and Columbia spread across huge plots of land. In more recent years, the National Broadcasting Company (NBC) opened a vast facility in "Beautiful Downtown Burbank" and the Columbia Broadcasting System (CBS) moved onto the old Republic Films lot in **Studio City.**

More significantly, the Valley turned into "L.A.'s bedroom," a community where single-story, ranch-style homes outnumber multiple dwellings by a ratio of at least two to one. After World War II, the Valley became one of the touchstones of the American dream, a place where anyone could afford to buy a nice house on a small lot, raise children and put in a good lawn.

Here in suburbia, however, there are a few problems. Architecture is almost uniformly boring. And the Valley's rich parents are guilty of excessively spoiling, exceedingly pampering, their children. Herein lies the socioeconomic basis for the Zappas' *Valley Girl* song. There is a tension between the generations, but the children aren't so much rebellious as they are parodies of their parents: obsessed with clothing, hair, fingernails, cars, shopping, credit cards

Workers posing in section of pipeline during aqueduct construction circa 1910.

and being at the right place in the right trend at the right time. Valley girls not only have their own aesthetics; they also have their own language.

The song's lyrics include numerous examples of Val Talk — phrases like "Bag your face," "Barf me out" and "Gag me with a spoon."

Touring the Studios

The Valley is far more than just a bedroom community over the hill from the "real world" of Los Angeles. Within its confines are some of the most popular tourist attractions in Southern California.

The **Universal Studios Tour** is unquestionably the single biggest draw in the San Fernando Valley. Though films may flop, Universal can always count on a steady flow of tourists. The 4½-hour tour is so popular, in fact, that during the summer new parties are taken every five minutes from 8 a.m. to 6 p.m., seven days a week! (The rest of the year, tour parties set out every 20 minutes daily with more limited hours.)

There are two parts to the studio tour. It begins on a "Glamourtrain," taking visitors on a constantly expanding series of thrills: a monster shark attacks the train, Cylons from *Battlestar Galactica* bombard the train with laser weapons, Conan the Barbarian wields his sword to protect passengers from a dragon. The train even passes through the Red Sea, parted for passengers courtesy of Moses.

This section serves to display numerous special effects and sets, and gives an understanding of sound stages, props and costuming. The tour ends with staged live shows and demonstrations by stuntmen and animal actors. The studio is located on Lankershim Boulevard at the Hollywood Freeway.

A short drive away is the **NBC Studio Tour** in Burbank (3000 W. Alameda Ave.). The 90-minute tour here is much more sedate than the Universal Studios tour, and a good deal more serious. The walk through the largest color studio in America leaves visitors with a sense of how hard it is to put together a television program. After the tour, many folks join the long line for admittance to *The Tonight Show* starring Johnny Carson.

The Valley's agricultural history is recalled in an orange crate label.

A Patch of Green

The largest urban park in America is **Griffith Park**, which effectively separates Burbank and Glendale from Hollywood and downtown Los Angeles. As municipal parks go, it is not exactly awash with charm. Neither is it a wonderful park for strolling. But it is rather enjoyable for drivers. How quintessentially Los Angeles!

The park, donated to the city by Col. Griffith J. Griffith, contains 4,063 acres (1,644 hectares) of land, much of it arid and mountainous. There are numerous attractions for those willing to pay the modest automobile admission fee. They include:

— The **Los Angeles Zoo,** with more than 2,000 species of mammals, birds and reptiles on its 113 acres (46 hectares). It is located near the junction of the Golden State (1-5) and Ventura (U.S. 101) freeways.

— **Travel Town** (5730 Crystal Springs Dr.), whose displays trace the evolution of various means of transportation.

— An **Equestrian Center** (Riverside Drive and Main Street) with 43 miles (69 km) of trails and international jumping and hunting schools.

— The **Greek Theatre** (2700 N. Vermont Ave.), a natural amphitheater that hosts ballets and rock concerts every summer.

— The **Griffith Observatory and Planetarium** (Mount Hollywood). The projector in the planetarium reproduces heavenly objects several times daily, while the **Hall of Science** has exhibits of meteorological achievements. On clear nights (except Mondays) from 7 to 10 o'clock, visitors may peer through the observatory's twin refracting telescope at the heavens and the city lights.

There are two branches of **Forest Lawn Cemetery** in The Valley, almost at opposite ends of Griffith Park. One is in Glendale, the other in **Hollywood Hills.** Brochures from the park — they avoid the term "cemetery" — quote founder Hubert Eaton as wanting to build "the greenest, most enchanting park you ever saw in your life." It's not exactly that, but it is breathtaking in its strangeness.

Both cemeteries are filled with exact replicas of famous churches, such as Wee Kirk o' the Heather and Boston's Old North Church (both in Hollywood

Tourists part the Red Sea at Universal Studios.

134

Hills). The Hollywood park also has halls dedicated to the patriotic history of America. Glendale's park features mammoth murals of the crucifixion and resurrection, a stained-glass rendition of Leonardo da Vinci's "Last Supper," and a reproduction of Michelangelo's David. Many famous Hollywood personalities are buried in these parks, among them W.C. Fields and Clark Gable.

Mansions and Missions

Glendale has other fine art works in its **Brand Library and Art Center**, 1601 W. Mountain St. in Brand Park. The Moorish-style mansion, built in 1904, is open afternoons Tuesday through Saturday.

The **Mission San Fernando Rey de Espana** is still alive and well at 15151 San Fernando Mission Blvd. in **Mission Hills** at the northern end of the Valley. The chapel and monastery, built in 1797, have been restored. Many Indian crafts and other artifacts have been preserved, including a 16th Century altar, detailed wood carvings which relate Bi-

ble stories, antique period furniture and a wine press. In Brand Park across the street from the mission are the original reservoir from which the *padres* took their water, an old soap works and a statue of Father Junipero Serra.

Other mission-era homes have also been rescued and renovated. **Los Encinos State Historic Park**, 16756 Moorpark St., Encino, contains several buildings and shops including the 1849 **De La Osa Adobe**. The **Leonis Adobe**, 23537 Calabasas Road, **Calabasas**, is a Monterey-style adobe ranch house dating from 1844. The **Andreas Pico Adobe** can trace its roots back to 1834. Arts and crafts of this era can be seen at the **Canoga Mission Gallery**, 23130 Sherman Way, **Canoga Park**. The surprise is not that these buildings and artifacts are so old, but that there's anything old to be found in the San Fernando Valley.

The fancier houses in The Valley can be found in Studio City, **Sherman Oaks**, Encino, **Woodland Hills** and Calabasas. While Beverly Hills and Bel Air claim the largest star populations in Los Angeles, there are plenty of celebrities here, too. They include comedian Bob Hope and singers Rick Springfield, Kim

_eft,
Singapore at
he Burbank
Studios.
Right,
souvenir of
a piece of
Americana.

Carnes and Michael Jackson (and the whole Jackson family).

The further from the hills one gets, and the closer to the desert, the hotter the temperature gets. Temperatures on The Valley side of the hills are usually above five degrees Fahrenheit (3°C) above those of downtown Los Angeles. They can go up another 10°F (5°C) on the "flats." Likewise, the "flats" population becomes poorer, more blue-collar and more Latino. (The Valley has a Latino population of about 17 percent.) Homes grow more tract-like and less interesting. On a hot day, the air is dusty and rancid.

In a way, neither the trendies who live in the hills nor the workers who eke out a living on the "flats" are really the heart and soul of The Valley. The true Valley people are ... well, let a Valley person explain.

'Valley People'

"I like to think of my parents as definitive Valley People," said Darryl Morden, a scriptwriter who grew up in the Valley. "When they were married in the early Fifties, they bought a small

house in **Van Nuys** on a quiet street. After I was born, and my sister was born, they moved to a larger house in Sherman Oaks."

Morden took another bite out of his waffle at **Du-par's**, a Studio City coffee shop popular with entertainment industry people. "They've spent a lot of time putting in gardens, a swimming pool, an electric garage-door opener. But they've been more concerned with the quality of their life than with the quality of their appliances. People like to say things are slower here than in Los Angeles, but that's not true. From where I live it takes me 15 minutes to get to Rodeo Drive, 20 minutes to get to downtown L.A. I can eat in restaurants in my neighborhood that are every bit as trendy as anything in Santa Monica. It's crazy to think of The Valley as just an annex of Los Angeles. This is as much a part of Los Angeles as the West Side and Hollywood. It's just a heck of a lot cleaner."

Du-par's is known as the "Polo Lounge of the Valley," a tongue-in-cheek moniker which comes from the large number of people from the nearby CBS Center who meet there to rub elbows, talk contracts and come up with sitcom ideas. Not far away, **Art's Deli** displays a framed letter from Frank Sinatra praising the eatery's corned beef. When Mimi Sheraton, restaurant critic of *The New York Times*, came to Los Angeles to study West Coast food trends, one of the handful of restaurants she visited was **La Serre** in Sherman Oaks. Ventura Boulevard, in fact, is one of Southern California's greatest restaurant strips as it runs through Universal City (**Fung Lum**, the world's largest Chinese restaurant), Sherman Oaks (**Camille's, Albion, Marrakesh** and **L'Express**, in addition to La Serre), Encino (**Hatsuhana, Bouillabaisse** and **Mon Grenier**) and **Tarzana** (**Café de la Paix** and **Le Sanglier**).

"I used to live on the West Side," said record company executive Jill Kaufman. "Parking was bad, three people were shot dead on my block. Life was interesting, but it wasn't good. Here I grow tomatoes and zucchini all summer, and chard and carrots all winter. It feels good to come over the hill in the evening and see the street lights going on. I don't like the heat, and I don't like the smog, but I do like living here. To me, it feels like home."

Left, Galleria shopping mall, Sherm Oaks. Right, belly dancer entertains at the annual Renaissance Faire, Agour

NORTH L.A.: A TOUCH OF MAGIC

North Los Angeles County, just over the San Gabriel Mountains from the Big Smog itself, is a sprawling, magical place.

Chock full of rugged canyons, spacious deserts and cold, clear mountain streams, it is a place in which John Wayne might have felt at home.

In a way, this region is an "intersection" of human history. Here is where California's first major gold strike took place. Here, also, is the site of the first landing of the National Aeronautics and Space Administration (NASA) space shuttle. Mostly, though, this great arc of canyonlands and desert has kept a low profile.

Anthropologists say North Los Angeles was inhabited for thousands of years by one gentle, wandering tribe of aboriginals after another, including the Alliliks of the 1700s. They lived off nuts, wild grains and local game. To this day, their simple petroglyphs can still be found on the canyon walls of the Vasquez Rocks. After the Indians came Spanish explorers and missionaries and, from the middle of the last century, the westward drift of settlers. Suburbanites came, too, but not until the 1950s; and now many a cornfield has been replaced by a condominium or ranch-style home.

In spite of time and suburban sprawl, North L.A. is still the sort of place where one can launch a rowboat, pitch a tent, snag a bass, pan for gold, go biking or hiking, or stalk spring wildflowers.

Lethal Loops And 'Star Wars' Scenery

Three major arteries lead out of metropolitan Los Angeles to the northern reaches of the country — Interstate 5 (the Golden State Freeway), Interstate 210 (the Foothill Freeway) and Interstate 405 (the San Diego Freeway). I-405 and I-210 join I-5 just beyond the town of San Fernando to cross together into the **Santa Clarita Valley**, a wedge-shaped area that once served as a Butterfield stagecoach station. The Magic Mountain Parkway exits I-5 at **Valencia** and runs smack dab into Southern California's third most popular amusement park: **Six Flags Magic Mountain.**

On the park's 200 landscaped acres (81 hectares) are 75 rides and attractions, including two sure-fire heart-stoppers. "The Colossus" is one of the largest, fastest wooden roller-coasters anywhere. "The Revolution" is a 60-mile (96-kilometer) per hour roller-coaster that whips and dips before blasting through a 360-degree vertical loop. Coupled with less lethal rides such as the "Roaring Rapids" and the "Log Jam" — both splashy and exciting, yet safe enough for children — these attractions have put Magic Mountain behind only Disneyland and Knott's Berry Farm in Los Angeles-area attendance figures.

The park is worth an outing of several hours. During the summer, though, it's best not to come until after 4:30 p.m., when both the heat and the crowds have diminished somewhat. From May 20 to Sept. 11, the park is open daily; it's open weekends and public holidays the rest of the year.

If the lunacy of Magic Mountain isn't other-worldly enough, the lunar landscape of **Vasquez Rocks County Park** might fill the bill. Located off the Agua Dulce exit from State 14, this sprawl-

Left, state flowers, California poppies, bloom in a field near Lancaster. Right, fall fruit harvest, Littlerock.

ing, sub-desert landscape is as near as most earthlings will get to the moon. Vasquez Rocks features eroded caves, textured boulders and tilted beds of sandstone. Countless television shows and films, including segments of *Star Wars*, have been shot here.

The park's namesake was a 19th Century *bandido*, Tiburcio Vasquez, who terrorized Southern California ranches then retreated with his gang to the safety of these rocks. Vasquez was led to the gallows in 1875, but there are rumors he hid a fabulous treasure somewhere in the park.

Silent Movies and a Swap Meet

Back on *terra firma* is the **William S. Hart County Park** (San Fernando exist, State 14). Hart, a silent-movie cowboy star, bequeathed his lavish Spanish-style mansion and his 300-acre (121-hectare) estate to Los Angeles County. The hilltop home has a great collection of Western memorabilia, and the wooded grounds below contain a children's zoo. There are free tours Wednesday through Sunday.

Bargain hunters' heaven is found at the **Saugus Swap Meet** (Soledad Canyon exit, State 14). Held Sundays at the old Saugus Speedway, the meet is actually a 42-acre (17-hectare) outdoor garage sale. After more than 20 years, it's *the* weekend social event in the Santa Clarita Valley.

Near **Newhall**, California's first commercial oil well was sunk in the 1870s. Operated by steam, it pumped 30 barrels of crude oil daily to a small nearby refinery, where it was converted to benzine and kerosene. A bronze plaque on Standard Oil property marks the site .

Travelers who stumble upon a great deal on a rubber raft can try it out in **Castaic Lake** (Castaic exit, 1-5). Fronted by wide, grassy beaches, picnic sites and fishing docks, the lake is very popular among sailors and sailboarders.

Bouquet, San Francisquito and Placerita canyons offer some of the best back-country roads in Southern California. **Bouquet** (San Fernando exit, I-14) is a winding, wooded mountain area with roadside picnic sites and hiking trails. **San Francisquito** (near Bouquet) is a river-molded canyon that's great to explore. Back in the Twenties, the St. Francis Dam collapsed here in what was

The Colossu at Magic Mountain.

at the time one of the worst disasters in American history.

Placerita (off State 14) features a 314-acre (127-hectare) nature reserve with an ecology center and guided trails. It was here in 1842 that one Francisco Lopez, on a day's excursion from Mission San Fernando, awoke from a siesta and began digging wild onions which, to his delight and amazement, had flakes of gold clinging to their roots! In the two years that followed, an estimated $100,000 is said to have been taken from the Placerita earth by frenzied miners. Today visitors are still encouraged to try their hands at gold panning.

Near the northwesternmost L.A. County community of **Gorman** — and technically just across the county line in Kern County — lie the partially reconstructed ruins of **Fort Tejon**, a U.S. Army outpost for 10 years in the mid 19th Century. Erected in 1854 to control the pass linking Los Angeles with the southern San Joaquin Valley, the fort became a stopover point for stagecoaches on the Butterfield Overland Mail route between L.A. and San Francisco. It was abandoned during the Civil War in 1864.

The Antelope Valley

Not an antelope has roamed the **Antelope Valley** in nearly a century. Today this 3,400-square-mile (8,806-sq-km) basin on the rim of the Mojave Desert — reached via State 14 and the Soledad Pass some 50 miles (80 km) north of downtown L.A. — is dedicated to the often-contradictory pursuits of agriculture and aerospace.

Antelope Valley's two biggest towns are **Lancaster** and **Palmdale**. The latter got its name from early settlers who erroneously thought the tall desert yuccas they found there were palm trees. The truth emerged later, but the name stuck.

More and more Angelenos are leaving the city and moving out to Antelope Valley's big sky country. That sky seems to be getting bigger all the time. There is talk that by the 1990s, a supersonic airport will be constructed here to complement already-congested Los Angeles International Airport.

Currently utilizing that big sky is **Edwards Air Force Base**. Most of America's major aviation advances have occurred at this huge desert test base,

Grazing land near Gorman.

reached by existing State 14 at **Rosamond**. Edwards offers a free 90-minute public tour (reservations requested) that takes visitors through aircraft hangars to the *U.S.S. Enterprise*, prototype of the space shuttle *Columbia*. There is also an aeronautics museum and a gift shop at the tour's end.

Edwards is the nation's second largest air base, and it is apparent why a desert site like this was chosen. The Mojave averages 350 cloud-free days a year for flying, an unlimited emergency landing area, and few residents to complain about sonic-boom disturbances.

The space shuttles are not Edwards' only claims to aviation fame: in autumn 1942, America's first jet aircraft, the XP-59A, took off from **Rogers Dry Lake** in the base precincts.

Five miles west of Rosamond, another site takes travelers from the future into the past. A fortune in gold has been removed since the 1890s from the sprawling hillside of the **Tropico Gold Mine and Museum**. A tour provides a fascinating glimpse at the miners' lives above and below ground.

Once a year, usually in late March, Antelope Valley's network of foothills explodes with great masses of orange and purple wildflowers. This incredible sight, which has been drawing carloads of Angelenos for decades, is best seen at the **California Poppy Preserve**. The state flower is also featured at the nearby **California Poppy Museum**, 13 miles (21 km) from Lancaster on Avenue I.

Poppies are not the only way folks get high in north L.A. County. Several soaring schools offer short introductory flights over the Mojave Desert from the quiet cockpit of a glider plane. (In Lancaster, try the **Great Western Soaring School** or **MacDuff's Flying Circus**; in Rosamond, **Aronson's Gliders**.) There are also a number of establishments with hot-air balloons for floating high over the desert. (Check out **L.A. Balloon Port** or **Desert High Ballooning**.) But those who seek noise and speed with their thrills can head for the racing drivers' school at the **Willow Springs Raceway** in Rosamond.

Alfalfa and Cherries

In the middle of Antelope Valley, rapidly falling victim to the endless onslaught of the sun, stands the empty

The flat expanses of Antelope Valley are ideal for ballooning.

142

shell of an amazing mansion. **Shea's Castle**, the one-time home of millionaire John Shea, was built between 1922 and 1924, modeled after a magazine photograph of a castle in Dublin, Ireland, that Shea provided his construction workers. When it was completed, Shea furnished the house with antiques from Europe and a pipe organ. He enjoyed living there for five years. Then the stock market crashed in 1929, and Shea lost everything. He leaped to his death from the Santa Monica Pier. Thomas Lee, a Los Angeles auto-racing buff who purchased the Castle, also committed suicide a few years later. Since then, the foreboding home stands shunned behind an eight-mile fence. No one wants it. Some say it is cursed.

The **Antelope Valley Fair and Alfalfa Festival** begins the last weekend in August. One of the California's largest down-home county fairs, it includes the state's original Rural Olympics — with tractor slalom, mule races and other pastoral recreations. By day an agricultural showcase, the fair at night becomes a rodeo and carnival midway. The fairgrounds are two miles from downtown Lancaster.

Near **Littlerock**, east of Palmdale on State 138, is the **Devil's Punchbowl County Park**. The tilting of rock beds caught between two major earthquake faults has created a geologic bowl, a surreal landscape ideal for hiking. A one-mile loop trail leads through this fascinating nether world and back to a small ecological museum.

Littlerock features numerous roadside stands loaded with peaches, pears, apples and cherries fresh from the trees. Those so inclined can pick the fruit themselves. The hub of the area's cherry picking activity, however, is the **Leona Valley**, about five miles (eight km) west of Palmdale. The season is late spring and early summer.

Travelers who miss the prime fruit season needn't despair. They may be just in time to ring in the autumn equinox at the **Valyermo Fall Festival** the last weekend of September. At the **St. Andrew's Priory**, home of 20 Benedictine monks, music, dancing and art displays continue for two full days. Valyermo is in the San Gabriel foothills southeast of **Pearblossom**; it is reached via Punchbowl Road, near Longview and Pallet Creek roads.

Another perfect landing at Edwards Air Force Base for the space shuttle *Columbia*.

Orange County, The Fun Capital

To many people, the world of make-believe is a cozy, safe, fun-filled place immeasurably more pleasurable than the real world. Rare is the adult who hasn't at some time longed to return to the simplicity of childhood. Perhaps this is why Orange County, with its population of 2 million plus, is one of America's most densely populated metropolitan areas.

Orange County, resting on Los Angeles County's southeastern flank, is the amusement capital of America. Here are Disneyland (the original "Magic Kingdom") and Knott's Berry Farm, two of the country's three most popular theme parks, as well as a plethora of other less colossal but equally enjoyable diversions.

Perhaps there are some folks who snicker at Disneyland, who can't believe any world can really be orderly, .clean ... and wholesome fun. At one of Disneyland's most popular attractions, "A Small, Small World," park visitors climb aboard a small boat which cruises past small mechanical dolls in native garb from around the globe. Sometimes even the cynics come away believing the dolls' message of brotherhood when they sing — in a falsetto, no less — "It's a smaaaalll world after all."

After visiting the Magic Kingdom for the first time, journalist Robert Ferrigno reported that he was amazed that cleanliness is one of Disneyland's greatest miracles. The biggest sanitation problems, he said, are the droppings deposited by the horses who pull the trolley cars. Using a stopwatch, he found that the average time between deposit and clean-up was 23 seconds. "Anywhere in America you could pass out on the sidewalk and not be picked up as fast as horse manure on the streets of Disneyland," he wrote.

The American Dream

It is easy for the more sardonic visitors to ridicule such fastidiousness and the amusement park's cornball humor and conservative preachments: good triumphs over evil, hard work is rewarded, self-reliance is the ideal races

Preceding pages, Sleeping Beauty Castle, Disneyland. Below, modernistic Town and Country complex at South Coast Plaza in Costa Mesa

146

Orange County suburban sprawl.

can mix as easily as a choir can sing. They also find it easy to poke fun at inland Orange County itself — a place which named its major airport after the late actor John Wayne, that symbol of no-nonsense manhood, gun-toting capitalism and unabashed American patriotism; a place where a television evangelist has built a drive-in church with a sanctuary crafted out of 10,660 panes of glass; the birthplace of a disgraced president, Yorba Linda native Richard M. Nixon; a place so fundamentally new that it seems to be without roots or culture, especially in contrast to San Francisco, New York City, and even sprawling Los Angeles.

But Orange County is anything but moribund. Without much of a past, it creates forms for the future and provides a high quality of life for its residents. It has two state universities and numerous colleges, a burgeoning cultural scene, excellent athletic facilities, theaters, hundreds of parks, sandy beaches, lakes and mountains. The county also offers exquisite restaurants, many of whose chefs number among the county's 75,000 Indochinese refugee population.

That's the good side of the coin. The bad side is that so many people want to enjoy Orange County's good life that the land is — acre for acre — some of the most expensive in the world. It's gotten so bad that the **University of California at Irvine** and many county firms have trouble recruiting out-of-state employees, shocked by the price tags attached to this nucleus of middle-class suburbia.

Lima Bean Heaven

Today freeways crisscross the county where Captain Gaspar de Portolá led the first Spanish overland expedition in 1769, through land covered with wild grass, sagebrush and tuna cactus. Seven years after Portolá's expedition, Juan Bautista de Anza and his men came to the region with livestock. Seeds hidden in the beasts' hides and wool soon gave root to wild mustard, thistles, hoarhound and castor beans. At about the same time, missionaries at San Juan Capistrano planted Concord grape vineyards, fruit orchards and gardens to meet their self-reliant needs.

By 1810, Antonio Yorba and Juan Peralta, who had been given a 62,512-acre (25,298-hectare) land grant by the Spanish, began to farm along the **Santa Ana River.** Like thousands of farmers who followed, they found that the land was some of the most fertile on earth.

Among the 19th Century pioneers who worked the land was a family named Segerstrom. They earned a comfortable living farming the broad, flat, nutritious lima bean. At one time, in fact, according to Orange County historian Jim Sleeper, the county was known as "The Lima Bean Bowl of America." When the Segerstrom family heirs developed the **South Coast Plaza** shopping center on former lima-bean land in **Costa Mesa,** they commissioned Japanese sculptor Isamu Noguchi to create a 28-ton monument titled "The Spirit of the Lima Bean." Comprised of 15 huge rust—colored rocks, it stands today in the modernesque courtyard of a business plaza across Bristol Street from the shopping center. South Coast Plaza, rapidly becoming the hub of western Orange County cultural pursuits, is surrounded by fine restaurants, cinemas and the South Coast Repertory Theater

with its soon-to-be-completed entertainment complex.

In 1857, Germans paid $2 per acre to purchase 1,165 acres ($2,330 for 479 hectares) to start a wine colony they called **Anaheim.** Oranges, however, gave the county its name. In 1870, the first orange seeds were pushed into the county's fertile earth and four years later, the first navel trees were planted. On land which now accommodates **California State University at Fullerton** (enrollment: 22,000-plus), the first commercial grove of Valencia oranges was planted in 1875. The Southern California Fruit Exchange, later renamed Sunkist, was organized in 1893.

Anaheim's grape industry was killed ·by disease and many orange groves have been felled by bulldozer blades. Orange County's most enriching crop today is strawberries, picked by members of the county's immense population of Mexican nationals.

Knott's Berry Farm

In 1920, farmer Walter Knott moved to **Buena Park.** Soon after, he began to raise boysenberries, the hybrid blackberry-raspberry creation of Anaheim nurseryman Rudolph Boysen. During the Great Depression year of 1934, Knott's wife Cordelia began selling chicken dinners — initially on her wedding china — for 65 cents a meal at the farm's roadside. She added jams, jellies and pies to the menu, and by the start of World War II customers were spending an hour or more in line outside the family's restaurant.

To occupy the guests and fulfill a dream, Knott recreated an 1848 gold town, complete with narrow-gauge railroad. **Knott's Berry Farm** grew from that point until by 1966 it was attracting 4 million visitors annually. That year, Knott, a staunch conservative, watched the completion of a $1 million replica of Philadelphia's Independence Hall, where America's Declaration of Independence was signed in 1776. A multi-million-dollar expansion of the park began in 1975.   ·

Knott died in 1981, but his estate carried on the work. In 1983, a new $10 million, six-acre section called Camp Snoopy opened for children between three and 11 years old. Particularly inviting to youngsters are the "Timberline Twister" roller coaster, the "Beagle

Left, *teppan-yaki* chef perform at Benihana restaurant. Right, thrill seekers rev on rides at Knott's Berry Farm.

Ballroom" (a tarpaulin filled with thousands of hollow plastic balls in which to burrow) and "Tubs of Fun" (spinning wooden washtubs).

The park's other attractions include the "Corkscrew," the "Log Ride" and the "Good Time Theater," which features entertainment varying from ice shows to mime Marcel Marceau. There are also many admission-free shows — Western stunts, can-can dancers, an old-time melodrama and revues — at different locales throughout the day.

In late October, just prior to Halloween (October 31), the park changes its name to "Knott's Scary Farm." Ghosts and goblins spring from behind every rock, tree and corner within and outside of the attractions.

Knott's Berry Farm is located at 8039 Beach Blvd. in Buena Park. Visitors should have no trouble finding it: there are directional signs scattered all over the northern part of Orange County.

Disneyland

As enjoyable as guests find Knott's Berry Farm, it is generally dwarfed in their imagination by **Disneyland,** the world's best-known theme park a few miles to the southeast. So that the one won't suffer by comparison to the other, it is often recommended that the tourist visit Knott's first.

Walt Disney, the Missouri farmboy-turned-movie mogul, opened Disneyland on July 18, 1955. Anaheim and Orange County would never be the same again. Orange groves were razed and the tourism business boomed, producing a string of motels with gaudy signs.

Disney, whose park initially had 18 attractions, promised that as long as man continued to have an imagination, his land would not be finished. His successors have been true to Uncle Walt's promise. In 1967, the year after Disney died, "Pirates of the Caribbean" opened. It has been one of the park's most popular rides since. In 1977, the high-speed "Space Mountain" ride opened. "Big Thunder Mountain Railroad" was added in 1979. By its 25th anniversary in 1980, the park had 59 attractions and a capital investment of $206 million.

Another $41 million was soon pumped into **Fantasyland** which, until

Wild spin at the Mad Hatter's Tea Party, Fantasyland

the revamped look was unveiled in 1983, had some of the park's most forgotten rides. "It's a Small World" has always been popular, but now Fantasyland will also line up customers at the renovated "Peter Pan's Flight" and "Mr. Toad's Wild Ride."

To reach Disneyland (1313 S. Harbor Blvd.) by car, the visitor can choose from a number of freeways. The Riverside (State Highway 91), Santa Ana (Interstate 5), Garden Grove (State 22) and San Diego (I-405) freeways all have Harbor Boulevard ramps — southbound from the former pair, northbound from the latter two. From the Orange Freeway (State 57), visitors should head west on Katella Avenue.

Avoiding the Rush

It's a good idea for the first-time visitor to arrive at Disneyland when the park opens (at 9 or 10 a.m., depending upon season and day of the week). Although the park suggests an orientation trip around the park by train, it is wiser to rush straight down **Main Street** (the park's entry corridor) to the most popular rides ahead of the crowds, thus avoiding at least one long wait in line.

Those who prefer fast, heart-stopping rides should scurry to **Tomorrowland's** "Space Mountain" or to the "Matterhorn" bobsleds haunted by abominable snowmen. Families with one or more children, or others who prefer serenity to sheer speed, should scamper to **New Orleans Square** to take the "Pirates of the Caribbean" ride and tour the "Haunted Mansion." A logical next step is a trek to nearby **Bear Country** to watch the "Country Bear Jamboree," a country-western music revue presented by 18 lovable mechanical bears. It's a lucky day if the lines are still short at **Adventureland's** "Jungle Cruise" or "Enchanted Tiki Room," where Pacific isle entertainment is provided by mechanical birds, flowers and supernatural icons.

Only when the lines have lengthened is it time to ride the train around the park. Only then should one return to Main Street to have a photo taken beside Mickey Mouse.

As the day wears on, to conserve energy, it helps to alternate standing in long lines and visiting attractions with shorter waits. In Tomorrowland, for ex-

Bird's-eye view of Fantasyland.

ample, after tackling the crowded "Space Mountain," one might consider discovering the world of the atom in "Adventure Through Inner Space"; or sitting in a carousel theater at the "America Sings" revue to listen to music performed by leading musicians and mouthed by mechanical animals. Another Tomorrowland rest stop is the "PeopleMover," a futuristic transportation mode which circles through several rides and which includes visual effects from the Disney movie, *Tron*.

If mom and dad want to rest on a shaded bench, but the kids can't sit still, Adventureland provides the "Swiss Family Treehouse" for young climbers. For a longer respite, **Frontierland** offers "Tom Sawyer Island." The children travel to the island by raft, then explore caves, cross a bridge of floating barrels, and investigate "Fort Wilderness."

Dixieland Romances

Disneyland at night is a romantic setting. Teenagers primp and promenade at such dance sites as "The Tomorrowland Terrace" and "The Space Stage." Post-teen couples seem to enjoy the more intimate setting provided by the "*Mark Twain* Steamboat," a stern-wheeler circling "Tom Sawyer Island" to the accompaniment of banjo-and-clarinet Dixieland music. On many nights, fireworks are sprayed above Fantasyland's "Sleeping Beauty Castle" and an electrical parade ambles down Main Street.

Unless a visitor has the marathon stamina required for a 12-hour visit, the best way to see Disneyland before and after dark is to leave at midday for a nap. Ticket-takers at the main gate will stamp hands so that visitors can return without an additional charge. Parking lot tickets are also good for free re-entry on the day of purchase. Closing times vary with longer hours during the summer and on New Year's Eve.

Day or night, the park offers inexpensive meals at such locales as the **Carnation Plaza Gardens,** where in the summer of 1983 visitors could purchase a fish burger, fries, salad and soft drink for $2.50.

Souvenirs are also reasonably priced. This is to Disneyland's credit; with a captive audience, high prices could easily be charged, particularly if greedy or

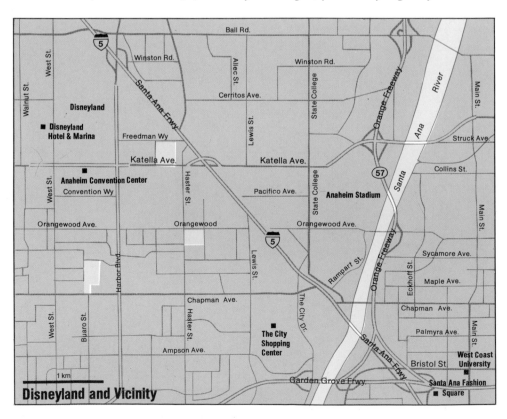

Disneyland and Vicinity

hungry children are in tow. What is lost in profit is gained several times over in good will.

Adult visitors shouldn't feel embarrassed about purchasing Mickey Mouse ears or a Donald Duck hat for their own heads. Everyone is a kid in Disneyland.

Lion Country

Disneyland and Knott's Berry Farm are the obvious destinations in Orange County. But there are many other attractions. Some of them are well publicized. Others are little known, even to Orange County residents.

Much of the recent publicity at Irvine's Lion Country Safari has been of a negative type. In late 1982, a two-year-old boy was critically hurt when a Siberian tiger allegedly sauntered out of its open cage, grabbed the boy by the head, and carried him 50 feet (15 meters). And in mid 1983, a park zoologist was crushed to death by a three-ton elephant named Misty. The elephant eluded capture for three hours, forcing the closure of nearby freeways.

Assuming another tiger or elephant

hasn't taken to the hills, necessitating a similar road closure, visitors can reach this wild animal park via Irvine Center Drive south from I-405, or by exiting I-5 south onto the Laguna Freeway and heading south on I-405 until the Irvine Center Drive on-ramp.

Irvine is also the location of **Irvine Meadows,** an amphitheater which books big-name entertainers. Another bowl offering concerts the likes of Barry Manilow and George Benson is the **Pacific Amphitheater,** located at the **Orange County Fairgrounds,** 88 Fair Dr., Costa Mesa.

The parking lot at these fairgrounds is virtually always packed because, in addition to the midsummer county fair and amphitheater shows, it hosts regular weekend swap meets — flea markets — which feature everything from modern gadgets to clothing to car parts.

The fairgrounds swap meet is the biggest in Orange County, but is far from the only one. Saturday and Sunday swap meets are common at drive-in theaters. Sometimes travelers passing through the area purchase space on a one-time basis to finance their journeying by peddling imported wares —

ebony carvings from Tanzania, for example, or Tibetan rugs from the Himalaya Mountains.

There are also canny travelers who try to double or triple their kitties at **Los Alamitos Race Track,** well known for its harness races. Despite the name, the track is located in Cypress (at 4961 Katella Ave.) rather than in neighboring Los Alamitos.

Stallions, Snakes, Weapons and Wax

There are other horses — in Buena Park, near Knott's — on whom no bets are placed. These are the three dozen white Andalusian stallions, bearing riders in costumes of Old Mexico and Renaissance France, who dance beneath chandeliers in a luxurious setting at the **Kingdom of the Dancing Stallions**, 7662 Beach Blvd.

Another Berry Farm neighbor (at 7671 La Palma Ave.) is the **California Alligator Farm,** one of the world's largest reptile collections and home of alligators, snakes, lizards and, curiously, monkeys.

More than $2 million worth of mili-tary memorabilia is displayed at the **Buena Park Museum of World Wars,** 8700 Stanton Ave. Reputedly, this exhibit of flags, uniforms, weapons, posters and medals is the largest of its kind in North America. Owner Ron Lane says his most valued possession is a small, gold-plated pistol confiscated from Nazi Field Marshal Hermann Goering by an American soldier in 1945. The pistol, says Lane, is one of three of its type: the others were owned by Adolf Hitler and Heinrich Himmler.

Star-struck visitors not lucky enough to spot celebrities in the flesh elsewhere in Southern California can at least see stars in wax at **Six Flags Movieland Wax Museum,** 7711 Beach Blvd. in Buena Park. The museum features 200 wax figures frozen for a moment in scenes from their movies and television programs. Movieland's "Black Box" offers horror movie sets in which the guest is bombarded by special effects.

The Buena Park-Anaheim axis also contains **Anaheim Stadium** (South State College Boulevard), home of the California Angels baseball team and the Rams football team, and host to many rock concerts. **Anaheim Convention**

The King of Beasts at Lion Country Safari, Irvine

Center (800 W, Katella Ave.) is always occupied by one or more conferences or exhibitions. In one hall might be the world's largest pet show, in another a television evangelist known for his faith healing and fundamentalist expostulation on Bible topics.

'Possibility Thinking'

Orange County has its own famous TV evangelist. The Rev. Robert Schuller preaches from the pulpit of the **Crystal Cathedral,** a **Garden Grove** congregation of the Reformed Church of America denomination. Known for his "possibility thinking" theology, Schuller started a new congregation in 1955 at the Orange County Drive-In Theater because he could find no suitable hall to rent to start his Protestant church. Orating from the tar-paper roof of the theater's snack bar, the pastor preached to a growing crowd despite the remonstrances of a minister friend for conducting worship services in a "passion pit."

Worshippers apparently were drawn to Schuller's creed: "When faced with a mountain, *I will not quit.* I will keep on striving until I climb over, find a pass through, tunnel underneath, or simply stay and turn the mountain into a gold mine, with God's help."

Today, Schuller — who lives in a luxurious home with a man-made waterfall in his back yard — rules over a Garden Grove complex (Chapman Avenue at Lewis Street) with office towers, an arboretum and the multimillion-dollar Crystal Cathedral, which contains one of the world's largest pipe organs. The auto-enclosed worshipper of drive-in movie days has not been forgotten: a gigantic glass door opens during services so that penitents have a choice of sitting in pews or bucket seats. A drive-in church sounds wacky to some, but in all fairness, it enables the handicapped, the elderly and the poorly dressed to attend services and give their donations to an usher who glides from window to window.

About 10,000 worshippers attend Schuller's church. In Costa Mesa, twice that number attend services at **Calvary Chapel** (3800 S. Fairview St.) to hear the Rev. Chuck Smith, a fundamentalist preacher who began his Orange County ministry by spreading the Gospel to

Reptilian repartee at Buena Park Alligator Farm.

beach bums and drug users. His services are now so crowded that the overflow must watch on a row of television sets in an adjacent hall that is itself filled to capacity.

Buddhists and Nudists

Orange County also has a mosque and synagogues, and for its large Asian population, Hindu and Buddhist temples. In Anaheim, a theater-in-the-round which once draw criticism for a program of bare-breasted women was converted by the Rev. Ralph Wilkerson, a Protestant preacher, into a sanctuary-in-the-round which retained the theater's name, **Melodyland.**

Bare breasts and other extremities are an everyday sight at the **McConville Nudist Camp,** located just north of Ortega Highway in the Orange County mountains. The family-oriented camp (no "Mr. Chubby Nude" contests here) has the usual nudist camp activities: swimming, volleyball and horseshoes. The camp was once the site of a wedding in which the bride, groom, attendants, ushers and minister were garbed only in their birthday suits. A newspaper called it "Southern California's weirdest wedding ceremony." Visits can be arranged by writing owners Flo and Wally Nilson at Post Office Box 131, Elsinore, California 92330.

For visitors who prefer to bathe at a place with more privacy, **La Vida Hot Springs** has indoor sunken tubs and outdoor swimming pools filled with therapeutic mineral waters pumped from an adjacent hill. The old-style resort has a few rooms for visitors and a masseur who has kneaded many a body into shape. La Vida is located at 6155 Carbon Canyon Road in the hills of **Brea,** a town known for its art gallery (1 Civic Center Circle) and numerous outdoor sculptures.

Along the eastern rim of Orange County are the **Santa Ana Mountains,** much of which are a part of **Cleveland National Forest.** Tucked into the mountains are the villages of **Trabuco Oaks, Silverado Canyon** (named for its defunct silver mines), **Modjeska Canyon** and **Irvine Lake.** The lake at the latter village is stocked with trout for fishing, and the national park also provides numerous opportunities for hunting,

Left, John Wayne still shows *True Grit* at the Movieland Wax Museum. Right, a modest newcomer at the McConville Nudist Camp

hiking and off-road vehicle riding.

There are three campsites in Orange County operated by the county government. They are **Featherly Park** (24001 Santa Ana Canyon Road, Anaheim), **Caspers Park** (33401 Ortega Highway, San Juan Capistrano) and **O'Neill Park** (30892 Trabuco Canyon Road, Trabuco Oaks). Down-on-their-luck transient families set up temporary residences at these camps and rotate among them when they have overstayed the maximum visit period.

There are two mountain wildlife reserves: the **Oak Canyon Nature Center** in the Anaheim Hills (6700 E. Walnut Canyon Road) and the **Tucker Wildlife Sanctuary** in Modjeska Canyon. Santa Ana has animals, too, at **Prentice Park Children's Zoo,** 1700 E. 1st St.

Motor buffs will want to visit Costa Mesa's **Briggs Automotive Museum** (205 E. Baker St. near John Wayne Airport). On display are more than 100 of the world's top autos, including the 1913 Peugeot three-liter Grand Prix racing car; Bobby Unser's "Eagle," which won the 1975 Indianapolis 500; and the Bugatti "Royale," one of the largest and most expensive cars ever built. At

Fountain Valley's **Mile Square Park** (16801 Euclid St.), vehicles of another kind race — wheeled craft propelled by wind caught in their sails.

Those who prefer to look to the more distant past enjoy **Bower's Museum** (2202 N. Main St.) in Santa Ana. It is noted for its Indian art and displays describing Orange County's Spanish heritage.

That past, too, is reflected in **Yorba Linda,** not solely at former president Nixon's boyhood home, a tourist attraction of sorts. Spookier by far is the **Yorba Cemetery,** built in the 1850s by the Yorba family. According to legend, on June 15 of every even-numbered year, the Pink Lady — a beautiful young woman killed in a buggy accident — appears at the cemetery. Outside the chain-link fence, several hundred people, skeptics as well as camera-toting believers, wait for hours, peering through the tombstones for a glimpse of the apparition in a glowing pink dress. She's due again in 1984.

Some people claim to have seen the Pink Lady. Others insist that the closest ghosts are those inhabiting the Haunted Mansion at Disneyland.

Vegetable farm resists urbanization near Lake Forest.

PLEASURES OF THE ORANGE COAST

Her name wasn't always Bix. Before she came to the coast of Orange County, before she sipped margaritas on patios facing a sailboat-filled sea, before she restyled her hair and her personality, she lived in a small town in Texas and her name was Ruth.

She fell in love with a building contractor — a millionaire on a business trip — who promised her orange sunsets, cool breezes and an even tan. She quit her job, packed her bags, traded glasses for contacts and headed west to the edge of the continent, to Newport Beach, Orange County, California.

But those changes were not enough. This migration required a total transformation. Even the name Ruth had to go. So he christened her Bix and set her name in gold on a necklace. To make themselves twins of a sort, the businessman changed his own name from Bob to Beaux and wore a matching gold necklace. And that is how they are known in Tiffany's, a Newport Beach dance club awash in perspiration, cigarette smoke, fine perfume, foreign accents and murmured come-ons.

Although changing one's name might be something of an extreme, people have long come to the Orange County coast — the Orange Coast — to alter their image and their outlook. The fancy bars are full of women who left the debris of failed relationships far behind in snowy Minnesota or Wisconsin or Michigan and came to California to let the sun burn its warmth into their chilled bones and damaged psyches. The bored of the world migrate here, too, looking for the social excitement and the business opportunities they could not find in the bush of the Australian Outback or the small-thinking burgs of Europe and America.

The migrant and the visitor find the starkest of contrasts here. For those with money or easy credit, there is a fast lane of multimillion-dollar homes on Lido and Linda isles, sports cars, yachts and yacht clubs, Mexican housekeepers, exquisite restaurants and, for those who so indulge, cocaine easily slipped into the county from Mexico, two hours by freeway to the south. And then there are the surfers and poets, living in garages, studios and battered trailers while they pursue the perfect wave or phrase. Between the two live the middle class, scraping up the money to make payments on the condo in Laguna Niguel or ante up the rent each month for an apartment in Corona del Mar or one on Balboa Island.

The Orange Coast offers them all a choice of pleasures. They can feast at a gourmet restaurant or roast a hot dog in a fire circle at Huntington Beach; drive Pacific Coast Highway at sunset in a shiny, chauffeured limousine or a Volkswagen whose paint has been dulled by too many saltwater-tinged breezes; drink rum concoctions aboard a yacht or body-surf across the water until the sand stings their chests.

Paradise Lost

A century and a half ago, the sunsets, mesas and sandy beaches belonged primarily to the Indians. In the hills near Newport Beach's Back Bay, they barbecued rabbits, squirrels and scallops and ate a mush of leeched-out acorns. Food and land were plentiful. Then the Spanish Catholic brothers arrived and mis-

Preceding pages, bikini contestants steal the show at Huntington Beach. Left, sunset surf on Balboa Peninsula. Right, a ritzy restaurant in Newport Center.

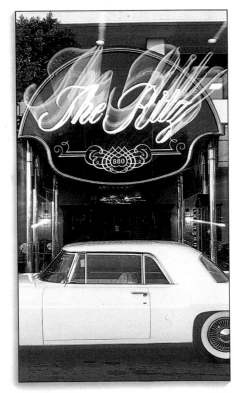

sionized the Indians. Disease decimated their numbers; others were brought to the mission to toil in the name of God. Meanwhile, the coast increasingly drew migrants and visitors in search of fertile land, a seaside view and adventure in a less-civilized realm.

In 1834, a Harvard College under-graduate — chaffing at authority, hungering for adventure, and suffering from a post-measles decline in his eyesight — dropped out of school and enlisted on a brig bound for the California coast. The son of genteel society became a common sailor working beside rough, blaspheming men. From his journal of that voyage from Boston around Cape Horn to California and back, Richard Henry Dana crafted the classic book, *Two Years Before the Mast*.

Dana's ship, *Pilgrim*, stopped along the coast near the Mission San Juan Capistrano so the men could collect hides. Dana was transfixed by what he saw: "High table-land, running boldly to the shore, and breaking off in a steep hill, at the foot of which the waters of the Pacific are constantly dashing... There was a grandeur in everything around, which gave almost a solemnity to the scene: a silence and solitariness which affected everything!"

Such eloquent praise was not forgotten. In 1924, developers named the area **Dana Point** and undoubtedly turned the author's prose into sales promotion.

A modern-day sojourner can find solitary places along the Orange Coast from Seal Beach at the county's north-ern border to San Clemente at the southern border. Aircraft from the **John Wayne Airport** (one of the world's busiest in number of flights) and Marine Corps' air stations in **El Toro** and **Tustin** might occasionally disturb his reverie, but the dominant sound heard on a Dana Point cliff is the immortal music of the sea.

Whereas Dana and his shipmates ex-plored the area on rented horses, the visitor today can investigate the Orange Coast's 42 miles (68 kilometers), by car, bus or bicycle, traversing the Pacific Coast Highway (State Highway 1).

The Watergate White House

Traveling north from the county's southern border just above the con-

Two visions of San Juan Capistrano Mission: left Father Serra points the way; and right, tourists explore corridors of history.

troversial **San Onofre Nuclear Power Plant**, the visitor's first stop is **San Clemente**, where former President Richard M. Nixon — an Orange County native — set up his Western White House on the 25.4-acre (10.3-hectare) **La Casa Pacifica** estate. In 1980, after 11 years' residence, Nixon and his wife Pat sold their Spanish-style home on Avenida del Presidente and moved to the East Coast.

Those who want to see the house where Nixon hosted heads of state, and where he agonized over the Watergate scandal, should walk down the beach to a point where the house can be seen on the cliffs, or else glance to the right while driving southbound on the San Diego Freeway (Interstate 5).

Merchants in the city of San Clemente don't hawk Nixon ashtrays, bookends or spoons. The city has no "Nixon Slept Here" billboards. However, Nixon's links to the city will be more obvious when the **Nixon Museum** is completed on a nearby 13-acre, $6.5 million plot of land.

For nine days every summer, San Clemente hosts the **La Cristianita Pageant**, dramatizing the first baptism of an Indian in California (in 1769 by Father Francisco Gomez). The pageant's three-act play features soldiers, priests, swordfights, Indian rites, dancing, singing and an on-stage waterfall. This performance is delivered in La Cristianita Bowl (on the Forster Ranch off Camino de Los Mares) three miles from where the actual event is said to have occurred in a wilderness clearing.

There are six California state beaches along the Orange Coast. At **San Clemente Beach** (not far from the Nixon estate at 225 Avenida Calafia) and **Doheny Beach** (34320 Del Obispo St.), visitors may camp for a nominal fee. State fish and game wardens patrol marine-life reserves — open to the public — in Doheny Beach, Dana Point, Laguna Niguel, South Laguna Beach, Laguna Beach, Irvine Coast (south of Corona del Mar) and Newport Beach. Snorkelers and scuba divers can look at, but not keep, underwater flora and fauna.

The Swallows Of
San Juan Capistrano

Capistrano Beach and Dana Point are just north of San Clemente along the

Sunday brunch at Las Brisas, Laguna Beach.

Pacific Coast Highway. Just inland on Del Obispo Street or I-5 is the town of **San Juan Capistrano**, home of the famous mission founded by Father Junípero Serra in 1776. Unlike Dana, today's visitor will find much more than a mission in decline when he makes his way to what is now the corner of Ortega Highway and Camino Capistrano.

The early mission, rebuilt since Dana's day, is a tourist magnet which attracts about 300,000 visitors annually. In mid 1984, work is expected to be finished on the Catholic congregation's replica of the **Old Stone Church**, the mission sanctuary destroyed in an 1812 earthquake. The church will be built in the shape of a Latin cross with seven domes. At the center of this cross will rise a giant dome housing a chandelier. It will be protected against any future temblor by a steel frame and 40 to 50-foot (12 to 15-meter) pilings driven into the earth.

No one knows what effect all of this will have on the annual migration of swallows. The mission's gardens are particularly crowded every March 19, St. Joseph's Day, when — according to a legend — the swallows return from their winter homes in Argentina to nest at the mission. Of late, pigeons have been more commonly sighted than swallows, those small birds with long, pointed wings.

The decline in the swallow population has been blamed on changes in the environment. Orange groves, where insects breed, have been uprooted for development and mud flats, which provide building material for the birds, have been covered with grass. One member of a San Juan Capistrano farming family recalls having seen more than 2,000 swallows fly past his home. Now it is not uncommon to hear that March 19 is the day the tourists — but not the swallows — return to San Juan Capistrano. Still, the occasion is great fun, with *mariachi* music, a parade and other festivities. Business is especially brisk at shops which display scarfs, teacups, glass bells and other knickknacks bearing likenesses of swallows.

Barbecued Ribs And the 'Last Supper'

From Capistrano, the Pacific Coast Highway continues north past Three

Left, artisan sculpts in glass at the Festival of Arts, Laguna Beach.

164

Arch Bay and South Laguna to **Laguna Beach**, known for its artists' colony, burgeoning gay population and landslides. In Laguna Beach, a person can get lazy: eat a croissant, sip cappuccino, catch some sunshine, and people-watch from a sea-facing bench along the promenade. More active types can dive through the air playing beach volleyball, wade into the water, wander through such art galleries as the **Vorpal** and the **Laguna Beach Museum of Art** (307 Cliff Dr.), window-shop at the stylish boutiques, or eat dinner at a restaurant serving Mexican seafood or Hawaiian-style barbecued ribs. One shouldn't expect to be alone in these pursuits, however. For just such simple pleasures, visitors and residents crowd Laguna Beach's narrow streets, particularly on summer days.

For seven weeks of July and August each year, townspeople recreate famous art works in the internationally known **Pageant of the Masters.** A half-century ago during the Great Depression, local artist Roy Ropp decided to promote the town's Festival of Arts exhibit with a program of *tableaux vivants*, representations of art works created by one or more persons who are mute, frozen and in costume. Now, about 500 volunteers create the nightly show of two dozen scenes before sellout crowds in the Irvine Bowl (650 Laguna Canyon Road). Special lighting and makeup techniques flatten the figures, so they seem two-dimensional. A typical program might include an Oriental woodblock by late 18th Century Japanese artist Kiyonaga, a Barnum and Bailey circus poster, Thomas Gainsborough's "Blue Boy," Leonardo da Vinci's "Last Supper" and Greek statuary, all formed for several minutes by persons trained not to scratch, sneeze, blink, swat or otherwise move any noticeable muscle.

Those not lucky enough to purchase a ticket in advance should plan on being at the bowl at noon the day of the show, when returned tickets go on sale. For the program, it is a good idea to bring binoculars (or be prepared to rent them) as well as a coat or sweater for warmth when cool sea breezes blow through the hills and the fog rolls in. Visitors should also allow time to visit the **Festival of Arts** show next door and the **Sawdust Festival** across the street from the Irvine Bowl.

Newport Beach

Bluffs overlook the Pacific Ocean north of Laguna Beach. On one bluff, a stable rents horses for rides along the beach. There's a beautiful sandy beach in **Corona del Mar.** Nearby are caves and tidepools to beckon the explorer. The town of Corona del Mar, actually a part of **Newport Beach**, has a shopping area along the Pacific Coast Highway with gourmet restaurants, singles' saloons and clothing shops, including several selling the wealthy's high-fashion hand-me-downs. Behind Spanish-style walls lies the two-acre **Sherman Library and Gardens**, a botanical garden with *koi* (Japanese carp) pond, fountains, driftwood sculptures, an outdoor tea garden, a tropical conservatory for the likes of orchids and Venus flytraps, desert plants and roses.

The high-class **Fashion Island** shopping center is north of Corona del Mar. It includes the **Bob Burns Restaurant,** home of some of the best live jazz north of Laguna Beach. In summer, the center hosts free outdoor jazz concerts.

Seaward, Newport Beach offers everything a sailor could ask, no matter how big or small the wad in his wallet. On **Lido and Linda isles,** some homes come equipped with docks for several yachts. (The late John Wayne lived in one of them.) And there are places where the low-cost sailor can push his inflatable kayak into **Lower Newport Bay** for a brisk respite from city life.

That bay is the site of the annual Christmas Boat Parade, the summer Character Boat Parade, the Bathtub Regatta and the start of the annual 125-mile (201-km) Newport to Ensenada (Mexico) race, all of which are traditionally viewed from a balcony filled with friends and a generous supply of intoxicants.

To go to **Balboa Peninsula**, visitors can turn south from Pacific Coast Highway to Newport or Balboa boulevards, or — more romantically — take the short ferry ride from **Balboa Island**, which can be reached from the Pacific Coast Highway by taking Jamboree Road south.

Like Laguna Beach, Corona del Mar and (to the north) Seal Beach, Balboa Island and the areas around the Balboa and Newport piers are great for indulging in chocolate-chip cookies, fruit drinks and ice cream. One way to work off a few of those calories is to rent roller skates and wheel down the cement walkway connecting the two piers. Skaters should be prepared, though, for the grating of their wheels on sand blown into their path.

At the base of **Newport Pier** is the weathered outdoor plywood market of the county's only dory fleet. More than a dozen boats go out to sea at dawn each day and bring back fresh rock cod, bonito, mackerel and sea trout.

Harbor tours leave Balboa Pavilion and take their passengers out to the breakwater, past the island homes of movie stars and other rich folks.

North on Pacific Coast Highway from Newport Beach and its components is **Huntington Beach**, the surfing capital of the Orange Coast and possibly all of California. Like **Seal Beach** to the north, Huntington Beach has a pier and the usual collection of grizzled fishermen flanked by nubile teenaged girls showing off the latest in swimwear. In the summer of 1983, Huntington Beach's annual bikini cotest was interrupted by a melee when some viewers tried to see what was beneath the skimpy garments.

Left, motorists drive ashore from the Balboa ferry Right, a wild ride through the Orange Coa surf.

THE SURPRISING INLAND EMPIRE

Many of the usual stereotypes about Southern California are confirmed or shattered by the area known as the Inland Empire.

No one is sure when this sobriquet was conferred. Many residents place the blame on an advertising campaign started by a local radio station in the 1940s. But if this area lying in San Bernardino and Riverside counties is indeed an "empire," it is a rich and varied one, with great historical, geographical and scenic diversity. Nature and circumstance give it setting; people give it color.

The Inland Empire is roughly bounded by the San Gabriel Valley on the west, Mount San Jacinto on the east, the San Bernardino Mountains to the north and San Diego County to the south. Visitors here must learn to think in reverse seasons. The native plants and shrubs covering the hillsides bloom from February through May. By summer they have taken on a stark, naked winter look, and remain dormant through the fall. The cycle then begins anew: green hills in winter and spring, brown in summer and fall.

Indians and Spanish

As long as 5,000 years ago, the Mission Indians (a name given to the native Americans by the Spaniards) lived in these interior valleys. They hunted and traversed the area, often seeking springs for sacred sites as well as for sustenance. Even today, many Indian reservations are scattered about the Inland Empire. One mile above the sprawling city of San Bernardino lies the **San Manuel Reservation** on San Creek. Twenty miles (32 km) southeast, above San Gorgonio Pass, is the **Morongo Reservation** with its fine museum. And there are numerous other reservations in Riverside County.

The first Spanish explorer to lead a party through this area was Pedro Fages in 1772. But it wasn't until 1810 that an attempt was made to build a mission. Father Francisco Dumetz, coming east from the San Gabriel Mission, stopped in this broad and beautiful valley near the mountain foothills. Taking up his

ecclesiastical calendar, he saw that it was the feast day of an Italian saint, San Bernardino of Siena. The mountains and the valley received his name.

Dumetz directed construction of a mission rancho, later called an *asistencia* (extension) of the San Gabriel Mission. Sporadic services were held until 1834. Now part of the San Bernardino County Museum system, the *asistencia* underwent complete restoration in the late 1930s.

By the 1840s, the Inland Empire was becoming known for its great cattle and horse ranches. Powerful families, such as the Yorbas and Lugos, carved up the acreage of the San Bernardino Valley. Seeking protection from rustlers, the Lugos employed Cahuilla Indian Chief Juan Antonio and his band of warriors to protect their interests. Juan Antonio became the "watchdog" of the valley, and in effect the commander of a pioneer police force.

Mormon Migration

In 1851, three years after California had become an American state thanks to the impetus of the Gold Rush, a large party of Mormons migrated to the Inland Empire. Although they remained only six years, their influence is still felt today.

Nearly 500 people in a caravan of 150 wagons left Utah in March 1851. A handful of them were non-Mormon "independents" who later sowed the seeds of discord. After a difficult trip, they arrived at the Cajon Pass (which separates the San Bernardino and San Gabriel mountains) and bought 36,000 acres (14,569 hectares) of land from Antonio Lugo for $77,000.

The Mormon settlement became a model for future development of the Inland Empire. Astute farmers, businessmen and city planners, the Mormons quickly set to work. They planted wheat and milled it; they harvested lumber and sold it. The town they founded in 1851 was named **San Bernardino**, after the valley. It was laid out by Elder H.G. Sherwood, the engineer who planned Salt Lake City.

In order to protect their political interests and assure their "theocracy in the wilderness," the Mormons lobbied for the creation of San Bernardino County in 1853. This area, formerly part of Los Angeles County, also in-

Preceding pages, a solitary ascent in the serene morning hours at Perris Valley. Left, cross-country skiers in the San Gorgonio Wilderness.

cluded land that today is in Riverside County. San Bernardino County became the largest county in the continental United States and retains the boast today with 20,117 square miles (54,115 sq km) of territory.

But rancor and land disputes between the Mormon and non-Mormon inhabitants divided the city of San Bernardino and soured the experiment. Matters came to a head when Mormon leader Brigham Young called the return of all the "faithful" to Salt Lake City in 1857. With the Mormons gone, a host of bargain hunters came to bid on their homes and businesses.

The years between 1858 and 1870 are called by some "the lawless decade." The vacuum of power was filled by a diversity of settlers, not all of them law-abiding. But San Bernardino still grew in importance. Its location at the foot of Cajon Pass, on the main road to Los Angeles from the east, made it an important transportation and distribution center. When the railroad was built in 1875, San Bernardino's economic future was secured.

The first orange trees were planted about the same time the first train arrived. Several important citrus colonies emerged and the valley thrived.

Rivalry Splits the Valley

The valley's two largest settlements, San Bernardino and **Riverside** (which grew around the 1840s Rubidoux Ranch on the banks of the Santa Ana River), engaged in seemingly ceaseless feuding. Political problems were solved with the creation of a separate Riverside County in 1893. The new county, stretching east all the way to the Colorado River, took sizable chunks out of both San Bernardino and San Diego counties. Never was a divorce a happier occasion. Even today, however, a strong rivalry remains between San Bernardino (population 120,000) and Riverside (population 170,000).

Before the label "Inland Empire" evolved, this two-county region was known as the Citrus Belt. Around Riverside, Redlands and Ontario, groves of oranges, lemons and other citrus fruits sprang up in the 1890s. Well-educated, ambitious and wealthy urbanites began throwing their destiny to the citrus industry. The land and climate

Turn-of-the-century fruit pickers, Riverside.

were perfect, the water inexpensive, and the railroads carried thousands of carloads of fruit yearly to the Eastern states. The need for low-wage labor was provided first by the native Indians, later by Chinese and Japanese immigrants, and finally by Mexicans. Today, the ethnic diversity of the Inland Empire is a legacy of labor history.

For the first half of the 20th Century, the Inland Empire saw change so gradual that to the casual eye it seemed frozen in time. But rapid change shook the region in the Fifties and Sixties. By the Eighties, the Inland Empire stood as one of the fastest growing areas in the United States.

The City of San Bernardino

San Bernardino itself has few visitor attractions today. The site of the **Mormon Stockade and Council House** can be seen at 3rd Street and Arrowhead Avenue. **California State College, San Bernardino**, is situated in the north end of the city. **Norton Air Force Base**, a missile center, is on the east side. **Glen Helen Regional Park**, 10 miles (16 km) northwest of city center, has 500 acres

Courtyard of the century-old Mission Inn.

(202 hectares) for camping, picnicking, boating and fishing. In 1983, it gained fame as the site of Southern California's big "US" rock concert.

San Bernardino's big event of the year is the **National Orange Show**, held for 10 days in mid March at the county fairgrounds, Mill and E streets. This show, which celebrates the end of the winter citrus harvest, has been held annually since 1915. It includes many special sports and entertainment events along with exhibits and festivities.

The west San Bernardino suburb of **Rialto** has a **Historical Society Museum** in the Christian Church Building, Riverside Avenue and 2nd Street. A wonderful example of craftsman-style wooden architecture, this 1907 structure features a tower with high-pitched dormers.

Colton, just south of San Bernardino, was settled in the 1840s by a group of New Mexico families encouraged to migrate to the Inland Empire to serve as a buffer against rustlers and marauding Indians. Flooding destroyed the settlement in 1862, but the **Agua Mansa Cemetery** survives as a reminder of that era.

East of San Bernardino is **Redlands**, founded in 1881 by two navel orange entrepreneurs from Connecticut, Edward G. Judson and Frank E. Brown. Searching for a guaranteed source of water, Brown, a civil engineer, secured land in the nearby Bear Valley surrounded by the San Bernardino Mountains. There he built the single-arch dam that created Big Bear Lake, now a popular recreation center. In 1885, the Bear Valley Mutual Water Company — still in business today — began dispensing the water carried 25 miles (40 km) by gravity flow from Big Bear Lake to Redlands.

The presence of water helped Redlands to expand rapidly. The colony became a mecca for many wealthy Eastern people who sought mild winters. Victorian mansions with lavishly landscaped grounds set among citrus groves were built around the turn of the century. Alfred and Albert Smiley, New York resort owners who lived in Redlands from 1890 to 1912, gave the colony national exposure. They created a 200-acre (81-hectare) botanical park (regrettably lost in the Sixties to an exclusive subdivision), a downtown park and a Moorish-style library.

The Elegance of Redlands

Among the outstanding mansions still standing is the **Kimberly Crest** home, built in 1897 for Mrs. Cornelia Hill of Marbletown, New York. A chateau-style house, it is surrounded by five acres of Italian gardens. From 1905 until 1979, Kimberly Crest was a private home. Now in the hands of a foundation, it is open to the public Thursday afternoons and the first Sunday of each month.

The 1890 **Morey House** describes itself as "America's favorite Victorian home." With its French mansard roof, onion dome, Queen Anne-style mill work and its five colors, it is easy to see why the Morey House has been chosen to appear in movies and advertising campaigns. The original interior woodwork is well preserved and features beautifully carved turned staircasess and ceiling moldings. There are public tours.

Smiley Park in the town center (4th and Eureka streets) features the **Lincoln Memorial Shrine**. Built in 1932 by philanthropist Robert Watchorn, it is the only library, museum and monument west of the Mississippi River honoring former U.S. President Abraham Lincoln. The shrine houses a collection of manuscripts, art, photos and other memorabilia from the Civil War period.

Also in Smiley Park is the **Redlands Bowl**, site of concerts and opera since 1924. More than 100,000 people annually enjoy the summer musical series which has featured such internationally known classical performers as Isaac Stern, Eleanor Marlow, Jerome Hines and the Aman Folk Ensemble.

The **San Bernardino County Museum**, located in Redlands at 2024 Orange Tree Lane, has displays of regional natural history, geology and pioneer artifacts. The museum also administers the **Asistencia Mission de San Gabriel**, the original (restored) San Bernardino mission. Two museum rooms and a wedding chapel recall valley life in the 1830s and 1840s. The mission is two miles west of downtown Redlands at 26930 Barton Road.

Little **Yucaipa**, east of Redlands off State 38, features a restored 1842 home called the **Sepulveda Adobe** (32183 Kentucky St.). There are period displays and furnishings. Yucapia also has a **Mountaintown** (38550 Oak Glen Road) which is a sort of taxidermist's zoo, with mounted animals from all over the world.

Apples are rarely associated with the Inland Empire. But **Oak Glen** — actually a series of valley ranches and restaurants near Yucaipa — has been a center of apple-growing since the 1870s. It was once a favored acorn-gathering area of the indigenous Indians. Thousands of people now flock to the area in the spring at apple-blossom time and in the fall during the harvest, when Gravenstein, McIntosh, King David and Delicious apples can be sampled and purchased. **Cherry Valley**, further down Oak Glen Road, contains the **Edward-Dean Museum of Decorative Arts** with a collection of priceless furniture and art.

Yucaipa was the site of one of the Inland Empire's more memorable historical incidents. In 1852, a gang of desperadoes led by "Red" Irving — so-called for his mat of orange hair and crimson nose from too much whiskey — was terrorizing ranchers and attacking *haciendas*. Juan Antonio, the Cahuilla chief who patrolled the valley, drove the gang into a box canyon near modern

Where it all began.

CALIFORNIA'S OLDEST WINERY

ESTAB. 1839

STORAGE TANK No. 43

CAP. 1404 GAL.

Yucaipa. The only outlaw who survived the slaughter by Juan Antonio and his braves was one who played dead.

Down by the Riverside

In the 1840s, a merchant and cattle baron named Louis Rubidoux purchased 6,700 acres (about 2,700 hectares) of land along the Santa Ana River. Descended from a famous French-Canadian family, Rubidoux became known as a generous, genial host. He spent money freely and spoke several languages, including Cahuilla. His ranch encompassed much of what is today downtown Riverside, and his name lives on at **Mount Rubidoux**. This 1,337-foot (408-meter) hill at the west end of downtown is capped by the Father Serra Cross and the World Peace Tower. Easter Sunrise services have been held here annually since 1909.

Riverside grew with the entire San Bernardino Valley. Juan Bandini and the large Yorba family controlled nearly 50,000 acres (some 20,000 hectares) of land; part of this was incorporated in 1886 as South Riverside, now **Corona**. It became known around the turn of the century for its outstanding lemon groves. In the early 20th Century, Corona was famed for its auto races, with such legendary daredevils as Barney Oldfield reaching unheard-of land speeds of 40 or even 50 miles per hour (65 to 80 km).

Today Riverside is still well known for its auto sports. The **Riverside International Raceway** (on Eucalyptus Avenue east of town) is the site of major national and international events, including the California 500 in early September and the Winston Western 500 in January.

Riverside is the home of the California orange. In the mid 1870s, Eliza and Luther Tibbetts took a shipment from Washington, D.C., of three orange saplings nurtured from the bud of a Brazilian seedless orange. From this infancy the local citrus industry exploded. One of these parent trees still lives in Riverside today in a small park at the intersection of Magnolia and Arlington avenues. Although its progeny are in the millions, it still blossoms and produces oranges more than a century after its planting.

Another remnant of the past is the

High-speed action on the motor circuit comes to Riverside and Ontario speedways.

Mission Inn (3649 7th St.), built in the 1880s by Frank Miller and a group of distinguished architects. A monument to Spanish revival architecture, it is officially registered as a United States historic landmark. Former U.S. President Theodore Roosevelt once stayed here, and Richard Nixon and his wife Pat spent their honeymoon in a penthouse suite.

Today the inn no longer serves as a hostelry, but is the focus of artistic and cultural curiosity. Miller built alcoves, balconies, terraces, outdoor patios, music rooms and art galleries. Many of the rooms have been refurbished, often with a Spanish Catholic theme: there are 900 bells, crosses and international dolls within. The St. Francis Chapel has a 200-year-old altar from Mexico and Tiffany windows. A tour of the delightful inn also includes such charming spots as the Cloister Wing and the Rotonda Internacionál, and the International Shrine of Aviators.

Another outstanding mansion from a similar era is the **Bettner House**, constructed in 1891 in Queen Anne style. Built on Magnolia Avenue by a wealthy widow, the house is today operated as a museum.

The **Riverside Municipal Museum** (3720 Orange St.) has exhibits on local history and Indian culture. At **March Air Force Base**, just southeast of town, there is an aircraft museum. The **University of California, Riverside**, has a delightful 37-acre (15-hectare) botanical garden specializing in dry-climate plants of Latin America, Australia and South Africa. In the **Temescal Valley** eight miles (13 km) southeast of Corona, the former South Riverside, are the privately owned **Glen Ivy Hot Springs**.

About 12 miles (19 km) west of Riverside is **Ontario**, the San Bernardino Valley's third largest city with a population of about 90,000. It was founded in 1882 by two Canadian brothers, George and William Chaffee, who established a "model colony" orange grove and named it after their home province. The Chaffees devised a revolutionary new irrigation system called a "mutual water company" which permitted water stock to go with acreage in a mutually held water company. Each share entitled the holder to a set amount of deliverable water. This avoided confusing water-rights issues

Hobie-cat sailors ply afternoon breezes as fishermen go after dinner at Big Bear Lake.

while assuring agricultural success in the Inland Empire.

Ontario today is the home of the Los Angeles area's second international airport. Another high-speed location is the **Ontario Motor Speedway**, like its cousin in Riverside an important stop on the national motor-racing circuit. There is room for 140,000 spectators in the stands and space for another 60,000 on the infield.

Ontario's northern neighbor is **Cucamonga**, whose name is Indian for "sandy place." The **Gausti Mansion** (800 N. Archibald Ave.), once surrounded by the world's largest vineyard, was built in 1900 by Secundo Gausti, owner of the Italian Vineyard Company. Several wineries remain in this area, and most are open to the public for tasting.

Balloons and Gunfights

Geographically, the biggest chunk of the Inland Empire is southeast of Riverside. On State Highway 74 about 17 miles (27 km) from Riverside is **Perris**, a major center for ballooning and other sky sports. Several outfits offer "champagne flights" in hot-air balloons, giving the public a rare opportunity to float silently through the atmosphere.

Perris is also the location of the **Orange Empire Railway Museum**. More than 140 trolleys and other railroad memorabilia are displayed daily.

Near **Rancho California,** just above the San Diego County line, is **Temecula**. This village has a **Frontier Museum Historical Center** with an exhibit of articles from the Old West. More remarkable are its dioramas of a gunfight, stagecoach and saloon with wax figures, and a larger-than-life bronze statue of John Wayne.

Lake Elsinore, once known as Laguna Grande ("Big Lake"), is 11 miles (17 km) west of Perris. Three investors launched the Elsinore Colony in 1883, naming it for the "pleasant sounding" Danish city in Shakespeare's *Hamlet*. Elsinore is now a popular resort area. In recent years, heavy rains have raised the lake level to unprecedented levels. Some people with lakeshore homes have found their homes surrounded by the lake.

Hemet, a bustling town of about 23,000 people, is 17 miles (27 km) east of Perris. Founded in a small mountain

ackpackers
epare to
ake camp in
e San
ernardino
ountains.

valley in 1893, it has become a retirement haven. Simple in its appearance but boasting considerable wealth, building after building on Florida Street houses either a bank or a savings-and-loan association.

Just outside of Hemet is the **Ramona Bowl** where the annual "Ramona Pageant" has been staged since 1923. Based on Helen Hunt Jackson's popular 1880s novel *Ramona*, it tells the sad love story of two Mission Indians in Mexican California. A local cast of 100, plus horses, put on the musical in late April and early May.

Maze Stone County Park is located a short distance northwest of Hemet. It contains a 15,000-year-old Indian petroglyph, in the form of a maze, on a large boulder.

San Jacinto, a charming century-old town in the San Jacinto foothills, is just north of Hemet. Along with **Idyllwild** further to the east, it is a popular base for backpacking and rock-climbing expeditions into the **Mount San Jacinto Wilderness**. Idyllwild is also the home of the summer **School of Music and the Arts** sponsored by the University of Southern California.

'The Rim of the World'

And then there are the mountains, mainly encompassed in the **San Bernardino National Forest** — established in 1893 by U.S. President Benjamin Harrison. Naturalist Francis Saunders observed: "They seem austere, barren and uninviting." As a first impression, that's true. Yet they divide the deserts of the north from the verdant valleys to the south. **Mount San Gorgonio**, the tallest peak in Southern California (below the Sierras) stands 11,499 feet (3,505 meters) from the desert floor. Both peaks are popular year-round outdoor recreation areas, attracting backpackers in the summer.

The foothills of the San Bernardino Mountains are covered with chaparral, a perennially green-gray shrub, with forests on the higher elevations. Because this range runs east-west, the light and shadow patterns created by the sun provide an unusual beauty.

Access to the mountains is by the **Rim of the World Drive,** State Highway 18 north out of San Bernardino city. First opened in 1915, this 101-mile (162-km) road features beautiful vistas, awesome

landscapes and numerous other attractions. The road begins at **Crestline**, once a logging area for the 1850s Mormon colony at San Bernardino. It is located at about 5,000 feet (1,500 meters) near **Lake Gregory**.

A short drive east is mile-high **Lake Arrowhead**. Now socially exclusive, it was created in 1891 with the damming of Little Bear Creek, and flourished as a popular resort in the Twenties. Today there are many fine homes along its shores built by Hollywood personalities and wealthy businessmen. Tourists are attracted by its shops, restaurants and hotel, as well as a sightseeing cruise on the lake.

It's Christmas throughout the year at **Santa's Village** in the nearby pine forests. For 27 years, Mr. and Mrs. Claus have maintained a residence here. In their village are rides such as the "Candy Cane Sleigh" and the "Whirling Christmas Tree," a toy shop, and small animals which youngsters can feed and pet.

Near **Running Springs**, where State 330 from Redlands joins the route, are two winter ski resorts. **Green Valley** caters to novice skiers, while **Snow Valley** — with a top elevation of 7,841 feet (2,390 meters) and a vertical rise of 1,141 feet (348 meters) — has 12 chair lifts and a lot of terrain for advanced skiers.

Big Bear Lake was created by a single-arch dam in 1883 to irrigate the orange groves of Redlands. Today, it is a summer and winter resort, featuring hunting and fishing, boating and horseback riding, camping and picnicking. There are skating, sledding and tobogganing in winter — plus skiing, of course. **Snow Summit** has 14 miles (22½ km) of runs from a top elevation of 8,200 feet (2,500 meters). Further east, the **Goldmine** ski area drops 1,500 feet (457 meters) from a top elevation of 8,600 feet (2,621 meters).

Near Big Bear is the wooded **Holcomb Valley**, the scene of frenetic gold mining in the 1860s. There were once two bustling towns here; now there are only memories. "Uncle Billy" Holcomb and Jack Martin discovered gold here in May 1860, and the news quickly spread. Pick-and-shovel prospectors swarmed in. The town of Belleville became the rough-and-ready hangout of such characters as "Hell Roaring" Johnson, a desperado who terrorized miners.

Climbers ponder the magnitude of Mount San Jacinto.

CALIFORNIA'S FIRST CITY: SAN DIEGO

"San Diego," the *Wall Street Journal* once observed, "is so laid back it sometimes seems comatose."

Untrue? Not necessarily. Unfair? Definitely.

The writer should have known better. San Diegans work hard at what they do best: enjoying themselves and their coastal city. And if the posture they assume in pursuit of enjoyment seems laid back, well, a true San Diegan probably wouldn't deny it.

But comatose is hardly the word to describe the changes that have occurred the past few years in California's second largest city. There's a pleasing new skyline and lifestyle downtown, the arts are flourishing and the population (now about 900,000) is climbing at a rate of about 42,000 a year. It is estimated that the population of San Diego County may reach 3.5 million by the year 2020. With northward expansion checked by Camp Pendleton Marine Base at the Orange County line, and southward growth stunted by the Mexican border, the only real room for affordable development is to the mountainous east.

So newcomers and long-time residents alike are making the most of their urban spaces. Cooling sea breezes help scrub the sky clean of pollutants and make for short-sleeve weather most of the year. San Diego is a nice place to visit, an even nicer place to live. The Convention and Visitors Bureau's trademark slogan seems to invite further arrivals: "San Diego feels good all over." But a popular bumper sticker summarizes the opinion of many other San Diegans toward their crowded future: "Welcome to San Diego. Now go home."

With the diverse and pleasing mix of activities that the city offers, however — ranging from cosmopolitan to, well, laid back — San Diego will find it hard to keep visitors away.

Historic Presidio Hill

California began in San Diego. Here, on July 16, 1769, Father Junípero Serra conducted a solemn mass dedicating California's first mission "to the glory of God." Father Serra, who subsequently moved north from San Diego to found California's famed mission chain, then dedicated the state's first military settlement, which surrounded and protected **Mission San Diego de Alcala.** This all took place on **Presidio Hill,** earning it the seldom-heard nickname, "The Plymouth Rock of the West Coast."

Today, Presidio Hill is flanked by Interstates 5 and 8 to the west and north, and even though the freeways' roar is omnipresent, a hike or drive up is worth the effort. From Taylor Street east of Old Town, a short, curving road marked **Presidio Hill Observation Point** turns off just before the 1-8 on-ramp. At the top of this road is a rarely visited city park consisting of a steep slope sometimes frequented by grass skiers (who have tractor-type treads on the bottoms of their skis).

From the top, there are terrific views of "mondo condo" **Mission Valley** — where the shopping malls and stacked residential units have been called "as close to being like Los Angeles as San Diego wants itself to be" — and **Mission Bay,** the city's man-made aquatic playground. Even on mildly clear days, the vista extends all the way to La Jolla (say

Preceding pages, San Diego's burgeoning downtown. Left, San Diego Bay and Shelter Island yacht harbor. Right, Mission San Diego de Alcala.

"La Hoya"), San Diego's seaside version of Beverly Hills. At the top of the park is a little monument dedicated to the white deer that used to roam the adjacent canyons. **Mission Hills** is now what the area is called. Some of San Diego's finest old Spanish and cottage-style homes line the broad streets framed by palm trees that seem to tumble out of those canyons.

This pocket of San Diego has changed little since the time of the missionaries. But everything around it has been on the move ever since — even the mission itself, which was relocated in 1774 to its present site five miles (eight kilometers) up Mission Valley when the Presidio area's lovely hillside proved unsuitable for crops.

Tombstones and Whales

Probably the best place to get a complete look at San Diego is from the southern tip of **Point Loma.** The drive out Cabrillo Memorial Highway leads through an expensive neighborhood with some fine ocean and city views. The scenery changes abruptly at the gate to the U.S. Navy's **Fort Rosecrans**

Military Reservation, home to a variety of military facilities including eerily beautiful Fort Rosecrans National Cemetery. The neat white markers marching down to the Navy station below are mute testimony to San Diego's deep military roots. The road ends at **Cabrillo National Monument,** named for Juan Rodriguez Cabrillo, the Portuguese explorer who discovered the point and upper California itself on Sept. 28, 1542. The visitor's center has displays explaining the city's discovery; daily programs about the monument itself are also presented.

A short stroll south is **San Diego Lighthouse,** first illuminated in 1853. Often obscured by fog, it was replaced in 1895 by a still-functioning Coast Guard lighthouse at the ocean's edge. There's also an observation point for watching the California gray whales on their southern migration from the Bering Sea to the warm waters of Scammon's Lagoon and Magdalena Bay in Baja California. From late December to early March, the behemoths are plainly visible from most of San Diego's coast. Numerous charters and private boats will shuttle adventurers out.

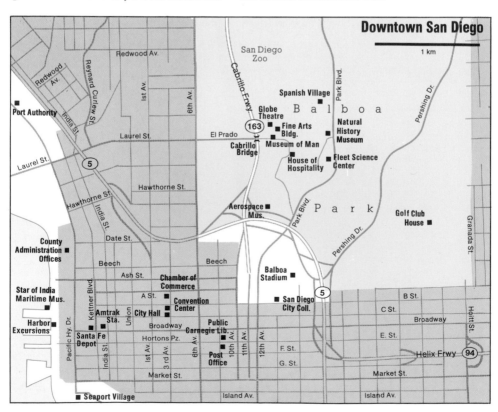

Heading back toward the city on Cabrillo Highway, a left turn on aptly named Hill Street leads into **Ocean Beach,** one of the city's oldest beach communities. Its reputation as a haven for hippie hold-outs is not undeserved; long-haired males and flowers-in-her-hair females are abundant in the flatlands near the beach and municipal fishing pier.

Sunset Cliffs Boulevard leads north to **Sea World,** where visitors come nose-to-dorsal fin with a happy clan of killer whales, dolphins, porpoises and other marine life from around the world. The brilliant new Penguin Encounter has quickly become the park's most popular attraction, but Shamu the whale, sharks and walruses still pack 'em in for a round of daily performances that would tire a vaudevillian. There are ample interpretative exhibits to satisfy those who prefer aquarium-type settings.

'Ducking Around the Bay'

Killer whales take a bow at Sea World.

North of Sea World on Ingraham Street is **Vacation Village,** a resort on carefully named Vacation Isle. The secluded village typifies just about everything the resort-goer seeks in San Diego: soft white beaches, lily-filled ponds, an immense heated swimming pool, rental sailboats and bicycles, plus fine dining. At the center of all this bliss is an observation tower that offers another excellent view of the city's coastline. For closer looks at 4,600-acre (1,860-hectare) Mission Bay without getting wet, Duck Tours' amphibious landing craft pick visitors up at land-locked hotels for guided tours. The tours have become the fashionable way to "duck around the bay."

Across Vacation Isle are **Mission Beach** and **Pacific Beach,** two of the most popular areas with out-of-towners and locals alike. Residents make a point of stating whether they're from North or South Mission. Homes in the latter are more exclusive because the neighborhood ends at Mission Bay's entrance channel, a wonderful place to watch boats or go fishing from the jetties. South Mission has **The Pennant** and **The Beachcomber,** side-by-side bars that are the ultimate San Diego beach hangouts — especially on Sunday afternoons, when it is presumed most of the tourists

have headed back to the inland valleys.

Pacific Beach is a tidy community nestled between the coast, Mission Bay and La Jolla. The ocean beach itself extends about four miles (6½ km), but is barely visible on a nice summer days when swarms of glistening bodies crowd the sand. The bay has miles of less-crowded beaches. but no waves except the wake from ski boats. Activities tend to center on the beach by **Crystal Pier** and in the area along Mission Boulevard and up Garnet Avenue, where the locals shop, dine and congregate.

Standard garb for most of the year in this locality is OP shorts, Hawaiian shirt (the gaudier the better), strapped-on sunglasses and stylish rubber sandals which are never referred to simply as "zoris." A deep-toned suntan is *de rigeur* of course. An optional extra might include Walkman-type headphones for tuning things out when jogging along the beach, bike-riding or just browsing in the bookstores.

Mission Boulevard continues north toward **La Jolla.** Mystery writer Raymond Chandler, who lived there, claimed the community was "a nice place for old people and their parents." La Jolla does have its fair share of senior citizens, but their numbers are at least equalled by the *nouveau riche* who can be observed running errands on their mopeds or in their Mercedes and always in their designer shirts.

La Jolla, 'The Jewel'

La Jolla means "The Jewel" in Spanish, and the name's literal and geographical meanings both apply. The town's scenic coastal edge meanders from **Tourmaline Surfing Beach** on the south to **Torrey Pines State Beach** on the north. In between are a number of easily accessible ocean-view sites across from homes that grow more gorgeous as one heads north up La Jolla Boulevard. **Bird Rock** is an interesting tidepool area at the end of a street with the same name. **Windansea,** at the end of Rosemont Street, is the locals' beach immortalized by Tom Wolfe in *The Pumphouse Gang.*

La Jolla Boulevard ends at Coast Boulevard, which rims central La Jolla's string of grassy beach parks, each with

Friday night crowd at The Pennant

its own blend of rocky bluffs, sand, palms and local color. **La Jolla Caves,** at the east end of Coast, are a snorkeler's haven and home of a local rite of passage. While snorkelers dart in and out of the ocean caves, teenagers above wait for waves to surge in, then take running leaps between the rock formations 20 feet (6½ meters) below.

Coast Boulevard climbs back up to **Prospect Street,** where La Jollans and visitors stroll, nosh, shop and dine. There are fine jewelry stores, boutiques, art galleries, restaurants, bars and hotels, including the elegant pink **La Valencia.** La Jolla extends several blocks southward in this same vein, with high-class department stores, gourmet food and antiques stores. For those with time to explore, the **La Jolla Museum of Contemporary Art** always has a well-publicized exhibit or two.

Treats for Body and Mind

Prospect proceeds north to Torrey Pines Boulevard and **La Jolla Shores,** one of the prettiest beach areas in San Diego. A fair hike to the north is notorious **Black's Beach,** once a legal nude

beach ("swimsuit-optional" is what the city called it) in an isolated area with high cliffs and a narrow shoreline. Numerous problems, including gaggles of gawkers, made the city rescind its blessing several years ago, but the all-over-tan bunch still makes its pilgrimages. It's an incongruous scene, really: nude bodies splayed out on the beach, colorful hang gliders riding the offshore breezes above, some of the biggest cliff-hanging homes in La Jolla nearby, and creepy looking guys training their binoculars on what they hope will be some action below. Sometimes those who visit wind up asking themselves: Was this strip really worth it?

La Jolla is also home of the **University of California of San Diego,** an affiliation that affords extensive cultural opportunities for the city. The new **La Jolla Playhouse,** on campus, is drawing raves for its brilliant design as well as its first-rate productions. Actor Gregory Peck, a La Jolla native, was a founder of the original off-campus playhouse, which went dark after several critically acclaimed but unprofitable years. Also a part of the campus is **Scripps Aquarium** a free-to-the-public attrac-

Smiling faces of La Jolla.

tion at Scripps Institution of Oceanography. An ongoing calendar of concerts, dance, theater and exhibitions keeps a large segment of San Diego's non-student populace shuttling regularly to UCSD.

The return trip to central San Diego includes two more panoramic points. From **Mount Soledad Easter Cross,** newly graded residential and commercial properties can be seen marching east to San Diego's future on the other side of I-5. A few miles south down Soledad Mountain Road, **Kate O. Sessions Park,** gives sweeping views of Mission Bay, the coast, the harbor and downtown. The sights are especially pleasing at sunset when the blue bay and sky turn bright orange.

The Past in the Present

A visit to **Old Town** often satisfies the traveler's desire for a trip south of the border. Much of the neighborhood falls within **Old Town State Historic Park,** a fairly accurate depiction of a mission-era Mexican plaza with early American influence. The park proper is off-limits to vehicular traffic. It includes such sites as the small room where the first edition of *The San Diego Union* was printed; **Whaley House Museum,** the oldest brick structure in San Diego; and **Casa de Estudillo**, a sprawling adobe residence that housed the original commander of the Presidio.

The tourist centerpiece of Old Town is **Bazaar Del Mundo,** another adobe rescued from neglect and converted into a lush complex of high-quality shops and restaurants. The bazaar and other shopping sections of Old Town blend together nicely despite the fact some of them were built new to look old. But the reverse happened at **Heritage Park,** a Victorian village where some of San Diego's earliest historic homes have been relocated, restored and given new life as shops and restaurants. The neatly manicured park is also home to the building that housed **Temple Beth Israel,** the city's first synagogue.

Bustling Balboa Park

San Diegans have always been proud of **Balboa Park,** a 1-400-acre (566-hectare) recreational and cultural oasis that grows more urbane as the city

A tender moment at the San Diego Zoo.

blossoms. On weekends, the park is an ever-changing wonderland of picnickers, roller skaters, families, art lovers, jugglers, mimes and Hare Krishnas — some seeking attention, most shying away from it. The **El Prado** and **House of Hospitality** areas, right in the center of things, are a good place to get acquainted with the park, its gardens and activities.

The park houses several excellent museums, including the **Aerospace Museum,** one of the most extensive of its kind in the nation; **Natural History Museum; Timken Art Gallery,** featuring European old masters and 19th Century American paintings; **San Diego Museum of Art; Reuben H. Fleet Space Theater and Science Center,** home of a spectacular multi-media Omnitheatre and the largest planetarium in the United States; and the **Museum of Man,** which emphasizes the Western Americas.

Most of the park's facilities are in Spanish Moorish-style buildings created for the Panama-California Exposition of 1915–16 and the California-Pacific International Exposition of 1935-36. One of the most interesting of the latter is **Spanish Village,** where dozens of

artists' studios ring a colorful, fading courtyard.

Theater is also a big part of Balboa Park's cultural makeup. In close proximity are **The Old Globe,** where works by Shakespeare, Oscar Wilde and others get the treatment they deserve in a modern version of Stratford-on-Avon's pride and joy; the **Cassius Carter,** a more intimate theater-in-the-round; the new outdoor **Festival Stage,** home of the annual summer Shakespeare Festival; and **Starlight Bowl,** an outdoor summer musical theater. Performances are unfortunately subjected to inescapable interruptions. The theater lies beneath the landing approach to San Diego's International Airport and performers have no choice but to stop until the aircraft noise subsides.

The park also is home of the city's most-visited attraction, internationally famous **San Diego Zoo.** Nearly 3,500 representatives of 760 species reside within this 100-acre (40-hectare) tropical garden. Most are in barless, moated enclosures in an attempt to recreate as much as possible the animals' natural homes in the wild. In addition to the

story ats at the nbarcadero.

STAR OF INDIA

usual assortment of elephants, lions, ti-gers, giraffes and bears, the zoo has more koalas — 30-plus at last count — than any other zoo in America. The cuddly creature has become the institution's unofficial mascot.

Water Balloons, Beer Cans and Victorians

Visitors can leave the park via Laurel Street, which runs through a neighborhood of restored Victorian houses and other old structures which lend a charm and elegance seen in few other parts of town. Laurel takes a steep dip on the way to Harbor Drive, the road to **Harbor Island** and **Shelter Island.** These man-made urban resorts are ideal for picnicking, strolling and viewing the glistening downtown skyline.

All of that is free. Those who want to drop some money will also find night clubs, restaurants, high-rise hotels and marinas where vessels of all sizes can be rented for sightseeing or fishing. On Wednesday evenings, for longer than anyone can remember, skippers have maneuvered their craft into **San Diego Bay** for the weekly "beer-can regatta."

Camaraderie and relaxation were the original intent of this typically San Diego ritual. But in recent years a sub-ritual — water balloon fights between crews of opposing vessels — has become the way to "do" the regatta.

A popular stop, before heading downtown via Harbor Drive, is the **Embarcadero.** Harbor cruises start from here, and there is a floating **Maritime Museum** aboard the *Star of India,* the oldest merchant vessel afloat (built in 1863 on the Isle of Man) and its sister ships, the steam yacht *Medea* and the ferryboat *Berkeley.* This attractive area is the waterfront's next growth area. Major hotels, restaurants and shopping zones are planned, an appropriate greeting for the cruise liners that are destined to call on San Diego within the decade.

A mile or so south is the waterfront's most popular redevelopment effort, three-year-old **Seaport Village,** a collection of shops, view restaurants and a municipal park-fishing pier jutting into the bay. Built on the site of the old Coronado Ferry landing, the village is a mixture of early Spanish, Victorian and California architecture rambling over 23

Tourists aboard the harbor cruise leave the Coronado Bridge in their wake.

bayside acres (nine hectares). This enormously successful venture is credited with bringing the middle class back to the waterfront. The upper class won't be far behind: a luxury hotel and pleasure-craft marina are under construction next door.

The Gaslamp Quarter

A good way to get to San Diego's new downtown is through its old downtown. Drivers headed southeast on Harbor Drive can turn left at Fifth Avenue and enter **The Gaslamp Quarter.** The brick-paved sidewalks, turn-of-the-century architecture, Victorian benches and gaslight-style street lamps are here to bring new life to the city's first true commercial district. This long-neglected neighborhood has undergone the transformation that occurs in many central cities: young, upwardly mobile artists, entrepreneurs and urbanites have moved in and renovated. City incentives helped smooth the way, along with The Gaslamp's designation as a historic district. A walk along Fifth Avenue takes in the **Stingaree Building,** site of a historic brothel raided early this century

in a futile effort to clean up downtown; the gilded **Louis Bank of Commerce Building,** with twin crow's-nest towers that once reigned as downtown's highest points; and the **Jewelers' Exchange Building,** headquarters for the city's wholesale jewelry market.

There's still a curious mixture of porno shops, dingy bars and transient hotels left over from the neighborhood's heyday as a playground for sailors on leave. All of that will probably remain even though the city's most ambitious inner-city project, **Horton Plaza** regional shopping center, is rising on 9.5 acres (3.8 hectares) between The Gaslamp and downtown's new high-rises. When completed in the spring of 1985, the plaza, named for San Diego visionary and developer Alonso Horton, will feature a deluxe hotel, major department stores, theater and more in a sophisticated ensemble expected to herald a new era in downtown living. Several new housing complexes have already proved popular, and their number should grow as San Diegans discover the joys of living two feet from work.

In downtown San Diego, one is likely to see a surfer toting his board, a

Commuters disembark Trolley at Gaslamp Quarter station.

bag lady and her day's catch, a pin-striped businesswoman on her way to exercise class, a pushcart vendor, sailors getting tattooed, and illegal aliens waiting for the next Greyhound bus north. Compared to some others, this downtown is a clean, compact area where all manner of financial and consumer needs are within walking distance. The skyscrapers don't exceed 27 stories. The people are friendly. There's an air of constant change as new businesses replace old, buildings get facelifts, and various improvement projects add their daily impact. Perhaps the best symbol of the new movement downtown is the **San Diego Trolley,** whose bright red cars whisk thousands of commuters daily between the **Santa Fe Depot** and 17 other stations south to the international border. The light-rail system has proved so successful in its first two years of operation that an eastern extension is on the drawing board.

Downtown also has its own version of Off-Broadway. Several eminently professional and affordable small theaters offer a wide scope of styles and subject matter. These include the **Gaslamp Quarter Theater** in that neighborhood,

the intimate **Bowery** in the basement of an old apartment hotel and **San Diego Repertory Theater** in what was once a church. Many of the actors and actresses have performed at the Old Globe and other major venues and represent an important ingredient in the reputation for professionalism that these theaters enjoy. The venues are popular among performers and theater-goers alike. San Diego is rapidly becoming a major American city in terms of its theater presentations.

Coronado and a
View Across the Bay

A pleasant way to wind up a San Diego visit is to travel to **Coronado,** an island-like community across the bay from downtown at the north end of the **Silver Strand Peninsula.** The ferry used to be the fastest way to get to Coronado. But it was replaced in 1964 by the **Coronado Bay Bridge,** a graceful 2.2-mile (3.5-km) archway. A return trip across this span yields a 360-degree look at the bay and city to the north, Point Loma and the coast to the west, downtown Golden Hill to the east, and Mexican border communities to the south. **North Island** at Coronado's western city limit is home of a massive naval air station, the noise of which is among the few negatives of Coronado life. The town is a handsome blend of cottages, custom homes, beach houses, condos and stately Victorians laid out in neat streets leading to the bay on one side and the Pacific on the other.

Near the luxurious Coronado Shores condominium complex is the **Hotel Del Coronado,** truly the crown of the area's beachfront resorts. Opened in 1888, "The Del" is a wealth of orange gables, cupolas and window peaks that have inspired many other structures in the San Diego area. Like any grande dame, she has her stories to tell. This was the first major American hotel to put electric lights in every room. The Duke of Windsor met his future Duchess here. *Some Like It Hot*, the Marilyn Monroe-Tony Curtis-Jack Lemmon comedy classic, and *The Stuntman*, starring Peter O'Toole, were filmed here. One of the guest rooms even has a ghost. The hotel's history is spelled out in detail in a series of display panels.

Left, Fat City, an art-deco night spot in the downtown area. Right, the historic Hotel Del Coronado.

A BIRD'S-EYE VIEW OF SAN DIEGO

EDITOR'S NOTE: In the decade since the fabulous San Diego Chicken fluttered into the American sports scene, he has become almost an institution throughout the country. Ted Giannoulas dons his colorful suit some 200 times a year and travels to sporting events throughout America to promote and publicize various teams and sports. He has been featured on television and magazine covers numerous times, and his portrait even graces the Kellogg's Corn Flakes box. But he remains true to San Diego, his adopted home. Herewith his somewhat feathered story.

There is a theory some people subscribe to: the entire North American continent is tilted to the southwest and everything loose rolls around there. It has been said that I am walking proof of this for San Diego.

Working a career in a chicken suit, albeit a lucrative one, I suppose means that I am nuts. Some say I'm also missing the bolts. But I love it. In a unique way, only San Diego could have given birth to an idea such as The Chicken and nurture it so well. It is a hint of what one can expect from living in San Diego or even visiting it.

Situated in a small corner of the United States, San Diego has a lifestyle that few cities anywhere can match. To me, no other place has such a country-club atmosphere.

The city's greatest asset is its weather. It simply brings out the best in San Diego's citizenry. We thrive on a healthy and fit lifestyle. That's why so many people move out here. San Diego's population, for the most part, consists of people transplanted from other areas of the country where they need domed stadiums to play their outdoor sports.

The climate brings an environment of relaxed festiveness. With that comes a spirit of new ideas with room for them to grow. That is the spirit of how The Famous Chicken was hatched here 10 years ago. It's also why San Diego is considered a major test market for new products.

The Chicken couldn't have started and succeeded elsewhere. Not in Los Angeles. Not in New York. Not in Chicago. There is a temperament here in San Diego that just isn't found anywhere else.

In Los Angeles, the idea of a chicken comedian wouldn't have been given the room to develop and grow, simply because it wouldn't have been socially accepted as chic by the so-called beautiful people ("Let's do lunch, baby").

New York would have rejected it at the start because it only has the patience for the finished product. It develops models. It is not a town for prototypes.

And while Chicago is a town of good times and amused people, its severe weather conditions would have stunted the character in the winter and the summer from getting about.

Today, as one who travels some 500,000 miles per year and performs regularly throughout the continent — including Los Angeles, New York and Chicago — I have obtained, you will excuse the expression, a bird's-eye view of the distinctiveness of San Diego compared to other towns.

I am not alone as a unique creature of San Diego. For example, I always make it a point to attend San Diego's "Over the Line" tournament every July. This is a beach gathering of weekend athletes and near-athletes who attempt to play a short form of softball. Sports aesthetics aside, this tournament (on a beach known as Fiesta Island) is many things to many people here: a pageantry of beautiful bikinied females, a perpetual happy hour, and of course the competition itself. It is San Diego adults at play on a backdrop of clean sand, clear water and open sun.

As one who came into San Diego from London, Ontario, Canada, I can say from the heart that this city pacifies anyone who longs for a piece of the weather back home. It is just a 45-minute ride for me if I want to drive from the warm beaches to the snowy mountainsides; or in another direction, to the heated desert.

The pace is a little slow around here. But that's by design, as if to savor each passing day. Furthermore, growth is designed at a limited speed. It took voters six years to finally approve a $94 million hotel and convention complex that is definitely needed for the tourism trade to develop to full potential.

San Diego has the usual array of parks, museums, animal emporiums

Ted Giannoulas' 'Chicken' has given him a golden egg.

and a definite abundance of postcard sites. But the area's charm is its strong point. Perhaps the best place for mingling is the Pacific Beach area. Down Garnet Avenue you'll find almost a carnival-like lure of fine restaurants, specialty boutiques and shops. Along the sidewalks by the surf, you'll find a pretty good show put on by a number of free-spirited talents. There are trick roller-skaters and souped-up car cruisers; dogs who catch Frisbees with their teeth and people who roast hot dogs over bonfires; joggers breezing by in designer workout fashions and others running past in cut-offs. The parking lots have Mercedes and old Chevys parked side by side. Here, no one looks at your checkbook. It's a melting pot of people bound by an area in which they like to mingle.

I love San Diego. I've had offers to take my chicken suit full-time to other cities but I prefer to live here. And even though I perform on the road more than half the year, I look forward each time to returning to my roost. The cost of living may be a bit more than in some other areas, but because of the weather and lifestyle, I'm sold on San Diego. Besides, this is where I emerged from my egg. The city has been good to me.

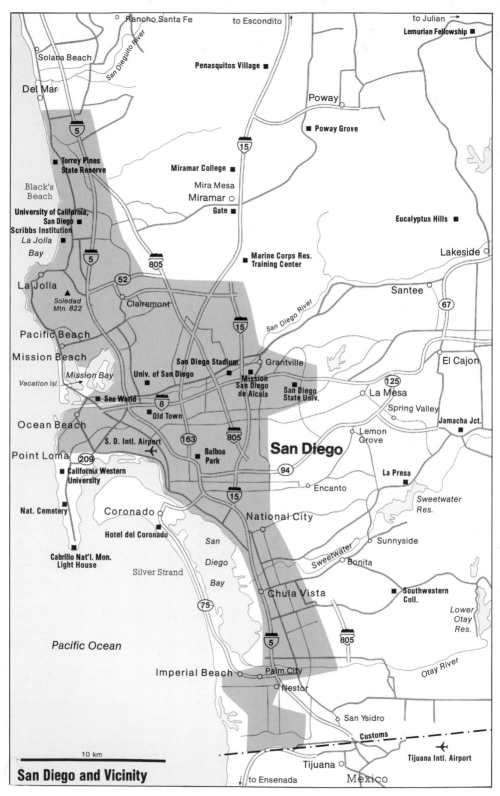

San Diego and Vicinity

Rancho Santa Fe
to Escondito
to Julian
Lemurian Fellowship ■

Solana Beach
Penasquitos Village ■

Del Mar
Poway
Poway Grove ■

Torrey Pines
State Reserve
Miramar College ■

Black's
Beach
Mira Mesa
Miramar ○
Eucalyptus Hills ■

University of California,
San Diego ■
Scribbs Institution
Gate ■

La Jolla
Bay
Marine Corps Res.
Training Center
Lakeside ○

La Jolla
Soledad
Mtn. 822
Clairemont
Santee
67

Pacific Beach
San Diego River
El Cajon

Mission Beach
San Diego Stadium
Grantville
125

Mission Bay
Univ. of San Diego
Mission
San Diego
de Alcala
San Diego
State Univ.
La Mesa

Vacation Isl.
Sea World
Spring Valley

Ocean Beach
Old Town
Jamacha Jct.

Point Loma
S. D. Intl. Airport
163
805
Lemon
Grove

California Western
University
Balboa
Park
San Diego
94
La Presa

Nat. Cemetery
209
Encanto
Sweetwater
Res.

Coronado
National City
Sunnyside

Hotel del Coronado
San
Diego
Bay
Sweetwater
Bonita

Cabrillo Nat'l. Mon.
Light House
Silver Strand
Southwestern
Coll.

Pacific Ocean
Chula Vista
Lower
Otay
Res.

75
Otay River

Imperial Beach
Palm City
Nestor

10 km
San Ysidro

San Diego and Vicinity
Customs
Tijuana Intl. Airport

Tijuana
to Ensenada
Mexico

196

SAN DIEGO —
THE COUNTY

San Diego County is a microcosm of the Golden State — its western boundary is totally ocean, its southern border is totally Mexico, and the east and north are laced with a combination of mountains and desert.

Stretching inland some 110 miles (176 kilometers) at its widest point, and northward 65 miles (104 km) from Mexico, San Diego County represents a diverse lifestyle, climate and landscape. And its two million-plus people are a cross-section of California ethnicity.

The North Coast

Stretching north of San Diego city along the coast are a string of Pacific Coast communities whose identities are much more interesting than the exit signs on Interstate 5 would indicate.

The first of these coastal towns beyond La Jolla is **Del Mar**, a beautiful spot with a sweeping hillside view of the Pacific. Site of the **Southern California**

Motocross racer flies toward the finish at the Carlsbad Grand Prix.

Exposition and national horse show over two weeks in June and July, and home of the **Del Mar Thoroughbred Club** racetrack, it is truly a community where "the turf meets the surf."

Actor Pat O'Brien and the late singer Bing Crosby rescued the struggling Del Mar racetrack in the early Thirties, pumping a huge amount of money into the facility and turning it into one of America's most popular racing-circuit venues. The season begins in July, a week after the big fair (which draws 700,000 people annually) has ended, and runs until mid September.

Del Mar is also the location of the **Torrey Pines State Reserve**, a natural habitat of the hardy evergreen which is twisted into strangely picturesque forms by Pacific winds. These same winds, rising off the cliffs at Torrey Pines Hang Glider Park, keep dozens of daring aerialists aloft whenever conditions are right. Sometimes onlookers can hitch a ride on a tandem rig with a licensed pilot.

A short distance farther north, beyond the seaside settlements of **Solana Beach** and **Cardiff-by-the-Sea**. **Encinitas** has another fine natural reserve: the **Quail Botanical Gardens**. Many rare plants are protected here, and there is a bird refuge in chaparral.

On the east side of I-5, inland some five miles (eight km), is the crown of North Coast communities — **Rancho Santa Fe**. Here is where the affluent of San Diego County's affluent live. Considered a country-style Beverly Hills, Rancho Santa Fe first became a popular retreat for many of Hollywood's celebrities in the late Twenties when actor Douglas Fairbanks and his wife, actress Mary Pickford, built their majestic **Fairbanks Ranch**. The ranch is the site of the 1984 Olympic equestrian events. Many other stars followed the Fairbanks to Rancho Santa Fe over the years, building plush homes in the hills (which are covered by a thick growth of native trees). Such stars as Victor Mature, Robert Young and Patti Page make their permanent homes today in Rancho Santa Fe.

At the top end of the county's North Coast are the communities of **Carlsbad** and **Oceanside**. Carlsbad, somewhat smaller with a population of 40,000, is a fast-growing city inhabited by middle-class families enjoying the best of country and city life in one place. A beach resort and commercial flower-growing center, the town is named after a Czechoslovakian spa city. There are mineral waters here, too. In late spring every year, motorcyclists from around the globe converge on Carlsbad for the U.S. Grand Prix of Motocross.

Oceanside, population 80,000, is known (much to the chagrin of its residents) as "Marine Town U.S.A." It sits at the southern gate to the huge **Camp Pendleton** Marine Corps training base, which extends along both sides of I-5 for the next 20 miles (32 km) northward, all the way to the Orange County line. Considered a buffer zone against the ever-expanding Los Angeles-Orange County megalopolis, Camp Pendleton is an occasional annoyance to Oceanside when hell-raising Marines are on liberty. But it is a blessing for the huge mountain and forest reserves it protects, capping this region with wonderful scenery.

Just outside Oceanside on State Highway 76, en route to Fallbrook, is the old **San Luis Rey Mission**, One of the 21 California missions built under the supervision of Father Junípero Serra, it was founded in 1798 by Father Lasuen and named for King Louis IX of France, a 13th Century crusader. It is the largest of all the missions, and has many historical artifacts and decorations. An annual fiesta is held in July.

North County

Inland northern San Diego County is known to locals simply as "North County." Its largest city is **Escondido** (population 65,000). Located in the rolling hills along I-15, Escondido (Spanish for "hidden") cannot be seen until the traveler is right in the city itself. Escondido is the center of California's avocado-growing industry; it also has a bustling business and manufacturing base which has made it one of the region's fastest growing cities.

California's winemaking tradition began here. Spanish missionaries first grew wine grapes in and around the Escondido area nearly two centuries ago. Since the Second World War, there has been a proliferation of wineries in North County. The Bernardo, Ferrara and San Pasqual wineries just outside of town are among those offering tours and tasting.

The San Luis Rey Mission

A short distance east of the city is the **San Diego Wild Animal Park**. More than 3,500 animals, representing species from Africa and Asia, are featured in the open park. There are animal and bird shows, various exhibits, and an electric monorail which takes visitors around the 1,800-acre (728-hectare) grounds. But mostly there are the animals — lions, elephants, giraffes and many others — who wander freely through the park.

Just two miles east of the wild animal park on State 78 is **San Pasqual Battlefield State Historic Park**, site of a major turning point in the United States' Mexican War of the 1840s. An unpretentious monument stands today as mute evidence of this so-called battle on Dec. 6, 1846. Historians now regard it as more of an embarrassing skirmish than a real act of war. More than 100 men and officers of the U.S. Dragoons, including scout Kit Carson, were ordered to "engage" a column of California Mexicans. The Dragoons had wet gunpowder, the Mexicans sharp lances, and the Dragoons were in big trouble — until Carson slipped away and returned with 200 U.S. Marines from San Diego.

Left, the world-famous Mount Palomar Observatory; and right, the locally famous Dudley's Bakery.

Lawrence Welk's Vacation Village, developed by the popular television orchestra leader, is located about five miles (eight km) north of Escondido on I-15. A beautiful mountainside resort hotel, dinner theater, golf course, trailer park and housing development occupy the site. The nightly combination dinner-broadway show is an entertainment bargain. Welk also has a museum featuring a 30-minute film on his life and various souvenirs he has collected along the way.

Palomar and Pala

Valley Center, a community to the north of Escondido on Road S6, is the gateway to massive **Palomar Mountain**. Rising 6,100 feet (1,859 meters) above sea level and stretching some 20 miles (32 km) in length, Palomar is the home of the Western world's largest reflecting telescope. The 200-inch Hale Telescope is within the **Mount Palomar Observatory**, owned and operated by the California Institute of Technology. It is world-famous for its many celestial discoveries of the past three decades. Open for limited tours and visitation

daily, the observatory includes the **Greenway Museum** with photographs of important sightings.

West of Palomar, on State 76 toward Oceanside, is the community of **Pala**. This village of 500 people proudly maintains its **Mission San Antonio de Pala**, an *asistancia* (extension mission) built in 1810. It is of special interest as the only California mission still serving Indians — it is on the **Pala Indian Reservation**. The Corpus Christi Festival, featuring an open-air mass, dances and games, has been held the first Sunday every June since 1816.

East of Palomar on State 76 is **Lake Henshaw**, where public camping and boating are especially popular among hunters and fishermen. The town of **Santa Ysabel**, located at the junction of States Highways 76 and 78, was the site of an all-but-forgotten mission, one of Father Serra's first four. Most travelers today are more apt to look for **Dudley's Bakery**. People from all over San Diego County flock to Santa Ysabel to buy Dudley's pastries and bread.

Seven miles (11 km) east on State 78 is **Julian**, a former mining town on the edge of the **Vallecito Mountains**. During a 10-year period just before the turn of the 20th Century, 2,000 resident gold miners dug more than $15 million in ore from the surrounding hills. Today Julian is a leisurely resort and trade center famous for its apple orchards, its autumn apple festival and its spring wildflower show. The **Eagle Mine** offers daily tours, and there is a **Pioneer Museum** open weekends. Julian is located near the **Cleveland National Forest** and **Cuyamaca State Park,** making it a favorite jumping-off point for outdoorsmen.

East County

East on I-8 from San Diego's Mission Valley, travelers climb a long hill past **San Diego State University** and enter the city of **La Mesa**, population 52,000. Often called "the Jewel of the Hills," La Mesa is home for many of San Diego's more affluent families. From the top of **Mount Helix**, reached by car via Fuerte Drive off I-8, there is a spectacular view in all directions.

Present-day historical points of interest include the old **McKinney House**, home of the city historical society. Built in 1908, it was first the home of a

A treat from the oven during Julian's annual autumn apple fest.

Methodist minister and later served as the city's first library.

The fully-restored passenger train that serviced this region in the 1920s is featured in the **Pacific Southwest Railway Museum** at the La Mesa Depot on Nebo Drive. This "Cannonball" train still operates excursion runs on special occasions.

The hub of the East County and the second largest city in San Diego County is **El Cajon**, population 95,000. El Cajon (say "El Ka-hone"), which means "the box" in Spanish, gets its name 'because it is surrounded by hills and mountains on all four sides and is nearly cut off from the cooling ocean breezes from the Pacific, just 20 miles (32 km) to the west. As a result, the temperature in El Cajon is nearly always 10 to 20 degrees (Fahrenheit) warmer than in San Diego. In the summer months, temperatures of over 100°F (over 38°C) are not uncommon.

The *padres* of mission San Diego de Alcala used the valley where El Cajon is now located to graze cattle. After the Americans settled into the county, the present city began to take shape in 1878, when Amaziah L. Knox built a five-room hotel and saloon to serve as an important stagecoach stop between San Diego and Yuma. The fledgling community became known as Knox Corners. Today, the old **Knox Hotel** still stands in **Judson Park** and is the home of the El Cajon Historical Society. The society maintains a museum which is open on Thursdays and Saturdays.

El Cajon is one of San Diego's finest cultural centers, with events held at the modern **Performing Arts Center**. The San Diego Symphony, the California Ballet and theater groups perform in the 1,200-seat auditorium.

Along State 94 some 40 miles (64 km) south is the county's border crossing at Tecate. The California side of this community is nothing more than a small shopping center and a post office, but on the Mexican side is a thriving community of 5,000 and a rather popular brewery named for the town.

Those traveling into Baja California Norte from San Diego County willing to avoid the crowded Tijuana border crossing will be pleased to know there is never a crowd in Tecate. In fact, there is seldom more than one Customs agent on duty, and he closes the border each

A thoughtful moment on the veranda of the Julian Hotel.

night about 11, earlier if there's no more traffic.

The easternmost community in the East County is **Jacumba**, once one of the most popular hot mineral-bath resorts in Southern California. Located just off I-8 (an old U.S. 80), Jacumba saw its glory days in the Thirties and Forties, when movie stars came to renew their bodies and health.

The South Bay

The South Bay region of San Diego County is a string of communities surrounding the lower end of San Diego Bay. National City, Chula Vista, Palm City, San Ysidro, Imperial Beach and Coronado make up these suburbs of greater San Diego — but don't tell any of the residents they live in "suburbs."

Portions of Palm City, San Ysidro and Imperial Beach are actually within the city limits of San Diego. Much of the industrial base for this region comes from the U.S. Navy and civilian maritime activities such as the huge **National Steel and Shipbuilding Company**. The Navy's largest surface vessel base is located in National City, and its Pacific

Surface Command is headquartered across the bay on Coronado Island.

National City and Chula Vista have growing commercial districts which depend heavily on Mexican shoppers coming across the border. The first shopping center ever built in America was the **South Bay Plaza** on National Avenue in **National City**. Opened in 1953, the center was the prototype which changed the face of American merchandising and shopping habits. National City has much of its past preserved in **Granger Hall**, which capsulizes the history of the South Bay.

Chula Vista, which means "cute view" in Spanish, has a population of 85,000 and is home for many retired and active-duty military personnel. The major city and commercial center for the South Bay, Chula Vista, is laid out to reflect "Hometown" U.S.A.

Palm City is far from that, but it is the home of a soaring historical controversy. According to records, John J. Montgomery flew the first heavier-than-air craft from atop a small hill, now known as **Airplane Park**, two years before the Wright Brothers made their flight at Kitty Hawk in 1903. The problem was that Montgomery never bothered to tell anyone east of the Mississippi about his feat and history has all but forgotten him — except in San Diego County. The wing of an airplane, jutting into the sky near the I-5 approach to San Ysidro and the Mexican border, is his monument. San Diego County's largest general-aviation airport, **Montgomery Field** in **Kearny Mesa**, bears his name.

San Ysidro, gateway to Mexico, is a booming community where it is of great benefit to be able to speak both English and Spanish. It is the busiest international border crossing in the world: some 40 million people pass in and out of the U.S. and Mexico here annually.

Imperial Beach, population 23,000, has beaches that lead right to the Tijuana Bullring to the south and the historic Hotel Del Coronado to the north. Imperial Beach has the dubious reputation of being "that little town down south where sailors and Mexicans live." There is indeed a rather large group of Hispanics and naval personnel living there, but the little town is changing. It has been discovered by the well-heeled of Los Angeles and Orange County who are buying up as much beach and adjacent property as possible.

Left, a Mexican resident of San Diego's South Bay. Right, a sunset flight over Black's Beach at Torrey Pines Hang Glider Park.

TIJUANA AND NORTHERN BAJA

Baja California is most Americans' introduction to Mexico. To some, it's paradise. To others, it's the pits. The truth, of course, lies somewhere between the tourist brochure puffery and years of girl-and-donkey-show stories.

The people of this region are as rich and poor, as warm and gracious, as enterprising and nationalistic as their *compadres* further south of the border. But by its very location, Northern Baja (as everyone on both sides of the border tends to call it) is a world unto itself.

U.S. citizens don't even need a passport if they're visiting for less than 72 hours or plan to go beyond the State Highway 1 checkpoint below Ensenada. If so, they must pick up a tourist visa in San Diego from any travel agent, the Mexican Consulate General, the Mexico Government Tourism Office or the Automobile Club of Southern California. Proof of nationality must accompany the visa. Drivers should carry some daily auto insurance, obtainable at any of the dozens of drive-throughs just north of the border. U.S. insurance is *not* valid in Mexico.

Eighteen miles (29 kilometers) south of downtown San Diego, Interstates 5 and 805 converge at the decidedly funkier Mexican side of the **International Border Crossing.** Here, the brown-skinned agents in their brown-tone uniforms casually wave drivers past their barren inspection booths, occasionally pausing to chat with friends or answer *gringos'* questions.

A few hundred feet south of the border, drivers encounter what has been called "a Mexican engineer's idea of an American interchange based on an American engineer's idea of a Mexican interchange." Straight ahead is the refurbished, tourist-oriented part of downtown **Tijuana** (say "tee-wanna").

On **Avenida Revolución,** Tijuana's renovated main drag, the visitor can still hop on a burro painted like a zebra, don a *sombrero* with "Drunk Again" scrawled on the brim, and pay a street photographer to make an instant postcard of the whole embarrassing scene.

There are enough bars and 50-cent margaritas to hang a person head-over-heels for the rest of his life. There are a

seemingly endless number of *mariachi* bands, discos and naughty, naked night clubs. It's not necessary to go looking for them; they make their presence known soon enough.

But for those who prefer loftier forms of stimulation, a superb way to learn about Mexico's heritage can be found less than a half-mile from the border. The new **Tijuana Cultural Center** on Avenida Paseo de los Heroes is a block of national pride in the heart of the city's redevelopment district. The museum in this futuristic-looking complex houses an outstanding collection of folk art, relics, handicrafts and artifact replicas. All are displayed on both sides of a 35-foot (11-meter) wide, mile-long indoor ramp.

Next door is another eye-popper, the 85-foot (26-meter) high **Omnitheatre.** Within the giant dome is presented a super-wide-angle film tour of Mexico's historical and cultural sites.

Across the street is Tijuana's closest rival to the suburban shopping malls found a few miles north. **Plaza Rio Tijuana,** the largest shopping center in northwestern Mexico, will gladden visitor's hearts and possibly empty their

Tijuana craftsman adds colorful touches to pottery in his shop.

wallets. Baja California is a free port, so most goods cost less than in San Diego. But shoppers should remember that U.S. Customs demands receipts for any daily purchases exceeding $400 per person.

Avenida Revolución and its side streets offer somewhat less cosmopolitan merchandise, although some of the city's finest clothing and jewelry shops are mixed among the *sarapes* and sandals. Mexican-made goods are priced in pesos, imported goods in U.S. dollars. If no price is posted, bargaining wins the prize.

Just southwest of Tijuana is the beach and the **Bullring-by-the-Sea,** newer and sturdier but far less popular than the rickety old bullring downtown. Bullfight season is May to September, with half the season held at each ring.

There are two routes south from Tijuana. The *Cuota* toll road, at $2.40 for a round-trip to Ensenada, includes some fine ocean scenery. It is recommended over the *Libre* free road, which parallels the *Cuota* as far as **Rosarito** (13 miles, or 20 km, from Tijuana), then dips inland.

Rosarito is a beach town whose grow-

ing popularity is evidenced by the hordes of "Yo (heart) Rosarito" bumper stickers seen throughout Southern California. It is no Mexican Riviera, but a recent proliferation of time-share resorts has pumped new life into the town, a long-time haven for American retirees who enjoy "mobile-home living."

A visit to the **Rosarito Beach Hotel** is obligatory. Guests of the 60-year-old former gambling palace have included Lana Turner, Mickey Rooney, Prince Ali Khan and other celebrities and heads of state. The hotel features glorious indoor murals by Matias Santoyo and a large swimming pool and bar area above the clean, wide beach.

Ensenada is another 30 miles (48 km) south, but worth the drive on the toll road. At the **El Mirador** exit, there is a bluff-top view of **Bahia de Todos Santos,** home of Ensenada's deep-sea charter fleet, naval drydock and various pleasure craft including the *S.S. Azure Seas* cruise liner from Los Angeles.

A few blocks from the bay is the main tourist shopping zone along **Avenida Lopez Mateos.** Merchants on the avenue display an astounding assortment of traditional Mexican crafts, from sandals sombreros and leather jackets to onyx chess sets, guitars and silverware. But prices are better in the "non-tourist" part of town off **Avenida Ruiz** a few blocks away.

No visit to Ensenada is complete without a stop at **Hussong's,** one of the oldest continually operating bars on the West Coast. Established in 1892, the wooden-frame cantina on Avenida Ruiz just east of Avenida Mateos is usually overflowing with *gringos* yukking it up and slurping down *cervezas* (beers) at record rates.

The return to California can be a bit tenser than the entry to Mexico. At the International Border Crossing, polished U.S. officers come out of their computerized hutches to make drivers sweat about the cigarettes in the trunk as if they were bricks of Acapulco Gold. The constant buzzing of a U.S. Border Patrol helicopter over nearby **Deadman's Gulch**, a notorious port of entry for illegal aliens, does little to soothe one's nerves. During busy American holiday periods, such as Independence Day (July 4) and Labor Day (early September), waits of up to two hours are not uncommon.

raditional othing and ather goods re only some the many roducts sold Tijuana's biquitous azaars.

SANTA CATALINA AND THE ISLANDS

It shouldn't really be there. Nature, having already endowed Southern California with enough scenic splendor and climatic favor, needn't have added the proverbial frosting on the cake by providing an island paradise as well.

Yet there lies **Santa Catalina Island**, 26 miles (42 kilometers) off the coast of Los Angeles. This eight-by-21-mile (13-by-33-km) piece of real estate lacks only television's tiny Tattoo to fulfill the traveler's postcard-perfect "Fantasy Island." A peaceful, unhurried life continues here, buffered by blue skies and warm breezes. Catalina exists serene and unimpressed with civilization, content to ignore progress in favor of conserving a pace which recalls simpler times.

Although it *is* possible to swim to Catalina — contests have occasionally been held with mixed success — easier access may be gained by air or sea from San Pedro, Long Beach or Newport Beach. Air travelers may spend the short flight gazing upon migrating gray whales below, while the seafarer's two-hour pilgrimage is sweetened with an arm's length view of the porpoises which seem to escort voyagers toward Atlantis.

While air travel is quicker, sailing is the preferred way to go. The lapping waves provide the most appropriate introduction to the gentle rhythm of California's only island resort. Breeching the early morning haze off the coast, one wonders if he hasn't been caught in some warp and transported somehow to the French Riviera, circa 1930, when entering the harbor at **Avalon,** Catalina's only town. The narrow beaches, grand private yachts and huge circular casino, which marks the harbor's entrance, encourage this reverie.

Stepping ashore, the quiet descends like an avalanche of whipped cream. Ears accustomed to car horns, buses, jet planes and the cacophony of city living are left at a loss. And the sunlight, while bright, seems to have lost its glare somewhere over the past 26 miles. With the few exceptions of those who ride electric carts, everyone walks. The time-warp consideration once again seems valid, for Avalon appears to be Smalltown, U.S.A., brought to the beach for summer vacation.

The natives, anything but restless, are identifiable by their tribal costume of bathing suits, T-shirts and sandals. All sport disquietingly uniform tropical tans. In contrast, visitors are adorned with cameras, hard-soled shoes and pale skins that a week in the Mojave wouldn't remedy.

It's All Not Here

Walking along **Crescent Avenue**, Avalon's main beachfront street, the visitor notices that no glass-and-chrome skyscrapers block the sun from the 2,000 year-round residents. Victorian hotels retain the charm employed in their construction 60 years ago, and side streets are sized for horse-and-buggies, not Oldsmobiles. Elderly residents occupy the plentiful benches which dot the streets, chatting casually about what a nice day it is or about the skimpy bikini on that young girl over there.

Conversations are uninterrupted by blaring portable stereos. They are prohibited from the beaches by city ordinance. Stepping slowly across the street

Left, a ketch from Newport Beach sails toward a weekend visit to Santa Catalina Island's Avalon Bay, right, dominated by its landmark Casino.

to pick up a paper or exchange gossip with a neighbor, citizens don't bother to look both ways: cars are prohibited in most of Avalon. In fact, automobiles are rare — their usage limited to islanders, 125 of whom are on a waiting list. Traffic lights, "Don't Walk" signs, freeway jams and parking jousts have all been left on the mainland.

Avalon is virtually a pedestrian's dream, a small village where nearly all points of interest are accessible by foot. Visitors may stroll through the many souvenir and clothing shops along Crescent Avenue (or as it's more commonly called, "Front Street"). Fresh seafood is the ticket at the many patio restaurants which face the sea. There are no McDonald's or Burger Kings here; nothing is fast, particularly the food service.

Beer and Polynesian drinks are favored beverages, consumed most enthusiastically by the natives. Jaded, perhaps, by the de-accelerated pace of this island Shangri-La, drinking has become a pastime cultivated by islanders. The analogy to the mythical land of *Lost Horizon* is further supported by the permanent exodus of island-born

as soon as they reach college age, abandoning Paradise in search of more worldly experiences. A real generation gap exists between Catalina's children and elderly.

Hotels and Tours

Visitors planning to stay awhile should make hotel reservations six months in advance. Occupancy soars to 10,000 or more from Easter to Labor Day. Housing, even for residents, is scarce — so scarce that government-financed developments had to be built to accommodate island employees who could not otherwise find shelter. Construction on Catalina is severely restricted by the Santa Catalina Island Conservancy which owns 86 percent of the island. Thus, its goal of preserving Catalina in its natural state is viewed with mixed emotions by those who must live in one-room dwellings.

There are about 40 hotels around the island, the most intriguing of which is the **Zane Grey Pueblo**. Perched on a hillside, the former home of the Western novelist offers rooms named after his works and provides a spectacular

The Wrigley Mansion on Mount Ada.

and romantic evening view of Avalon Bay. (Information on all Santa Catalina hotels can be obtained by telephoning 213-510-1520.)

The day-tripper is best left to his or her own devices in exploring Catalina. Tours which visit all parts of the island and its waters are available, but so are free guides to everything worth seeing. One of the big attractions is a glass-bottomed boat cruise to look at the ocean floor.

Once at Crescent Bay, an exploration of the 12-story **Avalon Casino** is in order. Built in 1929 by former island owner William Wrigley (the chewing-gum magnate), this impressive rotunda houses an art gallery, museum, 1,200-seat theater, and a ballroom that once swung to the sounds of Glenn Miller and Tommy Dorsey. The days of the big bands are gone, but the musical genre lives on. On the slopes of Mount Ada, across the bay from the casino, stands the beautiful **Wrigley Mansion.**

It's best on Catalina to take matters into one's own hands — or flippers, as the case may be. The clear azure waters of Avalon Bay yield rich kelp beds with aquatic life forms not often seen else-where. Skin divers can rent the necessary equipment (license required for scuba) and explore the northwest corner of **Crescent Bay** with its mysterious shipwrecks.

The Catalina Wilderness

The visitor can see all the attractions of Avalon in about half a day. But the *real* Catalina lies in the island's interior, a virtual pristine wilderness. Camping and hiking in this rugged land are permitted, and an overnight at **Little Harbor, Two Harbors** or the mountainous **Blackjack Campsite** is recommended. The less energetic can take a half-day motor tour of the island for $11.50.

The isolation of the Blackjack wilderness is broken only by a pay telephone, available for emergencies. What emergencies? Some campers have awakened to find a wild boar devouring their breakfast. Others have had surprise tête-à-têtes with 1,500-pound (680-kilogram) buffalo foraging in the brush. Such encounters do make one pause and reflect.

One might well wonder just what buffaloes are doing on Santa Catalina Is-

Bison graze n Catalina's undeveloped nterior.

land. Fourteen of the woolly beasts were brought to Catalina for co-starring roles in *The Vanishing American*, filmed here in 1924. Encouraged by the romantic nature of the island, the creatures have since multiplied their numbers to more than 400. The sight of these gargantuan beasts celebrating the rites of spring is something not easily forgotten.

Hollywood has frequently employed Catalina as a perfect "Old West" or "South Seas" location for years. The wrecked vessels used in the original *Mutiny on the Bounty* (1935) still lie on the sandy bottom of Avalon Harbor. The beach sand, incidentally, was imported from Orange County, and the seafront palms from Pasadena. Sending away for scenery was a practice that islanders adopted long ago.

After a trip to the island's interior, Avalon seems especially charming after sundown. Its harbor is gaily lit in the manner of a Mediterranean seaport; its streets are filled with shopkeepers and tour guides rejoicing the end of another busy day. Couples abandon their living-room televisions in favor of hand-in-hand strolls along the shore. They gaze upon the starlit sea while other visitors cruise upon it, smiling at the flying fishes on the harbor at night.

Meanwhile, college students drink to each others' health at **Big Mike's Tavern**. If the deliberate and preserved peacefulness of Catalina has any effect, and if such oaths can indeed come true, they may live to be 100.

The Channel Islands

If the Old Man of the Sea made Santa Catalina Island on his happiest day, when he wished nothing but goodwill toward men, then he made the rest of the **Channel Islands** while suffering the ravages of a monstrous hangover some 25 million years ago. These islands are desolate and foreboding. Rising out of a mysterious fog, their violent, uncharted reefs have for centuries been cemeteries for sailing men who dared too close.

Yet, while still accessible only by boat, and then only during brief lulls in the maelstrom, the Channel Islands offer a challenging and rewarding opportunity for the visitor.

Although within the area designated as the **Channel Islands National Park**,

A peaceful anchorage at Little Harbor on Catalina's windward si

the islands of **Santa Cruz** and **Santa Rosa** remain privately owned while **San Clemente** and **San Nicholas** islands offshore San Diego are owned by the U.S. Navy. Except for Catalina, the remaining Channel Islands are virtually uninhabited although the nearest to the continent — tiny **Anacapa Island** — is a mere 14 miles (22 km) off the coast of Oxnard.

Navigating the hazardous channel once a day from Ventura, Island Packers of the National Park Service will deposit visitors on Anacapa. Five miles long — actually three islands in one — Anacapa contains only one square mile of land and may be appreciated only after a long climb up a steep stair. But once there, Anacapa offers long-forgotten sensations: the smell of fresh sage, the serenade of the meadowlark, and (when the wind is right) complete and utter quiet.

All is brown and desolate here, save for native flora which a sudden spring shower may turn green and lush. Sea lions thrive along the shore, protected by the sea's inhospitality to man, seemingly amused by the presence of human visitors on the cliffs above.

California sea lion, denizen of the rocky Channel Islands.

Rangers who inhabit and administer the islands for the National Park Service have adopted the same friendly-yet-cautious attitude. Pleased to accommodate travelers, these guardians' primary responsibility is to maintain the delicate ecosystem in spite of civilization's occasional forays.

Camping is available through the National Parks Service, but visitors must bring their own water, food and a tent strong enough to protect against chilling winds which cut to the bone. Scuba diving and exploration of Anacapa's many tidepools are permitted by license, presenting exciting plant and invertebrate life in its prehistoric state. But like a visit to a china shop, everything must be put back precisely as it was discovered. Preservation is taken *seriously* here.

San Miguel, the westernmost island of the chain, lies battered by the ferocity of the elements, unprotected by the mainland. Northwesterly gales have sandblasted the island, voiding its terrain and leaving the most dangerous approach to any of the Channel Islands. The sheer rocks and submerged reefs serve as headstones to the many navigators who lost their lives along these craggy shores. Gulls, sea lions and seals rule now, roaming unimpressed among the ghost forests of calcified vegitation. Juan Rodriguez Cabrillo, Spanish discoverer of California and the Channel Islands, walks among the spirits here, reputedly buried on San Miguel, although his gravesite has never been found. **Santa Barbara Island**, accessible only by private boat, is little more than a lunar landscape.

The two privately owned Channel Islands, Santa Cruz and Santa Rosa, may be visited by permission and are well worth the effort. Santa Cruz, at 62,000 acres (25,000 hectares), is the largest island and contains the most diverse topography, pocked with enormous sea caves and steepled with numerous peaks. Deep wooded canyons provide exploratory digs for tracings of the Chumash Indians who once inhabited the scarred terrain. To the southwest, Santa Rosa Island lures the curious with its lazily angled cliffs, its interior hospitable only to the cattle which graze there, oblivious to the significance of the exposed bones of dwarf mammoths which long ago strode along these fertile hills.

CENTRAL COAST: A QUIET CHARM

Unrushed, contemplative, friendly: these are adjectives frequently used to describe the stretch of California coastline from Ventura north to San Simeon.

Usually known as the Central Coast, it is in some ways a forgotten part of the state. To many people, "central" means the San Joaquin Valley's flat farmland, and "coast" implies the beaches from Malibu south. But here on the Central Coast, there is quiet, scenic charm. The drive along U.S. Highway 101 and State Highway 1, though not as unrelentingly spectacular as Big Sur and other areas further north, is always lovely and less despoiled than many other populated parts of California.

Concentrated within this coastal region of about 200 miles (320 kilometers) are the restored remnants of a significant chapter in California's historical development: the missions. Five of the state's 21 missions, founded by Franciscan *padres* from Spain, are located along the Central Coast. Their locations were neither mistake nor coincidence. The *priests* were creating a chain linking the state from San Diego to Sonoma, and they chose prime sites with good water sources, fertile farm and pasture lands, pleasant surroundings, an occasional harbor, and always a supply of Indians who could provide farm labor once they became Christians.

The mission heritage has not been forgotten elsewhere in California, but the Central Coast has woven that era more tightly into its modern fabric than other areas. U.S. 101 parallels the famous **El Camino Real,** the King's Road, once a narrow Indian trail, then widened to a rutty road for the *padres.* Today it is a smooth, modern thoroughfare. Travelling up the coast along El Camino Real, the visitor becomes a modern missionary rediscovering the state.

San Buenaventura

As if to guarantee that the historical connection won't be forgotten, El Camino Real is frequently marked by mission-type bells hung along the roadway. One of the first is at the southern gateway to the town of **Ventura.** At this point, U.S. 101 has finally reached the ocean after crossing a rather dull stretch of overdeveloped, smoggy land.

Ventura is the site of the **San Buenaventura Mission,** the last mission founded under the leadership of Father Junípero Serra. Early California explorer Juan Rodriguez Cabrillo had first discovered this shoreline in 1542 when Indian canoes greeted his ship, but it wasn't until 1782 that Father Serra erected his church. He named the mission after a 13th Century Tuscan follower of St. Francis. The name was later shortened to Ventura, and the town dubbed itself "The Poinsettia City" for the popular Christmas plants it nurtures.

The mission, which once maintained extensive grazing land and fabulous gardens, now lies at the edge of an area called **Old San Buenaventura.** Its quaint shops are reminiscent of pioneering days. Close to the mission are modern buildings created in mission-style architecture, and nearby are a historical museum and an excavation project. Prehistoric Indian artifacts have been uncovered here, as well as the foundations of five early buildings.

Elsewhere in Ventura, a town of

Preceding pages, a windswept view of Morro Rock. Left, Santa Barbara Mission and its head pastor, Father Virgil. Right, the emblem of El Camino Real.

215

more than 60,000 supported primarily by the oil industry and agriculture, are the 1857 **Ortega Adobe** and the **Chinatown-Figueroa Mall,** center of the Chinese community in the 1870s. But most of Ventura's activity is centered on the oceanfront. The town is the embarkation point for cruises to the nearby Channel Islands. It has an extensive marina and long stretches of beach and dunes.

East of Ventura, there are dramatic mountain vistas along State Highway 33. The first important stop on this route is the small town of **Ojai** (say "oh-hi"), nestled among the hills

Glossed Horizon

Ojai has managed a rare, eccentric mix of people and interests. Some residents are wealthy country-club types who relish Ojai's renowned classical music festival in June and its famous spring tennis tournament. Others are "health nuts" drawn to the area for the healing powers attributed to its several hot springs; or philosophers who have established numerous esoteric institutes among the oak trees of this community

of 7,000. Artists are drawn to Ojai's quiet rural atmosphere and scenic beauty: east of town on Ojai Avenue is the vantage point from which Ronald Colman viewed Shangri-La in the movie classic *Lost Horizon*. Small farmers still maintain their acreages in the area around town.

Ojai's charmless business strip is surrounded by verdant groves of oranges and avocados, country clubs and golf courses, and a well-known health spa, **The Oaks.** Close by is **Lake Casitas,** site of the 1984 Olympic rowing and canoeing competitions.

What initially drew people to the area in the 1870s — besides the discovery of oil — was Eastern journalist Charles Nordhoff's glowing description of a town with mild temperatures, natural mineral baths and an outstanding climate for agriculture. Initially named Nordhoff after the newsman, the town gained its current moniker in 1917. It supposedly meant "The Nest" to native Indians, although a Toledo, Ohio, glassmaker named E.D. Libby was responsible for the name change. Libby also helped turn the town into a resort with Spanish architecture and an empha-

Offshore oil rigs glow in the Santa Barbara Channel.

sis on the arts and sports.

Northeast of Ojai along State 33 is the **Wheeler's Gorge** camping area. It's the beginning of the stunning **Los Padres National Forest,** a mecca for backpackers and campers. West of Ojai, State 150 winds along some of the 60 miles (97 km) of Lake Casitas' shoreline, then through hilly orchards and back to U.S. 101. This route is full of impressive vistas. But so is the invigorating stretch of U.S. 101 north of Ventura that travellers miss when they take the Lake Casitas route.

Where State 150 meets U.S. 101, Ventura County ends and Santa Barbara County begins. The fields of **Carpinteria** are filled with lemons, beans, walnuts and olives. But the town's pride is having "The World's Safest Beach." One wag claims that's "because no one ever uses it." Others suggest that its natural reef breakwater, where skin divers search for lobsters and abalone; its lack of rip tides; and its rockless beaches warrant the title.

The block-long town of **Santa Claus** is frozen in perennial winter. A large plaster Santa and a snowman beckon visitors to stop for date shakes, live lobsters and other goodies at **Santa's Kitchen.** But no, Virginia, there's no Mission Santa Claus in town.

Surprising Santa Barbara

As the highway enters **Santa Barbara,** There's a surprising splash of greenery — much of it borrowed from other countries and climes. As California chronicler Carey McWilliams noted, when people learned that anything would grow in Southern California, *everything* was planted here, most conspicuously eucalyptus and palm trees. McWilliams called the latter "an abomination, a blot on the landscape, hideous beyond description."

Most would disagree, especially when driving along Santa Barbara's five miles (eight km) of palm-lined beachfront. It is one of the most inviting ocean stretches in the United States. At its eastern end are dozens of beach volleyball courts, across from Santa Barbara's strip of luxury hotels. To the west, the hotel rates go down a bit, but the beach continues its unmarred expanse, further brightened on weekends with art festivals along the boardwalk. At night,

Left, Santa Claus greets visitors in Santa Claus. Right, the Santa Barbara Wharf.

those twinkling lights offshore might resemble a distant shore, but they're actually oil derricks, a reminder of the millions of gallons of black goo that covered the pristine beaches in 1969's widely publicized environmental disaster.

But Santa Barbara has been lucky enough to avoid many of the misfortunes that plague other mid-sized cities. It started its existence fortuitously hemmed in by mountains on one side and a treacherous sea on the other. Because of its year-round sun and pleasant climate, it became famous as a rich man's resort by the 1890s. In fact, by the 1920s the neighbouring town of **Montecito** reportedly had the largest concentration of wealth in the nation.

An earthquake nearly destroyed Santa Barbara in 1925, allowing it to be rebuilt in a uniform Spanish colonial style favouring white walls, red-tiled roofs, rounded archways and iron grill-work. The style was inspired by the 1915 San Diego Panama-California Exposition, and has remained the hallmark of the town. Santa Barbara has been cited as one of the best examples of how architecture can be regulated to the lasting benefit of a city.

Mission and Museum

Of course, the Spanish heritage had even earlier roots in Santa Barbara. A *presidio* (army fortress) was founded in 1782, and a mission was built in 1786. Father Serra had died by then; Father Fermin Francisco de Lasuen was in charge. Originally, the mission was an unpretentious adobe structure, enlarged three times. After the third version was destroyed by an earthquake in 1812, it was rebuilt to look like a drawing of a church made by the 1st Century B.C. Roman architect Vitruvius. The hybrid mixture of Spanish and Roman elements produced what is considered the most beautiful of all the California missions. It is a majestic pink building with a mission arcade, a belltower and a Roman pediment supported by six Ionic columns.

Located high above the town, with a view of the ocean, the **Santa Barbara Mission** is still one of the town's chief attractions. A self-guided tour includes a visit to the mission's cemetery and chapel, still in use today. About a block away is Santa Barbara's **Museum of**

Natural History, where visitors can learn about the Chumash Indians.

The Chumash (or Canalinos) were a series of tribes that stretched from Morro Bay in the north to Malibu in the south. In some places, they succeeded the earlier, more primitive Oak Grove people (7000 to 3000 B.C.). Jointly ruled by men and women and ministered to by shamans, the Chumash were an industrious people. "Only lazy people get up after the sun" was a Chumash saying. Good weather and abundant food gave them plenty of time for leisure, during which they performed rituals and created myths and complex song-and-dance cycles.

But in the late 18th Century, as everywhere along the California coast, Spanish missionaries came and set about to "Christianize" them. The Indians contracted European diseases for which they had no immunity; they became addicted to alcohol; and their elaborate culture and economy collapsed. Their numbers dwindled from 30,000 to just 1,250 by 1910.

The museum has preserved remnants of the Chumash culture — baskets, bowls, charms, beads (their monetary unit) and tools. One of the most spectacular Chumash relics, a modern recreation of their structurally remarkable wood-plank canoe, is not located in the museum, however. Reinforced by only a single crossbeam, the 20-foot (six-meter) *tomol* could carry 10 persons back and forth to the Channel Islands for fishing and trade. The canoe can be seen in the **Santa Barbara County Courthouse,** the most grandiose building in the city. Constructed in the late 1920s, it is a magnificent Spanish-Moorish castle, decorated inside with murals, mosaics, woodcarvings and tile. Filling in the square of the L-shaped building is an exquisite sunken garden shaded by tall trees.

The courthouse is just a block from State Street, the city's main thoroughfare. Although the north end of the street is filled with newer shopping centers, the southern part carries out the city's Spanish motif with many blocks of red-tile roofs, rounded porticos, wooden balconies and adobe-like walls. The streets inspire leisurely strolls past a variety of shops and restaurants, as well as nearby historic adobes such as **Casa de la Guerra,** made famous in the book *Two Years Before the Mast,* and a

A rooftop view of residential Santa Barba

classic-style **Museum of Art.** In August, the city celebrates **"Old Spanish Days"** with an outdoor breakfast in historic **El Paseo** arcade and with traditional costumes and dances.

Even away from the State Street area, there is no dearth of restaurants in Santa Barbara. This is a town that relishes good food as much as a good tan. Three of the best restaurants are plopped in an otherwise-deserted cul-de-sac just across the road from the **Andrée Clark Bird Refuge,** a lagoon located a winding drive southeast from **East Beach.**

Starting there, visitors might want to circle Santa Barbara at least once before leaving: south to Montecito and its Beverly Hills-style shopping and dining center; up into the ocean-vista hills along Almeda Junípero Serra, past the Mediterranean elegance of the **El Encanto Hotel** and the famous **Brooks Institute of Photography;** past the mission and 1½ miles into **Mission Canyon,** where the **Botanic Gardens** display an array of native California vegetation; down to the beach and north along Cliff Drive through the rolling estates of the **Hope Ranch.**

Ranches and Beaches

Two routes lead out of Santa Barbara to the north. State 154 winds into the **Santa Ynez Mountains** and through the **San Marcos Pass.** This is where Capt John Fremont led his troops on his way to capture Santa Barbara in the mid-19th Century U.S. war with Mexico. It's now an area known for its spacious horse ranches.

The highway leads past **Lake Cachuma,** a man-made, trout-stocked lake formed in 1953, and through tiny towns like **Santa Ynez** and **Los Olivos,** a former stagecoach stop that prides itself on its historic 1886 **Mattei's Tavern.** Near where State 154 joins U.S. 101, Zaca Station Road offers access to one of the few *natural* lakes in this part of California, tiny **Zaca Lake.** An isolated 1½-acre jewel nestled in a bowl of tree-studded mountains, the lake is a good place to do absolutely nothing except maybe swim, sail, canoe, fish, hike, ride horses or play tennis. It offers camping and 18 rustic cabins built in the 1940s, as well as an excellent restaurant.

Those who leave Santa Barbara on U.S. 101 travel along the coast, passing

Viewing tower atop the Santa Barbara Courthouse.

lemon groves, circling hawks and a number of state beaches. The first town is **Goleta,** home of the **University of California, Santa Barbara.** Known to many as a laid-back surf-and-party campus, it briefly spoiled its reputation in the turbulent Sixties when students burned down a branch of the Bank of America in neighboring **Isla Vista.**

Further along the coast are **El Capitan State Beach; Refugio State Beach,** a delightful cove surrounded by palms; and **Gaviota State Beach,** which sports a fishing pier.

The home of U.S. President Ronald Reagan, **Rancho del Cielo,** is located about 30 minutes north of Santa Barbara off U.S. 101. Access to the ranch is via Refugio Road, an inland turnoff opposite signs pointing to the state beach. But security won't let unknown visitors too close to the ranch.

Pea Soup and Danish Pastries

The vegetation becomes greener as the road curves inland and winds through hills to **Buellton,** a town whose fame is built on pea soup. **Andersen's Pea Soup Restaurant** is a memorable

stop on any traveler's itinerary. The Andersen family originally operated the Electric Cafe, celebrating the unusual use of an electric stove 50 years ago. Other than Andersen's (which also operates an inn), Buellton is known for its thoroughbred and Arabian horse-breeding ranches, just east of town along State 246. This pine tree-lined road also leads to another anomalous locale — the Danish-revival town of **Solvang.**

Solvang was a planned community, established by a group of Danish educators in 1911 as the site of a folk school. The original residents were farmers and carpenters, and they maintained Danish traditions in their isolated enclave. But in 1947, the *Saturday Evening Post* published an extensive article on the town, and entrepreneurs moved in overnight to create a Disneyland-type shopping-and-eating village with a Danish theme.

Everything in Solvang has been given a provincial Danish look and flavor, from the motels (the Hamlet, the Viking and so on) to the ubiquitous bakeries. All are marked by thatch-like roofs, pointed towers and painted cross-beamed walls called *bindingsvaerk,* as

Left, picture-perfect fun in a State Street tavern window, Santa Barbara. Right, a misty morning mood at a Buellton breeding farm.

well as some wooden storks on rooftops. The town becomes even more Danified the third weekend every September when its **"Danish Days"** festival is held. Costumed singers, dancers and musicians wander the streets, where an open-air breakfast of *aebleskiver* (ball-shaped pancakes) and *medisterpolse* (sausage) is served.

Solvang has other things going for it, including a developing outdoor **Theaterfest** that's gaining good notices for its portrayal of Shakespeare, musicals and Broadway classics. Pre-Danish history is maintained at the **Mission Santa Ines.** The last mission to be built in the Chumash area (1804), it has been lovingly restored to a rosy pink, with copper-tiled roof, a long arcade and a three-belled tower.

This mission wasn't especially successful, either in converts or agricultural production, but it gained some measure of fame when it was torched by Indians in an 1824 revolt. The same arsonists helped douse the flames! The revolt also took place at the Santa Barbara Mission and the **Mission de la Purisima Concepción,** 20 miles from Santa Ines west along State 246.

Founded in 1787, La Purisima Concepción was never an important mission in the chain. But today, thanks to restoration work started by the Civilian Conservation Corps in the 1930s, it offers visitors the best impression of mission life at the height of Spanish power and prosperity before Mexican rule led to the secularization of the missions. Surrounded by 900 acres (364 hectares) of parkland, the arch-less mission displays an excellent collection of artifacts and, during the summer months, holds demonstrations of various mission crafts.

La Purisima Concepción is located near **Lompoc,** which is noted for its seed-supplying flower fields (there's a **Flower Festival"** in June) and its proximity to the **Naval Missile Facility,** where missiles jet over the Pacific leaving colorful trails in sunset skies.

Wine and Clams

From Lompoc, the traveler can proceed north on State 1 or return via State 246 to U.S. 101. The federal route wends its way northward past rolling blond hills and farmland. Paralleling it to the east is another scenic road, State 176, which can be reached about five miles (eight km) north of Buellton. It offers winding country roads, one-store farm towns and wine-producing vineyards. Stops at these wineries, including the **Zaca Mesa Winery** and the **Rancho Sisquoc Winery,** can sweeten any journey.

With a final straight stretch through strawberry fields, State 176 arrives in the town of **Santa Maria,** there rejoining U.S. 101. Like Lompoc, this town is surrounded by fields of flowers, but its main source of employment is **Vandenburg Air Force Base.** The base, which may be toured one day a month by reservation, is being developed as a launch site for U.S. Air Force space shuttles. There aren't many sights in the town, with the possible exceptions of the **Allen Hancock College** Theaterfest, the historical museum and the speedway. Its real merit to the traveler is its central location. Founded at the intersection of four ranches in 1875, Santa Maria has a number of high-quality accommodations for the weary.

From Santa Maria, U.S. 101 continues inland. It rejoins the coast and State 1, near **Pismo Beach,** a resort

Timely souvenirs adorn the wall of a Solvang sho, left, while locals dance in the streets right, during the annual Danish Days

known primarily for its clams and its sand dunes.

The Pismo clam, which ranges up the Big Sur coast as far as Monterey, has a heavy circular shell that grows to the size of a dinner plate and weighs as much as 1½ pounds (nearly 700 grams). The meat has a distinctive, sweet flavor. In the past, these clams were easy to obtain, dug from the sand with large forks at low tide. Now Pismo Beach has been seriously depleted of just the thing that once made it the world's clam capital. "You get a clam these days," says one resident, "you make it a meal for three." Nonetheless, clams can still be found in unrestricted areas. If they're at least 4½ inches (11.4 cm) in diameter, they're keepers.

Unlike the clams, Pismo's dunes are doing just fine despite years of use by recreational vehicles which drive merrily over the hilly piles of sand. **Pismo Beach State Park** has about six miles (10 km) of shoreline dunes, running south to the tiny beach community of **Oceano.** Only certain areas are open to dune buggies and other all-terrain vehicles. But any motorist may drive on the beach itself! The rest of the park includes areas for surfing, surf fishing, pier fishing and muskrat-watching.

Further south are the **Guadelupe Dunes,** a habitat for the endangered California least tern and California brown pelican. These dunes are no longer open to drivers. They are currently being excavated in order to locate 22 sphinxes, each seven by 15 feet (2.1 by 4.5 meters), buried in the sand after Cecil B. deMille completed his 1923 movie epic, *The Ten Commandments.* The photogenic dunes in the Pismo-to-Guadalupe area have also appeared in several other films, including Rudolph Valentino's *The Sheik.*

Pismo is rapidly expanding, with housing areas and motels sprouting up on the east side of the main road. A quieter beach town is **Avila Beach,** just north of Pismo and a few miles west off U.S. 101. Except for the obtrusive oil tanks on the cliff above the harbor, the town is picturesque, with wide sandy beaches and water temperatures kept comfortably warm by a sheltering cove. The ocean views quickly disappear further north as the highway proceeds past **Shell Beach** and **Diablo Canyon,** site of a controversial nuclear power plant.

San Luis Obispo

The next major town is **San Luis Obispo,** situated in a rather forested area below the **Santa Lucia Mountains.** Some observers describe the community's population as a blend of rodeo rednecks and hippie computer types. The town also has a case of "the cutes," making it an increasingly attractive place to visit — less ritzy than Santa Barbara, with an inexpensive but intriguing variety of restaurants, Victorian homes and a youthful shopping area.

It's no surprise that San Luis Obispo's history began with a mission. **San Luis Obispo de Tolosa,** founded by Father Serra in 1772, was originally built out of logs and tule. The thatched roof was repeatedly torched by Indians, leading the missionaries to come up with a major innovation: fireproof roof *tiles,* a theme quickly adopted by the rest of the missions in the chain.

The town grew up around the mission. The restored and modernized building is now situated in the downtown area, surrounded by a landscaped plaza, an old adobe house and the **County Historical Museum.** The mission

Wine-tasting under the oaks at the Ballard Canyon winery near Solvang.

has a museum as well, housed in the original *padres'* living quarters.

Just a block away is Higuera Street, one of the main streets for shopping and eating. It includes a small arcade in a restored creamery. This sector has the flavor of a hip college town, due to the proximity of **California Polytechnic State University, San Luis Obispo** ("Cal Poly SLO") and **Cuesta Community College.**

Streets near the main shopping area are laced with well-cared-for Victorian homes, craftsmen's bungalows and colonial revival-style dwellings. The chamber of commerce publishes a free walking tour of 38 "heritage homes," ranging from quaint cottages to multi-room mansions.

Oddly enough, the main visitor attraction in San Luis Obispo is a hotel just south of town, the **Madonna Inn.** Seen in all its pink-and-white gingerbread splendor from U.S. 101, the Inn, built in 1960 and frequently renovated since, is a favorite for honeymooners with its elaborate fantasy suites (each one different), rock-hewn fireplaces and ornate bathrooms. Much of it was created out of huge boulders. It looks like a large ranch house gone delightfully mad.

West of San Luis Obispo, past the small town of **Los Osos,** is the **Montaña de Oro State Park,** a spacious wilderness area along 1½ miles of rugged coastline. It offers hiking, surf fishing and camping.

Morro Rock and Morro Bay

Travelers in a hurry to get to the San Francisco Bay area head north from San Luis Obispo inland on U.S. 101. Those with more time, however, prefer State Highway 1, which clings to a magnificent coastline all the way to the Monterey Peninsula. Though this route is sometimes closed just below Big Sur due to landslides, there are few (if any) finer drives in California.

About 15 miles (24 km) north of San Luis Obispo on State 1, a massive rock formation juts from the ocean. This monolith, actually the last in line of nine prehistoric volcanic peaks in the area, is **Morro Rock.** The bay surrounding it, and the town that grew on its hinterland, are both called **Morro Bay.**

The rock was named by Cabrillo on

his discovery voyage up the California coast in 1542. Gaspar de Portolá's party camped near it on their road to Monterey in 1769. It later became a landfall for Spanish galleons sailing in coastal waters. Of course, the Chumash Indians and their predecessors had discovered it long before: archaeologists have found artifacts dating back 47 centuries B.C.

The 576-feet (176-meter), rock was once even larger than it is today. Earlier in the 20th Century, the great monolith was used as a quarry. But in 1969 it was given national monument status. Once an island at high tide, like France's Mont-Saint-Michel, Morro Rock since the 1930s has been reachable by car at any hour. There's a small beach beside the rock.

The endangered peregrine falcon, a species nearly wiped out by the side effects of the pesticide DDT, nests on the rock. To protect the birds (and human adventurers), climbing on the rock is prohibited. The town also bans firearms, lest any insensitive sharpshooter take aim at Morro Rock's treasured feathered friends. The entire community, in fact, has been declared a bird sanctuary. Some 250 different species have been spotted here.

The town of Morro Bay centers around the waterfront. At the **San Francisco Wharf** or along the **Embarcadero,** seafood lovers can eat fish to their stomachs' delight. The marine delicacies are hauled in by the town's own commercial fishing fleet. Many boats invite sportsmen (and women) to catch their own perch or flounder, or in the winter to catch a glimpse of migrating gray whales. The "Clam Taxi" ferries passengers to the bay's **Sand Spit,** a finger of sandy dunes emerging from the south part of the bay; here one can sunbathe, surf-fish or dig for the elusive Pismo clam.

Morro Bay also has a well-kept, unusual state park on the south side of town that includes camping, a roadside golf course (built in the 1930s by Works Progress Administration laborers), an excellent natural history museum and eucalyptus-shaded bay views along its narrow beaches. In October when the "forest" of eucyalptus blooms, the park becomes a haven for the orange-and-black monarch butterfly.

Only one thing mars the peaceful beauty of this little fishing town, but it's a big one. In fact, it's the first thing people notice after the rock: the **Pacific Gas and Electric** power plant, with its three 450-foot (137-meter) smokestacks rising from the edge of the bay like giant filter-tipped cigarettes. The plant was built in 1953, replacing a World War II naval training base.

Charm and Harmony

Cayucos, a charming town just north of Morro Bay, truly provides a get-away-from-it-all experience. The site of a prosperous deep-water wharf in the late 19th Century, it is now just a residential oceanfront town a few blocks wide. It has a few small, clean-looking motels, several places to eat and shop for antiques, and an uncrowded public beach and fishing pier.

Back on State 1, the coast begins to get more rugged, intimating the grand cliffs in the miles ahead. White-topped rocks seem as perfectly placed in the water as pebbles in a Japanese garden, and horses and cattle lazily graze on clifftop farmland.

It seems appropriate that the next settlement is a village called **Harmony,**

offering a wedding chapel so that couples can start their married life "in Harmony." The town also has a couple of restaurants and art galleries. It used to exhibit a toilet seat that reportedly was sat upon by Rudolph Valentino. The seat was stolen years ago, and recently it was further discredited by information that it never held Valentino's bottom at all, but was merely used by Pola Negri and Marion Davies!

The three Hollywood actors were on their way to San Simeon. Going north, they first passed through a forested area and the town of **Cambria,** a handsome, arty enclave. The coast in this area — a sea otter refuge for the next 100 miles (161 km) — has brilliant turquoise-green water near the shore, and the roadside is brightened by red, orange and yellow ice plants. From this point, travelers face a continuing onslaught of increasingly spectacular natural beauty.

Hearst's Incredible Castle

But nothing really prepares a person for what awaits at the top of a hill high

Morro Bay: left, a pelican's eye view of the PG&E smokestacks; and right, Morro Rock guards the harbor.

above the little village of **San Simeon.** It was here that newspaper tycoon William Randolph Hearst built his vacation mansion. He called it La Cuesta Encantada, "The Enchanted Hill"; but everyone else refers to it as **Hearst Castle,** and it's the No. 2 visitor attraction in California, behind only Disneyland.

Hearst's father, George, who had struck it very, very rich in gold, silver and copper, had originally bought 40,000 acres (16,188 hectares) of the Piedras Blancas Ranch in the 19th Century. Running from San Simeon Bay through the Santa Lucia Mountains, the ranch cost 70 cents an acre. The senior Hearst later expanded his land holdings to 275,000 acres (111,291 hectares) and 50 miles (80 km) of oceanfront. He used the ranch as a family campsite, calling it "Camp Hill."

But his son, who inherited the ranch after his parents died, had more grandiose ideas. William Randolph, who added to the family fortune by building a media empire that included dozens of newspapers, magazines and two film studios, decided to build a house on Camp Hill to serve as a museum for his extensive art collection. "He didn't

need a house to live in," points out a tour guide at San Simeon today. "He needed a hobby." Hearst hired Julia Morgan, a favorite family architect and the first female graduate of the École des Beaux Arts in Paris, and together they worked for 28 years to bring his dreams to fruition.

And what dreams they were, especially since money was absolutely no object. Often Hearst would start a room design with an *objet* he owned — say, a 400-year-old, 83-foot (25-meter) long carved wooden ceiling from Italy — then have the room built to fit it. Using the remains of European castles and cathedrals, he and Morgan blended carvings, furnishings and art work from different eras and countries into a single room, yet somehow unified them into a convincing, and often breathtaking, whole.

The grounds were an equally amazing conglomeration of plants and animals from all over the world. At one time, Hearst maintained the largest private zoo and animal reserve in the world, with everything from yaks to lions to kangaroos to bears. Even today, zebras graze on the land just below the castle.

85,000 acres (34,399 hectares) of which are still owned by the Hearst family and used for cattle ranching. (In return for a $50 million tax write-off, the family donated the castle to the state of California. Its official name today is "Hearst-San Simeon State Historical Monument."

Hearst still hadn't finished building his monument when he died in 1951, but the result in no way seems incomplete. The hill includes three guest houses — each looking like a Mediterranean villa fit for royalty — and a main house that's a town-towered mansion with 38 bedrooms. It also includes an 83-foot assembly hall (built around that Italian ceiling), a Gothic dining room, an indoor mosaic pool called "The Roman Bath" and a movie theater with giant Greek-inspired caryatids along the walls. Outside, Hearst built a marble-lined "Neptune Pool" — probably the highlight of the entire place — that holds 345,000 gallons (1.3 million liters) of water and looks out onto the ocean below.

There are four separate tours of the castle, each one replete with dropped names of Hollywood celebrities who visited Hearst here: Charles Chaplin, Douglas Fairbanks, Mary Pickford, Hedda Hopper, Gary Cooper, Clark Gable and Cary Grant, to name a few. Tour One is the best for first-timers. Advance reservations are suggested.

San Simeon is an appropriate place to end a tour of California's Central Coast. Although it isn't on El Camino Real, and there's no mission in San Simeon, the regal Hearst Castle certainly has many of the trappings of a mission.

Hearst filled his enchanted hill with religious paintings and the architecture of medieval churches, including a Rubens tapestry of the Catholic church triumphant over the pagans of Rome. The main house itself resembles nothing quite so much as a cathedral or a particularly grand mission.

It is a secular mission, to be sure. Hearst hardly subscribed to the ascetic disciplines of the Franciscan fathers. "Pleasure is worth what you can afford to pay for it," he wrote. But perhaps in his own way, using money rather than prayer, William Randolph Hearst was trying to make contact with divinity.

One wonders what Father Serra, who started the whole California mission movement, would think.

Hearst Castle towers over its gardens, left; the Neptune Pool right, is one of its spectacular attractions.

THE SOUTHERN SAN JOAQUIN

Driving north from Los Angeles, the wayfarer enters a different world. It begins with a dramatic descent of the Grapevine, a stretch of Interstate 5 that loses almost a mile of elevation in five minutes. It's a free-fall drop, a decompression-champer adjustment from the heady world of Los Angeles to the down-to-earth San Joaquin Valley.

The ears begin to pop as the foot eases off the gas pedal. The car speeds up anyway, whizzing past the trucks that have slowed down for safety. Stretching ahead is a seemingly endless checkerboard of fields divided occasionally by freeways, service roads and cement canals. At night, the string of highway lights is visible for 30 miles (48 km) — all the way to Bakersfield.

The southern San Joaquin Valley is an area of hard-working people with conservative values honed by years of a day's pay for a day's work. There are no world-renowned tourist attractions like Disneyland, not even any tour buses; but there is a side of California the timid visitor won't see, a glimpse into an area that exemplifies California's diversity.

The hub of the southern valley is **Bakersfield**, the largest city between Los Angeles and Fresno. The area also includes several small agricultural towns, a national forest, some of the country's most challenging whitewater rapids and a town that expects frequent earthquakes for the next five years. The small towns, most located near the two major highways (I-5 and State Highway 99) that bisect the valley, dot the plate-glass-flat land that produces everything from table grapes to almonds, tomatoes to cotton. In fact, this valley is the No. 1 cotton-producing region of America.

This quiet, desolate land appealed to the Yokut Indians, a peaceful tribe who inhabited the southern valley until the European settlers arrived. The Yokuts were largely an agricultural tribe, the first to recognize the potential of the land's bounty. The Yokuts believed that after death their spirits moved into the giant oak trees that lined the valley.

Bakersfield was largely swampland until Col. Thomas Baker, an engineer in the state militia, received an 87,000-acre (35,208-hectare) grant in 1863.

Baker began growing alfalfa on some of the drier land, and travelers began stopping at "Colonel Baker's field."

Gold mines in the hills and fights over water rights bred conflicts among the early settlers, who included Anglos, Armenians, Orientals, Mexicans and Basques. The Basques were drawn to the valley in the late 1800s when the area emerged as the key sheep-raising part of the state. Skilled as shepherds, they took the sheep into the mountains for "summering," returning to the plains in the cooler weather.

The winds of political change blew through the valley in the early 20th Century. The Great Depression led to the "Dust Bowl" invasion of the Thirties, as penniless farmers packed their families and belongings in their trucks and headed for a better life. (John Steinbeck chronicled the shift in *The Grapes of Wrath*.) There were more "Okies" than there was work, however, and their dreams turned to dust once again.

An Oily Reputation

Many found work in the oil fields. Like many other oil-producing regions,

The San Joaquin Valley leads the nation in production of cotton, left; and right, one of the valley's hard-working farmers.

side enterprises such as saloons, dance halls and bawdy houses flourished when the oil was flowing. Fistfights and gunfights were common, often over oil leases after large finds were made along the Kern River. These kinds of activities gave Bakersfield and Delano the reputation of being "wide-open" towns.

The valley has always had oil to fall back on. There are only three American *states* with more oil reserves than Kern County. The oil pumps, bobbing day and night in a slow but constant motion, are everywhere, blending into the environment whether they're next to a ranch or a restaurant. Near Visalia, some have been decorated. A favorite looks like Snoopy from the comic strip *Peanuts.*

The oil fields also provide the valley with some of its most stunning night scenes. Giant flames dance 50 feet (15 meters) in the air from the top of derricks as natural gas is burned off. Refineries and wells cast enough light to give the illusion of daylight.

The area's other natural asset is the sun, unshaded by clouds for most of the year. Putting the sun and soil to work required water, lots of it. But since rainfall is typically less than seven inches (178 millimeters) a year, nature wasn't much help. The early history of the valley was scarred with fights over the water rights to the Kern River, although they didn't have the high drama and shenanigans of Los Angeles disputes. Eventually two water systems — the Central Valley Project (1951) and the State Water Project (1973) — were constructed to help farmers.

One mustn't assume that the arid-looking land holds no water. In fact, the water table below the fertile soil is rising every year. But it's actually harmful to crops due to accumulated mineral salts. Some agriculture pessimists fear that the brackish water will eventually destroy farming in the valley, in the same way it was eradicated in ancient Egypt.

'Garden of the World'

For today, at least 200 agricultural commodities are produced in the valley. Such success would be quite a shock to the Spanish priest who reported in 1816 that "there is no fit land for sowing crops here because everywhere is sand." He should have listened to the

Citrus groves east of Bakersfield.

great 16th Century French prognosticator Nostradamus, who knew about the bounty of the San Joaquin before it was discovered. In what is often interpreted as his "big California quake" prediction, he saw the "New City" (Los Angeles) near "the garden of the world" (the San Joaquin) being "seized and plunged into a tub" (the Pacific, certainly the largest tub in the immediate area).

The earthy industries have molded the southern valley residents into a practical bunch. Bakersfield is considered so typically American in attitudes and composition that it's often used for marketing studies of new products. Like many other towns in the valley, it appears unglamorous to the outsider, a "why-would-anyone-want-to-live-here" kind of place. As such, Bakersfield has been the butt of jokes for years, and natives have that slightly defensive attitude common to residents of frequently ridiculed cities such as Buffalo and Cleveland.

The other favorite topic for humor is the weather, and the harsh climate is the single biggest factor discouraging visitors. In what is sometimes called "the San Joaquin blast furnace," August temperatures routinely top 100 degrees Fahrenheit (38° Centigrade). Residents defend the weather by saying "...but it's dry heat." (The humidity is usually under 20 percent). But to the visitor, the outdoors can seem like a dry strength-sapping sauna. There is scant hope for a shower: clouds usually take the summer off.

The winter weather offers another extreme — the Tule fog, some of the thickest moisture outside of London. Unlike the low cloudiness found on the California coast, this winter blanket doesn't always burn off as the day goes on. It sometimes hangs on for weeks in January.

'Nashville West'

Bakersfield's most familiar contribution to culture has been in the field of country music. The city known as "Nashville West" was the training ground for *Hee Haw* star Buck Owens (who still lives there) and singer Merle Haggard. Owens and Haggard honed their skills in the many small, rough-and-tumble country bars (some with

Sunrise on
Lake
Isabella.

sawdust on the floor) that thrived in the Fifties and Sixties.

Today only a few country clubs (**Trout's, The Funny Farm** and **Wild Bill's**) are open, and it's unlikely the next Buck Owens will be performing.

The influence of the early settlers can be tasted in Bakersfield's famous Basque restaurants, where high-protein and carbohydrate feasts are served at low prices. It's all family-style, with guests seated at long banquet tables and large platters of steaks and other foods passed around. There is only one seating time for either lunch or dinner. The most authentic Basque fare is offered at **The Noriega Hotel** or the **Pyrenees**.

The best bargain in town is **Pioneer Village**, a museum that asks only a $1 donation. It is considered to be among the best historical recreation projects west of the Rockies. It was the dream and lifelong work of the late Richard Bailey, who with the help of volunteers secured more than 40 original structures from Bakersfield's early days and moved them into this 15-acre (six-hectare) site north of town. A self-guided tour down the streets of the village includes a visit to a furnished Victorian mansion, a schoolhouse, a saloon and a railroad station.

Winding through Bakersfield from northeast of the city is the **Kern River**, which provides some of the most challenging whitewater rapids in the western states over three stretches: the Forks of the Kern (May to July), the upper Kern (May to early July) and the lower Kern (June to September). The rapids are rated class IV and V; the most dangerous rating is VI, but those are so treacherous that experts station rescue teams downstream.

Fortunately for neophytes, there are guided tours available, offering everything from a "get-your-paddle-wet" 90-minute jaunt to three-day trips that provide spectacular campfire meals at the end of a long day on the river. Those who are feeling particularly adventurous should head for the Forks, which was only recently opened to public tours. The sole access is a three-mile trail (mules are used to carry the rafts), and it's secluded from the highway for that wilderness feeling. The U.S. Forest Service in Porterville has a complete list of outfitters.

At Miracle Hot Springs, visitors can

Left, headwaters of the Kern River; and right, rafters prepare for a whitewater journey downstream.

watch rafters float by while soaking in spring-fed hot pools right on the bank of the Kern.

Fishermen may want to stop in the **Lake Isabella-Kernville** area, between the upper and lower Kern, where a flood-control dam built in the early Fifties created the largest freshwater lake in Southern California. Kernville was once located where the lake itself is now, before it was moved by the government. In late autumn, if the water is low, it is possible to wander among the old foundations and find remnants of the former village.

History and Wilderness

North of Bakersfield in the valley are a flock of small agriculture-based towns, with names such as **Pixley** and **Goshen.** Scattered among them are a few attractions worth searching for.

It takes some navigational skill, but **Colonel Allensworth State Historic Park** provides a unique look at one man's vision for his race. The agricultural colony of Allensworth was founded in 1908 by an ex-slave who wanted Blacks to have political and economic independence. After the colonel's death, Allensworth fell on hard times. It was scheduled to be bulldozed over in the 1960s before the state stepped in and began restoring the buildings. (Some are still in disrepair.) To get there, mobile explorers must take State 99 to Tulare County Road J22 and turn left, then proceed south on State 43.

Near **Porterville** is the **Sequoia National Forest.** It features a stunning redwood grove, the Kern Plateau, the Golden Trout Wilderness and numerous giant sequoias (naturally) over a 1.2-million-acre (485,000-hectare) area. The fall colors are as stupendous as can be found anywhere, and winter sports such as skiing and snowmobiling are made possible by the high altitude.

When it comes time for the evening meal, the southern valley has a few excellent restaurants off the beaten freeway. **Ducor** is home to **The Dutch Frontier**, which imports its lobsters from Australia and its steaks from Iowa. **Hanford**, a charming town with a beautiful Central Square, has the **Imperial Dynasty**, a gourmet Chinese restaurant that serves what *Travel/Holiday* magazine described as the world's best escargot.

Autumn colors the Sequoia National Forest.

238

DEATH VALLEY AND THE MOJAVE

Somewhere in the heart of the **Mojave Desert**, tucked between the **Tin Mountains** and **Wingate Pass**, a 19th Century Indian treasure lies hidden in a cave guarded by a balanced rock.

It is a treasure of gold and loot whose value is beyond the imagination. To some it is a treasure worth searching for, maybe even worth dying for.

Some swear the tale of Paiute Indian gold is absolutely true. Others say it's a myth, a whopper, a tale spun from whole cloth. But that's the way of things in this Mythic badland northeast of Los Angeles: the line between what's real and what's not fades with time and distance in the Mojave. Heat, hardship and prospectors' legends all form one rich tapestry of desert existence.

Even if the Paiutes didn't bury their plunder in the desolate Tin Mountains, the Mojave Desert is packed with many other treasures — more varied, and even more accessible — than most travelers realize.

In a single weekend, Mojave visitors can camp in the "Grand Canyon of the West," explore a mysterious desert castle, scale a dormant volcano, tee off from the lowest spot on earth, explore historic mining towns, and see the excavated site of man's earliest beginnings on the North American continent.

'Something Awesome'

"I cried the first time I drove through the Mojave," said one of the naturalists assigned to Death Valley National Monument. "God knows, it wasn't the beauty of the place. But there was something awesome about it. I still remember wondering, 'Can anything be this big?'"

The Mojave (named after a southwestern Indian tribe, pronounced "mo-*hahv*-ee") lies between U.S. Highway 395 and Interstate 40, snuggled against the Nevada state border. It has come to mean different things to different people. Since the back-to-the-land movement of the 1960s, the Mojave Desert has become a battleground of conflicting interests between backpackers, miners, ranchers, scientists, environmentalists and off-road vehicle groups.

Most of the time, the federal Bureau of Land Management must referee the fights.

What generates such an interest in the huge, hot Mojave? Most Californians who travel here do so to escape the confines of urban life. They also come to experience for themselves the truth about one of the most desolate, challenging landscapes in the Americas.

Land of the Dead

The legends surrounding Death Valley, the heart of the Mojave, are inarguably true. Take it from the Australian bicyclist who, under an unrelenting summer sun and temperatures exceeding 125°F (52°C), pedaled the length of the hostile valley in a record seven hours, 16 minutes, and vowed never to return. Or consider the Democratic party campaign worker who, in a burst of enthusiasm, promised to roller-skate Death Valley if Jimmy Carter was elected President in 1976. She kept her promise, but more than once regretted her bravado. Death Valley, which chalks up a few casualties every summer, nearly bagged two more.

Centuries ago, explorer Juan Bautista de Anza experienced the Mojave's natural furnace and in his diary referred to the region as *Tierra del Muertos*, literally, "Land of the Dead." Those words came back to haunt the first settlers who had the misfortune of wandering into Death Valley in 1849 on their way to the Gold Rush.

These days Mojave Desert travel, regardless of the season, is infinitely easier and safer, with well-supervised roads and good accommodations. (Death Valley has two inns and a luxury hotel.) The climate between November and April is ideal for outdoor travel, while May through October burn with heat like the North African Sahara.

Author John Steinbeck, criss-crossing America in the recent Sixties, approached this mythic no-man's land to experience for himself the heat, the loneliness, the all-encompassing silence of this final natural barrier of the last century. He left impressed. "Death Valley," wrote Steinbeck, "is a great and mysterious wasteland. A sun-punished place ... with something concealed, waiting."

A fascinating two or three-day trip can be made from Los Angeles through the Mojave to Death Valley and back. Perhaps the best route is to set out from the San Fernando Valley on State Highway 14 through Lancaster and return via I-15 and Barstow.

Mojave: Miners and Mules

At the junction of State Highways 14 and 58 is the small desert town of **Mojave.** From borax to the B-1 bomber, it has seen more history than most settlements many times its size.

Located just a short distance from **Edwards Air Force Base**, Mojave is part of the Antelope Valley aerospace boom. As such, it is earmarked to become one of the high-technology desert centers of the 21st Century. Its current role is very much that of a bedroom community for the aerospace workers, as well as those employed in agriculture and railroads. The winter season is busiest in Mojave; that's when weekend skiers, heading to and from Sierra slopes, pack the motels and roadside cafes.

A century ago, Mojave certainly didn't depend on automotive power for

Red Rock Canyon State Recreation Area.

its existence. It looked to miners and mule power. From the 1870s until just before World War I, Mojave was a gritty, rough-and-ready Western rail town from which prospectors shipped fortunes in gold, silver, lead, tungsten and zinc. Those were the days of the famous Twenty Mule Teams, when 100-foot (30-meter) spans of these beasts of burden lugged giant ore wagons into town with great fanfare. They carried borax, a chemical salt whose trade name as a cleanser — Boraxo — later became a household word in America.

By coincidence, the host of a Fifties television show sponsored by Boraxo, *Death Valley Days*, also became a household name: Ronald Reagan. But that's not Mojave's only link with the film industry.

For there's an improbable little museum in town, the **Hollywood Stuntmen's Hall of Fame**. It is run by veteran TV and movie stuntman John Hagner, 57, who's been falling off cliffs, buildings and moving trains for more than 30 years.

Hagner's Hall of Fame (admission: $1) has a photo gallery of stunt people, a small theater showing action film clips, and a forecourt of handprints and footprints of stunt people *a la* Mann's Chinese Theater. Hagner even conducts amateur stunt classes. The fee is only $100 and the bruises are free. The museum itself is open weekends.

'Grand Canyon of the West'

North of Mojave some 25 miles (40 kilometers) along State 14 is the **Red Rock Canyon State Recreation Area**. This unusual camping and picnic spot is one of the important geological treasures of Southern California, but it's just enough off the beaten path to be one of the area's best-kept secrets. Nicknamed "Grand Canyon of the West," it's actually more akin to Utah's Bryce Canyon. Great, brightly colored columns of sandstone rise off the desert floor on either side of the highway.

Formed after the last Ice Age, these sculpted towers in the foothills of the eastern Sierras were once the home of a desert Indian tribe now known only as "the old ones." Much later, about the middle of the last century, traffic picked up considerably when desert prospectors began discovering gold nuggets on

Descent from the barren summit of Mount Whitney.

the surface of dry stream beds. A mini-boom followed, and before long some $16 million in ore had been removed, including one five-pound (2.27-kilogram) nugget.

On weekends, state rangers give guided nature walks. Picnic tables and some 50 primitive campsites are provided for tenters and recreational-vehicle enthusiasts. There are no concessions at the park, however, so visitors must bring their own food and water.

The Living Ghost

Randsburg, a 19th Century ghost town that isn't a ghost, is about 20 miles (32 km) due east of Red Rock Canyon on U.S. 395. Named for one of the big gold boomtowns of South Africa, Randsburg is living proof that lightning can strike the same place twice ... er, three times.

From 1895 to 1947, this hilltop enclave — and two others just over the hill, **Johannesburg** and **Atolia** — struck it rich first with gold, then with silver, and finally with tungsten. Gold fever struck in the 19th Century's final decade

with the discovery of the Yellow Aster mine, which yielded $20 million in paydirt before it was exhausted.

After the mine's owners celebrated their good fortune on San Francisco's Market Street with a marching band, stories of Yellow Aster's success raced up and down the California coast. Turn-of-the-century Randsburg was as wild and woolly as any Western boomtown, with saloons and dance halls, scoundrels and rogues. Local legend says one of the town gunmen took second place to the Randsburg vigilantes and was buried cradling a bottle of whiskey in each arm.

Today Randsburg is a small but thriving mining community. Among the ramshackle remains of the original wood-and-corrugated iron buildings on the main street is the **Desert Museum**. Open weekends, it contains a small but fascinating collection of mining and geological artifacts. Also open are the town saloon, dance hall and barber shop, which have been quaintly converted to shops offering rocks, bottles and mining curios. The **Randsburg General Store** is open every day, selling everything from dungarees to dynamite!

Remembrance of the 20 mule team.

Thirsty wayfarers can sip a chocolate soda at the same swivel-chaired soda fountain that was hauled into town by mules a century ago.

Over the hill in Johannesburg (locals call it "Jo-burg"), another remnant of the boomtown days — the **Owl Hotel** — still stands on U.S. 395. The Owl was the hub of the miners' red-light district, and was famous enough to have warranted a bronze plaque commemorating the deeds of its residents:

To the Owl Hotel, where the action was. (This is) *dedicated to Hattie, Little Eva and the girls of the line. While the men dug for silver,* (the girls) *dug for gold.*

China Lake and Trona

Paleontologists have given the world such famous fossil finds a Java Man and Peking Man. There are those who suspect that, once day, a China Lake Man may be discovered beneath the rock and sagebrush of these Mojave flatlands.

Recent discoveries of Stone Age tools indicate human habitation in North America is older than anyone previously suspected. Scientists originally believed the first paleo-Indians didn't cross the Bering land bridge into the New World until the end of the last glacial period, 11,000 to 14,000 years ago. Now, as a result of discoveries at **China Lake**, some scientists are tempted to say that humans migrated from Asia at least 40,000 years ago, and perhaps as long as 100,000 years ago.

China Lake is a dry lake near **Ridgecrest** off U.S. 395. It is best known as the focus of the important **China Lake Naval Weapons Center**. Near the main gate of the naval station is the small **Maturango Museum**, open weekend afternoons. The museum occasionally conducts public field trips to study aboriginal rock inscriptions found at China Lake, perhaps the best collection of them in California.

Not far from China Lake, near the banks of the equally dry **Searles Lake**, are the **Trona Pinnacles**. This great pincushion of ancient limestone columns in the middle of the Mojave Desert is as rare as it is bizarre. The spooky stone spires are "national natural landmarks," probably the outstanding example of tufa formations in North America and a marvelous moonscape to

The Furnace Creek Inn.

explore for hikers and rock climbers of all ages.

Geologists believe the 50 to 150-foot (15 to 46-meter) high spires, which resemble cave stalagmites, are the handiwork of organic calcium deposits (tufa) that grew at the rate of a foot every century when an Ice Age lake covered the area.

Access to the Trona Pinnacles is via State 178 north from Johannesburg. They are found in a two-square-mile area on the west side of Searles Lake, a bleak and awesome bit of real estate seemingly untouched by the hand of man. Camping is permitted at the Pinnacles. Motorists can get local directions in the community of Trona.

Ninety-four miles (151 km) north of Johannesburg on U.S. 395 is **Lone Pine**, a picturesque village that has often been used as a location for Hollywood westerns. From here, **Mount Whitney** — at 14,494 feet (4, 418 meters) the highest peak in the continental United States — is accessible, if one wants to stretch the meaning of that word. It's a two to three-day, 11-mile (18-km) challenge from the end of Whitney Portal Road to reach the summit.

After the climb, a good place for a break is **Keeler**, a ghost town about 10 miles (16 km) from Lone Pine.

The Lowest Spot on Earth

That same highway, State 190, is the main artery through **Death Valley National Monument.**

Long ago, Indians knew this hostile valley as *Tomesha*, "Ground Afire." Little would they have suspected that *Tomesha*, instead of being a place to be shunned, would become one of the most visited natural attractions in the American West.

Ever since Death Valley was established as a national monument by decree of President Franklin D. Roosevelt in 1933, it has attracted greater and greater audiences, and increasingly international ones. Winter or summer — it doesn't seem to matter much — sightseers, hikers and amateur naturalists come to scramble up the sand dunes near **Stovepipe Wells**, marvel at the view from **Zabriskie Point**, gasp at ancient **Ubehebe Crater**, study old mines and ghost towns, look perplexedly at abandoned charcoal kilns, and snap whole photo albums of themselves

at humble **Badwater**, 282 feet (86 meters) below sea level, the lowest spot on earth.

Summers are unmerciful in Death Valley. Yet on any given morning, the valley floor shimmers in the heat, creating marvelously mysterious, floating mirages.

Death Valley's temperatures are exceeded only in the Libyan Sahara. This depression — 120 miles (193 km) long and four to 16 miles (6½ to 26 km) wide — is the result of a geological phenomenon. Eons ago, the deep gap between the **Panamint and Funeral mountains** was formed by a folding of the earth's crust. Gradually erosion wore rock debris away from the mountains and filled the valley floor. The ice ages left it flattened and swathed in a vast cool sea, which evaporated to leave alternating layers of mud and salt. Cut

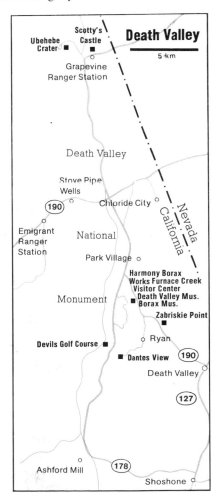

Contours in the sand near Stovepipe Wells.

off from cooling breezes by the surrounding mountains, this basin has been left to parch with an average annual rainfall of less than two inches (50 mm).

Autumn through spring, the climate is made to order for exploring Death Valley. Daytime temperatures range in the 60s and 70s Fahrenheit (about 15 to 25°C), chillier at night; skies are usually bright and rain-free.

Summers are another story. The *average* daily high in July for the past half-century has been 116°F (47°C). It commonly soars past 120°F (49°C), and once hit a national high of 134°F (57°C). In short, May to October is one continuous heat wave. As one year-round resident puts it: "Death Valley is heaven eight months of the year, and four months of sheer hell."

So rigorous is the summer climate that American and foreign automobile manufacturers make a point of conducting hot-weather tests in the valley. It's the sort of oven-like heat that neither man nor beast can ignore. Death Valley naturalists say birds won't fly, nor snakes emerge from their burrows, during the scorching summer days.

Despite the harshness of Death Valley's environment, about 900 different species of plants grow in the national monument, some throwing down roots 10 times the height of a man. In many ways, Death Valley's human population of 200 or so seems just as indomitable, enduring terrific heat and isolation. (The nearest supermarkets are in Las Vegas, Nevada, 140 miles — 225 km — away, and local television reception is mediocre.)

Furnace Creek

Years ago, it was traditional for all concessions to close down in the summer. "What tourist would want to endure such heat?" asked the proprietors. Quite a few, apparently — particularly European and Asian visitors eager for a Western adventure. Nowadays, **Furnace Creek Ranch** and the Stovepipe Wells motel complex stay open throughout the year, and neither is ever empty.

Furnace Creek is a good focal point for a visit to Death Valley. Located not far from Badwater, it features a national monument **Visitor Center** open daily throughout the year, and until 9 p.m.

Early-morning light on Zabriskie Point and the snow-capped Panamint Range.

from November to April. The Furnace Creek Ranch has an 18-hole golf course which is indisputably the lowest on earth. It doesn't necessarily follow that golfers' scores are that low.

There's one other golf course in Death Valley: the **Devil's Golf Course**. But no one could hire a caddy to wander through this bizarre expanse of rugged salt crystals pushing up from hundreds of feet underground.

Overlooking Badwater to the east is **Dante's View** (elevation 5,475 feet or 1,669 meters). The scene from here is quite spectacular, with high mountains looming in the background. **Telescope Peak,** the highest point in the Panamint Range (11,049 feet or 3,368 meters), towers directly above Badwater.

Among Death Valley's other natural beauty spots are Zabriskie Point, southeast of Furnace Creek in the **Black Mountains,** with another awesome view; **Artists Drive** and the **Golden Canyon,** vivid displays of color among odd outcroppings; and Ubehebe Crater, an extinct volcano at the north end of the national monument.

At the **Harmony Borax Works** near Furnace Creek, an old cleanser-processing plant has been restored to show visitors the 19th Century manufacturing method.

Scotty's Castle

In the near proximity of Ubehebe Crater is a man-made phenomenon — a graceful yet flamboyant oddity and living epitaph to one American millionaire's penchant for spending money.

This is **Scotty's Castle,** a 25-room, $2 million Spanish palace that stands poised like a prospector's dying mirage. Operated by the National Park Service, it is easily Death Valley's biggest visitor attraction.

The adage, "A man's home is his castle," may have been written about Chicago millionaire Albert Johnson, who made his fortune in mining before he was 35. In the early 20th Century, he was charmed into investing thousands of dollars in a fruitless search for gold by an affable roustabout named Walter Scott, better known in these parts as "Death Valley Scotty." After years of waiting for Scott to strike his fortune, Johnson's patience ran out — but not before he had grown so fond of Death

Scotty's Castle.

Valley that he decided to build a summer retreat there.

Work on the castle began in 1926 at the foot of a natural spring-fed canyon at 3,000 feet (about 900 meters) elevation. Construction materials from as far away as Europe were transported in by ship, truck and train. Some 2,000 workmen completed the castle in 1931.

Long before it was finished, though, Death Valley residents — as well as newspaper readers across the United States — got wind of the mysterious desert castle. Word was that the castle was being financed by Scotty's secret gold mine. The truth remained a joke between Johnson and Scott to their dying days.

A facsimile of a Spanish-Mediterranean villa, Scotty's Castle contains beautiful continental furnishings and *objets d'art*. It might have been graced with gardens, swimming pool and other expensive refinements. But midway during construction, Johnson lost heavily in the 1929 Wall Street crash. Nevertheless, the Chicago financier and his wife lived on and off at the castle for many years until his death in 1948. "Death Valley Scotty," the good-natured rogue, also lived there, of course. He died in 1954, and his grave lies along a trail just behind the castle.

Today, the castle is open daily to public inspection. There are hourly tours.

To Bury a Burro

On nights when the moon is full, the howl of coyotes lingers through the hot, dusty valley. The cry is mournful and loud, but it is nothing compared to the sounds of controversy over how to deal with another wild Death Valley creature — the burro.

About 2,500 burros run wild in Death Valley and the surrounding mountains. They're raising hell with the desert ecology, say National Park Service biologists. Something must be done. But what?

The question has come down to this: Are the Death Valley burros lovable creatures to be saved at any cost? Or are they pests to be exterminated? There is no simple answer. In fact, there are an estimated 15,000 wild burros roaming America's Western deserts. Their fate has been the subject of court battles and legislative fights.

Heliostats reflect the future at Solar One near Barstow

A $6 million-a-year federal program has relocated more than 4,000 burros since 1976. But no one knows what to do with the rest.

Early Men and Gunfighters

State 190 exits Death Valley National Monument not far from the Nevada border, and joins State 127 at the tiny community of **Amargosa**. It's a scenic 83-mile (134-km) drive south (via **Tecopa Hot Springs**) to **Baker** and I-15. From Baker, another 50 road miles (80 km) take the traveler to **Calico.**

Some of the earliest traces of man on the North American continent were discovered on this windblown desert. Paleontologists are still carrying on the work of the late Dr. Louis Leakey, leader of a team of scientists who came upon a prehistoric "tool factory" estimated to be some 200,000 years old. The so-called **Calico Early Man Site** is open for public viewing, with guided tours Wednesday through Sunday. Arrangements can be made with the federal Bureau of Land Management office in nearby Barstow.

The town of Calico was established by silver miners in the 1880s. A clever restoration of that boomtown is the **Calico Ghost Town**. Half history, half Hollywood and all fun, Calico is an appealing Western amusement park where visitors can explore mining tunnels, ride the ore train, and browse through the dry-goods shops. During the annual **"Calico Days"** festival, the second week of October, Calico hosts the United States National Gunfight Stunt Championship.

Just west of Calico is **Barstow**, a bustling desert town, part-suburb and part-military community. Situated at the junction of Interstates 15 and 40, it has a five-mile (eight-km) stretch of motels, gas stations and grocery stores that make it an excellent base for desert adventures.

Barstow has figured in Western history since the 19th Century Indian wars. Today, some 40 miles (64 km) northeast of the town at **Fort Irwin**, the U.S. Army conducts combat training that's just short of warfare.

Solar One, a large experimental solar-power generating station, is in **Daggett,** six miles (10 km) east of Barstow on

Soaring enthusiasts take advantage of the flat expanse of the Lucerne Valley.

I-40. Southern California Edison employs reflecting heliostats to generate energy; a visitors center explains how. The power company also operates a giant wind-powered generating station near Palm Springs.

Crater and Caverns

It's 77 miles (124 km) east via I-40 to the hamlet of **Amboy**, where on the horizon is the 1,000-year-old **Amboy Crater**. A dormant volcano, its symmetrical cinder cone rises 200 feet (61 meters) above the floor of the desert badland. Unofficial trails lead from the road to the crater rim. The trail penetrates sometimes-jagged lava rocks, so hikers must take care. From road to crater's base, it is a 30 to 45-minute walk; another steep 20-minute climb to the rim follows. There is no water en route.

About as close to the middle of nowhere as one can get in California are the **Mitchell Caverns** and **Providence Mountains State Recreation Area.** Some 100 miles (161 km) east of Barstow via I-40, then another 17 miles (27 km) north from the Essex exit, this red-dirt

high desert region offers primitive camping and hiking. Tours of two of the caverns, El Pakiva and Tecopa, are offered weekday afternoons (except summer) and weekends (year-round). They contain several rare cave formations as well as the requisite stalagmites and stalactites.

Almost due south of Barstow on State 18 is **Apple Valley**, which may be the dude ranch capital of Southern California. Dozens of ranches are located here. Perhaps the most popular is the **Apple Valley Inn**, a 28-acre (11-hectare) resort where locals flock on Saturday nights for an outdoor Western steak fry and a Sunday brunch.

Located on the north side of the San Bernardino Mountains, Apple Valley lies on the path followed by 18th Century Spanish missionaries. Back then, they stopped to refresh themselves at what is now **Mojave Narrows Regional Park**, an 860-acre (348-hectare) oasis and a favorite stop for hikers, campers and rock climbers. Paiute Indians once sheltered their families among the rocks.

Not far away, former television cowboy and crooner Roy Rogers has his popular **Western Museum**. Inside the reconstructed stockade, the Old West lives again. Thanks to taxidermists, so do Trigger and Bullet. Roy's co-starring horse and his faithful dog are there .

Surviving in the Desert

The Mojave Desert is just a few hours drive from Los Angeles. It is so close and so accessible that travelers often are amazingly casual about what to expect in this alien environment. Smart travelers take plenty of precautions.

The Mojave covers an enormous amount of land — roughly that of the states of Massachusetts, Connecticut and Rhode Island combined. It's easy to get lost and, with conventional vehicles, even to get stranded off the main roads.

Visitors who have never experienced summer desert heat, and who haven't a clue how to pace themselves, should be warned: It is quite literally life-threatening to be under the desert sun too long.

"You lose the thirst impulse," said Shirley Harding, museum curator at the Death Valley National Monument. "People have died out here with a full canteen of water beside them."

Left, land sailors line up for winds on a dry-lake bed east of Victorville. Right, living history at Calico Ghost Town.

PALM SPRINGS
TO THE COLORADO

Where the high Mojave Desert greets the lower Colorado Desert, the landscapes speak.

They make stark statements in shades of brown and beige, arid platitudes punctuated by snow-capped mountain peaks. What might be perceived as nature's harshness really offers an enveloping sense of warmth and tranquility to those who learn to know the many moods of California's southern desert.

This desert area is one of great contrasts — hot and cold, lush and sparse, populous and barren. Urbanization hasn't extended its tentacles here yet. There are cities, but no metropolises. There are people, but no crowds. And there are three separate wildernesss designations (totaling more than 500,000 acres) where the impudent roadrunner, the majestic desert bighorn sheep and the wedge-snouted, fringe-toed lizard are the main residents. Man is only a visitor.

Southeastern California's upper reaches (those between Interstates 10 and 40) are indeed parched and mainly unpopulated. Further south, however, the region comes to life. It stretches beyond the shimmering Salton Sea to the Colorado River and the state of Arizona. In the west, the resort-oriented Coachella Valley surrounding Palm Springs is a favored destination of "newlyweds and nearly deads" — or so one cynic has said.

Palm Springs

While it is true that the abundance of sunshine and recreational opportunities make the **Palm Springs** region appealing to honeymooners, retirees and the wealthy, there is an ever-increasing middle class. They, too, are captivated by the accessibility of myriad activities and terrains. On a hot summer day, with temperatures topping 100 degrees Fahrenheit (38° Centigrade) in the shade, a 15 to 20-minute ride on the **Palm Springs Aerial Tramway** will carry sojourners 8,516 feet (2,596 meters) up **Mount San Jacinto**, where snow can still be found in July amid a peaceful alpine atmosphere. In the winter, cross-country skiers enjoy the mountaintop

terrain, and there are annual dog-sled races.

Many people know Palm Springs (population 32,000) by two of its more luxurious features — lush golf courses and celebrities' homes. Bob Hope's house, built on a ridge over-looking the swimming pool-dotted **Coachella Valley**, was likened by one writer to a Trans World Airlines' terminal. It is not quite that large, but it is as large as a fair-sized department store and easily visible from the desert floor.

Hope — along with such other celebrities as Frank Sinatra, Kirk Douglas, Red Skelton, Dinah Shore and the late Jack Benny — has brought fame to Palm Springs, along with fortune. But long before the Hollywood luminaries and Midwest business tycoons lived here, the area was inhabited by the Agua Caliente Indians, a band of the Cahuilla. Their name, which means "hot water" in Spanish, came from the ancient mineral springs on which the resort city rests.

Every other square mile of Palm Springs, in fact, is part of the **Agua Caliente Indian Reservation**, a checkerboard arrangement devised by the Unit-

Preceding pages, Joshua Tree National Monument. Left, sun worshippers at Anza Borrego's Palm Canyon. Right, Bob Hope sinks another putt at Palm Springs.

ed States government when it sought to give a right-of-way to the Southern Pacific Railroad. The result is a hodge-podge of development, a continuing squabble over who has the right to zone Indian land. About 100 separate members of the Agua Caliente each own land worth more than $2 million.

Sacred Ground

San Jacinto — the mountain that shelters Palm Springs and furnishes its beneficial climate — was once a seasonal hunting ground for the Indians, who fled the desert floor when the heat became unbearable. They believed the mineral springs possessed healing powers and thus were sacred.

The area holds many legends. One of the more popular involves Tahquitz, an early Cahuilla medicine man reputed to have great supernatural powers. Tahquitz, so the legend goes, began using his powers to harm his tribe, and therefore was driven out. Swearing revenge, he stormed into the San Jacinto Mountains, climbing high into the canyon which now bears his name (and where much of the original version of the movie *Lost Horizon* was filmed). Tahquitz is said to still watch over the area through the translucent walls of his cave. During the day, he stirs up great clouds of sand and dust into which the unwitting sometimes disappear. At night he searches for souls and carries them deep into his cave. He prefers virgins, of course. The Indians believe he often appears as a giant meteor.

Near to **Tahquitz Canyon** are the so-called **Indians Canyons,** popular spots for hiking, picnicking and nature-loving. **Palm Canyon**, 15 miles (24 km) of rocky ravine lined with stately palm trees, has often been a movie location. **Andreas Canyon**, five miles (eight km) south of downtown Palm Springs, is favored by desert horseback riders. **Murray Canyon**, a short hike from Andreas, is a good resting place. Washingtonian palm trees, believed to be 1,500 to 2,000 years old, form a shaded setting for meandering brooks and rugged outcroppings at all three canyons. Reached by a toll road at the end of South Palm Canyon Drive, the canyons are usually open to sightseers from October to June.

By the mid 1860s, many non-Indians

Spectators pack the stands at the annual mid February international tennis classic at La Quinta.

256

knew about the desert's mineral springs. Railroad surveyors discovered them in 1853, stagecoaches in the 1860s. Tourism was not far behind. In 1886, Dr. Welwood Murray, a canny Scotsman who today has a downtown library named after him (not to mention the canyon), built the **Palm Springs Spa Hotel**, its first lodging house.

Two years earlier, John Guthrie McCallum had become the first permanent white settler. He laid out the first irrigation system, planted figs, citrus, alfalfa and vineyards. Later residents called McCallum "Judge," an honorary title but one befitting his position as an attorney and the community's founder. Palm Springs flourished. In the Twenties, it became a popular hideaway for movie stars and executives. After all, "The Springs" were only 105 miles (169 km) east of Los Angeles.

On New Year's Eve 1928, **El Mirador Hotel**, built by oilman P.T. Stevens, opened in a then-isolated location in the northern part of the city. Skeptics snickered, but Stevens knew what he was doing, and the 200-room grand hotel hosted the toast of filmdom along with such serious-minded folk as Albert Ein-

stein. In 1931, the *Amos 'n' Andy* radio program, a favorite of President Franklin D. Roosevelt, was broadcast from the hotel's Byzantine-Moorish tower. El Mirador was taken over by the federal government as an Army hospital during World War II, had many glory days in the Fifties and Sixties, then was closed in 1973 when bought by its neighbor, Desert Hospital.

El Mirador played a part in the genesis of the famed **Palm Springs Racquet Club**. Since the hotel had only one tennis court at the time, actors Charlie Farrell and Ralph Bellamy often had to wait to play. Having their own court seemed a solution, so they bought 200 windswept acres a few blocks north of the hotel for $30 an acre. The club opened on Christmas Day 1933 with two courts and a small dressing room. A swimming pool and snack bar followed. So did movie stars such as Humphrey Bogart, Marlene Dietrich, Douglas Fairbanks, Henry Fonda, Clark Gable, Greta Garbo, Carole Lombard, Paul Lukas, Mary Pickford, Ginger Rogers and Spencer Tracy.

Palm Springs fostered the image of a "Playground of the Stars and Presi-

Relaxing in a jacuzzi at La Quinta Hotel.

dents." Though tennis brought the original acclaim, it soon became known as the "Golf Capital of the World." Today there are more than 50 golf courses in the Coachella Valley from Palm Springs east to Indio.

The Culture Vultures

In Palm Springs, it is easy to buy one's way into the social structure. A large contribution to charity or a fancy party guarantees a photo in the local society pages. No doubt, most visitors think of Palm Springs as a collection of hotels (the word "motel" is *verboten*), restaurants, nightclubs, swimming pools and bejeweled women walking poodles.

Perhaps because of this stereotype, "culture" is a word taken seriously by many in Palm Springs. Residents are somewhat sensitive to criticism. They are — with reason — vastly proud of the **Desert Museum**, an $8.5-million arts center at the base of the San Jacinto Mountains near the Desert Fashion Plaza.

The Denney Western Art Wing houses an ever-expanding collection of American sculptures, paintings, graphics and photography. The McCallum Natural Science Wing (named after the "Judge") has four extensive galleries devoted to desert landscape, climate, plant and animal life. Also in the bi-level structure are the Annenberg Art Wing and the 450-seat Annenberg Theater. (Funds were donated by Walter Annenberg, publisher and former ambassador to the United Kingdom, and his wife, Lee.) The Walt Disney Gallery, the Helena Rubenstein Children's Art Studio and the (Frank) Sinatra Sculpture Court round out the museum.

Annenberg and Sinatra live a few miles down State Highway 111 in **Rancho Mirage**, a bedroom community of country clubs, golf courses and tennis courts. Former U.S. President Gerald Ford and Leonard Firestone, industrialist and former ambassador to Belgium, also reside there, side by side on a fairway at Thunderbird Country Club. The Annenberg estate is a few blocks away at the corner of Frank Sinatra and Bob Hope drives. (Having a street named after a person has become the desert's ultimate status symbol.) Annenberg had his own nine-hole golf course built, so the story goes, because he was de-

nied membership in one of the local country clubs. It must be a good course. U.S. Presidents Dwight Eisenhower, Richard Nixon and Ronald Reagan have golfed there.

Rancho Mirage's **Mission Hills Country Club** hosts the annual Nabisco Dinah Shore Invitational ladies golf tournament, as well as prestigious tennis tournaments. **Tamarisk Country Club** in Rancho Mirage is a Bob Hope Desert Classic course every other year. (It alternates with **Eldorado Country Club** in **Indian Wells**.) The three other mainstay courses are Indian Wells, Bermuda Dunes and La Quinta country clubs.

Palm Desert, with its huge **Town Center** shopping center and its boutique-lined **El Paseo**, has been waging a concerted effort to lure visitors down valley from Palm Springs. Aside from the ever-burgeoning country clubs with the attendant recreational facilities, this town features the **Living Desert Reserve**, 900 acres (364 hectares) of open desert surrounded by the **Santa Rosa Mountains**. The reserve's botanical gardens contain species from several types of North American deserts.

15 minutes aboard the Palm Springs Aerial Tramway brings visitors from desert heat to winter snow.

Indian Wells is well on its way to becoming a completely gated city with entry to its country clubs only to those with connections. But it's worth a note because former President Eisenhower spent many of his final winters at Eldorado Country Club, working on his memoirs after a daily round of golf.

La Quinta is a hidden community nestled in a Santa Rosa Mountain cove that's becoming less and less hidden. Landmark Land Company, a real-estate and golf-course developer, has taken over the venerable **La Quinta Hotel**, which oozes with European charm; built up the golf course to 36 holes; and added a tennis club whose partners include professionals Arthur Ashe and Roscoe Tanner. Every February, the ATP/La Quinta pro tennis tourney attracts top international stars like Czechoslovakia's Ivan Lendl. Spanish-style cottages dot the spacious lawns of La Quinta which, in stagecoach days, was a travelers' resting place.

The Dates of Indio

East of La Quinta is **Indio**, once a railroad boom town, now the gateway to the richly agricultural lower Coachella Valley. Indio may bear an inferiority complex when it thinks of its wealthier neighboring communities, but it is the home of the National Date Festival, held annually in February. The festival features an Arabian Nights pageant, exhibits, shows and even ostrich and camel races.

The area around Indio, because of climate and soil, is the only place in the United States where dates are grown. Some 4,000 acres (about 1,600 hectares) yield 25,000 tons annually with a crop value of more than $30 million. Several date gardens welcome visitors. One of them shows a film called *The Sex Life of a Date* — for purely educational purposes, of course.

The date palm was introduced to the United States by Spanish missionaries in the late 18th Century, but it wasn't until after 1900 that the U.S. Department of Agriculture experimented with plantings from Egypt, Algeria and Iraq in the Southern California desert. Healthy date trees today yield up to three pounds of fruit per leaf, or about 300 pounds (136 kilograms) of dates per season.

n unlikely
ttraction
r desert
sitors:
og-sled races
gh above
alm Springs.

South of Indio and north of the Salton Sea is **Lake Cahuilla**. Created from the adjacent waters of the **All America Canal**, the lake is stocked with rainbow trout, striped bass and catfish. For non-anglers, there are hiking and equestrian trails, shady picnic spots, special campsites and a children's play area on the sandy beach — away from fishermen.

What can be said of the **Salton Sea?** To be honest, it was all a big mistake. When engineers attempted in 1905 to divert Colorado River water to the Imperial Valley, the river changed course and reflooded the ancient Salton Basin, 235 feet (72 meters) below sea level. This formed a sea of 360 square miles (968 sq km) with royal blue water filling the area where the Coachella and Imperial valleys merge.

Sportsmen love it. The sea's saltiness creates a buoyancy popular with water skiers and swimmers. It also provides a habitat for salt-water game-fish. Adjoining marshlands are a refuge for migrating birds and a haven for bird watchers. The **Salton Sea State Recreation Area** is an 18,000-acre (about 7,300-hectare) park with both developed and primitive campsites. There is a large boat basin at **Varner Harbor**. And geology buffs have a field day with ancient shorelines and layers of marine fossils visible along the base of the Santa Rosa Mountains.

The Salton Sea, 38 miles (61 km) long and nine to 15 miles (14 to 24 km) wide, is flanked by State 111 on the east and State 86 on the west. Local residents like to avoid the latter road, a two-lane thoroughfare they have dubbed "the killer highway" because of the unusually high number of fatal traffic accidents it records.

Anza-Borrego Park

The northeastern tip of **Anza-Borrego Desert State Park** is only a couple of miles from the Salton Sea. The largest state park in California, it contains some 600,000 acres (243,000 hectares) of Colorado Desert, and extends nearly to the Mexican border. The park is chock full of canyons and *arroyos* (dry gullies) easily reached by car. It also has its share of badlands, inhospitable except to the jackrabbits, coyotes, kangaroo rats and chuckwalla lizards who call them home. Camping is permitted

Left, a date palm, fruit of the desert right, visitors race camels the annual Indio Date Festival.

260

almost everywhere.

Off-road vehicle enthusiasts delight in roaring around **Ocotillo Wells**, on State 78 at the park's eastern edge. A state vehicluar recreation area, its dunes, washes and hills offer special challenges to drivers.

More than 150 species of birds have been sighted in Anza-Borrego park. The vegetation is equally varied, ranging from junipers and pines at the 5,000-foot level (1,500 meters) to palm trees at sea level. A three-mile hike from **Campfire Center** to **Palm Grove** reveals plants used by the Cahuilla Indians for medicines, dyes and food.

The town of **Borrego Springs**, 90 miles (144 km) south of Palm Springs, is entirely surrounded by the northern part of the park. In the spring, the Borrego Valley showcases the glory of nature's beauty with blooming wildflowers and brilliantly vibrant cacti. From Borrego Springs to the Salton Sea, the Erosion Road provides an engaging excursion through washes and badlands. Long ago this area was covered by the ocean, which left a rich history of sediments and geologic formations.

South of the Salton Sea, State 86 leads past the **U.S. Naval Aerial Gunnery Ranges** to some of the richest farmland on earth. This is the **Imperial Valley**, centered around appropriately named **El Centro** ("The Center"). Irrigation has turned what was once desert into a cornucopia of lettuce, tomatoes, melons, sugar beets and other vegetables and fruit.

East of El Centro, home of 24,000 people, is little **Holtville**, where the California Angels baseball team holds its spring training. South of El Centro about 10 miles (16 km) is the boisterous border town of **Calexico**. Its sister city is **Mexicali**, capital of the Mexican state of Baja California Norte. The town names were supposedly coined by a land promoter. Only a fence separates the two communities. Days are peaceful, but nightlife can get rowdy.

The Colorado River

About 58 miles (93 km) due east of El Centro is **Yuma**, Arizona, a desert town built on the banks of the Colorado River where it enters Mexican territory. The Colorado forms the entire eastern border of Southern California from

Overlooking the Badlands, Anza Borrego Desert State Park.

Mexico to Nevada. Several dams built across it have created reservoirs while providing hydroelectric power for the metropolises of Los Angeles and San Diego.

From **Brawley** at the north end of the Imperial Valley, State 78 heads east toward the Colorado, crossing the barren-but-beautiful **Chocolate Mountains** and skirting the **Cibola National Wildlife Refuge**. Where the highway meets Interstate 10 at the Arizona border is the emerging recreation center of **Blythe**; it is situated at the southwestern corner of the **Colorado River Indian Reservation**, which also includes the hydroelectric town of **Parker**, Arizona.

Many people prefer to park their vehicles in Parker when they come to explore the river. Parker is considerably less tourist-oriented than **Lake Havasu City**, Arizona, 40 miles (64 km) north. But the cool blue Colorado River is the same — open year-round for fishing, boating, water skiing, rafting, tubing, swimming and just lolling about.

On the California side of the river (State 62) is the **Parker Power Plant**, open to public visits. There is a local **Indian Tribes Museum** with a fine basketry collection; a nearby living ghost town, **Oatman**; and the **Buckskin Mountain State Park**, backdropped by jagged cliffs. Two miles west of the river is the California community of **Earp**, named after the legendary Old West lawman and gunfighter, Wyatt Earp.

The **Parker Dam** is actually about 15 miles (24 km) north of Parker. Completed in 1938, the dam is the world's deepest. Sixty-five percent of its 320-foot (97-meter) height is below the riverbed. Water stored by the dam is pumped into the **Colorado River Aqueduct**, which can deliver 1 billion gallons (3.8 billion liters) of water daily to thirsty Southern California urbanites.

Lake Havasu, 46 miles (74 km) long, and no more than three miles (five km) wide, is the reservoir behind the dam. Those who don't want to drink the water enjoy playing in it. Along Arizona State Highway 95 between Parker and Lake Havasu City are recreational-vehicle parks, marinas and campgrounds with room for tens of thousands of visitors. Water sportsmen from outboard boaters to yachtsmen, water skiers to sailboarders, love the lake. There's fishing for bass, bluegills, trout and crappies. Small game popu-

lates the rugged southeastern (Arizona) shore of the lake that constitutes **Lake Havasu State Park**. Birds are everywhere, as the entire body of water is contained with the **Lake Havasu National Wildlife Refuge**.

Jet-boat excursions from Lake Havasu City take adventurers through **Topock Gorge**, past the California town of **Needles**, to a gambling casino in Nevada a good 50 miles (80 km) upriver. (Comic-strip readers recognize Needles from *Peanuts* as the home of Spike, the real-estate salesman brother of Snoopy, the whimsical beagle.) Rockhounds search through the terrain for agate, jasper, turquoise, quartz and black obsidian known locally as "Apache tears."

Lake Havasu City, nonexistent as recently as the late Sixties, has exploded into a resort center of 15,000 population. Developed by the late millionaire Robert P. McCulloch Sr., its most famous landmark is the original **London Bridge**, which no doubt has caused many British visitors to be overcome by nostalgia. The bridge was rescued from falling down (into England's Thames River) by McCulloch, who expended

Fauna and flora of the Colorado Desert: left, a collared lizard, and right, an *echinocereus* cactus bloom.

$2.4 million of the fortune he made in chain saws and other machinery. McCulloch had the bridge shipped piece by piece to Long Beach, then trucked to the lakefront community he created.

The bridge now arches over a one-mile channel dredged to divert water from the lake, under the bridge and back into the lake. Beneath the bridge (but not under water) is an acre of land deeded to the City of London and featuring English shops, restaurants and other reminders of the British Isles. McCulloch died in 1977, but his promotional monument lives on, a bridge over mostly untroubled water.

Twentynine Palms

It's a drive of about 150 miles (240 km) across barren desert plains from Lake Havasu through the Turtle and Sheep Hole mountains, to **Twentynine Palms**. This oasis on State 62 serves a dual function: it is headquarters for the **Joshua Tree National Monument** and site of the enormous **United States Marine Corps Center**, largest of its kind in the world. War games are routine here, but it's unlikely that a visitor will be able to view them first-hand unless he is a congressman or general.

The town of Twentynine Palms itself has many more than 29 palms. But that was the number here in the 1970s when the town was named. Now with a year-round population of 7,500, it is located where the Mojave and Colorado deserts in the high desert area where the Mojave and Colorado deserts collide.

Joshua Tree National Monument, 467,000 acres (189,000 hectares) of eerie geological formations and granite monoliths, is administered by the National Park Service with offices at the **Mara Oasis** just south of Twentynine Palms. Indians once lived at this oasis, and later prospectors and homesteaders. Helpful park rangers conduct nature walks on autumn and spring weekends. There are nine campgrounds and several picnic areas within the national monument; dirt roads and hiking trails connect points of interest. The monument, a popular rock-climbing area, takes its name from the greenish-white spring-blossoming Joshua tree that grows as tall as 40 feet (12 meters).

Geology Falls Road, through 18 miles (29 km) of unpaved terrain, displays the

A British import at Lake Havas — London Bridge.

264

might of nature in shaping the earth. Nine self-guided trails lead through huge, twisted rock formations and statuesque pinnacles. The golden eagle and other forms of animal and plant life seldom seen elsewhere are found here.

Joshua Tree National Monument is a vast, unspoiled land that recalls the meaning of the term "wilderness," as defined in the federal and California state wilderness acts — "a place ... where earth and its community of life are untrammeled by man, where man himself is a visitor who does not remain."

Biblical Statues And Six-Shooters

It's less than 50 miles (80 km) via State 62 from Twentynine Palms back to Palm Springs. About 20 miles along the route, **Scenic Mountain** affords a panoramic view of the **Yucca Valley**. This 40-acre (16-hectare) former retreat of composer Jimmy Van Heusen, an Academy Award-winning songwriter who inked many tunes recorded by Frank Sinatra, has been converted into a gourmet restaurant. The view from

4,000 feet (1,220 meters) is worth the price of the meal itself.

In the pickup truck-filled Yucca Valley is an even more unusual location — **Desert Christ Park**. Sculptor Antone Martin spent the last nine years of his life creating 11 New Testament scenes in stone, plus a 16-ton, 10-foot statue of Jesus Christ. Martin said he wanted his work "to stand through the ravages of eternity," so he modeled the construction after the only buildings that survived the atomic attack in 1945 on Hiroshima, Japan.

Four miles north of Yucca Valley is a community as close to the Old West as can be found in this high-technology day and age. It's **Pioneertown,** a former outdoor movie set used for many Westerns, including those starring Gene Autry and Roy Rogers. There's plenty of room for camping, and several local hangouts for meeting down-to-earth folks. Six-shooters must be checked at the doors.

Desert Hot Springs, south of Yucca Valley and about three miles north of I-10, is a spa city which (unlike Palm Springs) encourages the less-than-wealthy to stay longer. Residents of the

town, used to the label "the poor man's Palm Springs," like to point out that there is an extra hour of sunshine each day in Desert Hot Springs. Without Mount San Jacinto blocking the sun's late rays, Desert Hot Springs has more time for tennis, golf, swimming, hiking, horse back riding, sunning and soothing tired muscles. Natural hot springs are almost bubbling, but they are cooled to between 102°F and 110°F (39°C to 43°C) for therapeutic and recreational dips.

There are two remarkable attractions nearby. **Cabot Yerxa's Old Indian Pueblo** (67616 E. Desert View Ave.) is designed in ancient Hopi Indian style, or so it is said. It is four stories high, 7,000 square feet (650 sq meters) in area, with 35 finished and 45 unfinished rooms, 150 windows and 65 doors, 17 of which lead to the outside. Yerxa started building it when he was 58 years old from rocks, cement, lumber and nails. By the time he completed it, he was 81. It remains as it was when Yerxa died, stacked high with Indian artifacts, eclectic furniture, even mementoes of the Alaskan gold rush. In one word, it is weird.

The **Kingdom of the Living Dolls** has hundreds of hand-crafted dolls in au-

thentic costumes, placed in historical settings from prehistory times to 1900. There are dolls in a Southern plantation, in a medieval castle, in a Turkish mosque. It took Betty Hamilton, the dolls' Danish-born creator, 18 years to assemble her kingdom.

There's one more delightful stop for travelers before returning to the relaxation of Palm Springs. Eight miles (13 km) west of Desert Hot Springs on I-10 is a settlement called **Cabazon**. Here stand two of the most unusual sights in Southern California.

Gazing moodily over the highway and surrounding terrain are larger-than-life-sized replicas of dinosaurs — a *brontosaurus* and a *tyrannosaurus rex*. They weight more than 40 tons each and stand out against the horizon like two gigantic sentinels guarding antiquity. The *brontosaurus*, 45 feet (14 meters) high and 150 feet (46 meters) long, has a three-floor interior with a museum containing fossils, Stone Age artifacts, Indian arrowheads and an Old West gun collection. Standing 65 feet (20 meters) high, the *tyrannosaurus* is still unfinished; when complete, it will have view platforms in its mouth and tail.

Left, a *brontosaurus* stands sentinel over I-10 at Cabazon; and right, experimental power — a giant wind generator near Desert Hot Springs.

'THE INDUSTRY': MOVIES AND TELEVISION

Hollywood, dream city to much of the rest of the world, is in reality a rather tawdry collection of middle-class homes and nondescript business avenues that serve as the hub of Southern California's vast motion picture and television industries.

The city trades vigorously on its storied past — when the stars actually lived in the canyons and hills north of fabled Sunset Boulevard and caroused in such glamorous watering holes as the Trocadero, Ciro's, Macambo and the Garden of Allah, none of which still exist. People were then in the

value translates into millions of tourist dollars, even more at the box office. And symbolically — forget the local economic and geographic facts — Hollywood is still the biggest dream city on earth.

It's impossible to conceive of Southern California without its celebrity merchants. Before motion pictures, before Jewish glove merchants came west to make movies and become studio czars, Los Angeles was known for its orange groves. And before the orange groves, the city's sense of identity was most closely allied with its 19th Century

picture business as those of other cities were into grain or bonds.

In Hollywood's myth-making days, circa 1915 to 1950, the business of glamour belonged to a network of huge studios. Most of these studies are still churning out glamour, but no longer from Hollywood. They are down the road in a sprawling amorphous area known as Greater Los Angeles. Today, in fact, only one major studio (Paramount) and one television network (CBS) have their offices in Hollywood proper.

The Dream City

Nevertheless, the facade of Hollywood is of incalculable importance. Its symbolic

Spanish culture. It was the introduction of motion pictures in the 1920s and the star system — which produced Chaplin, Pickford, Fairbanks, Valentino, Keaton — that permanently married the motion-picture industry to Southern California.

But the halcyon days of the Silver Screen ended a generation ago. The television industry, with corporate headquarters in New York, has been for more than a quarter of a century the dominant entertain-

Preceding pages: actors cast as Asian tribesmen stand guard on set of Columbia Pictures' *Bring 'em Back Alive*. Above, film crew prepares to shoot sequence. Right, 1920s comedy team monkeys around on set.

ment industry in Los Angeles. TV and theatrical films, encompassing independent stations and countless independent production houses, today influence lifestyles more than any other industry. In fact, in Los Angeles, the pervasive entertainment industry is known simply as "The Industry."

Seven major studios dominate the film industry: Metro Goldwyn Mayer/United Artists in Culver City, 20th Century-Fox in Century City, Paramount in Hollywood, and four studios in the San Fernando Valley — Columbia Pictures, Warner Bros. and Walt

that vie to sell programs to the networks or to fashion movies for distribution by the major studios.

Even though the overwhelming number of people in Los Angeles have nothing to do with these companies and make their living like people do all over the world "The Industry" is the dominant economic and social force in Los Angeles. Besides the sheer impact in dollars, the film and television industries also affect the L.A. populace by the huge reservoir of unusual types of people they draw.

Disney Productions in Burbank and Universal Pictures in nearby Universal City.

Also in the otherwise dreary city of Burbank sits NBC. Almost totally hidden from view is ABC in the northeastern part of Los Angeles. CBS (Television City, as it is known) is in the center of Los Angeles.

These are the giants, employing thousands of workers, surrounded, in turn, by other lesser studios such as Warner Hollywood (where Sam Goldwyn used to have his Goldwyn Studios), Hollywood General, Gower-Sunset Studios (where Columbia was based during Harry Cohn's reign), and Francis Ford Coppola's bankrupt Zoetrope Studios. Sandwiched among these fiefdoms are many fiercely competitive production companies

Easterners love to sneer about the nuts and crackpots in Los Angeles, — perhaps best typifield in American literature by Nathanael West's corrosive Hollywood novel, *The Day of the Locust*. The city has always been a magnet for creative people. Whether talented people came for the money — as William Faulkner and F. Scott Fitzgerald, who wrote movie scripts in the late Thirties and early Forties — or whether they were drawn by the muse, the effect over the years of so many popular artists on the community-at-large has given Hollywood a bizarre and fanciful image. The fact that the majority of writers, actors, musicians and assorted promoter types never find a stable income — that they are, in fact, out of work most of the year — is the underbelly of Hollywood that "outsiders" seldom hear about.

The Labor Unions

Creative types are no doubt a separate breed than most Angelenos. This is exemplified, strangely enough, in labor unions. Unions do not have a strong history in Los Angeles. But one of the most tightly unionized industries in Southern California is the entertainment industry. The Screen Actors Guild (SAG) — which once elected a president named Ronald Reagan — and the American Federation of Television and Radio Artists (AFTRA) total more than 100,000 members nationwide, with the majority in Los Angeles. No one acts before

talkies, has been inextricably tied to the history of the labor movement in Hollywood.

In the Thirties and Forties, that history was bloody, corrupt and tumultuous. The studio chiefs, such as Harry Warner at Warner Bros. and Louie B. Mayer at MGM, fought labor organizers with police and hired goons outside the studio gates. There was Mafia influence at the studios; Chicago hood Willie Bioff, installed as the leader of the IATSE in Hollywood, took payoffs from studio presidents to keep down union demands. Strikes in 1945 and 1947 turned Tinseltown into a latter-day version of union-management battles at steel mills in Pittsburgh.

At the same time, in a decade spanning the mid Forties to the mid Fifties, Holly-

a camera if he or she is not in the union. And normally an offer of employment from a producer is a prerequisite to join either SAG or AFTRA.

Directors have their Directors Guild of America and screen and television writers have their Writers Guild of America. Non-union talent finds it *extremely* difficult to land work. Behind-the-camera workers such as grips, gaffers, film editors, carpenters, plasterers, publicists, costumers, art directors, sound men and cinematographers are represented by the powerful International Alliance of Theatrical Stage Employers (IATSE). Studio drivers are in the Teamsters. In short, the history of motion pictures, at least from the early days of the

wood endured its gloomiest era, that of the communist witch hunts. Ten Hollywood writers, including Dalton Trumbo, went to jail. The House Un-American Activities Committee, feeding on hysteria about Reds, enjoyed a field day. Careers in Hollywood collapsed overnight. Many picture people cooperated with the witch-hunters and went to Washington, D.C., to name names and thus save their careers. Many didn't cooperate and were literally exiled from the business. Half the town was suspected of being

Left, actresses Joan Collins and Linda Gray of TV's *Dynasty* at an Emmy Awards ceremony in Pasadena. Right, L.A. television crew arrives to film a horse race at Del Mar.

communist. It was Hollywood's Dark Age.

To make matters worse, it was the dawn of the age of television, and motion-picture houses across the country were shutting down as the studios realized too late that they had misjudged TV, and that millions of moviegoers were staying home glued to the tube.

Meanwhile, the TV networks, like the first East Coast picture studios before them, saw that Hollywood and not New York would be the production center of the future. The drain of talent from New York to Hollywood has continued ever since.

With the advent of television, the old studio contract system began to crack. Soon, stars, writers and directors became free agents, able to make the best deal to work for anybody. In perhaps the most symbolic exit of a major figure, Mayer at MGM lost a power play with stockholders in the early Fifties and was gone. Suddenly a new breed — in MGM's case, Dore Schary — was calling the shots.

The Rich and Famous

Some of Hollywood's rich and famous moved to the "suburbs," specifically Beverly Hills. But most of the stars in the Thirties stayed in Hollywood, with several — such as Sidney Greenstreet, Peter Lorre, opera singer Lawrence Tibbet, and Clark Gable and Carol Lombard (who were in pre-marital seclusion) — residing in Laurel Canyon just a stone's throw above the Sunset Strip and the legendary Schwab's drugstore where Lana Turner, according to the myth makers, was discovered in her tight sweater sipping a malt.

But all that was to change. The big money in town was moving west, toward the Pacific Ocean and the setting sun. Geographically, the entertainment people, as if tilted toward the seashore in the Forties and Fifties, began invading Beverly Hills, Bel Air, Malibu and Pacific Palisades. Beverly Hills today has the highest per capita income in the country, after Greenwich, Connecticut, New York's wealthiest suburb. A lot of that money is made in deals inked after umpteen martinis at the Polo Lounge of the Beverly Hills Hotel.

This is the fantasy land where people who make movies, record albums and television shows live like royalty. This world is so gold-hatted that it's déclassé to have east-west tennis courts because of the slant of the setting sun.

What's the effect of all this on Southern California? One good example is the little lady who sits in her canvas chair under an umbrella every day on Sunset Boulevard in Holmby Hills. She sells maps to the stars' homes. So do others on Sunset all the way into Hollywood. They are part of the trail to the California dream.

But in a ravenous town like this, permanence is an illusion, change is swift, security is tenuous. The average tenure of a studio executive is 18 months at the majors. The average annual income of a member of the Screen Actors Guild is around $4,000. Most members of the Writers Guild fare little better. The IATSE craftsmen are lucky to be employed half the year. Millions are spent at the networks on development of projects that never get shot; and if they do get made into "pilots," most never get aired.

These failures still feed the masses. All these unmade or unseen projects provide work for thousands of people, including those who write about "The Industry."

Among Hollywood's oldest traditions are its two trade papers, *Daily Variety*, founded in 1933, and *The Hollywood Reporter*, founded in 1931. Today, with an influence out of all proportion to their circulation, more than 20,000 people in the entertainment industry read the "trades" every weekday morning. Egos wax and wane at the mention of their names in the papers — or at their omission.

In a high-profile community like Hollywood, it's never business as usual. It's always a myth with a banner headline.

THE L.A. SOUND

If ever the term "melting pot" could be used in describing a city's very own musical character, Los Angeles is surely the place. L.A. spawned or nurtured music style ranging from rhythm-and-blues to folk to surf music to rock 'n' roll and beyond, and all this since World War II.

Los Angeles' many contributions to the popular musical culture of America can be traced back to the mid-Forties. The country's upbeat post-war mood inspired many people to direct their thoughts toward recreational pursuits.

Despite this positive mood swing, an atmosphere of despair prevailed in the city's lower-income areas, such as Watts and Compton. Some of the more astute and creative residents of these areas sought to escape from their plight through music. Among them were saxophonist Big Jay McNeely, pianist Joe Liggins, bandleader Roy Milton and vocalist Margie Evans, all of whom combined the technique and exuberance of the big bands of the early Forties with an urgency and despair in delivery and lyrical content that reflected their personal situations. Their styles were the forerunners of what came to be known as rock 'n' roll music.

From Rhythm-and-Blues To Rock 'n' Roll

Rhythm-and-blues was bred in many clubs throughout the Los Angeles area, the most notable being the Le Parisien at the corner of La Brea and Washington boulevards. The small, gray concrete building provided an intimate atmosphere that served as an ideal showcase for established musicians as well as up-and-coming talent. Patrons of the Le Parisien often found themselves in the company of some of rhythm-and-blues' most respected artists, including Bobby Bland, Sam and Dave, Joe Tex and Jimmy Witherspoon. Until its closing in 1982, the Le Parisien was the most popular rhythm-and-blues club in Los Angeles.

As people of many different ethnic and cultural backgrounds migrated to Los Angeles, the city's music drew from a variety of genres and inspirations. The rhythm-and-

Sha Na Na, whose music is a throwback to the "Happy Days" of the 1950s and 1960s, rock around the clock at the Greek Theatre.

blues of the Forties gave way in the mid-Fifties to the "doo-wah, doo-wah" sound. But there was also growing social consciousness in this era and a greater emphasis on lyrical content. Some performers bypassed the offerings of professional songwriters in favor of their own material, which they performed with exuberance. Los Angeles became the musical home of singers/songwriters such as Jessie Belvin, Elta James, Richard Berry, Young Jessie and Donald Woods, as well as vocal groups such as the Six Teens and the Penguins. They helped make Los Angeles a leader in popular music of the time, challenging not only the status quo of the occasionally stoic record industry (also based in Los Angeles), but also the creative juices of performers of other musical genres as well.

Rock 'n' roll was quickly embraced by a number of Los Angeles radio stations, most of which were started by disc-jockeys who combined effervescent personalities with an unabashed enthusiasm for this new means of musical self-expression. Their prominent position in the local media made many of them "messiahs" in the eyes and ears of their listeners, inspiring a fad that has since become an American tradition — cruising.

Cruising involves a group of friends driving an automobile or van on a popular street in search of a good time. Car radios have always been an integral part of cruising, a fact realized in the Fifties by local disc-jockey Art Laboe. Noticing that cruisers often made local drive-in restaurants their destination, Laboe began broadcasting at a popular Los Angeles drive-in, soon drawing a crowd of faithful followers. Many of them would shout record requests to Laboe from their cars. Cruising such popular boulevards as Sunset, Hollywood, Whitter and Van Nuys remains a favorite pastime among many teenagers to this day.

Folk Music And The Surf Sound

The late Fifties and early Sixties were periods of rapid development and change in America. And as a leading cultural center, California was quick to reflect this change in its music. The growing rebellion by the younger generation against a repressive society, and the political awareness brought about in part by the 1960 election of the cha-

275

rismatic John F. Kennedy to the presidency, necessitated a realistic yet positive outlook in the popular mood, and called for a change in popular music. The most logical outlet for this expression was folk music, a centuries-old form whose timelessness was insured by its ability to exemplify the human experience more succinctly than any other form.

Being a center of utopian ideology as well as cultural development, Los Angeles was quick to develop a folk music of its own, one that highlighted such unique virtues as the city's year-round summer, diverse aesthetic pursuits and high lifestyle. The answer was surf music, characterized by an upbeat rock 'n' roll setting and harmonious, exuberant vocals that extolled L.A. life — including fast cars and innocents in love. The move-

Television was quick to capture the essence of the surfing culture, broadcasting on the beach such popular rock 'n' roll programs as Dick Clark's *Where the Action Is* and *Malibu U*, the latter hosted by rock 'n' roll legend Rick Nelson. Beach-goers fortunate enough to be on the sand during the telecasts could mingle with the likes of Paul Revere and the Raiders, the Crossfires (later known as the Turtles) or Jackie and Gayle.

The Home of Folk-Rock

Nonetheless, America was once again to experience a drastic mood swing in the mid-Sixties. The assassination of John Kennedy in 1963, coupled with the escalating civil-rights movement and the growing disen-

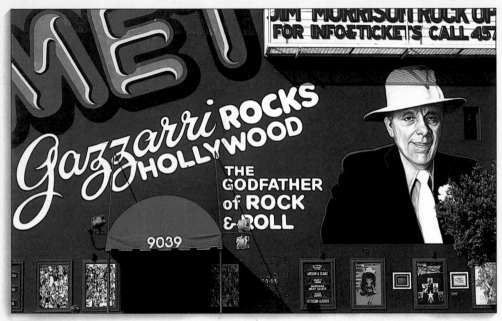

ment was led by The Beach Boys and Jan and Dean, whose slant towards realism in their lyrics (combined with subtle humor) helped give outside admirers a more balanced view of L.A. life.

The Beach Boys and Jan and Dean not only popularized surf music, but also served to create a whole new California culture. Many duly-inspired artists such as the Surfaris, Annette Funicello, Dick Dale, the Fantastic Baggys, Sandy Nelson, the Rip Chords and Carol Connors recorded worthwhile originals in the surf music idiom of the early Sixties. Their spirit was reflected in Hollywood by the motion picture industry with such films as *Beach Blanket Bingo*, *Ride the Wild Surf* and *How to Stuff a Wild Bikini*.

chantment with the U.S. involvement in Vietnam, led to a greater concern among the populace regarding the state of the nation. Again, Los Angeles was among the first to note this growing awareness.

The first change came with the development of folk-rock. Throughout 1964 and 1965, innovators such as the Inner Tube (later known as the Association), the Mamas and Papas, Shelby Flint, Bob Lind, Sonny and Cher, the Beefeaters (a group that eventually evolved into the Byrds), the Grass

Left, Gazzari's is one of the oldest surviving rock 'n' roll clubs on Sunset Strip. Right, sound technicians in a recording studio find the right mix for a major artist.

Roots and Love helped develop the style by incorporating the lyrical impact of the folk idiom into the driving rhythm of rock 'n' roll. Interestingly enough, some of the first champions and practitioners of folk-rock were the same artists who just two years earlier were extolling the virtues of California via surf rock. The Beach Boys and Jan and Dean made some of the most inventive folk-rock records of 1965–1966, as did the Surfaris, Fantastic Baggys, vocalist P.F. Sloan, the Rip Chords and the Turtles.

The unifying spirit of folk-rock quickly blossomed into a local music scene bursting with a camaraderie rarely seen in musical circles. The Sunset Strip became the most popular hangout for the musicians who championed the movement, inspiring club

from the Whisky sits the Roxy, which gained its fame at the beginning of the folk-rock era by being a meeting place for the likes of Donovan, Mama Cass Elliot and members of the Beau Brummels. The Roxy's laid-back atmosphere was a fertile breeding ground for musical ideas. More recently the Roxy has alternated between functioning as a theater (it was home of the *Rocky Horror Show*) and acting as a showplace for new-wave music.

Tex-Mex and Garage-Band

As if oblivious to the rising awareness brought about by rock on Los Angeles' west side, Spanish-influenced East Los Angeles was rapidly developing a musical sound of its

owners to open their doors to this new talent. By far, the most popular of these clubs was the Whisky a Go Go. Located on the Strip, the Whisky consisted of a small stage, a dining area with a capacity of about 100 persons, and a balcony bar that gave the club a sort of Old West feel, the perfect atmosphere for performer-audience interaction. It was not uncommon to walk into the Whisky and witness a performance by the likes of Johnny Rivers or Trini Lopez, the Byrds, the Doors, Love, Fleetwood Mac or the Everly Brothers. Though the Whisky a Go Go finally closed in August 1982, the club is currently undergoing remodeling, and will probably reopen in 1984.

Fewer than four blocks down the Strip

own. The subtle blend of *mariachi*, country and rock 'n' roll known as "Tex-Mex" rock became immensely popular in Southern California in 1964 and 1965. Largely inspired by the late Richie Valens, the East Los Angeles music scene produced a number of prolific talents, including The Midnighters, Cannibal and the Headhunters, the Blendells, the Premiers and the Sisters. (Valens, a native of nearby Pacoima, achieved legendary status upon his death with singers Buddy Holly and J.P. "Big Bopper" Richardson in a 1959 plane crash.)

The neat style of the Sixties has been referred to as garage-band music, perhaps the most potent, vital and exuberant form of musical expression to hit L.A. Garage-band music is primarily the basic raw energy of rhythm-and-blues coupled with a lyrical aggressiveness (again the folk influence) and frantic delivery inspired by the intensity of the style. Los Angeles had a superlative selection of practitioners of this musical genre — including the Monkees, Seeds, Standells, Stark Naked and the Car Thieves, Yellow Balloon, Painted Faces, Palace Guard, Mourning Reign, Paul Revere and the Raiders, the Music Machine, Avengers, Road Runners, Grains of Sand and the Four Making Do.

The popularity of garage-band music (so named because of the common practice of bands rehearsing in their garages) led to the establishment of a number of clubs catering to the new sound. One of the better ones

was It's Boss, located on the Sunset Strip, about one-half mile east of the Whisky a Go-Go. Known as Ciro's during the surf music heyday, It's Boss usually featured any local act fortunate enough to have a chart record at the moment. Today it is known as the Comedy Store; many successful comedians were given their first performing breaks there.

Another popular rock 'n' roll club was Doug Weston's Troubador, located on Santa Monica Boulevard in West Hollywood. Weston had a policy of signing performers to contracts for a certain number of appearances at his club. He would hold the contract until the performer became a star; the performer would then come back to play for

packed houses. Even Elton John performed there. Today it draws a heavy metal crowd.

Television also played a big role in the success of the music industry in the mid-Sixties with the arrival of such shows as *Shindig*, *Hollywood a Go-Go*, and Dick Clark's *American Bandstand*, which moved west from Philadelphia. This was also the beginning of the popular outdoor rock concerts, with The Beatles playing Hollywood Bowl and Dodger Stadium in consecutive years, followed by the Rolling Stones and other music giants.

The New-Wave Explosion

But despite its many musical attributes, Los Angeles is not without its musical regrets. The early Seventies brought a sharp decline in aesthetic creativity from local music writers. Then in the late Seventies, new wave blossomed. With venues such as Madame Wong's, Whisky and the Starwood (known many years ago as P.J.'s), Los Angeles became the home of groups such as the Go-Go's, Plimsouls and Germs. The new-wave explosion was unlike anything seen since the mid-Sixties.

Other forms of music such as rockabilly began to hit. New clubs such as the Lingerie on Sunset in Hollywood opened. New groups such as the Blasters, X, Circle Jerks and Berlin made it big. Even restaurants such as Barney's Beanery (another former hangout of the Mamas and Papas and the Byrds) and fast-food joints such as the Oki-Dog (a rowdy new-wave crowd) became hangouts for musicians once again.

Los Angeles, along with New York and Nashville, is considered one of the homes of the music industry. Performers too numerous to mention either got their start in L.A. or migrated there to learn the trade and make it big.

One reason they all came to L.A. was that most of the major record companies are based there. The executive offices of Capitol, Columbia, Warner Bros., Motown (it left Detroit in the Seventies), A & M, Electra, Atlantic, Arista, and even some flourishing independents such as Rhino are in Los Angeles.

Says one music magazine editor: "Groups know that if you come out to California, you'll always get record-industry people in to see you if the word spreads.

Left, music superstar Stevie Wonder puts a bearhug on actor Eddie Murphy at L.A.'s Hard Rock Cafe. Right, singer Pat Benatar, whose new-wave vocals rock America.

The sun has barely risen, but already the parking lot surrounding the three-story, cinder-block building is three-quarters full. As the people steadily trickle in through the double doors and head for one of several levels inside, each individual is focused on his own task, yet all minds share a common purpose: the making of the Southern California body.

This particular health club is in West Los Angeles. But it could be any one of hundreds in Southern California. Dozens of exotic-looking weight machines fill the mirrored main workout rooms — one each for men and women. On the uppermost floor, a line of enclosed racquetball courts is fronted by a phalanx of computerized stationary bicycles that can simulate leisurely Sunday afternoon rides or killer uphill struggles.

From the room on the left comes the grunting of men and women and the clinking of steel plates. To the right, the heavy bass of disco music means an aerobics class is in perpetual motion. Sporting carefully coordinated tights, leotards, leg warmers and headbands, the faithful bounce, kick and stretch to the music and the exhortations of well-proportioned instructresses.

A narrow, carpeted running track, hanging from the ceiling between the floors, is well used. So are the 25-metre long pool and the spacious whirlpools, saunas and steam rooms.

Given the plethora of health clubs from San Diego to San Bernardino to Santa Barbara, it seems that everyone in Southern California is a member of one somewhere. There is no small amount of truth in the cliché characterization of Southern Californians as being preoccupied with *The Look*, always striving to build *Body Beautiful*. A survey of the chic sidewalk cafés in Beverly Hills and the beach cities leaves an observer thinking the Southland is populated solely by actors and models — and those trying to look the part.

Joggers' Heaven

In an area so fertile and lucrative for sports, the fan is also the player.

In search of "The Look": left, an aerobic dancer at a Los Angeles health club; and right, a wrestler works out at The Golden Door in Escondido, near San Diego.

San Vicente Boulevard, which winds through the affluent West L.A. suburb of Brentwood and across the northern border of Santa Monica to famed Palisades Park, offers another crash course in the sports culture. Along this stretch of San Vicente, traffic is separated by a wide grassy divider that a generation ago carried streetcars. The grass itself is bisected now by single-file coral trees, named for their fiery blossoms.

Today this is joggers' heaven. When combined with the 1½ miles of Palisades Park, perched atop the cliffs looking out over the

Pacific Ocean, the boulevard offers a five-mile (eight-kilometer), grass-covered running strip interrupted only rarely by pavement and even less often by traffic signals. Part of the 1984 Olympic marathon (a 42-km race), will follow this scenic path.

Like San Vicente, other areas of Southern California are prime running spots — San Diego's Balboa Park, for example. This running lifestyle is obvious on virtually any weekend, when 10-kilometer races draw from a few hundred to several thousand competitors. The passing pageant is so diverse in size, age, style, dress and level of conditioning that it may seem running shoes and a determination to finish are the only common denominators.

Culver City, a community of 40,000 adjacent to West L.A. each December hosts the second-oldest continuously conducted marathon in the United States. A few miles north and usually on the same Sunday morning, perhaps the most glamorous 10-km race on the West Coast winds through the fabled streets of Beverly Hills.

San Diego hosts the annual Mission Bay Marathon. But the city's most popular race may be a half-marathon — the America's Finest City race, held every August. More than 6,500 runners, including several world-class men and women, answered the gun in the 1983 race. The 13.1 mile (21-km) event also has developed into a top draw for corporate running teams, which compete for a team title.

Nowadays the cycling hordes have a new shrine in the Los Angeles Harbor-area town of Carson: a velodrome built for the 1984 Olympics. It is located on the campus of California State University, Dominguez Hills.

The Beach Bangers

No doubt most people come to the beach to work on their tans or to frolic in the breakers. But hundreds or even thousands are attracted by the high-class volleyball competition. Just about anywhere along the coast, four people can string up an eight-foot-high net, lay out a court using rope staked at the four corners, and play a beach

They may have been born in Hawaii, but triathalons came to California to grow up. The islands still host the premier "Ironman" race, but cannot match the Mainland in offering chances to compete in this growing and grueling sport that combines open-water swimming, cycling and running. During one representative month, 13 triathalons of varying lengths were scheduled from Lake Tahoe to Mission Viejo (Orange County) to Mission Bay.

Southern California is also bicycle crazy, as indicated by the number of clubs. Members of the Marina del Rey Bicycle Club, Pacific Cyclists, Foothill Cycle Club and many others can be found pedaling in the mountains, coast roads and even off-road.

volleyball game. Some pretty famous athletes, such as basketball great Wilt Chamberlain, frequently join in.

For the competitive, summer brings a series of tournaments for two-person teams at all levels from novice to the "AA pros," hosted by beaches from San Diego to Malibu. Many beach bangers have made it to the U.S. Olympic team over the years, then return to join the beach ranks in weekly combat.

But it's way out there in the blue — in the

Left, a Windsurfer takes to the waves off Newport Beach. Right, the Los Angeles Rams football team lines up against the San Francisco 49ers in professional action.

water, that is — that aficionados of the sport most closely identified with Southern California can be found. The surfing spots immortalized in the songs of The Beach Boys now are seeing a second generation of devotees riding a new generation of boards. Design technology has replaced the nine-foot, blunt-nosed planks with more buoyant, maneuverable, dagger-tipped boards that often do not stand as tall as their riders.

Many of the best surfers hop up and down the Southern California coastline competing in a series of Grand Prix events sponsored by makers of surfing-related products. The contests are part of the year-long surfing world tour that tests waves and riders from Australia to South Africa. Since California rarely provides waves to rival the monsters in

coalesced into a patent for something they called a Windsurfer.

The acceptance and proliferation of their invention — a plastic board equipped with small centerboard, a pivoting mast and a wishbone-shaped boom — has outlived the partnership. Schweitzer still owns the patent and the Windsurfer Company, but he and Drake now find themselves on opposite sides of a legal action.

Thousands of the boards have been produced by Windsurfer and by other firms, with or without permission. The brightly colored, wedge-shaped sails have become an institution of summer. Sailboards (as they are properly known) can ply across a lake or a protected harbor, or can take on the open ocean with pounding waves to test the rider's

Hawaii, West Coast surfers learn to pack their shorter rides with every slashing maneuver the smaller waves offer.

Ironically, just as surfing was being absorbed into the national consciousness during the early Sixties — aided by The Beach Boys' tunes and a short-lived string of "beach blanket" movies — an idea was germinating that eventually would blossom into a sports industry to rival the Hawaiian-born surfing craze.

Two Southern California aeronautical engineers with a love of sailing and skiing pondered a way to sail a one-man craft while standing up. When one of the engineers, James Drake, joined forces with a friend who surfed, Hoyle Schweitzer, concepts

acrobatic imagination.

The sport comes of age in 1984, when the first Olympic sailboard competitors slice through the waters of Los Angeles Harbor as part of the 1984 Summer Games.

Professional Sports

Inextricably linked to the participant-sports lifestyle in Southern California are the professional teams that entertain and inspire.

Any examination of the area's pros from the top down could start at only one place: Dodger Stadium. Having bailed out of Brooklyn (New York) in 1958, where they had spent decades as the beloved "Bums," the Los Angeles Dodgers can claim the title of the most financially successful sporting venture in American history.

Drawn by the Dodgers' colorful play, by their annual contention for the National League championship and a spot in the World Series, and by the club's canny community relations, the faithful pour through the Dodger Stadium turnstiles each year at a rate that would make any two rival teams envious. Pulling in nightly crowds averaging 40,000 or more throughout a six-month season has become a Dodger tradition that has defied every other baseball team and every other sport. They have twice drawn more than 3 million a year in home attendance.

The Dodgers have rewarded their fans with a handful of league and divisional titles over the past decade, and in 1981 captured their first world championship since the glory days of Sandy Koufax and Don Drysdale in the mid-Sixties.

An hour's drive south on the Santa Ana Freeway from Dodger Stadium is the fortress of Southern California's only American League entry. In the two decades of their existence, the California Angels have yet to bring the World Series to Anaheim Stadium. Perhaps more importantly, however, they did bring big-time sports to Orange County.

The trail to Orange County blazed by the Angels in the Sixties was followed 15 years later by Los Angeles' original entry in the National Football League — the Rams. Before meeting his death in the Florida surf, Rams' owner Carroll Rosenbloom set the stage for his team to leave the L.A. Coliseum (after three decades) in favor of new facilities at Anaheim Stadium and possibly greener pastures among the football-hungry masses in burgeoning Orange County. The Rams made their only trip to the Super Bowl following the 1979 season, losing to the Pittsburgh Steelers.

A somewhat similar scenario was played out two years later in Oakland on the east side of San Francisco Bay, where the Raiders gave their fans a Super Bowl title in 1981, then packed up and headed south to fill the void left by the Rams in the venerable Coliseum. It took two years' worth of court battles before the move was allowed, since the NFL and city of Oakland wanted the black-shirts to stay put. The Raiders climaxed their first year as Southern Californians by defeating the Washington Redskins in the 1984 Super Bowl.

San Diego has sported a pro football team twice as long as a major league baseball club. But neither the NFL Chargers nor the National League Padres has brought a world title home to the border city.

The Chargers have teetered on the doorstep of the Super Bowl for years, but never have taken the final step into the January showdown for NFL supremacy. Since their early days as a charter member of the old American Football League, the Chargers relied on a passing attack that could always put points on the board by the dozen. Quarterback Dan Fouts, born and raised in California, was the NFL's most valuable player for the 1982 season.

The Padres, meanwhile, have had to struggle for acceptance and respectability alongside their longer established northern neighbors, the Dodgers and the San Francisco Giants. While never contending for a division title themselves, the Padres have continually improved. They have earned a reputation for spoiling the late-season pennant drives of their rivals.

Basketball and Ice Hockey

On the basketball court, few teams can match the steady success of the Los Angeles Lakers. Conversely, the San Diego Clippers' history in the National Basketball Association is distinguished by a steady lack of achievement.

The Lakers left Minneapolis and followed the Dodgers west as the Fifties came to a close. Soon the team was a perennial contender. But the Lakers' failure in several championship series (usually against the Boston Celtics) earned them the tag of sports bridesmaids — until the record-breaking season of 1971-72. Their first crown topped off a campaign that featured a record 33-game winning streak. With a completely different cast of coaches and players, headed by superstar center Kareem Abdul-Jabbar, the Lakers added titles in 1980 and 1982.

Further south, since joining the NBA as an expansion entry in the Seventies, the Clippers have gone through a string of owners, coaches and players without finding a winning combination.

Such also has been the legacy of the Los Angeles Kings, Southern California's entry in the National Hockey League. The rabidly loyal following of ice-hockey fans who flock to The Forum in Inglewood each winter are still waiting for the Kings to make a real run at the Stanley Cup, symbolic of the NHL championship.

An exhausted high school runner is congratulated by another competitor, left. Following pages, thousands compete in a 10-kilometer run through the strets of L.A.

I Love You California

Words by
F. B. SILVERWOOD.

Music by
A. F. FRANKENSTEIN.

Will Farrand Wilson.
May 19th 1913.

Marziale.

Copyrighted 1913 by F. B. Silverwood.

Mary Garden stopped Grand Opera
to make this California song famous

SOUTHERN CALIFORNIA MUSIC CO.
DISTRIBUTORS
332-334 SO. BROADWAY   LOS ANGELES, CAL.

SPIRIT OF HOPE: L.A.'S 1932 OLYMPICS

It was the worst of times. But it was the best of Olympics.

When Los Angeles was awarded the 1932 Olympics, it was the Roaring Twenties (1923, to be exact), a time of euphoria after the nervous years of World War I. Los Angeles had just completed the 76,000-seat Coliseum, partially in anticipation of hosting the Olympics, and the city was at the apex of its post-war building boom.

By the time the Games took place, though, the world was wallowing in depression, and it almost looked like Los Angeles

at the Coliseum (its seating capacity had been expanded for the Games) had been sold. Athletes from some 40 nations marched into the stadium, having scraped up the travel funds. Brazil's athletes came on a coffee boat that stopped at various ports to sell its goods and finance the Olympic trip.

Los Angeles proceeded to put on a remarkable Olympiad — athletically, aesthetically and socially. Its success, especially in the midst of such hard times, had much to do with the hospitality of the city, and with the innovation and ingenuity of its organizers led

would have to answer the question, "What if we gave an Olympics and nobody came?" European and South American nations, carefully counting scarce monies, wondered if they could afford to send athletes halfway around the world to the West Coast of the United States. Impoverished residents of Los Angeles wondered if they could afford to buy tickets to the Games, even though they cost only $1 or $2.

By January 1932, scarcely any tickets had been sold, and the Los Angeles organizers still didn't know how many countries would actually attend the Games. But by April, ticket sales began to pick up. By June they had exploded, and on July 30, 1932, the last of 105,000 tickets to the opening ceremonies

by William May Garland.

The Los Angeles Games were the first to provide an Olympic Village to house athletes. Built on a 250-acre (101-hectare) hillside area in Baldwin Hills, the Village consisted of 500 plywood cabins (many sold as beach cottages after the Games), a post office, fire station, hospital, telegraph office, theater, and dining halls run by chefs familiar with each nation's cuisine. (The Village *didn't* include any of the nearly 200 women Olympians among its 2,000 temporary resi-

Left, a ticket for 1932 competition; prices are considerably higher in 1984! Right, the '32 Olympic Village was the first ever constructed expressly for athletes.

dents, though. They stayed in Hollywood's elegant Chapman Park Hotel.)

In past Olympics, each country had housed its athletes separately, but the reasoning behind the Village concept was financial: since the countries could barely afford boat fare, they appreciated being offered inexpensive lodging and food ($2 per person per day). The athletes appreciated even more the camaraderie engendered by the Village, where they could meet and mingle with fellow competitors and experience the true international spirit of the

into a cycling velodrome with a banked wooden track. (The wood was later used to panel the interior of a house in Pasadena.) The Olympic Auditorium in downtown Los Angeles, privately built in 1925, was leased to the Olympics for wrestling, weightlifting and boxing. (After the Games it became the property of the Los Angeles Athletic Club.) The State Armory — constructed in 1912 and now an exhibit hall for the Museum of Science and Industry in Exposition Park — served as the fencing venue. Shooters competed at the range of the Los Angeles

Games. The Olympic fans liked the Village too, as they could congregate outside the gates to grab autographs or glimpses of their heroes, or merely gaze out at the magnificent view of the city below, twinkling with jewel-like lights at night.

The 1932 organizers took out a $1 million bond issue from the state (which they later repaid) to support the Games. They didn't waste taxpayers' money building elaborate new sites for the events (other than the Coliseum, which was already serving as a football stadium, and the swim stadium adjacent to it). Los Angeles simply, and less expensively, modified the facilties it already had. Pasadena's Rose Bowl, known for its annual New Year's football game, was transformed

Police Academy in Elysian Park.

The city of Long Beach did have to dredge its lagoon an additional 500 meters to accommodate the rowing races. Although the course is no longer suitable for Olympic competition, it's still a favorite practice spot for rowing events.

The streets of Los Angeles became Olympic sites for the marathon and the 100-kilometer bicycle race. But the center of action was definitely the Coliseum, which held not only track and field, but gymnastics, an American football exhibition and some equestrian events as well.

In men's track and field, eight world records were set, but spectators remembered the competitive excitement of certain races meter race, called by hyperbolic sportswriter Braven Dyer "the greatest 400-meter race ever run on this planet," was a vivid duel between American Bill Carr (the winner) and Ben Eastman. The 5,000-meter race featured a valiant, unexpected challenge to Finnish superiority in distance races by the University of Oregon's Ralph Hill. He twice tried to veer around Finland's Lauri Lehtinen in the home stretch but was blocked each time and lost. Cries of foul were heard in the Coliseum, but announcer Bill Henry calmed the disappointed American fans with the words, "Remember, please, these people are our guests."

Babe Didrikson's Olympics

World records were set in all six of the women's track and field events, all but one by Americans. And even that one, the 100 meters, was won by a woman who lived in America under the name Stella Walsh but competed for her native Poland as Stanislawa Walasiewicz.

The heroine of women's track and field — and of the entire 1932 Games — was clearly Mildred "Babe" Didrikson, the tomboyish super-athlete from Beaumont, Texas. Didrikson came to L.A. fresh from an amazing performance at the national track and field championships, where in three hours she had won six events, set four world records, and won the *team* championship although she was the sole member of her squad. Not surprisingly, she had gained quite a swelled head, and arrived in Los Angeles bragging that she could win any event, even though she was only allowed to enter but three. This didn't endear her to her U.S. teammates, but the fans loved her.

And she almost made good on her boasts. First she won the javelin, then the 80-meter hurdles (in a still-disputed photo finish with Evelyn Hall). She missed a third gold in the high jump, despite clearing the same height as her rival Jean Shiley. Babe was bumped to second place when the judges decided she had illegally "dived" head-first over the bar. Nonetheless, the 1932 Olympics had served as the world's introduction to Babe Didrikson. Her continued excellence in a variety of sports after that (especially golf) later earned her the title, "Woman Athlete of the Half Century."

As the U.S. women had swept the diving medals, so did the U.S. men. But in men's swimming, it was a Japanese show almost all the way. The only American man to win a swimming gold medal was Clarence "Buster" Crabbe, who parlayed that victory and

his rugged good looks into an acting career as Tarzan and Flash Gordon.

Americans also triumphed in men's gymnastics (winning 15 medals, including five golds); in wrestling (three golds and two silvers), in yachting (two golds, one silver); and rowing (three golds). The eight-oared rowing match turned out to be one of the highlights of the Games. Some 80,000 people lined the rowing path to watch a to-the-wire duel between the United States and Italy. As the American team, made up of University of California at Berkeley students, passed the Italians in the last stretch, a roar went up from the partisan crowd that was (recalls one observer) "like thunder."

Of course, athletes from a number of other countries did quite well in the 1932 Games, though it must be remembered that these were the times before there was an Eastern Bloc dedicated to athletic supremacy. The British were fine runners (as they were in the 1924 *Chariots of Fire* Olympics), the Italians excelled in cycling and fencing, the French in equestrian sports and weight-lifting, the Swedes in the modern pentathlon and wrestling, the Hungarians in gymnastics.

In all, it was an Olympics that achieved the worldwide athletic interplay that is the Olympic mission. But since it was in Los Angeles — the film capital of the world — it had a decidedly Hollywood flair as well. Athletes were invited to fancy luncheons and balls, to a reception with Douglas Fairbanks and Mary Pickford at their Pickfair mansion, and to a popular morning radio program. For Jean Shiley, a trip to actor Conrad Nagel's beach house was almost as good as beating Babe Didrikson. "He was the sexiest man I'd ever seen," she remembered 50 years later.

The Olympics changed nearly every competitor's life. Many on the U.S. team later moved to Los Angeles, impressed by the great weather. And people from small towns, who had little money at the time, got a chance to make contact with people and cultures they might never have known.

The Olympics changed the city of Los Angeles as well. No more would it be a place known just for oranges and movie studios. It has gone *international*, providing a spirit of hope to the world in the darkest of times.

As the Olympics return to Los Angeles in 1984, it won't be a unique arrival. It will be as if an old friend has returned.

Babe Didrikson nips Evelyne Adams Hall by a neck in the controversial finish of the 80-meter hurdles at the 1932 games.

THE 1984 OLYMPIC GAMES

When the Olympics return to Los Angeles in 1984 after a 52-year hiatus, it will be a dream come true for those citizens who have labored four decades to bring them back. Hopefully, these Olympics will be as innovative — and as successful — as their predecessor.

It was the success of the 1932 Olympics, capped by the $1 million surplus that the Olympic Committee returned to the state of California after the Games — that inspired Southern Californians to start lobbying for another Los Angeles Olympiad just seven years after the first one had ended. William May Garland, who had presided over the 1932 Olympic Committee, was elected to head the Southern California Committee for the Olympic Games (SCCOG). He served in that capacity until his death in 1948, aided by a variety of Olympic boosters and wealthy businessmen.

To raise money for SCCOG, the committee sponsored the annual Coliseum Relays, an international track meet that showcased top athletes and performances for 30 years. But while the Relays were going well, the Olympic bid was not. There were no Olympics in the years of World War II, and Los Angeles didn't make any headway in the Fifties. In the Olympiads from 1960 to 1972, Los Angeles couldn't even win the support of the U.S. Olympic Committee. Detroit was selected as the American candidate city in those years.

Finally, the USOC authorized Los Angeles to make a bid to the International Olympic Committee (IOC) for the 1976 Olympics. However, Moscow made a last-minute entry into the bidding for that year and, as a compromise, the IOC selected Montreal.

The First 'Private' Olympics

Moscow then got the nod for 1980, but in 1977 Los Angeles became the favorite for the 1984 Games. Suddenly several other U.S. cities expressed interest in the Games: Atlanta, Boston, Chicago, New Orleans and, most seriously, New York. New York's presentation to the USOC was expensive and traditional. It promised to build lavish

A Singaporean archer aims for the bull's eye in pre-Olympic trials at El Dorado Park, Long Beach. Only the best will qualify.

new facilities for the Games, paid for by the government, and projected a closing deficit of $200 to $300 million. Los Angeles, on the other hand, took an entirely different tack unique among recent Olympic hosts. The Games would be privately financed, with very few new facilities, and would even show a slight profit when the torch was extinguished.

Well aware of the financial disaster suffered by Montreal in 1976 (a $1 billion construction deficit), the USOC put its trust to Los Angeles and its iconoclastic plan. And then it was time for the American city to compete for the Games internationally. But when the only other candidate — Tehran, Iran — withdrew, there was no competition.

Los Angeles should have been a shoo-in at that point, but its unorthodox financing plan — and especially its requirement that the city not be held financially liable, as the IOC demanded — led to a year of frustrating negotiations. At one point, Mayor Tom Bradley formally requested the City Council of Los Angeles to withdraw its Olympic bid. Finally, with no other contenders for the 1984 Games, the IOC agreed to suspend Rule 4 of its charter and accept that the liability in 1984 would be shared by the local organizing committee and the USOC, but *not* the Los Angeles taxpayer.

The contract for the 1984 Olympics in Los Angeles was signed on Oct. 20, 1978. The new Los Angeles Olympic Organizing Committee (LAOOC), now chaired by Paul Ziffren, set about the task of preparing for the first "private" Olympic Games.

LAOOC selected travel-agency entrepreneur Peter Ueberroth as president of the committee. He entered his new job with "a cardboard box with $300,000 in debts, no employees, no phones, no plan" — and no key to the door of the committee's first office because LAOOC couldn't pass a credit check.

'The Corporate Games'

The 1984 Olympics have been dubbed "The Corporate Games" because of the sponsorship factor: 30 large corporations have each donated at least $4 million to the Olympic cause.

In past Olympics, the host city solicited any number of advertisers to sign up as the "Official Olympic This" or the "Official

Olympic That." At the 1980 Winter Games in Lake Placid, New York, for example, there were 381 official sponsors. But they contributed a total of only $9 million for the use of the Olympic name.

The Los Angeles Games severely limited the number of sponsors, but upped the ante. Not only were the sponsors required to donate a large sum of money; they generally will provide services to the LAOOC as well. IBM, for example, has computerized the Games; AT&T supplies phone lines; Transamerica is insuring the Olympics. The most prominent use of sponsorship monies, besides the $225 million for American television rights paid by ABC, has been the building of the only two new facilities for the Games: the 7-Eleven Velodrome for cycling

The Olympic Villages, unlike those in recent Olympiads, will be as far−flung as the sites. One will be at UCLA, one at USC, and one at the University of California in Santa Barbara (not far from Lake Casitas). All will use existing university dormitories. Some people have complained that spreading out the athletes will ruin the experience of camaraderie engendered by the one - village concept. Others realize that these cost - efficient Games required the committee to make the most of existing facilities. "We invented the concept of the Olympic Village [in 1932]," John Argue, the longtime head of the SCCOG has said. "We're disinventing it."

The work of the LAOOC over the past

and the McDonald's Swim Stadium. Despite the use of the sponsors' names in current advertising, the LAOOC promises that advertisements will be kept *out* of the venues during the Games.

Corporations have supplied other important elements of the Games: ARCO has built practice tracks at local universities; other corporations are contributing to Olympic youth programs. Indeed, anyone can contribute to the youth and make Olympic history: $3000 buys one kilometer in the Olympic torch relay, and the money will be given to youth sports.

The LAOOC, in its thriftiness, has built only two new facilities and has mostly made do with existing sports facilities.

five years has inspired both admiration and criticicism. Despite assurances that taxpayers won't pay a cent for the Olympics, some people are afraid local governments will have to increase their budgets to meet Olympic needs. LAOOC counters with reports that the Games will *add* revenue to local governments.

Other criticisms leveled against the Los Angeles Olympics have less to do with the LAOOC than with the city itself. Smog, for example, has been cited as a threat to

Left, L.A. Coliseum, site of the 1984 track and field competition. Right, Sam the Olympic Eagle, official mascot of the '84 Games, is flanked by runners at a dedication.

athletes' well-being. The organizers have tried to take this into consideration, scheduling events at the most smog-free hours of the day, but undoubtedly there *will* be smog.

Another concern is traffic, that infamous Los Angeles menace. Transportation planners have determined that the worst jams will occur near the Coliseum, where three events (track and field, boxing, swimming and diving) will sometimes be taking place simultaneously, and in Westwood, the already-crowded shopping area bordering UCLA. Ticket holders will be encouraged to take buses to these venues and the others. Special signs and routing will be designed to diminish the hassle. However, the freeways may be overwhelmed at various times. A particular freeway to avoid will

lowed the deaths of 269 persons when a Korean airliner was downed over Soviet air space in September 1983.

Ueberroth, however, has staunchly sought to separate the Olympics from politics, going so far as to denounce the 1980 Olympic boycott by the United States and to encourage citizens and governments not to penalize athletes for the actions of their national leaders. He hopes that all eligible nations will participate in the 1984 Games.

As the 1932 Olympics helped Los Angeles emerge as an international city, the 1984 Games will once again focus attention on the West Coast. Within the city, perhaps a new enthusiasm will be generated for amateur sports that will carry on past the Games. The widespread youth programs, which teach

be Interstate 405 (the San Diego Freeway), along which no fewer than seven Olympic venues are sited.

Political Threats

Two other unfortunate Olympic-related problems are major concerns to the Los Angeles organizers: terrorism and international politics. Elaborate security systems are being designed to thwart terrorism. Politics has already affected participation in pre-Olympic events. China withheld its athletes from several contests in protest against the defection of tennis player Hu Na, and the Soviet Union cancelled out of several competitions after negative backlash fol-

youngsters about unfamiliar Olympic sports, may help the U.S. increase participation in those sports.

And once again, Los Angeles can serve as a beacon of hope in troubled times. In 1932, the Games took place in the midst of depression. In 1984, the world is again in difficult economic straits, and is torn apart by wars in numerous areas of the globe.

Yet in the summer of 1984, people from around the world can meet for two weeks of harmonious, exciting, inspiring competition. The swords won't pierce flesh; the guns won't be aimed at people. Just as the ancient Greeks stopped their conflicts during the Olympics, so too will athletes in Los Angeles.

OLYMPIC SCHEDULES

ARCHERY
(El Dorado Park, Long Beach)

Aug 8 — 70m (women) and 90m (men), 10 a.m. to 12:45 p.m. 60m (women) and 70m (men), 2:30 to 5 p.m.

Aug 9 — 50m (women) and 50m (men), 10 a.m. to 1 p.m. 30m (women) and 30m (men), 2:30 to 5:15 p.m.

Aug 10 — 70m (women) and 90m (men), 10 a.m. to 12:45 p.m. 60m (women) and 70m (men), 2:30 to 5 p.m.

Aug 11 — 50m (women) and 50m (men), 10 a.m. to 1 p.m. 30m (women) and 30m (men), 2:30 to 5:15 p.m.

BASEBALL
(Dodger Stadium)

July 31 — 2 games (preliminaries), 4 to 11 p.m.
Aug 1 — 2 games (preliminaries), 4 to 11 p.m.
Aug 2 — 2 games (preliminaries), 4 to 11 p.m.
Aug 3 — 2 games (preliminaries), 1 to 8 p.m.
Aug 4 — 2 games (preliminaries), 10 a.m. to 5 p.m.
Aug 5 — 2 games (preliminaries), 1 to 8 p.m.
Aug 6 — 2 games (semifinals), 1 to 8 p.m.
Aug 7 — 2 games (finals), 4 to 11 p.m.

BASKETBALL
(The Forum, Inglewood)

July 29 — 2 games (preliminaries, men), 9 a.m. to 12:30 p.m. 2 games (preliminaries, men), 2:30 to 6 p.m. 2 games (preliminaries, men), 8 to 11:30 p.m.

July 30 — 1 game (round robin, women), 1 game (preliminary, men), 9 a.m. to 12:30 p.m. 1 game (round robin, women), 1 game (preliminary, men), 2:30 to 6 p.m. 1 game (round robin, women), 1 game (premliminary, men), 8 to 11:30 p.m.

July 31 — 1 game (round robin, women), 1 game (preliminary, men), 9 a.m. to 12:30 p.m. 1 game (round robin, women), 1 game (preliminary, men), 2:30 to 6 p.m. 1 gam (round robin, women), 1 game (preliminary, men), 8 to 11:30 p.m.

Aug 1 — 2 games (preliminaries, men), 9 a.m. to 12:30 p.m. 2 games (preliminaries, men), 2:30 to 6 p.m. 2 games (preliminaries, men), 8 to 11:30 p.m.

Aug 2 — 1 game (round robin, women), 1 game (preliminary, men), 9 a.m. to 12:30 p.m. 1 game (round robin, women), 1 game (preliminary, men), 2:30 to 6 p.m. 1 game (round robin,

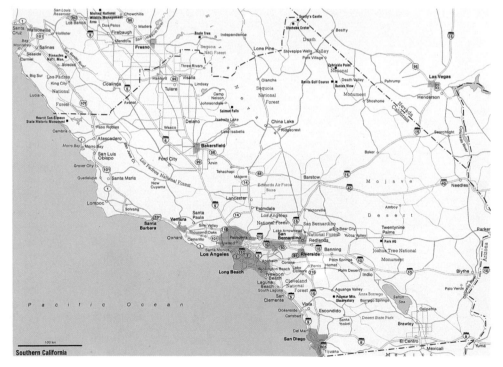

Southern California

women), 1 game (preliminary, men), 8 to 11:30 p.m.

Aug 3 — 1 game (round robin, women), 1 game (preliminary, men), 9 a.m. to 12:30 p.m. 1 game (round robin, women), 1 game (preliminary, men), 2:30 to 6 p.m. 1 game (round robin, women), 1 game (preliminary, men), 8 to 11:30 p.m.

Aug 4 — 2 games (preliminaries, men), 9 a.m. to 12:30 p.m. 2 games (preliminaries, men), 2:30 to 6 p.m. 2 games (preliminaries, men), 8 to 11:30 p.m.

Aug 5 — 2 games (round robin, women), 9 a.m. to 12:30 p.m. 1 game (semifinal, men consolation), 2:30 to 4:15 p.m. 1 game (round robin, women), 1 game (semifinal, men consolation), 6:30 to 10 p.m.

Aug 6 — 2 games (quarterfinals, men), 10 a.m. to 1:30 p.m. 2 games (quarterfinals, men), 5 to 8:30 p.m.

Aug 7 — 2 games (finals: 1-4 places, women), 5 to 8:30 p.m.

Aug 8 — 2 games (semifinals, men), 10 a.m. to 1:30 p.m. 2 games (semifinals, men), 5 to 8:30 p.m.

Aug 9 — 2 games (finals: 9-12 places, men), 10 a.m. to 1:30 p.m. 1 game (final: 3-4 places, men), 7 to 8:45 p.m.

Aug 10 — 2 games (finals: 5-8 places, men), 10 a.m. to 1:30 p.m. 1 game (final: 1-2 places, men), 7 to 8:45 p.m.

BOXING
(Los Angeles Sports Arena)

July 29 — Preliminary bouts 11 a.m. to 2 p.m., 6 to 9:30 p.m.

July 30 — Preliminary bouts 11 a.m. to 2 p.m., 6 to 9:30 p.m.

July 31 — Preliminary bouts 11 a.m. to 2 p.m., 6 to 9:30 p.m.

Aug 1 — Preliminary bouts 11 a.m. to 2 p.m., 6 to 9:30 p.m.

Aug 2 — Preliminary bouts 11 a.m. to 2 p.m., 6 to 9:30 p.m.

Aug 3 — Preliminary bouts 11 a.m. to 2 p.m., 6 to 9:30 p.m.

Aug 4 — Preliminary bouts 11 a.m. to 2 p.m., 6 to 9:30 p.m.

Aug 5 — Preliminary bouts 11 a.m. to 2 p.m., 6 to 9:30 p.m.

Aug 6 — Preliminary bouts 11 a.m. to 2 p.m., 6 to 9:30 p.m.

Aug 7 — Quarterfinal bouts 11 a.m. to 2 p.m., 6 to 9 p.m.

Aug 8 — Quarterfinal bouts 11 a.m. to 2 p.m., 6 to 9 p.m.

Aug 9 — Semifinal bouts 11 a.m. to 2 p.m., 6 to 9 p.m.

Aug 11 — Final bouts 11 a.m. to 2 p.m., 6 to 9 p.m.

CANOEING
(Lake Casitas, Ventura County)

Aug 6 — 500m heats (men & women), 7:30 to 10:45 a.m. 500m repechage (men & women), 4:30

to 6:45 p.m.

Aug 7 — 1,000m heats (men), 500m (women), 7:30 to 10:45 a.m. 1,000m repechage (men), 500m repechage (women), 4:30 to 6:45 p.m.

Aug 8 — 500m semifinals (men & women), 7:30 to 10:30 a.m.

Aug 9 — 1,000m semifinals (men), 500m semifinals (women), 7:30 to 10:30 a.m.

Aug 10 — 500m finals (men & women), 8 to 10:30 a.m.

Aug 11 — 1,000m finals (men), 8 to 10:30 a.m.

CYCLING
(California State Univ., Dominguez Hills)

July 29 — 190km individual road race (men), 9 a.m. to 2 p.m. 70km individual road race (women) (held in Mission Viejo, Orange County), 3 to 5:30 p.m.

July 30 — Individual pursuit qualification; 1 km time trial final, 10 a.m. to 1 p.m.

July 31 — Individual pursuit quarterfinals; Sprint repechage, Points race qualification, 10 a.m. to 3 p.m.

Aug 1 — Individual pursuit semifinals & finals; Sprint quarterfinals; Points race qualification, 10 a.m. to 3 p.m.

Aug 2 — Sprint semifinals; Team pursuit qualification & quarterfinals, 10 a.m. to 3 p.m.

Aug 3 — Sprint finals; Team pursuit semifinals & finals; Points race final, 10 a.m. to 3 p.m.

Aug 5 — 100km road race team time trial (held on Artesia Freeway, State 91), 8 a.m. to 1 p.m.

DIVING
(University of Southern California)

Aug 5 — Springboard preliminaries (women), 10 a.m. to 12:30 p.m. Springboard preliminaries (women), 3 to 5:30 p.m.

Aug 6 — Springboard finals (women), 4:30 to 6 p.m.

Aug 7 — Springboard preliminaries (men), 10 a.m. to 1 p.m. Springboard preliminaries (men), 4 to 6:30 p.m.

Aug 8 — Springboard finals (men), 4:30 to 6:30 p.m.

Aug 9 — Platform preliminaries (women), 10 a.m. to 12 noon. Platform preliminaries (women), 4:30 to 6:30 p.m.

Aug 10 — Platform finals (women), 4:30 to 6:30 p.m.

Aug 11 — Platform preliminaries (men), 10 a.m. to 12 noon. Platform preliminaries (men), 3 to 5 p.m.

Aug 12 — Platform finals (men), 11 a.m. to 1 p.m.

EQUESTRIAN
(Santa Anita Park, Arcadia)

July 29 — Three-day event, dressage test, 8 a.m. to 6 p.m.

July 30 — Three-day event, dressage test, 8 a.m. to 6 p.m.

Aug 1 — Three-day event, endurance test (held at Fairbanks Country Club, San Diego

County), 10 a.m. to 6 p.m.

Aug 3 — Three-day event, jumping test, 11:30 a.m. to 2:30 p.m.

Aug 4 — Jumping training competition, 2 to 6 p.m.

Aug 7 — Team jumping competition, 10 a.m. to 2 p.m.

Aug 8 — Team dressage competition, 2 to 6 p.m.

Aug 9 — Team dressage competition, 2 to 6 p.m.

Aug 10 — Individual dressage competition, 2 to 5 p.m.

Aug 12 — Individual jumping competition, 7 a.m. to 2 p.m.

FENCING
(Long Beach Convention Center)

Aug 1 — Foil: individual preliminaries (men), 9 a.m. to 6 p.m.

Aug 2 — Foil: individual preliminaries (men & women), 9 a.m. to 5 p.m. Foil: individual finals (men), 8 to 11 p.m.

Aug 3 — Foil: individual preliminaries (women); Sabre: individual preliminaries (men), 9 a.m. to 5 p.m. Foil: individual finals (women), 8 to 11 p.m.

Aug 4 — Foil: team preliminaries (men); Sabre: individual preliminaries (men), 9 a.m. to 5 p.m. Sabre: individual finals (men), 8 to 11 p.m.

Aug 5 — Foil: team preliminaries (men & women), 9 a.m. to 6 p.m. Foil: team finals (men), 8 to 11 p.m.

Aug 7 — Foil: team preliminaries (women); Epée: individual preliminaries (men), 9 a.m. to 6 p.m. Foil: team finals (women), 8 to 11 p.m.

Aug 8 — Sabre: tam preliminaries (men); Epée: individual: preliminaries (men), 9 a.m. to 5 p.m. Epee: individual finals (men), 8 to 11 p.m.

Aug 9 — Sabre: team preliminaries (men), 12 noon to 6 p.m. Sabre: team finals (men), 8 to 11 p.m.

Aug 10 — Epée: team preliminaries (men), 10 a.m. to 4 p.m.

Aug 11 — Epée: team preliminaries (men), 10 a.m. to 6 p.m. Epée: team finals (men), 8 t0 11 p.m.

GYMNASTICS
(University of California, Los Angeles)

July 29 — Compulsory exercises (men), 9:30 to 11:30 a.m., 2 to 4 p.m., 6:30 to 8:30 p.m.

July 30 — Compulsory exercises (women), 10 a.m. to 12:45 p.m., 5:30 to 8:15 p.m.

July 31 — Optional exercises (men), 9:30 to 11:30 a.m., 2 to 4 p.m., Optional exercises: team finals (men), 6:30 to 8:30 p.m.

Aug 1 — Optional exercises (women), 10 a.m. to 12:45 p.m. Optional exercises: team finals (women), 5:30 to 8:15 p.m.

Aug 2 — All-around finals (men), 5:30 to 8:30 p.m.

Aug 3 — All-around finals (women), 5:30 to 8 p.m.

Aug 4 — Apparatus finals (men), 5:30 to 8:30 p.m.

Aug 5 — Apparatus finals (women), 5:30 to 7:30 p.m.

Aug 9 — Rhythmic preliminaries (women), 6:30 to 10:30 p.m.

Aug 10 — Rhythmic preliminaries (women), 6:30 to 10:30 p.m.

Aug 11 — Rhythmic finals (women), 8 to 10:30 p.m.

HANDBALL (Team)
(California State University, Fullerton)

July 31 — 3 games (preliminaries, men), 11 a.m. to 3:30 p.m., 6:30 to 11 p.m.

Aug 1 — 3 games (round robin, women), 6:30 to 11 p.m.

Aug 2 — 3 games (preliminaries, men), 11 a.m. to 3:30 p.m., 6:30 to 11 p.m.

Aug 3 — 3 games (round robin, women), 6:30 to 11 p.m.

Aug 4 — 3 games (preliminaries, men), 11 a.m. to 3:30 p.m., 6:30 to 11 p.m.

Aug 5 — 3 games (round robin, women), 6:30 to 11 p.m.

Aug 6 — 3 games (preliminaries, men), 11 a.m. to 3:30 p.m., 6:30 to 11 p.m.

Aug 7 — 3 games (round robin, women), 6:30 to 11 p.m.

Aug 8 — 3 games (preliminaries, men), 6:30 to 11 p.m.

Aug 9 — 3 games (round robin, women), 6:30 to 11 p.m.

Aug 10 — 2 games (finals: 9-12 places, men), 11 a.m. to 2 p.m. 2 games (finals: 5-8 places, men), 6:30 to 9:30 p.m.

(The Forum, Inglewood)

Aug 11 — 2 games (finals: 1-4 places, men), 2 to 5 p.m.

HOCKEY (Field)
(East Los Angeles College, Monterey Park)

July 29 — 3 games (preliminaries, men), 1:45 to 6:45 p.m.

July 30 — 3 games ((preliminaries, men), 1:45 to 6:45 p.m.

July 31 — 2 games (preliminaries, men), 8:30 to 11:45 a.m. 1 game (round robin, women), 1 game (preliminary, men), 2:30 to 5:45 p.m.

Aug 1 — 1 game (preliminary, men), 1 game (round robin, women), 8 to 11:15 a.m. 2 games (preliminaries, men), 1 game (round robin, women), 1:45 to 6:45 p.m.

Aug 2 — 2 games (preliminaries, men), 8:30 to 11:45 a.m. 1 game (round robin, women), 1 game (preliminary, men), 2:30 to 5:45 p.m.

Aug 3 — 1 game (round robin, women), 1 game (preliminary, men), 8 to 11:15 a.m. 2 games (preliminaries, men), 1 game (round robin, women), 1:45 to 6:45 p.m.

Aug 4 — 2 games (preliminaries, men), 8:30 to 11:45 a.m. 1 game (preliminary, men), 1 game (round robin, women), 2:30 to 5:45 p.m.

Aug 5 — 1 game (preliminary, men), 1 game (round robin, women), 8 to 11:15 a.m. 2 games (preliminaries, men), 1 game (round robin, women), 1:45 to 6:45 p.m.

Aug 6 — 2 games (preliminaries, men), 8:30 to 11:45 p.m. 1 game (preliminary, men), 1 game (round robin, women), 2:30 to 5:45 p.m.

Aug 7 — 1 game (preliminary, men), 1 game (round robin, women), 8 to 11:15 a.m. 1 game (round robin, women), 2 games (preliminaries, men), 1:45 to 6:45 p.m.

Aug 8 — 2 games (semifinals, men), 7 to 10:30 p.m.

Aug 9 — 2 games (semifinals, men), 8 to 11:15 a.m. 1 game (round robin, women), 2 games (semifinals, men), 1:15 to 6:15 p.m.

Aug 10 — 1 game (final: 11-12 places, men), 1 game (round robin, women), 8 to 11:15 a.m. 2 games (finals: 7-10 places, men), 1 game (round robin, women), 1:15 to 6:15 p.m.

Aug 11 — 3 games (finals: 1-6 places, men), 9:15 a.m. to 2:45 p.m.

JUDO
(California State University, Los Angeles)

Aug 4 — Extra lightweight, 4 to 8 p.m.
Aug 5 — Half lightweight, 4 to 8 p.m.
Aug 6 — Lightweight, 4 to 8 p.m.
Aug 7 — Half middleweight, 4 to 8 p.m.
Aug 8 — Middleweight, 4 to 8 p.m.
Aug 9 — Half heavyweight, 4 to 8 p.m.
Aug 10 — Heavyweight, 4 to 8 p.m.
Aug 11 — Open category, 4 to 8 p.m.

MODERN PENTATHLON
(Coto de Caza, Orange County)

July 29 — Riding, 9 to 11 a.m., 4 to 6 p.m.
July 30 — Fencing, 8 a.m. to 8:30 p.m.,
July 31 — Swimming, 2 to 4 p.m.
Aug 1 — Shooting, 9 a.m. to 12 noon. Running, 5 to 6 p.m.

ROWING
(Lake Casitas, Ventura County)

July 30 — Elimination heats (women), 7:30 to 10 a.m.

July 31 — Elimination heats (men), 7:30 to 10:30 a.m.

Aug 1 — Repechage (men & women), 7:30 to 10:30 a.m.

Aug 2 — Semifinals (men & women), 7:30 to 10:30 a.m.

Aug 3 — Finals (7–12 places, men & women), 8 to 10:30 a.m.

Aug 4 — Finals (1–6 places, women), 8 to 10 a.m.

Aug 5 — Finals (1–6 places, men), 8 to 10:30 a.m.

SHOOTING
(Prado Park, Chino)

July 29 — Free pistol; Sport pistol; Clay target-trap; 9 a.m. to 4 p.m.

July 30 — Small-bore rifle, English match; Clay target-trap; Running game target; 9 a.m. to 4 p.m.

July 31 — Clay target-trap; Running game target; Air rifle; 9 a.m. to 4 p.m.

Aug 1 — Small-bore rifle, 3 positions; Rapid-fire pistol; 9 a.m. to 4 p.m.

Aug 2 — Small-bore rifle, 3 positions; Rapid-fire pistol; Clay target-skeet; 9 a.m. to 4 p.m.

Aug 3 — Air rifle; Clay target-skeet; 9 a.m. to 4 p.m.

Aug 4 — Clay target-skeet; 9 a.m. to 3 p.m.

SOCCER (Football)
(Rose Bowl, Pasadena)

July 29 — Preliminary match, 7 to 9 p.m.
July 30 — Preliminary match, 7 to 9 p.m.
July 31 — Preliminary match, 7 to 9 p.m.
Aug 1 — Preliminary match, 7 to 9 p.m.
Aug 2 — Preliminary match, 7 to 9 p.m.
Aug 3 — Preliminary match, 7 to 9 p.m.

(Other preliminary matches will be played July 29 to August 3 at Harvard University in Cambridge, Massachusetts; the U.S. Naval Academy at Annapolis, Maryland; and Stanford University in Palo Alto, California.)

Aug 5 — Quarterfinal match, 7 to 9 p.m.
Aug 6 — Quarterfinal match, 7 to 9 p.m.

Other quarterfinal matches will be played August 5 and 6 at Stanford University.)

Aug 8 — Semifinal match, 6 to 8 p.m.

(Another semifinal match will be played August 8 at Stanford University.)

Aug 10 — Final match (3-4 places), 7 to 9 p.m.
Aug 11 — Final match (1-2 places), 7 to 9 p.m.

SWIMMING
(USC: McDonald's Swim Stadium)

July 29 — Heats: freestyle (women), 100m breaststroke (men), 400m individual medley (women), 200m freestyle (men), 8:30 to 11:30 a.m. Finals: 100m freestyle (women), 100m breaststroke (men), 400m individual medley (women), 200m freestyle (men), 4:15 to 6 p.m.

July 30 — Heats: 100m butterfly (men), 200m freestyle (women), 400m individual medley (men), 200m breaststroke (women), 4 x 200m freestyle relay (men), 8:30 to 11:30 p.m. Finals: 100m butterfly (men), 200m freestyle (women), 400m individual medley (men), 200m breaststroke (women), 4 x 200m freestyle relay (men), 4:15 to 6 p.m.

July 31 — Heats: 400m freestyle (women), 100m freestyle (men), 100m backstroke (women), 200m backstroke (men), 4 x 100m freestyle relay (women), 8:30 to 11:30 a.m. Finals: 400m freestyle (women), 100m freestyle (men), 100m backstroke (women), 200m backstroke (men), 4 x 100m freestyle relay (women), 4:15 to 6 p.m.

Aug 2 — Heats: 400m freestyle (men), 100m butterfly (women), 200m breaststroke (men), 100m breaststroke (women), 4 x 100m freestyle relay (men), 800m freestyle (women), 8:30 to 11:30 a.m. Finals: 400m freestyle (men), 100m butterfly (women), 200m breaststroke (men), 100m breaststroke (women), 4 x 100m freestyle relay (men), 4:15 to 6 p.m.

Aug 3 — Heats: 200m individual medley

(women), 200m butterfly (men), 100m backstroke (men), 4 x 100m medley relay (women), 1500m freestyle (men), 8:30 to 11:30 a.m. Finals: 200m individual medley (women), 200m butterfly (men), 800m freestyle (women), 100m backstroke (men), 4 x 100m medley relay (women), 1,500m p.m.

Aug 4 — Heats: 200m individual medley (men), 200m butterfly (women), 200m backstroke (women), 4 x 100m medley relay (men), 8:30 to 11:30 a.m. Finals: 200m individual medley (men), 200m butterfly (women), 1,500m freestyle (men), 200m backstroke (women), 4 x 100m medley relay (men), 5 to 7 p.m.

SYNCHRONIZED SWIMMING
(USC: McDonald's Swim Stadium)

Aug 6 — Duet routines preliminary, 10 a.m. to 2 p.m.

Aug 9 — Duet routines final, 1:30 to 2:30 p.m.

TENNIS
(University of California, Los Angeles)

Aug 6 — 16 matches, 9 a.m. to 5:30 p.m.

Aug 7 — 16 matches, 9 a.m. to 5:30 p.m.

Aug 8 — 16 matches, 9 a.m. to 5:30 p.m.

Aug 9 — 8 matches (quarterfinals), 9 a.m. to 5:30 p.m.

Aug 10 — 4 matches (semifinals), 9 a.m. to 5:30 p.m.

Aug 11 — 2 matches (finals), 10 a.m. to 2 p.m.

TRACK AND FIELD
(Los Angeles Memorial Coliseum)

Aug 3 (morning session) — Heptathlon: 100m hurdles, high jump. Qualifying: triple jump, shot put (women). 1st round: 400m hurdles (men), 400m (women), 100m (men). 2nd round: 100m (men). 9:30 a.m. to 1 p.m.

(Evening session) — Heptathlon: shot put, 200m. 1st round: 800m (women), 800m (men), 10,000m. Finals: 20km walk, shot put (women). 4 to 8:15 p.m.

Aug 4 (morning session) — Heptathlon: long jump. Qualifying: javelin throw (men). 1st round: 400m (men), 100m (women). 2nd round: 400m (women). 9:30 a.m. to 1 p.m.

(Evening session) — Heptathlon: javelin throw, 800m (final event). 2nd round: 100m (women), 800m (men). Semifinals: 100m (men), 800m (women), 400m hurdles (men). Finals: triple jump, 100m (men). 4 to 8:15 p.m.

Aug 5 (morning session) — Qualifying: javelin throw (women), hammer throw. 1st round: 400m hurdles (women), 110m hurdles. Final: marathon (women), finish. 8 a.m. to 12:30 p.m.

(Evening session) — Qualifying: long jump (men). 2nd round: 110m hurdles, 400m (men). Semifinals: 100m (women), 400m (women), 800m (men). Finals: 100m (women), javelin throw (men), 400m hurdles (men). 4 to 7:30 p.m.

Aug 6 (morning session) — Qualifying: pole vault, 1st round: 200m (men), 3,000m. 2nd round: 200m (men). 9:30 a.m. to 12:30 p.m.

(Evening session) — 1st round: 3,000m steeplechase. Semifinals: 110m hurdles, 400m hurdles (women), 400m (men). Finals: 110m hurdles, hammer throw, 400m (men), 800m (women), long jump (men), 800m (men), javelin throw (women), 10,000m. 4 to 8:15 p.m.

Aug 8 (morning session) — Decathlon: 100m, long jump, shot put. Qualifying: discus throw (men). 1st round: 200m (women), 1,500m (men). 2nd round: 200m (women). 9:30 a.m. to 1 p.m.

(Evening session) — Decathlon: high jump, 400m. Qualifying: long jump (women). 1st round: 5,000m. Semifinals: 200m (men), 3,000m, 3,000m steeplechase. Finals: 200m (men), pole vault, 400m hurdles (women), 400m (men). 4 to 8:30 p.m.

Aug 9 (morning session) — Decathlon: discus throw, 110m hurdles, pole vault. Qualifying: high jump (women). 1st round: 100m hurdles, 1,500 (men). Semifinals: 200m (women), 1,500 (women), 5,000m. Finals: 200m (women), long jump (women).

Aug 9 — Decathlon: discus throw, 110m hurdles, pole vault, javelin throw, 1,500m (final event). Qualifying: high jump (women). 1st round: 100m hurdles, 1,500 (men). Semifinals: 200m (women), 1,500m (women), 5,000m. Finals: 200m (women), long jump (women). 9:30 a.m. to 8 p.m.

Aug 10 (morning session) — Qualifying: high jump (men), discus throw (women). 1st round: 4 x 400m relay (women), 4 x 400m relay (men), 4 x 100m relay (women), 4 x 100m relay (men). 9:30 a.m. to 12:30 p.m.

(Evening session) — Semifinals: 100m hurdles, 4 x 400m relay (men), 4 x 400m relay (women), 1,500m (men). Finals: high jump (women), discus throw (men), 100m hurdles, 3,000m, 3,000m steeplechase. 4 to 7:45 p.m.

Aug 11 (morning session) — Qualifying: shot put (men). Semifinals: 4 x 100m relay (women), 4 x 100m relay (men). Final: 50km walk (start and finish).

(Evening session) — Finals: discus throw (women), 4 x 100m relay (women), high jump (men), 4 x 100m relay (men), 4 x 400m relay (women), 4 x 400m relay (men), shot put (men), 1,500m (women), 1,500m (men), 5,000m. 4 to 8 p.m.

Aug 12 — Final: marathon (men), finish included in closing ceremony of Olympic Games.

VOLLEYBALL
(Long Beach Sports Arena)

July 29 — 2 matches (preliminaries, men), 10 a.m. to 2 p.m. 2 matches (preliminaries, men), 6:30 to 10:30 p.m.

July 30 — 2 matches (preliminaries, women), 10 a.m. to 2 p.m. 2 matches (preliminaries, women), 6:30 to 10:30 p.m.

July 31 — 2 matches (preliminaries, men), 10 a.m. to 2 p.m. 2 matches (preliminaries, men), 6:30 to 10:30 p.m.

Aug 1 — 2 matches (preliminaries, women), 10 a.m. to 2 p.m. 2 matches (preliminaries, women), 6:30 to 10:30 p.m.

Aug 2 — 2 matches (preliminaries, men), 10 a.m. to 2 p.m. 2 matches (preliminaries, men), 6:30 to 10:30 p.m.

Aug 3 — 2 matches (preliminaries, women), 10 a.m. to 2 p.m. 2 matches (preliminaries, women), 6:30 to 10:30 p.m.

Aug 4 — 2 matches (preliminaries, men), 10 a.m. to 2 p.m. 2 matches (preliminaries, men), 6:30 to 10:30 p.m.

Aug 5 — 2 matches (semifinals: 5-8 places, women), 10 a.m. to 2 p.m. 2 matches (semifinals: 1-4 places, women), 6:30 to 10:30 p.m.

Aug 6 — 2 matches (preliminaries, men), 10 a.m. to 2 p.m. 2 matches (preliminaries, men), 6:30 to 10:30 p.m.

Aug 7 — 2 matches (finals: 5-8 places, women), 10 a.m. to 2 p.m. 1 match (final: 3-4 places, women), 4 to 6 p.m. 1 match (final: 1-2 places, women), 8:30 to 10:30 p.m.

Aug 8 — 2 matches (semifinals, men) and 1 match (final: 9-10 places, men), 9 a.m. to 3 p.m. 2 matches (semifinals, men), 6:30 to 10:30 p.m.

Aug 10 — 2 matches (finals: 5-8 places, men), 6:30 to 10:30 p.m.

Aug 11 — 1 match (final: 3-4 places, men), 12 noon to 2 p.m. 1 match (final: 1-2 places, men), 6:30 to 8:30 p.m.

WATER POLO
(Pepperdine University, Malibu)

Aug 1 — 2 games (preliminaries), 8:30 to 11 a.m. 2 games (preliminaries), 1:30 to 4 p.m. 2 games (preliminaries), 7:30 to 10 p.m.

Aug 2 — 2 games (preliminaries), 8:30 to 11 a.m. 2 games (preliminaries), 1:30 to 4 p.m. 2 games (preliminaries), 7:30 to 10 p.m.

Aug 3 — 2 games (preliminaries), 8:30 to 11 a.m. 2 games (preliminaries), 1:30 to 4 p.m. 2 games (preliminaries), 7:30 to 10 p.m.

Aug 6 — 2 games (preliminaries), 8:30 to 11 a.m. 2 games (preliminaries), 1:30 to 4 p.m. 2 games (preliminaries), 7:30 to 10 p.m.

Aug 7 — 2 games (preliminaries), 8:30 to 11 a.m. 2 games (preliminaries), 1:30 to 4 p.m. 2 games (preliminaries), 7:30 to 10 p.m.

Aug 9 — 2 games (final round), 8:30 to 11 a.m. 2 games (final round), 1:30 to 4 p.m. 2 games (final round), 7:30 to 10 p.m.

Aug 10 — 2 games (final round), 8:30 to 11 a.m. 2 games (final round), 1:30 to 4 p.m. 2 games (final round), 7:30 to 10 p.m.

WEIGHTLIFTING
(Loyola Marymount University, Westchester)

July 29 — Flyweight (up to 52 kg), group B, 2 to 4 p.m. Flyweight group A, 6 to 9 p.m.

July 30 — Bantamweight (up to 56 kg), group B, 2 to 4 p.m. Bantamweight, group A, 6 to 9 p.m.

July 31 — Featherweight (up to 60 kg), group B, 2 to 4 p.m. Featherweight, group A, 6 to 9 p.m.

Aug 1 — Lightweight (up to 67.5 kg), group C, 11 a.m. to 1 p.m. Lightweight, group B 2 to 4 p.m. Lightweight, group A, 6 to 8 p.m.

Aug 2 — Middleweight (up to 75 kg), group C, 11 a.m. to 1 p.m. Middleweight, group B, 2 to 4 p.m. Middleweight, group A, 6 to 8 p.m.

Aug 4 — Light heavyweight (up to 82.5 kg), group C, 11 a.m. to 1 p.m. Light heavyweight, group B, 2 to 4 p.m. Light heavyweight, group A, 6 to 8 p.m.

Aug 5 — Middle heavyweight (up to 90 kg), group C, 11 a.m. to 1 p.m. Middle heavyweight, group B, 2 to 4 p.m. Middle heavyweight, group A, 6 to 8 p.m.

Aug 6 — First heavyweight (up to 100 kg), group B 2 to 4 p.m. First heavyweight, group A, 6 to 9 p.m.

Aug 7 — Second heavyweight (up to 110 kg), group B, 2 to 4 p.m. Second heavyweight, group A, 6 to 9 p.m.

Aug 8 — Super heavyweight (over 110 kg), group B, 2 to 4 p.m. Super heavyweight, group A, 6 to 9 p.m.

WRESTLING
(Anaheim Convention Center)

Greco-Roman Style

July 30 — Preliminaries (48, 62, 90 kg), 12 noon to 3 p.m. and 6 to 8:30 p.m.

July 31 — Preliminaries (48, 52, 62, 74, 90, over 100 kg), 12 noon to 3 p.m. and 6 to 8:30 p.m.

Aug 1 — Preliminaries (52, 57, 68, 74, 82, 100, over 100 kg); Semifinals (48, 62, 90 kg), 12 noon to 3 p.m. Preliminaries (52, 57, 68, 74, 82, 100, over 100 kg); Finals (48, 62, 90 kg), 6 to 8:30 p.m.

Aug 2 — Preliminaries (57, 68, 82, 100 kg); Semifinals (52, 74, over 100 kg), 12 noon to 3 p.m. Preliminaries (57, 68, 82, 100 kg); Finals (52, 74, over 100 kg), to to 8:30 p.m.

Aug 3 — Preliminaries (57, 68, 82, 100 kg), 12 noon to 3 p.m. Semifinals and finals (57, 68, 82, 100 kg), 6 to 8:30 p.m.

Freestyle

Aug 7 — Preliminaries (48, 62, 90 kg), 12 noon to 3 p.m. and 6 to 8:30 p.m.

Aug 8 — Preliminaries (48, 52, 62, 74, 90, over 100 kg), 12 noon to 3 p.m. and 6 to 8:30 p.m.

Aug 9 — Preliminaries (52, 57, 68, 74, 82, 100, over 100 kg); Semifinals (48, 62, 90 kg), 12 noon to 3 p.m. Preliminaries (52, 57, 68, 74, 82, 100, over 100 kg); Finals (48, 62, 90 kg), 6 to 8:30 p.m.

Aug 10 — Preliminaries (57, 68, 82, 100 kg); Semifinals (52, 74, over 100 kg), 12 noon to 3 p.m. Preliminaries (57, 68, 82, 100 kg); Finals (52, 74, over 100 kg), 6 to 8:30 p.m.

Aug 11 — Preliminaries (57, 68, 82, 100 kg), 12 noon to 3 p.m. Finals (57, 68, 82, 100 kg), 6 to 8:30 p.m.

YACHTING
(Olympic Yachting Center, Long Beach)

July 31 — First race, 1:30 to 6:30 p.m.
Aug 1 — Second race, 1:30 to 6:30 p.m.
Aug 2 — Third race, 1:30 to 6:30 p.m.
Aug 3 — Fourth race, 1:30 to 6:30 p.m.
Aug 6 — Fifth race, 1:30 to 6:30 p.m.
Aug 7 — Sixth race, 1:30 to 6:30 p.m.
Aug 8 — Seventh race, 1:30 to 6:30 p.m.

GUIDE IN BRIEF

Traveling to Southern California

By Air

The area's largest airport is Los Angeles International (LAX), located on the west side of Los Angeles. LAX handles the major international, domestic, and regional carriers. Some of the international carriers serving LAX include AeroMexico, Argentine Airlines, Air Canada, Air France, Air New Zealand, British Airways, China Airlines, Continental Airlines, KLM-Royal Dutch Airways, Qantas Airways, Pan American World Airways, Scandinavian Airlines and Trans World Airlines.

The terminal buildings at LAX are arranged in an oval. Arrivals are on the lower level; an upper level for departures has been built in anticipation of the increased airline traffic that the '84 Olympics will bring. The 'C' bus stops at each terminal building and then shuttles out to a large parking area before repeating its trip around the oval. Taxis that will bring you to any part of the city are easily available from here. Charges are determined by the meter: $1.90 for the first 0.2 mile (0.3 kilometer) and $1.40 for each additional mile (1.6 kilometer). For those more budget-conscious, there are always the public buses. Service numbers 88, 220, 607, 608, 834, 869 and 871 link LAX with various parts of the city. Call the **Southern California Rapid Transit District** (RTD) for information. Limousine and private bus services are also available. Read notes in **Transportation** section.

By Land

Continental Trailways and Greyhound bus companies bring visitors into Southern California from points all across the country. Both offer unlimited mileage passes at $186 for seven days, $240 for 15 days, and $347 for 30 days. The pass is half-priced for children under 12, and free of charge for children under five.

Amtrak provides train service throughout Southern California. Los Angeles' Union Station is one of the architectural landmarks of the city. The "Coast Starlight" is a deluxe train connecting Los Angeles with San Francisco, Portland and Seattle. The "Coast Starlight" offers bedrooms for couples and families, and has a special bedroom available for handicapped persons. For more information, call (800)648-3850.

If you are traveling by car, you are apt to be confused by Southern California's many freeways. The following guide may help. Nevertheless, a good map and fair amount of patience are absolute necessities!

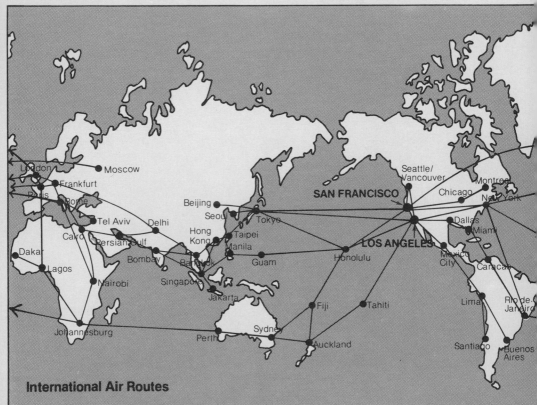

International Air Routes

The principal north-south byways in Southern California are:

• Interstate 5 (the Golden State and Santa Ana freeways), which covers the distance from Canada to Mexico via Seattle, Sacramento, Los Angeles and San Diego.

• Interstate 15, which transits San Bernardino and San Diego after a long passage from Montana's Canadian border, via Salt Lake City and Las Vegas.

• U.S. Highway 99, which wends an easterly route from Sacramento via Fresno and joins I-5 south of Bakersfield.

• U.S. Highway 101 (the Ventura and Hollywood freeways), which proceeds south down the Pacific coast from Washington state, crosses San Francisco's Golden Gate Bridge, and ends in downtown Los Angeles.

• U.S. Highway 395, which follows the eastern edge of the Sierra Nevada and ends in the city of San Bernardino.

• State Highway 1 (the Pacific Coast Highway), which hugs the coast from San Diego through the California beaches to San Francisco and further north.

The principal east-west byways are:

• Interstate 8, which departs from I-10 at Casa Grande, Arizona and ends in San Diego.

• Interstate 10 (the San Bernardino and Santa Monica freeways), which begins on America's East Coast in Jacksonville, Florida and proceeds through New Orleans, Houston, El Paso, Tucson and Phoenix before cutting through Los Angeles and ending in Santa Monica.

• Interstate 40, which connects Knoxville, Tennessee, with Barstow via Memphis, Oklahoma City and Albuquerque.

Other important freeways in Los Angeles are:

• Interstate 210 (the Foothills Freeway), from San Fernando, through the San Fernando and San Gabriel valleys to Pomona. (It continues to San Bernardino from San Dimas as State 66.)

• Interstate 405 (the San Diego Freeway), which covers Los Angeles and Orange counties from San Fernando to Santa Ana via Westwood and Long Beach.

• Interstate 605 (the San Gabriel River Parkway), Monrovia to Long Beach via Whittier.

• State Highway 11 (the Harbor Freeway), Pasadena to Long Beach via downtown Los Angeles.

• State Highway 55 (the Newport Freeway), east Anaheim to Newport Beach.

• State Highway 57 (the Orange Freeway), Pomona to Santa Ana.

• State Highway 60 (the Pomona Freeway), downtown Los Angeles to Beaumont via Pomona and Riverside.

• State Highway 91 (the Riverside Freeway), Torrance to San Bernardino via Anaheim and Riverside.

• State Highway 118 (the Long Beach Freeway), East Los Angeles to Long Beach.

Travel Advisories

Most visitors, upon entering the United States, must have a passport and visitor's visa, and if they are from (or have passed through) an infected area, a health record. Canadian citizens entering from the Western Hemisphere need not have a visa or a passport. Neither do Mexican citizens who possess a border pass.

At the Nevada, Oregon and Mexican borders, the State Department of Food and Agriculture inspects all produce, plant materials and wild animals to see if they are admissable under current quarantine regulations. To avoid a lengthy inspection, do not bring any agricultural products into California.

Most hotels will honor foreign traveler's checks that are in dollars. Most of them, however, will not exchange money, so it's best to have this done at the airport, especially if you arrive on a weekend. Unlike in Europe, not all banks will exchange foreign currency. The larger banks do, but there is no rule.

In most states, a sales tax is added to retail goods. California charges 6½ percent sales tax, but they don't tax all goods. You're a genius if you can understand the logic behind the tax laws; most people simply memorize them. There is a tax on books, for instance, but no tax on magazines. If you buy a hamburger and eat it in the restaurant they will tax you, but if you eat the hamburger in your car they cannot tax you. If you fail to make sense of these laws, you will be in the same boat as the natives.

Getting Acquainted

State Song and Nickname: *California, Here I Come* and "The Golden State."
State Flower: Golden Poppy
State Motto: "Eureka! (I have found it!)"

Climate

Southern California is one of the few areas in the world where you can ski in the morning and surf in the afternoon. It is not uncommon for the temperature to vary 30 to 40 degrees Fahrenheit (17 to 22°C) as you travel a short distance from high mountains to low deserts to the beaches. The change of seasons is not as dramatic as it is elsewhere. The winters are mild, with a rainy season that lasts from January through March. In the summer months the humidity is usually low so that discomfort is rare. The famous Los Angeles smog is at its worst in August and September.

Month	(°C)	(°F)
January	18.3	65
February	19.4	67
March	20.0	68
April	20.5	69
May	22.2	72
June	23.8	75
July	27.7	82
August	28.8	84
September	28.3	83
October	25.6	78
November	22.8	73
December	20.6	69

Earthquakes

Earthquakes do occur here. Check the local directories for Civil Defense inundation maps and related emergency information regarding such harzards.

The 1971 San Fernando Valley quake with its epicenter in Sylmar measured 6.4 and killed 64 persons and caused more than a billion dollars in property damage.

Seismologists believe that there is at least a 50 percent chance of an earthquake measuring more than 7.0 to hit the Los Angeles areas by the year 2010. Federal disaster experts fear that the casualties and damage will constitute the worst catastrophe since the Civil War and "will surpass any natural disaster thus far experienced in the United States."

Casualties are expected to be minimal if the quake occurs at night when most people are at home. But the worst scenario would be if it occurred during the evening rush hour, with many people on the freeways. The most dangerous place to be in will be any of the unreinforced masonry buildings built before the 1933 earthquake. Building codes have been strengthened since then, so that most newer buildings are reasonably safe The safest place is one-story family homes.

Experts expect that Los Angeles will be virtually isolated for the first 72 hours after a quake, with air, rail and highway transportation at a standstill as well as power outages and breakdowns on water and telephone systems. They anticipate that neighbors will have to rely on one another to share food and first aid supplies. Schools have stockpiled food and supplies to care for children for several days.

Plans have been made to move in military doctors in case of emergency, and television crews have even prepared for a potential earthquake with specific assignments for staff members. Some cameramen even take their equipment home nightly in case road closures make it impossible for them to get back to the station.

Clothing

Dress in Southern California is decidedly casual. Rare is the restaurant that requires jackets and ties for men.

Unless you are going to visit the mountain areas, the moderate climate makes heavy clothing unnecessary. Wool sweaters or lightweight overcoats are sufficient for winter evenings, and a light jacket will be adequate for evenings in the summer. If you plan to spend a lot of time in the sun, be sure to bring lotion to protect yourself from sunburn.

Time Zone

Southern California is within the Pacific Time Zone, which is two hours behind Chicago, and three hours behind New York. On the last Sunday in April the clock is moved ahead one hour for Daylight Savings Time, and on the last Sunday in October the clock is moved back one hour to return to Standard Time.

Without Daylight Savings Time adjustment, when it is 12 noon in Southern California it is ...

10 a.m. in Hawaii
3 p.m. in New York and Montreal
8 p.m. in London
9 p.m. in Bonn, Madrid, Paris and Rome
11 p.m. in Athens and Cairo
12 midnight in Moscow
1:30 a.m. (the next day) in Bombay
3 a.m. (the next day) in Bangkok
4 a.m. (the next day) in Singapore, Taiwan, Hong Kong
5 a.m. (the next day) in Tokyo
6 a.m. (the next day) in Sydney

Etiquette

It is courteous to show your gratitude for help given to you, and in the service trade nothing is more appreciated than a tip.

The accepted rate for porters at the airports is 50 cents per bag. Hotel bellboys and porters usually get tipped 35 cents per bag or suitcase. A doorman should be tipped if he unloads or parks your car. It is not necessary to tip chambermaids unless you stay several days in a small hotel.

Depending on quantity and quality of service rendered, 15 to 20 percent is the going rate for most other help; taxi drivers, barbers, hairdressers, waiters and waitresses. Make the bartenders happy with 10 to 15 percent. In some restaurants, tips or a service charge is included in the bill if the group is large. No tipping in cafeterias.

Business Hours and Public Holidays

Most businesses are open from 9 a.m. to 5 p.m. Some department stores open at 10 a.m., and many stores stay open until 9 p.m. Los Angeles is famous for its 24-hour restaurants. A few super-markets also open round-the-clock. Banks often close by 3 p.m., although some stay open later, especially on Fridays. Banks are closed on weekends.

Most businesses and banks close for the following holidays: (dates are for 1984)

New Year's Day	January 1
Washington's Birthday	February 20
Easter Sunday	April 8
Memorial Day	May 28
Independence Day	July 4
Labor Day	September 3
Thanksgiving Day	November 29
Christmas Day	December 25

Some businesses and banks close on:

Lincoln's Birthday	February 12
Good Friday	April 6
Columbus Day	October 10
Election Day	November 6
Veteran's Day	November 11

Credit Cards

Most restaurants and hotels honor Visa, Master Charge and American Express credit cards; many also accept Diner's Club and Carte Blanche cards. However, stores and gas stations usually accept Master Charge and Visa only.

Liquor Laws

The legal age for both the purchase and the consumption of alcoholic beverages is 21; proof of age is often required. Alcoholic beverages are sold by the bottle or by the can in liquor stores, in some supermarkets and many drug stores. Alcoholic beverages are sold by the drink (from 6 a.m. to 2 a.m.) at most restaurants, nightclubs and bars. Some of these establishments are licensed to serve beer and wine only. One quart of alcohol may be imported from another country.

Embassies and Consular Services

There are 53 foreign consulates located in the Los Angeles area; refer to the Appendix for a listing.

Tourist Information

When in doubt, use the telephone. The fastest way to obtain assistance is simply to dial "0" for the operator. If operators cannot help, they usually give you another number where assistance may be obtained.

The **Greater Los Angeles Visitors and Convention Bureau** operates two Visitors Information Centers: In downtown Los Angeles; Atlantic Richfield Plaza, Level B, Sixth Street at Flower, (213) 628–3101 and in Hollywood; Pacific Federal Building, Hollywood Boulevard at Highland, (213) 466–1389. A 24-hour recorded message of current events of interest can be heard by dialing (213) 628–5857.

For tourist information in Southern California communities, please refer to listing of centers in appendix.

Transportation

Air Travel (Domestic)

There are several airports in Southern California. While the largest is Los Angeles International Airport, you may find it more convenient to use one of the other airports.

Los Angeles International Airport (LAX), one of the busiest in the world, handles major international, domestic and regional carriers. Read notes on "Traveling to Southern California by air."

San Diego International Airport handles several international carriers, as well as a wide range of domestic and regional carriers.

Ontario International Airport handles domestic and regional flights.

Palm Springs Airport handles a wide range of domestic and regional carriers.

Hollywood-Burbank Airport handles domestic and regional carriers.

Ventura County Airport in Oxnard, **John Wayne Airport** in Orange County, **Santa Barbara**

Airport and **San Luis Obispo Airport** handle regional flights.

See the appendix for a listing of the airline companies (with their telephone numbers) whose planes call at Southern Californian airports.

Buses

In Los Angeles, the **Southern California Rapid Transit District** (known as the RTD) offers a tourist pass that entitles you to unlimited travel for $2 a day (minimum three days). For information call (213) 626–4455. A tourist kit is available from the RTD by writing **Tourist Kit Department**, RTD Marketing, Los Angeles, CA 90013. Also, the RTD offers a self-guided tour brochure that routes you to every major Los Angeles attraction.

In San Diego, the **San Diego Transit Company** offers complete bus service; for bus route information, call (619) 233–3004. **The San Diego Trolley** runs every 15 minutes from downtown San Diego to the Mexican border for $1. For information, call (619) 231–1466.

There are as many kinds of bus tourist services as there are private bus companies in Southern California, each running its own routes and offering different package tours. Full information on their itineraries may be obtained at their offices. The appendix includes a listing of a few of these bus charters.

A good network of public bus routes also makes traveling easy. Rates of these public buses are fixed at 50 cents for a ride in a basic local, 25 cents for a downtown minibus and between 50 cents to $1.75 for a freeway express. Call RTD for information.

Many of the major hotels have bus service to the airport; check the hotel guide for further information. Also read "Traveling to Southern California by air."

Trains

Southern California is so spread out that the usual mode of transportation is car or bus. **Amtrak**, however, does provide extensive service between major Southern California cities (and is probably the easiest way to travel between Los Angeles and San Diego). For information, call (800) 648–3850.

Taxis

For medium distances of a few miles, taxis are a convenient and reasonably priced alternative to public or private buses or walking. Taxi services are provided by City Cab (870–3333), Independent Cab (385–8294), Red Top Cab (395–3201), United Independent (653–5050) and Yellow Cab (481–2345).

Taxis should be called in advance for pick-up, but in some urban areas, they can usually be hailed directly on the streets. They are readily available at major hotels.

For long distances, taxis are expensive. For rates, read notes in "Traveling to Southern California by air" section.

Limousines and Helicopters

Offering similar package tours as the private bus companies, are the many private limousine and helicopter companies. Addresses of a few of them are given in the appendix.

Car Rentals

A complete listing may be found in the Yellow Pages of the phone directory. The larger companies, however, are listed in the appendix of this section.

Pages of the phone directory under "Automobiles — Rental." Reservations are advised. The larger companies, however, are listed in the appendix of this section.

There are dozens of automobile rental agencies throughout Southern California — Avis, Budget, Dollar, Hertz and National. Rental offices are in most cities and at all airports. Basic charges range from $25 to $55 per day; most companies offer unlimited mileage and special weekend rates. Shop around for the best rates and features. Often, smaller local rental companies offer less expensive, more desirable conditions than the large national firms. Be sure to check insurance provisions (usually an extra $5 per day for full coverage) before signing anything.

Most rental agencies require you to be at least 21 years old (sometimes 25); and to hold a valid driver's license and a major credit card. (Some will take a cash deposit, often as high as $600, in lieu of a credit card.) Foreign travelers may need to produce an international driver's license or a license from their home country. Drivers must abide by local and State traffic regulations.

Motoring Advisories

Unless otherwise posted, the speed limit on California highways is 55 miles (88 km) per hour, and in residential and business districts, the speed limit is 25 to 35 miles (40 to 56 km) per hour.

In addition to street signs advising no-parking hours and special tow-away zones, the color of the curb governs the kind of parking permitted. Red curbs mean no parking at all. Yellow curbs indicate limited stops (usually for trucks only) for loading and unloading of passengers or freight. White curbs, usually found at entrances to hotels and restaurants, are limited to short-term stopping only. Green curbs also indicate parking for limited periods only, usually 10 to 30 minutes. Blue curbs are reserved for the disabled. It is not advisable to ignore any of these signs. Police are strict on illegal parking, summoning tow trucks for vehicles found in No Parking areas or found blocking driveways. You'll need plenty of cash or at least a major credit card to bail your car out. Towing fees and fines are steep.

Hitchhiking is not advised. Picking up hitchhiking strangers is also potentially dangerous. Local newspapers regularly recount stories of robbery and rape that begin with an extended thumb.

When traveling into the mountain areas, especially during the winter months, it is advisable to phone ahead for road conditions. At times, chains will be required on the tires.

Desert Traveling:

The single most important precaution a desert traveler can make is to tell someone before leaving his intended destination, planned route and anticipated time of return. It is best to mark one's route on a duplicate map and leave it with a friend, relative or local ranger.

Drivers should also take account of the time of week they are traveling. This may affect the availability of fuel. Most small town stations remain open on weekends; nevertheless, it is a good idea to top off one's tank whenever possible. Death Valley National Monument has three gas stations, all open daily.

No one, of course, should forget to carry water. "Water is life in the Mojave," the experts say. "You cannot bring too much of it." It's a basic

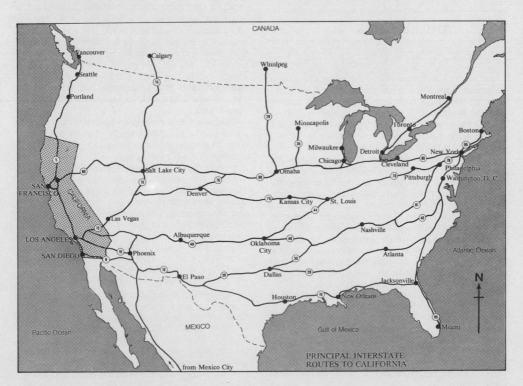

PRINCIPAL INTERSTATE ROUTES TO CALIFORNIA

necessity for desert travel. Sojourners should plan on a minimum of one gallon (about four liters) per person per day, with five gallons kept in reserve for the trip. A stranded desert traveler would last only about 36 hours in the summer without water, even less if he left his car. The killer is dehydration.

Travelers should also be warned not to freely drink natural water discovered en route in the desert. Even spring water should be boiled or purified before drinking.

Drivers should give their vehicle a thorough check-up before leaving for the desert. This includes checking tires, fan belts, coolant hoses, and fluid levels in the battery, radiator crankcase and transmission. And one should expect the unexpected. A California State Highway Patrolman says summer desert travel pushes cars to the extreme.

"I've seen tires blow, engines quit, parts come unglued, hoses burst," the patrolman said. "Sometimes automatic transmissions get so hot the car's floor-boards have caught fire."

If one's car breaks down, or if the traveler is injured or lost, there is one rule to follow: *Stay where you are and wait for help.* Even experienced desert hikers are in danger of losing their ways when overcome by fatigue, heat or disorientation. Since the days of the first settlers, and before them the Indians, the watchword has been the same: "Be prepared."

Accommodations

Southern California offers the complete gamut in accommodations; from the elegant European-style L' Ermitage, with its original artwork adorning the walls and its exclusive dining room, to inexpensive motels renting rooms by the week (famous for housing the hopeful actor or actress who has just moved out from Cleveland).

In Los Angeles, the most expensive **hotels** are situated downtown and in Beverly Hills and afford the best access to shopping and public transportation. They are particularly well-suited to the international traveler, and many of these hotels are attractive landmarks in their own right. The concierge on duty at most of the finer hotels arranges your theater tickets, tours, telex, seats at sporting events, limos with bilingual drivers, and airline reservations. He recommends restaurants, can speak foreign languages and helps exchange money in a dozen different currencies.

For those not impressed by the stylish glamour (with matching prices) of the larger hotels, the **small hotels** are a good alternative. Providing basic comforts with a personal touch, these small hotels are popping up in areas not "central" to the city; in Orange County, in the San Fernando Valley and on the west side of Los Angeles. If you don't have a car, you may be wise to stay near Wilshire Boulevard, as this busy street passes through downtown, Beverly Hills, Westwood and the beach.

If you are traveling by car and don't intend to spend much time in your lodgings other than sleeping, **motels** are the best solution. In San Diego, there are several wonderful golf and tennis resorts in the inland hills (foremost among them is **La Costa**, with its famous spa facilities), and dozens of motels scattered along the beach. Degree and quality of accommodations vary, but most motels are bare bones. A restaurant or coffee shop, swimming pool and sauna are often on the premises. Room facilities would include a telephone, TV and radio but do not hesitate to ask the motel manager if you may inspect a room before agreeing to take it. Other than their accessibility by auto, the other attraction of motels is their price; they are even less expensive in the outlying areas. Most of them have toll-free telephone numbers for making and confirming reservations.

Country inns have become extremely popular in the last decade throughout the United State. Most cluster in scenic areas and being situated in beautiful rural settings, they do a thriving business with city dwellers in search of a romantic weekend retreat. Converted from mansions and farmhouses with five to 15 rooms, these inns offer the traveler a highly individual experience; no two inns are alike, and in most inns no two rooms are alike. Many residents have opened their homes to strangers. For those accustomed to the strict uniformity of large hotels and motel chains. the inns provide a hospitable and quaint alternative.

Many inns have shared bathrooms and only a few have televisions or telephones in the rooms. Most include breakfasts with the room rental; hence the name, bed-and-breakfast inns. Prices vary from inn to inn and could be anywhere between $20 and $80 per night. Call or write in advance — the inns are particularly popular on weekends and in the summer. All serve breakfasts, from coffee and croissants to hearty, full-course meals.

California has a chain of **hostels**; some are located inside old lighthouses. Hostels are clean, comfortable, *very* inexpensive ($5 per night) and although suitable for people of all ages, they are definitely for the "young at heart."

Beds are provided in dormitory-type rooms. Hostelers carry their own gear (knife, fork, spoon, sheets or sleeping bag, towel, washcloth) and are expected, following breakfast each day, to take 15 minutes to help at such communal tasks as vacuuming, sweeping, chopping firewood and stoking the fireplace. Hostels are closed daily from 9:30 a.m. to 4:30 p.m., so most guests fill their days with nearby outdoor adventures. Reservations are highly recommended.

Campgrounds sprinkled throughout California provide an ample choice of outdoor accommodations for the mobile traveler. They range from primitive areas marked off for tents and sleeping bags, to elaborate facilities with utility hook-ups for home-on-wheels recreational vehicles (RVs), restaurants and planned activities. Many also provide lodgings complete with separate bathrooms, kitchenettes and room service. There are even campgrounds for nudists.

Most state parks, forests, national parks, monuments and seashores offer primitive camping facilities, a place to park your car, a sectioned-off spot under the trees or along the river for sleeping, public rest rooms within walking distance, and outdoor cooking facilities. Fees range from $1 to $4 per site. Most public campgrounds are busy from mid June to early September and are allotted on a first-come-first-serve basis. Again, advance reservations are advisable.

Private campgrounds have blossomed around many of the popular parks and commercial attractions. Costing an average of $5 per person, the grounds usually have sites for RVs, a coin laundry, flush/pit toilets and a play area for the children. Sometimes they also have restaurants, grocery stores and swimming pools. The largest private campground association is Kampgrounds of America with its 600-odd nationwide camps. A list of their facilities costs $1 inclusive of postage and handling. Write to Kampgrounds of America, P.O. Box 30162, Billings, Montana 59114.

In using the listing in the appendix, please keep in mind that, it is only a small selection of lodgings in Southern California. Your travel agent can give you more complete information. Due to highly fluctuating costs, it is difficult to chart the price trends and say decidedly what is available for the real low-budget travelers, and on the other end of the scale, for those who indulge in luxury. The rates given in the listing behind are for double occupancy and are subject to change.

Communication

Postal Services

At the time of this writing, postage rates are as follows:

letters inside the United States, or to Mexico and Canada, are 20 cents for the first ounce and 17 cents for each additional ounce;

postcards inside the United States, or to Mexico and Canada, are 13 cents;

surface letters to other foreign countries are 30 cents for the first ounce and 17 cents for each additional ounce;

airmail letters to other foreign countries are 40 cents for each half-ounce;

postcards to foreign destinations are 19 cents for surface mail and 28 cents for airmail; and

aerograms require 30 cents postage.

Stamps may be purchased at any post office; most are open from 8 a.m. to 5 p.m. on Monday through Friday and from 8 a.m. to noon on Saturdays. Stamps may also be purchased from vending machines located in hotels, stores, airports and bus and train stations.

The main post office in Los Angeles is at 900 N. Alameda Ave., (213) 688–2290; and in San Diego, it is at 2535 Midway Drive, (619) 293–5410.

Telephones and Telegraph Messages

Coin-operated telephones are literally everywhere — in hotels, restaurants, shopping centers, gas stations and often in lit booths on street corners. To operate, deposit a dime (in other states you will be asked to deposit 15 to 25 cents). Once you get a dial tone, you may dial the seven-digit number. If the call is long distance, you may dial direct by dialing the three-digit area code before the number. An operator will then tell you how much to deposit into the phone. If you wish to place the call through an operator, simply dial "0". Directions are usually printed on the phone, and are always included in the first few pages of the phone directory.

When making a call from your hotel room, simply dial the hotel operator and they will place the call for you. You will be billed for your calls when you check out of the hotel.

Telegraph facilities are available through Western Union or Telex. Consult the phone directory in your area and call the appropriate company for information.

News Media

Newspapers and Magazines

The Los Angeles Times is one of the most widely read newspapers in the country. There are several regional editions (for instance, the San Diego edition gives local San Diego news plus the same national and international news as the other regional editions), and there is probably no better entertainment section in the country than in the Times' Sunday "Calendar" section.

Other large daily papers are The Los Angeles Herald Examiner, The Daily News, The San Diego Union, The San Diego Tribune and the Orange County Register.

Los Angeles Magazine, Palm Springs Life, San Diego and Orange Coast are monthly regional magazines that have lively feature articles on Southern California culture, as well as listings of restaurants and current happenings. California Magazine is a feature-oriented magazine covering the entire state.

Where Magazine is available in many hotels; it contains lists of restaurants, nightclubs and cultural activities.

In Los Angeles, two weeklies, *LA Weekly* and *The Reader*, are available for free. They regularly review plays, movies, art openings, musical concerts, and fashion, and are complete in their listing of cultural activities.

In Los Angeles, foreign and foreign-language publications are available at the following bookstores:

The Spanish Bookstore, 2326 Westwood Blvd., 475–0453.

La Cité des Livres (French books), 2306 Westwood Blvd., 475–0658.

German & International Book Store, 1767 N. Vermont Ave., 660–0313.

For foreign periodicals in Los Angeles, try the newsstands in Century City, at the corner of Pico and Westwood boulevards, at the corner of Hollywood and Las Palmas boulevards and in Santa Monica on Ocean Avenue near Santa Monica Boulevard.

Radio and Television

The most widely listened-to radio stations in Southern California are KABC-AM for news and information, KUSC-FM for classical music, KMET-FM and KISS-FM for mainstream rock 'n' roll, and KROQ-FM for new-wave music. KKGO-FM is one of the country's premiere jazz stations.

The three major television networks, CBS, NBC and ABC, have affiliates that reach most of Southern California. For less commercial programming, there is PBS, the public television network which survives on grants and donations. Recently, Southern California has been flooded with cable TV services offering round-the-clock programs in sports and movies.

For information about obtaining tickets to a television show taping, call:

ABC-TV Shows	(213) 557–7777
CBS-TV Shows	852–4002
Merv Griffin Show	461–4701
Metromedia Television Shows	462–7111
NBC-TV Shows	840–4444
Lawrence Welk Show	451–5727

Radio Stations in Southern California

AM	station	city	format
550	KAFY	Bakersfield	
570	KLAC	Los Angeles	
590	KFXM	San Bernardino	
600	KOGO	San Diego	rock
640	KFI	Los Angeles	
710	KMPC	Los Angeles	
760	KFMB	San Diego	
790	KABC	Los Angeles	talk, news
910	KOXR	Oxnard	
920	KDES	Palm Springs	
920	KVEC	San Luis Obispo	rock
930	KHJ	Los Angeles	country
980	KFWB	Los Angeles	
990	KBLS	Santa Barbara	rock
1010	KCMJ	Palm Springs	
1070	KNX	Los Angeles	
1130	KSDO	San Diego	news
1150	KPRZ	Los Angeles	
1150	KBAI	Morro Bay	rock
1170	KCBQ	San Diego	country
1190	KEZY	Anaheim	
1230	KGEO	Bakersfield	
1240	KSON	San Diego	country
1330	KFAC	Los Angeles	classical
1340	KATY	San Luis Obispo	country
1350	KNTB	Bakersfield	
1360	KGB	San Diego	rock
1410	KERN	Bakersfield	
1450	KPSI	Palm Springs	
1490	KDB	Santa Barbara	rock
1560	KDMC	Bakersfield	
1580	KDAY	Santa Monica	black

FM	station	city	format
88.3	KSDS	San Diego	jazz
89.9	KCRW	Santa Monica	eclectic
90.7	KPFK	Los Angeles	classical
91.5	KUSC	Los Angeles	classical
91.9	KVCR	San Bernardino	
93.1	KNX	Los Angeles	mellow
94.1	KLYD	Bakersfield	
94.1	KFSD	San Diego	classical
94.7	KMET	Los Angeles	rock
95.5	KLOS	Los Angeles	rock
96.1	KUNA	San Diego	
97.1	KHTZ	Los Angeles	mellow
98.1	KIFM	San Diego	mellow
100.3	KIQQ	Los Angeles	
100.7	KFMB	San Diego	
101.1	KRTH	Los Angeles	oldies
101.5	KGB	San Diego	rock
102.7	KISS	Los Angeles	
103.3	KRUZ	Santa Barbara	
103.5	KOST	Los Angeles	
104.3	KBIG	Los Angeles	
105.1	KKGO	Los Angeles	jazz
105.5	KNAC	Long Beach	rock
105.9	KWST	Los Angeles	rock
106.5	KPRI	San Diego	rock

TV Stations in Southern California

channel	station	city	affiliation
2	KNXT	Los Angeles	CBS
3	KEYT	Santa Barbara	ABC
4	KNBC	Los Angeles	NBC
5	KTLA	Los Angeles	independent
6	KSBY	San Luis Obispo	NBC
7	KABC	Los Angeles	ABC
8	KFMB	San Diego	CBS
9	KHJ	Los Angeles	independent
10	KGTV	San Diego	ABC
11	KTTV	Los Angeles	independent

12	XEWT	Tijuana	Spanish
13	KCOP	Los Angeles	independent
28	KCET	Los Angeles	PBS
34	KMEX	Los Angeles	Spanish

Health and Emergencies

In the event you need medical assistance, consult the local yellow pages for the physician or pharmacist nearest you. In large cities, there is usually a physician referral service whose number is listed.

There is nothing cheap about being sick in America. Make sure you're covered by medical insurance while traveling in California. An ambulance costs around $200; an emergency room treatment costs a minimum of $50; and an average hospital bed costs at least $300 per night. If costs are a concern, turn first to the country hospital which gives good service and will not charge patients who are indigent.

Most hospitals have 24-hour emergency rooms. No matter what your problem is, you usually end waiting longer at these "emergency rooms" than you feel you should but the eventual care and treatment is thorough and professional.

Below are but a few of the larger hospitals and more popular 24-hour drugstores:

Hospitals

Cedar-Sinai Medical Center, 8700 Beverly Blvd., 855–5000
City of Hope, 1500 E. Duarte Blvd., 359–8111
Hollywood Presbyterian Medical Center, 1300 N. Vermont Ave., 660–3530
UCLA, 10833 LeConte Ave., 825–3901
USC, 1200 N. State St., 226–2622

Drug Stores

Thrifty, 3rd and Vermont, 381–5257
Kaiser Permanente, 4867 Sunset Blvd., 667–8301
Kaiser Permanente, 1050 W. Pacific Coast Highway, 539–1650
Kaiser Permanente, 9400 E. Rosecrans, 920–4211

Security and Crime

Los Angeles and San Diego, like any large cities, have their share of crime, and it is advisable for visitors not to linger in non-commercial areas after dark. Whenever possible, travel with another person while sightseeing or shopping — particularly at night. Women, especially, should not walk in deserted or poor areas alone.

If you witness a crime or need the assistance of a police officer, dial "0" and ask the operator for the police.

No California city is in the Top 10 of America's most crime-ridden cities. Only Oakland is in the Top 20. In general, it is safe to walk the streets during the day.

If driving, lock your car and never leave luggage, cameras or other valuables in view. Lock them in the glove compartment or in the trunk. At night, park in lighted areas.

Never leave your luggage unattended. While waiting for a room reservation, a cab or a rental car, always keep your property in plain view. Rather than carrying your bags around with you, ask the front desk at a hotel, the hostess at a restaurant, or the security guard at a department store if you could check in your luggage with them. Most hotels provide a storage service free of charge. Never leave money or jewelry in your hotel room, even it is only for a short time. Always turn in your room key at the desk when going out.

Try to carry only the cash you need. Use credit cards and traveler's checks whenever possible and avoid displaying large amounts of cash when making purchases.

Useful Telephone Numbers
(Los Angeles)

Police	625–3311
Fire	384–3131
	262–2111
Ambulance	483–6721
Paramedics	262–2111
	677–1181
Child Abuse Hotline	989–3151
Suicide Prevention Hotline	381–5111
Rape Hotline	262–0944

Dining Out

If it's true that Southern Californians dine out an average of two or three times a week, it follows that there must be an awful lot of restaurants around, and there are. New ones come in waves; in the late 70s there was the Szechuan explosion where everyone got their first taste of *mu shu pork*, and fast on its tail came the *sushi* revolution and the popular *California roll*. Southern California would have to be the nation's leader in fast-food places; they include more historic **Tommy's** (known for their chili burgers) and **Carny's** (a railroad car on the Sunset Strip) and **Fatburger**. The state-of-the-art restaurant would therefore be a fast-food *sushi* dive ("It shouldn't take long to serve raw fish"), and yes, there are a few around.

The most prevalent ethnic food is Mexican, and there are at least four dozen good Mexican restaurants in the area. Popular Mexican dishes are *tacos* (thin corn *tortillas* folded and stuffed with beef, pork, or chicken, lettuce and cheese) and *carne asada* (tender butterfly steak). One sign of a good Mexican restaurant is if it makes good *albondigas*, or spicy meatball soup.

Steak and lobster restaurants abound, and usually they have salad bars where you can take a plate and create your own salad from among dozens of ingredients.

Another popular Southern California institution is "Happy Hour," which is usually between 4 and 7 p.m., when the price of beer, wine and hard drinks is reduced. A lot of restaurants serve hot appetizers in their bar area on an all-you-can-eat basis, *for free*. A popular trick among used-to-be-starving artists is to eat for free at a different Happy Hour bar each night.

Los Angeles is a city where you can shop at midnight or have your hair done at 3 a.m., so it shouldn't be surprising that there are many 24-hour restaurants. Several are delicatessens with extensive menus. The most characteristic all-night haunt is **The Pantry** downtown. It's been a landmark for over 50 years.

When in Southern California, one cannot forget the fast-food chains and franchises, and prevalent are **McDonald's, Burger King, Carl's Jr., In-and-Out,** and **Jack-in-the-Box**, all of which serve burgers and fries. **Del Taco** and **Taco Bell** specialize in Mexican delights and **Der Wienerschnitzel** and **H. Salt Esq.** whose fish and chips are popular among locals.

See the appendix for a small selection of the many and various restaurants in Southern California.

Shopping

For those with expensive tastes, the three-block stretch of **Rodeo Drive** between Santa Monica and Wilshire boulevards in Beverly Hills will certainly not let you down. Rumored to be the most expensive commercial real estate in California, Rodeo Drive features such fine stores as **Gucci, Cartier, Courreges, Bally of Switzerland,** the **Elizabeth Arden Salon**, and **Giorgio**, where men can have a whiskey and shoot pool while their wives shop. The window displays are superb, and on a Sunday afternoon the street will be filled with window shoppers.

The rest of Beverly Hills offers fine shopping as well, from the recently opened **Nieman-Marcus** to the finest of the Los Angeles-based department stores, **Robinson's**. Beverly Hills has five bookstores; **Hunter's, B. Dalton's, Crown, Doubleday** and **Brentano's**.

Downtown Beverly Hills is straddled by two large shopping malls: to the east, on Beverly and La Cienega boulevards, is **The Beverly Center** with dozens of fine boutiques, department stores, restaurants and 14 movie theaters. This is a mall for the chic, and if you want to see what kinds of fashions are in, just watch the people in the Beverly Center. To the west of Beverly Hills is **Century City**, home of the **ABC Entertainment Center** (which contains the Schubert Theatre for plays and the Plitt Theatre for movies) and a large shopping center highlighted by **Bullock's, Robinson's**, and first-class fashion boutiques such as **Ann Taylor**.

An area that is more hip than chic is West Hollywood. There are stores along Melrose Avenue that look like large costume emporiums; West Hollywood is an eccentric's paradise with lots of unisex shops, and a few kinky lingerie shops.

Westwood Village is adjacent to UCLA and is a movie lover's seventh heaven: there are 18 movie theaters within a four-block radius. It's one of the few places in the city where people walk the streets — and in it's own way it is similar to Berkeley or Greenwich Village in that you can browse through **Tower Records**, buy a novel at **Hunter's Books**, and sit down at an outdoor cafe with friends at 10 in the evening. Mimes, magicians and musicians often give street performances on weekends.

Near downtown Los Angeles is **Olvera Street**, one of the city's oldest streets, with many shops selling Mexican crafts. Nearby is **Little Tokyo**, where you can buy clothes and crafts in the largest Japanese shopping area in the country.

Southern California has over 50 indoor malls for the convenience of shoppers. The largest of these malls is **Del Amo** in Torrance. This mall is so big that it has not one, but two **B. Dalton** bookstores!

Other large modern malls: **South Coast Plaza** in Costa Mesa near Newport Beach, **The Galleria** in Sherman Oaks, **Fashion Valley** in San Diego, **La Jolla Village Square, The Glendale Galleria**, and **Santa Monica Place** near the ocean. Each of these malls have several large department stores and hundreds of smaller speciality shops in addition to restaurants and fast-food counters.

On Wednesday mornings in Santa Monica, the downtown streets are blocked off so that farmers and craftsmen can sell their goods at the weekly outdoor market. It's a good chance to pick up produce or knickknacks at good prices.

If you want to avoid the stereotyped coffee mugs and other commercial souvenirs, and return home with authentic made-in-California gifts, take a trip to the farm country. Apple wine, blackberry jam, dried fruits and herbs, fresh honey, jojoba oil ... there are hundreds of products that you can buy direct from the producer, saving yourself money while visiting a real, working farm.

Tours and Attractions

Los Angeles

FARMER'S MARKET, 6333 West Third, (213) 833-9211.

A sprawling marketplace with over 160 individually owned shops and restaurants. Souvenirs, fresh fruits and vegetables, handmade baskets, imports and more in a labyrinthine setting.

Hours: 9 a.m. until dusk.

GRIFFITH PARK OBSERVATORY PLANETARIUM THEATRE, 2800 East Observatory, (213) 664-1191, (213) 997-3624.

Located in the 4,000-acre park, the observatory houses a 500-seat planetarium theatre and the Hall of Science.

Hours: In summer 1 p.m. to 10 p.m. Sun. to Fri., 11:30 a.m. to 10 p.m. Sat; in winter 2 to 10 p.m. Tues. to Fri., from 11:30 a.m. Sat., from 1 p.m. Sun.

LITTLE TOKYO, First at San Pedro Street, (213) 626-5116.

Little Tokyo is the social, economic, cultural and religious center of the largest Japanese-American community in the mainland United States. The Japanese Village Plaza has 26 shops and 14 restaurants.

Hours: Most shops open 10:30 a.m. to 7 p.m.

LOS ANGELES ZOO, 5333 Zoo Drive, (213) 666-4090.

A large aviary, a Reptile House and a Children's Zoo are featured in this sprawling 113-acre zoo.

Hours: 10 a.m. to 6 p.m. in summer, 10 a.m. to 5 p.m. in winter.

Admission: adults $3, children and seniors $1.

MARINELAND, Rancho Palos Verdes, (213) 541-5663, (213) 377-1571.

Shows featuring dolphins, sea lions and killer whales in beautiful outdoor amphitheaters overlooking the Pacific. Exotic marine life from around the world is displayed in "Passages Beneath the Sea", a multi-aquarium exhibit. You can rent snorkeling equipment and dive into Baja Reef with its thousands of harmless tropical and local fish.

Hours: 10 a.m. to dusk. Closed on Mondays and Tuesdays during winter.

THE QUEEN MARY AND THE SPRUCE GOOSE, Pier J, Long Beach, (213) 435-4747.

The Queen Mary is the world's largest passenger boat at more than 1,000 feet long. During the Second World War, the ship was used to transport troops and Hitler offered a quarter of a million dollars and the Iron Cross as a reward for her sinking. Many U-boats tried, but they never came close because this ship was the world's fastest until 1952. Tour the engine room, the wheelhouse and the salons decorated in the art deco style. Entertainment, shops and restaurants are found aboard the ship and in neighboring Londontowne Plaza.

The Spruce Goose is Howard Hughes' legendary "flying boat" whose wingspan is longer than a football field. Visit the cockpit and flight deck, and watch movies on the construction of the plane and Hughes' flying career in Hollywood.

Hours: 10 a.m. to 4 p.m. daily.

WILL ROGERS STATE PARK, off Sunset Boulevard in the Pacific Palisades.

Once home to the famed humorist, this ranch house is now open to tourists. Polo matches take place on weekends on the large lawn below the house. Hike a half-mile up the trail behind the house and you'll have a majestic view of the ocean, the hills and the city. Adjacent to the house is a large lawn with a sand trap and a green that Will Rogers once used to practice golf on. It's now used primarily for picnics. One of the choice places to spend a Sunday afternoon.

San Diego

BALBOA PARK, in the center of San Diego, (619) 239-0512.

A 1,074-acre park housing museums, art galleries, theaters, sports facilities and grounds for hiking or picnicking. It's also the home of the world famous San Diego Zoo, and the botanical gardens. The Reuben H. Fleet Space Theater and Science Center, Hall of Champions, Museum of Man, Natural History Museum, San Diego Museum of Art and the Timken Gallery are all in the park.

MARITIME MUSEUM, (619) 234-9153.

Comprised of three ships moored alongside the Embarcadero. Visitors can tour the 100-year-old *Star of India* (the oldest merchant vessel afloat), the ferryboat *Berkeley* (saved thousands of people in the 1906 earthquake by ferrying them to Oakland), and the steam yacht *Medea* (built in 1904 for a wealthy Scotsman).

Hours: 9 a.m. to 8 p.m. daily.

PALOMAR OBSERVATORY, Palomar Mountain, (619) 742-3476.

Located 66 miles (107 km) north of San Diego, the telescope is at the summit of the 5,565-foot mountain. In addition to the dome gallery, where you can view the 200-inch telescope, there is an exhibit hall with photographs of nebulae and star clusters taken through the telescope.

Hours: 9 a.m. to 5 p.m. daily.

SAN DIEGO OLD TOWN, 2645 San Diego Ave., (619) 237-6770.

Old Town was the first European settlement in California, and many of its buildings have been restored. The settlement dates back to 1821, and highlights include the Casa de Estudillo and the *San Diego Union* newspaper office.

Hours: Tours led by rangers of Old Town State Park depart daily at 2 p.m. from the Machada y Silvas Adobe.

THE SAN DIEGO ZOO, (619) 231-1515.

This zoo ranks among the best in the world. Many of the 3,400 animals are allowed to roam in barless, moated enclosures which resemble their natural environment. A 40-minute guided bus tour will give you a total perspective of the zoo and allow you to pick your areas of concentration. Don't miss the walk-through aviary, nor the koalas (there are more than 30, the largest collection outside of Australia). There is a Children's Zoo built to the scale of a four-year-old, complete with a netting paddock.

Hours: Open every day of the year; from 9 a.m. to 7 p.m. July through Labor Day; 9 a.m. to 5 p.m. Labor Day through Oct., and March through June; 9 a.m. to 5 p.m. Nov. through Feb.

Admission: adults $8, children (below 16 years) $3.75.

SEA WORLD, 1720 South Shores Rd., (619) 226-1221.

Features six major shows and dozens of exhibits containing marine life from around the globe, including the world's largest live shark exhibit. The star attractions are the charming Shamu, a three-ton killer whale and the penguins. Throughout the park are more than 1,300 birds from all over the world.

Hours: 9 a.m. until dusk daily.

Admission: adults $10.55, children (3 to 11 years) $7.50.

WILD ANIMAL PARK, (619) 231-1515.

Located 30 miles (48 km) northeast of San Diego, this 1,800-acre wildlife preserve has a home base in Nairobi Village, where you can see animal shows or visit the gorilla grotto. A 50-minute monorail ride takes you through the sweeping plains and veldts where you'll see elephants, zebras and tigers in something akin to their natural habitats.

Hours: 9 a.m. to dusk daily, except in summer months when visitors may enjoy entertainment in Nairobi Village until 11 p.m.

Admission: adults $8.75, children (under 16 years) $6.50.

Orange County Inland and Coast

DISNEYLAND, Harbor Blvd. at Santa Ana Freeway, Anaheim, (213) 626-8605, (714) 999-4123.

Over 200 million people have visited this magical kingdom. Enter the park and you are on **Main Street U.S.A.** with its turn-of-the century buildings, shops, marching band, horseless carriage ride and Penny Arcade. In **Adventureland**, you may take a "Jungle Cruise," tour the "Haunted Mansion," or go on the cavernous "Pirates of the Caribbean" ride, which is one of the most imaginative in the park. In **Frontierland**, the "Mark Twain Steamship" paddles through the Rivers of America. The "Matterhorn" is a sleek roller coaster in **Fantasyland**, where you can also see life from a different perspective in "It's a Small World." Perhaps thee most popular attraction in the park is "Space Mountain," the roller coaster that flies through darkness and finally explodes into outer space. Naturally, it's in **Tomorrowland.**

Disney characters, such as Mickey Mouse and Pluto, stroll the grounds and will be glad to pose for a picture with children. In the summer, there are nightly fireworks. Disneyland has many services including Lost and Found, First Aid, and a Pet Kennel. There is a Baby Center for preparing formulae, warming bottles and changing diapers. Unfortunately, there are no babysitting services. Strollers and wheelchairs are available, and the park is designed for the handicapped.

Hours: Mid March to mid September, 9 a.m. to 12 midnight daily. Mid October to mid March, 10 a.m. to 6 p.m. Wed. to Fri., to 7 p.m. Sat. and Sun., closed Mon. and Tues.

Admission: adults $12, junior (12-17 years) $10.50, child $9.

KNOTT'S BERRY FARM, 8039 Beach Blvd., Buena Park, (714) 827-1776.

Family fun in this Old West Ghost Town, colorful Fiesta Village and jazzy Roaring Twenties area. More than 130 rides and attractions including the speedy "Montezuma's Revenge," the "Parachute Sky Jump" and a chance to pan for gold. The Good Time Theatre holds 2,100 people and features top entertainment. Fine restaurants and shops within the park.

Hours: In summer, 9 a.m. to 12 midnight Sun. to Thurs., to 1 a.m. Fri. and Sat.; in winter, 10 a.m. to 9 p.m. weekends, 10 a.m. to 6 p.m. weekdays. Closed on Wednesdays and Thursdays except for holidays and vacation periods.

San Fernando Valley

NBC STUDIO TOUR, 3000 West Alameda Ave., Burbank, (213) 840-3537.

A totally unstaged one-hour narrative walking tour of a television studio. You'll learn about set construction, special effects, make-up and wardrobe, and visit the sound stage of *The Tonight Show*.

Hours: 9 a.m. to 4 p.m. except major holidays.

Admission: adults $3.50, children (5-11 years) $2.75. Children under 5 years, free.

UNIVERSAL STUDIOS TOUR, Universal City, (213) 508-3794.

Here's a chance to get a behind-the-scenes glimpse of how movies are made. Take the two-hour surprise-filled tram tour past movie sets and through the back lot, and then watch the shows in the Entertainment Center. Especially good is the Stunt Show.

Hours: 8 a.m. to 6 p.m. in summer, 9 a.m. to 4

p.m. for the rest of the year.

Admission: adults and children more than 12 years $10.95, children $7.95, seniors $8.45.

Palm Springs

MOORTEN BOTANICAL GARDENS, 1701 S. Palm Canyon Dr., Palm Springs, (619) 327–6555.

Nature trails among 2,000 varieties of giant cacti, flowers and succulents.

Hours: 9 a.m. to 5 p.m. daily.

THE PALM SPRINGS AERIAL TRAMWAY, State Highway 111 and Tramway Road, Palm Springs, (619) 325–1391.

The tramway takes you from the desert to the mountains as it ascends a mile in less than 18 minutes. At the top there is a breathtaking view and nearby is the 13,000-acre Mt. San Jacinto State Park with campgrounds and winter skiing. The Alpine Restaurant on top features prime rib.

Hours: Tram departs every half hour from 10 a.m. Mon. to Fri. and from 8 a.m. on weekends. Tram fare (round trip): adult $7.95, children $4.95.

Other Cities

JOSHUA TREE NATIONAL MONUMENT, Twentynine Palms.

Basically a wildlife sanctuary, it covers more than 870 square miles (2,253 sq km) east of Los Angeles. Numerous different kinds of flora abound including the rare Joshua Tree. Camping facilities are also available.

LION COUNTRY SAFARI, 8800 Irvine Center Drive, Laguna Hills, (714) 837–1200.

A large wildlife preserve and theme amusement park located mid way between Los Angeles and San Diego.

Hours: in summer, 9:45 a.m. to 5 p.m.; in winter, 9:45 a.m. to 3:30 p.m.

SIX FLAGS MAGIC MOUNTAIN, Magic Mountain Parkway, Valencia, (805) 255–4826.

Located 25 miles north of Los Angeles, this 260-acre amusement park features the mighty Colossus (a huge wooden roller coaster), the Revolution (a 360-degree vertical loop roller coaster), and the Roaring Rapids (whitewater rafting ride). There is also a Dolphin Show, a Marionette Show, a High Diving Show and a Children's Village with a petting zoo. Shows, concerts, restaurants.

Hours: the park opens at 10 a.m. daily, the Children's Village every weekend all year and daily from May 21 to Sept. 11.

THE HEARST CASTLE, San Simeon Village, (805) 927–4621. (For information on toll-free ticket, call (800) 952–5580).

Available are three two-hour tours of the gardens, pools and interior of the castle of the famed publishing baron, William Randolph Hearst. Located 30 miles north of Morro Bay in the foothills rising from the ocean, the castle is a wonderland of hedonism in the middle of nowhere. The rooms are filled with valuable pieces of art from all periods. Tour reservations a must.

Admission: adults $8, children $4.

The Missions of California

In 1769, Father Junipero Serra established the first of his 21 missions in San Diego. The chain of missions stretches all the way north to Sonoma. The missions were situated to be a day's ride apart, which was 30 miles in those days. The more popular missions among visitors are:

Mission San Diego de Alcala, 10818 San Diego Mission Rd., San Diego, (619) 281–8449. Oldest of the missions, with original records available for viewing.

Mission San Luis Rey, 4050 Mission Ave., San Luis Rey, (619) 757–3651. Largest of the missions, located near Oceanside north of San Diego.

Mission San Juan Capistrano, Ortega Highway at Camino Capistrano, San Juan Capistrano, (714) 493–1111. A famed summer home of the swallows, it includes a museum and diorama of early mission life.

Mission Santa Barbara, Laguna St., Santa Barbara. A candle has been burning on the altar since 1786; museum, gardens and beautiful view of Santa Barbara.

Cultural Activities

Museums

Briggs Cunningham Automotive Museum, 250 East Baker, Costa Mesa, (714) 546–7660.

Collection of autos from the turn of the century to the present.

George C. Page Museum, 5801 Wilshire Blvd., Los Angeles, (213) 936–2230.

Prehistoric fossils recovered from the La Brea Tar Pits, the world's richest source of Ice Age mammals and bird fossils.

Open: 10 a.m. to 5 p.m. Tues. to Sun.

Admission: Adults $1; children, seniors and students 50 cents.

The Huntington Art Gallery, 1151 Oxford Rd., San Marino, (213) 792–6141.

Contains mostly 18th and 19th Century British art — paintings, drawings, sculpture, ceramics, silver and furniture. Contains Gainsborough's "Blue Boy," and Constable's "View on the Stour," as well as other masterpieces of the period. The art gallery was originally a residence for the family, so the art is displayed in settings similar to those for which the art was created.

Open: 1 to 4:30 p.m. Tues. to Sun.

Admission: Free.

The J. Paul Getty Museum, 17985 Pacific Coast Highway, Malibu, (213) 454–6541.

Tremendous collection of Greek and Roman antiquities housed in a replica of an ancient Roman villa that stood on the slopes of Mount Vesuvius overlooking the Bay of Naples. This museum stands on the slopes of Malibu with a breathtaking view of the Pacific. In addition to the marble and bronze sculptures, you'll see tapestries, chandeliers, vases—and even a few rooms of comparatively modern items from the 15th and 16th Centuries. Lunch available at the Garden Tea Room.
Open: 10 a.m. to 5 p.m. Tues. to Sat., from September to June; 10 a.m. to 5 p.m. Mon. to Fri., from June to September.
Admission: Free, but since this is a residential neighborhood, parking reservations must be made in advance.

La Jolla Museum of Contemporary Art, 700 Prospect St., La Jolla, (619) 454–3541.
The works of Warhol, Lichtenstein, Stella and other important contemporary artists are on display.
Open: 10 a.m. to 5 p.m. Tues. to Fri., 12:30 p.m. to 5 p.m. Sat. and Sun.
Admission: Adults $2, children 50 cents.

Los Angeles Children's Museum, 310 N. Main Street, Los Angeles, (213) 687–8800. (To schedule tour groups, call (213) 687–8825.)
A "hands-on" museum integrating art, science, humanities and technology, where children (and adults) touch, shape, explore and use objects.
Open: From September to June, 10 a.m. to 4:30 p.m. Sat and Sun., 2:30 to 4:30 p.m. Wed.; from June to September, 11 a.m. to 4:30 p.m. Mon. to Fri., 10 a.m. to 4:30 p.m. Sat. and Sun.
Admission: Adults $3.50, children under 14 years and seniors $1.75.

The Los Angeles County Museum of Art, 5905 Wilshire Blvd., Los Angeles, (213) 867–6111.
Works by Picasso, Rembrandt, and El Greco give it its world-class stature, but the museum's real strengths are the Exotic Art collection (Nepal and Tibet) and the traveling collections. At any given time there will be five or six temporary shows going on, and they may range from tapestries to copper engravings to photographs. The museum also has a superb film series, showing rarely seen classics.
Open: 10 a.m. to 5 p.m. Tues. to Fri., 10 a.m. to 6 p.m. Sat. and Sun.
Admission: Adults $1.50; children, students and seniors 75 cents; children under five years, free.

Mission San Diego de Alcala, 10818 San Diego Mission Rd., San Diego, (619) 281–8449.
In 1769, Padre Junipero Serra established the first of his 21 missions in San Diego. The buildings date from 1813 and were restored in 1931. The Father Luis Jayme Museum at the mission has some of the original mission records as well as early liturgical robes and books. Also in San Diego County is Mission San Luis Rey.
Open: 9 a.m. to 4 p.m. daily.
Admission: Adults $1

Museum of Neon Art, 704 Traction Ave., Los Angeles, (213) 617–1580.
The one-and-only. Neon, electric and kinetic art.
Open: 12 noon to 5 p.m.
Admission: $2.50.

Museum of Science and Industry, 700 State Drive, Los Angeles, (213) 744–7400.
Continually changing exhibits examine man in relationship with his environmnt. Communications, Computers, Transportation, Hall of Health—a virtual haven for the curious.
Open: 10 a.m. to 5 p.m. daily.
Admission: Free.

The Natural History Museum of Los Angeles County, 900 Exposition Blvd., Los Angeles, (213) 744–3411.
Fossil dinosaurs, pre-Colombian artifacts, Southwest history and much more in this huge 35-hall museum that's been a popular attraction for 70 years. Films are screened on Saturdays at 2 p.m., and chamber music is performed on Sundays at 2 p.m.
Open: 10 a.m. to 5 p.m. Tues. to Sun.
Admission: Adults $1; children, seniors and students, 50 cents.

Norton Simon Museum of Art, 411 W. Colorado Blvd., Pasadena, (213) 449–6840.
Through family and corporate foundations, Norton Simon has assembled one of the finest art collections in the world. On display are works by Picasso, Goya, Rembrandt and Degas; also works from the Baroque and Rococo periods. The Museum Bookshop is a superb art bookstore that also sells prints.
Open: 12 noon to 6 p.m. Thurs. to Sun.
Admission: Adults $2; children, seniors and students, 75 cents.

Palm Springs Desert Museum, 101 Museum Drive, Palm Springs, (619) 325–7186.
More than 1,000 American Indian artifacts, including some of the finest examples of rug making and basketry in the world. Lectures, films, field trips.
Open: 10 a.m. to 4 p.m. Tues. to Fri., 10 a.m. to 5 p.m. Sat and Sun. Closed on Mondays.
Admission: Adults $2.50, children $1.25.

The Real Thing Museum of Coca-Cola Memorabilia, 11650 Riverside Dr., North Hollywood, (213) 980–3444.
Pure Americana: a museum of artifacts (dating back to 1891) used to promote a soft drink. It's a tribute to advertising, and a fascinating look at 20th Century America. Absolutely charming.
Open: 11 a.m. to 4 p.m. Mon. to Sat.
Admission: Free.

San Diego Museum of Art, (619) 232–7931.
Houses collections of great Dutch, Flemish, Italian, Spanish Renaissance and Baroque paintings. Also works by Degas, Picasso, Munch, Monet and Braque.
Open: 11 a.m. to 4 p.m. Mon. to Sat.
Admission: Adults $2.50, children 50 cents.

Art Galleries

The nature of the art scene in Southern California is quick-changing. In West Hollywood a style can go in and out of fashion while you're waiting for a bus. West Hollywood has the greatest concentration of galleries, and is where the avant garde resides. Laguna, Palm Springs and La Jolla are three areas where artists congregate and galleries abound. Art Openings are popular and usually occur between 7 and 9 p.m. on the opening night of a new exhibit. Wine and cheese are traditional, and the artist will usually be in attendance to explain a nuance you might have overlooked.

Art Space, 10550 Santa Monica Blvd., Los Angeles.
LA Artcore, 652 Mateo St., Los Angeles.
Galerie Helene, 8232 W. 3rd St., Los Angeles.
The Richard Mann Gallery, 665 N. La Cienega, Los Angeles.
Jan Baum Gallery, 170 S. La Brea, Los Angeles.
Molly Barnes Gallery, 750 N. La Cienega, Los Angeles.
Flow Ace Gallery, 8373 Melrose Ave., Los Angeles.
Stephen White Gallery, 752 N. La Cienega, Los Angeles.
Traction Gallery, 800 Traction Ave., Los Angeles.
Kirk deGooyer Gallery, 1308 Factory Place, Los Angeles.
Knowles Gallery, 7420 Girard Ave., La Jolla.
Old Town Circle Gallery, 2501 San Diego Ave., San Diego.
Thomas Babeor Gallery, 7470 Girard Ave., La Jolla.
Gallery of Two Sisters, 1298 Prospect St., La Jolla.

Music, Dance and Theaters

Los Angeles has one of the finest symphony orchestras in the world; the renowned **Los Angeles Philharmonic**. Their winter home is the **Dorothy Chandler Pavilion** in **The Music Center**, 135 N. Grand, 972–7211 or 241–9413. Their summer home is **The Hollywood Bowl**, 2301 N. Highland Ave., Hollywood, 876–8742. **The Ahmanson Theater** and **The Mark Taper Forum** are also part of the Music Center. At all of these, you will be treated to lavishly mounted productions, thus explaining why tickets are expensive. The atmosphere is definitely dressy. Performing at the Music Center from May to October is **The Los Angeles Civic Light Opera**.

You will find world-famous soloists, such as Pincas Zuckerman and Jakob Gimpel, rendering their favorite pieces at **The Ambassador Auditorium**, 300 W. Green St., Pasadena, 577–5511. Between September to May, chamber groups take over.

The **Los Angeles Ballet** performs at **The Wilshire Ebell Theater**, 4401 W. Eighth St., Los Angeles, 939–1128.

For Broadway fans, there are (among many others) the **Schubert Theaters**, 2020 Avenue of the Stars, Century City, 553–9000; and the **Pantages**, a famous Hollywood landmark at 6233 Hollywood Blvd. The first one is famous for its stage of musicals such as *Chorus Line* and *Dreamgirls*. Tickets are expensive but worth it.

The **Westwood Playhouse** at 10886 LeConte, Westwood, 553–9000 is a versatile theater that presents mime troupes and one-man shows as well as musicals.

A bit on the avant-garde side is **The Roxy Theater** at 9009 Sunset Blvd., Hollywood, 276–2222. The former rock club is trying its hand at theater with much success.

John Anson Ford Theater, 2580 Cahuenga Blvd., Los Angeles, 972–7428, the **Huntington Hartford**, 1615 N. Vine St., Hollywood, 462–6666, and the **Wilshire Theater**, 8440 Wilshire Blvd., Beverly Hills, 653–4490, are three other Los Angeles theaters with over 1,000 seats.

Some of the smaller top-notch theaters are the **Landmark Alliance Theater**, 6817 Franklin Ave., Hollywood, 851–5982, **Cast Theater**, 804 N. El Centro Ave., Los Angeles, 462–0265, and **The Odyssey Theater**, 12111 Ohio Ave., W. Los Angeles, 826–1626.

On the UCLA campus, **Royce Hall** (825–2953) is a 2,000-seat auditorium that features a distinguished fine arts series including world-famous soloists and dance companies.

There are scores of theaters in Los Angeles, and a complete listing is available on Sundays in the *Los Angeles Times,* "Calendar" section.

In San Diego, the nationally-acclaimed **San Diego Opera** attracts performers such as **Beverly Sills** and **Luciano Pavarotti**. The season runs from mid October through May, and each summer two Verdi operas are performed. For information, call (619) 232–7636. Performances are downtown at the **Civic Theater.**

Also playing at the Civic Theater from November until May is the **San Diego Symphony.** In the summer, the symphony plays at various outdoor locations throughout the San Diego area. For information, call (619) 239–9721.

The landmark **Old Globe Theater**, in the Simon Edison Center for the Performing Arts, (619) 239–2255, stages a summer Shakespeare Festival on its outdoor Festival Stage.

Libraries

Every city and town in America has a public library. Libraries vary enormously in quality and service, but a few generalities can be made. The larger cities have library systems, built on a main branch which offers major collections and special services. Neighborhood branches around the city offer smaller collections.

In the larger cities, the library systems offer services to the blind, deaf and physically handicapped, youth and children's services include special collections and story telling. In addition, some of these systems offer special local history collections, and foreign language books. Some have business branches devoted to periodical and book selections on subjects relating to international business.

Use of all libraries is free. Non-residents are not

allowed to check out books, but can read all you want inside the building from reference materials to daily newspapers and foreign-language periodicals. Listing of neighborhood branches can be found in the White Pages of the telephone directory under *city government*.

The UCLA Library System, 405 Hilgard Ave., Westwood, 825–1323, contains 18 separate libraries, including a superb music library and the extensive University Research Library.

The **Central Library**, 630 W. 5th St., Los Angeles, 626–7461, is an enormous library that has a California history room and a genealogy room as well as a special children's library. In the patent library you can look up the patent for the Frisbee or the yo-yo.

The Huntington Library, 1151 Oxford St., San Marino, 792–6141, has the earliest known manuscript of Chaucer's *Canterbury Tales* and is a mecca for serious scholars.

The Beverly Hills Public Library, 444 N. Rexford, Beverly Hills, 550–4721, is where some of the top novelists and scriptwriters do their research. Multimedia collection includes fillms, records and cassettes.

The Palm Springs Public Library, 300 S. Sunrise Way, Palm Springs, (619) 323–8291, has over 78,000 volumes and has over 250 current magazines. Extensive multimedia collection.

Bookstores

The two largest chains in America, **B. Dalton** and **Waldenbooks**, are strongly represented in Southern California, and any sizeable indoor shopping mall is bound to have one or both of these stores. A third chain, **Crown Books**, sells remainder books and best-sellers at discount.

The "Big Daddy" of the B. Dalton stores is located at 6734 Hollywood Blvd., 469–8191. Extensive fiction selection, plus large sections on cinema and computers. Don't miss the Bargain Book section on the third floor where you can pick up a coffee table book of Picasso or Monet illustrations at a big discount.

A few of the independents, most notably **Papa Bach's** (11317 Santa Monica Blvd., W. Los Angeles, 474–2378), **Chatterton's** (1818 N. Vermont Ave., Los Angeles), and **Small World Books** (1407 Ocean Front Walk, Venice, 399–2360) aim for a more literary clientele.

A haven for film buffs is **Larry Edmund's Cinema and Theatre Bookshop**, 6658 Hollywood Blvd., Los Angeles, 463–3273. In the rear is their fabulous collection of Hollywood stills from movies going back to the twenties. The right hand wall has one of the most complete inventories of plays anywhere. Screenplays, biographies, used books and magazines. You could spend a whole afternoon here easily.

Movies

First-run movies, fresh from Hollywood, are being screened for the first time. Most American theaters show exclusively first-runs — some showing them at slightly reduced price after the first

wave of popularity is over. Most theaters offer afternoon matinees on Wednesday, Saturday and Sunday at discounted ticket prices. Tickets range from $4 to $5 in the evening, $2 to $3 for matinees.

Being the home of the movie industry, it would seem appropriate that Los Angeles has a lot of movie theaters, but none can match "Cineplex," the 14-theater complex in the **Beverly Center**. Movies often open in **Westwood**, where there are more movie theaters per square mile than anywhere else in the world.

To find out what's playing and at what time, read the "Calendar" section of the *Los Angeles Times* or the "Style" section of the *Los Angeles Herald Examiner*. The *L.A. Weekly* and *The Reader* also publish complete movie listings on a weekly basis.

United Artists Theaters and **Mann Theaters** are the most widespread of the theater groups; other prominent chains are **General Cinema Theaters, Edwards Cinemas, Pacific Theaters, SRO Theaters** and **AMC Theaters.**

The **Laemmle Theaters** present first-rate foreign releases as well as artistic American movies.

There are several excellent revival theaters in Southern California; they play different movies every night of the week. Famous are the **Nuart**, the **Rialto**, the **Beverly** in Los Angeles, and the Art Theatre in Long Beach. The ticket price for these movie theaters is a couple of dollars less than first-run theaters. Most revival movies are shown on a double bill (two movies for the price of one).

Only the large cities have theaters that specialize in foreign films, subtitled for American audiences. In addition, universities often screen such classics on campus

Festivals and Events

Filling the annual calendar are festivals, events and tournaments. Some of these are causes for grand celebrations while others are observed on a smaller scale, but none fails to attract a large turn-out of local townsfolk who flock to watch or support or participate in the true American spirit.

For exact information on time and venue, it is best to call up any one of the tourist information centers listed in the appendix of this section or check the daily press for a listing of the events. Do this at time of visit only due to frequent changes in these programs which are definitely not to be missed if you wish to catch a glimpse of the local color.

January

Tournament of Roses Parade & Rose Bowl Football Game, Pasadena.

This spectacular parade is a must for out-of-towners. It features floats made up solely of roses. Get there early because good seats are hard to come by; many people spend the night camping out on Colorado Blvd. For advance tickets to the parade, write Tournament of Roses Association, 391 S. Orange Grove Blvd., Pasadena, CA 91105.

International Folk Dance Festival, Los Angeles.
A chance to watch experts from around the world—or to participate.

Greater Los Angeles Auto Show, Los Angeles Convention Center.
A chance to preview the new cars and see what the manufacturers have planned for the future.

Sunkist Invitational Track Meet, Los Angeles.

Southern California Boat Show, Los Angeles Convention Center.

Beverly Hills Dog Show, Sports Arena.

San Diego Open Golf Tournament, La Jolla.
The world's best golfers compete on a beautiful seaside golf course. Call (619) 291–5372.

San Diego Invitational Rugby Tournament, San Diego.
48 teams compete for the championship. Call (619) 299–8130.

February

Mardi Gras—Olvera Street, Los Angeles.

National Date Festival, Indio.

Chinese New Year, Los Angeles.
Traditionally a colorful event, with crowds filling the streets to see the fireworks and dancing.

Laguna Beach Winter Festival, Laguna Beach.

Pacific Indoor Rodeo, Long Beach.

World of Wheels, Custom Car & Hot Rod Show, Los Angeles Convention Center.

Los Angeles Open Golf Tournament, Los Angeles.
The tournament in which Arnold Palmer once took a "12" on the eighteenth hole, winning him a place in the hearts of duffers all over the world. Palmer also won the tournament in subsequent years.

March

Beverly Hills Ball, Beverly Hills.

Ocean Beach Kite Festival, San Diego.
Awards in two categories: decoration and flying. Call (619) 223–1175.

Los Angeles Lite Marathon, Los Angeles.

Renaissance Week, Oxnard.

St. Patrick's Day Parade, Los Angeles and San Diego.

St. Patrick's Spring Dart Classic, San Diego.
One of the country's most prestigious dart tournaments. Call (619) 469–6128.

Return of the Swallows, San Juan Capistrano.

World Championship Gold Panning Contest, Knott's Berry Farm, Buena Park.

Filmex, Los Angeles.
An international film festival with new releases, seldom-seen classics, and tributes to Hollywood greats. There's always one all-night marathon that separates the devotees from the dilettantes.

April

The Freeway Series, Los Angeles.
A 3-game series between the city's two major league baseball teams, the Dodgers and the Angels, on the eve of the new season. The season lasts from April to October. In San Diego, the Padres begin their season.

Peg Leg Liars Contest, Borrego Springs.
A yarn-spinning contest around a campfire on Sunday evening at Peg Leg Monument with the best liar winning. Call (619) 767-5311.

Heritage Days, Bakersfield.

Ice Capades, Los Angeles.
Ballet on ice with music and light show.

Tournament of Champions, Carlsbad.
Only those golfers winning a tour event in the last 12 months are eligible. It's golf's equivalent of the All-Star game. Call (619) 438–9111.

Lilac Festival, Palmdale.

National Mime Week, Los Angeles.

Easter Promenade, San Diego.
Judges drive in classic autos throughout downtown, then select the city's best-dressed men and women with a fashion show following. Call (619) 234–0331.

National Orange Show, San Bernardino.

Toyota Grand Prix, Long Beach.
The winding beachside boulevards turn into Monte Carlo for one of the largest prizes in racing.

May

Cinco de Mayo, Olvera Street.
Celebration of this Mexican holiday is one of the liveliest days of the year in Los Angeles.

Gordon Bennett Balloon Race, Fountain Valley.

Renaissance Pleasure Fair, Agoura.
Strolling minstrels, harpists and 16th Century costumes on weekends throughout May. Call (213) 889–3150.

National Horse Show, Del Mar Fairgrounds.
Thousands of show horses. Admission: $3. Call (619) 755–1161.

Seventeen Tennis Tournament, Mission Viejo.

Westwood Sidewalk Art & Craft Show, Westwood Village.
Everything from stained glass to handmade jewelry to decorative toilet seat covers.

UCLA-Pepsi Track Meet, Draice Stadium, UCLA.

Los Angeles Civic Light Opera, Los Angeles.
Shows run through November.

Tecate-Ensenada Bike Ride, Mexico.
A 73-mile race through the desert backroads attracting 10,000 riders from throughout North America. Call (619) 275–1384.

Fiesta de la Primavera, San Diego.
Celebrates the city's past with mariachis, troubadours, fiddle contests, Buffalo barbecue and more. In Old Town. Call (619) 237–6770.

June

Asian Cultural Festival, Los Angeles.

Community Fair, Santa Barbara.

Craft Heritage Fair, Los Angeles.

Old Town Art Fiesta, San Diego.

San Diego Opera Verdi Festival, San Diego.

Santa Anita National Horse Show, Arcadia.

Whale Festival, San Pedro. Call (213) 548–7562.

Winston Cup Stock Car Race, Riverside.

National Shakespeare Festival, San Diego.
Old Globe Theatre's professional repertory of three Shakespearean plays.

Southern California Exposition, San Diego.
A mini world's fair with displays of every sort; livestock, flowers, rides and lots of hot dog stands. Call (619) 275–2705.

July

Art-A-Fair, Laguna Beach.

County Fair, Santa Barbara.

Festival of Arts & Pageant of the Masters, Laguna Beach.

Hollywood Bowl Summer Festival, Hollywood.
Beginning with a Fourth-of-July extravaganza, the Bowl offers classical, jazz and pop concerts through August.

Fourth of July Fireworks.
Celebrations take place in dozens of communities; you can see four displays at once in Pacific Palisades Park overlooking the ocean in Santa Monica.

Malibu Festival of Arts and Crafts, Malibu. Call (213) 456–9025.

National Horse and Flower Show, Santa Barbara.

Festival of the Bells, Mission San Diego de Alcala.
Anniversary of the founding of California's first mission. Call (619) 281–8449.

Old Miner Days, Big Bear Lake.

Orange County Fair, Costa Mesa.

Ringling Brothers Barnum & Bailey Circus.
Various Southern California sites, primarily The Forum. Call (213) 673–1300.

Summer Festival of Arts & Crafts, Santa Fe Springs.

Del Mar Thoroughbred Club Racing Season, Del Mar.
An hour north of San Diego just inland from one of the finest beaches in California. Racing through September.

August

Character Boat Parade, Newport Beach.

International Surf Festival, Hermosa Beach, Manhattan Beach and Redondo Beach. Call (213) 545–4502.

Pro football season.
Three area teams compete in the National Football League; Los Angeles Rams, Los Angeles Raiders and San Diego Chargers. The season ends with the Super Bowl in January.

Old Spanish Days Fiesta, Santa Barbara.

San Bernardino County Fair, Victorville.

Score Off-Road World Championships, Riverside.

World Body Surfing Championship, Oceanside.
Three-day competition. Call (619) 439–7325.

The San Fernando Valley Fair, Northridge. Call (213) 363–8181.

Pamplonada, Tecate, Mexico.
Annual running of the bulls through the streets of Tecate.

September

Festival of Art Outdoor Show, Santa Catalina Island.

Hispanic Heritage Week, Los Angeles.

Cabrillo Festival, San Diego.
Celebrating Cabrillo's discovery of the West Coast in 1542 including a reenactment of the landing. Call (619) 293–5450.

Kern County Fair and National Horse Show Classic, Bakersfield.

Thunderboat Regatta, San Diego.
Hydroplane races in Mission Bay. Call (619) 692–4001.

Los Angeles County Fair, Pomona. One of the largest county fairs in the world. Rides, food and judging of everything from collies to chocolate chip cookies.

Los Angeles City Birthday, Olvera Street, Los Angeles.
This celebration take places on the sixth.

Mexican Independence Day, Los Angeles.

Oktoberfest, Big Bear Lake.

World Championship Beach Volleyball, Redondo Beach. Call (213) 245–3778.

October

Budweiser Grand Prix, Riverside.

Golden Days, Azusa.

Los Angeles Lakers (Basketball) and **Los Angeles Kings** (Hockey), The Forum, Inglewood.
Seasons last through May.

Los Angeles Philharmonic.
One of the top dozen in the world, it begins its indoor season at the Music Center. Call (213) 972–7211.

Sandcastle and Sandsculpture Contest, Corona del Mar.

Point Magu Air Show, Point Magu.

Los Angeles Street Scene.
A weekend-long block party featuring musicians, dancers and artisans. Call (213) 626–0458.

Festival of the Californias, San Diego.
Features arts and crafts, concerts and food. Call (619) 232–3101.

November

All Western Band Review, Long Beach.

Hollywood Christmas Parade, Hollywood.
Probably the earliest Christmas parade in the country; it happens the Sunday after Thanksgiving. Call (213) 469–2337.

Baja 1000 KM, Baja California Peninsula. Biggest of all off-road races. Call (213) 889–9216.

Mother Goose Parade, El Cajon.

New York City Opera.
This group visits Los Angeles for a month of performances at the Music Center.

Stamp Expo Pacific, Los Angeles Convention Center. Heaven for stamp collectors.

Fiesta de la Cuadrilla, San Diego.
Square and round dance festival. Call (619) 273–5639.

December

Christmas Parades (in various Southern California communities).

Santa's Holiday Village, Long Beach.

Santa Anita Thoroughbred Racing, Arcadia.
The season lasts until April. Call (213) 574–7223.

Christmas at Pioneer Village, Bakersfield.

Lighted Boat Parades in various Southern California marinas; for the one in Marina del Rey, call (213) 822–0555; in San Diego, call (619) 291–5985.

Day at the Docks, San Diego.
Waterfront festival with boat rides, entertainment, food and more. Call (619) 222–1144.

Las Posadas, Mission San Luis Rey.
Traditional Mexican Yuletide ceremony. Call (619) 757–3651.

Snow World at Sea World, San Diego.
A chance to watch how awkward Californians are in snow. Nine hundred tons of man-made snow dumped on this theme park, complete with 20-foot slope for sliding. Call (619) 222–6363.

Nightlife

Entertainment is taken seriously in Los Angeles. The very top performers work the established clubs and concert halls, but right below them, hoping to join their ranks, are scores of talented artists who have come to Los Angeles from all over the world. Here, in the home of the music and film industry, they hope to get "discovered" by an agent or a producer who can vault them to stardom. The comedy clubs are particularly good, as are the new-wave dance clubs.
There are a number of nightclubs on Sunset Strip (or simply "The Strip"), which is a portion of Sunset Boulevard easily recognized by its cluster of monumental billboards (between Doheny and La Cienega). Going east you pass into Los Angeles' equivalent of a red-light district. The

women you see in tight pink shorts or scant evening gowns — even if it's a cool evening — are there to negotiate their services with strangers. Don't be shocked if you see male prostitutes, and even a few adolescents.

West Hollywood is known for both its new-wave clubs and gay bars, while **Marina del Rey** is famous for its "singles" bars.

Concerts are held at **The Forum**; the **Irvine Meadows**, the **Pacific**, and the **Universal** amphitheaters; the **Beverly** and the **Greek** theaters; and several other large auditorium-type settings. The appendix gives a listing of the more intimate clubs, many of which have dance floors.

It should be remembered, however, that there are too many places to ever be able to offer a complete list and besides, places go in and out of business within a few months. It is wise to check before going. Also read the Guide in Brief section on "Cultural Activities."

Sports

Spectator Sports

Southern California has some of the finest teams in professional sports.

Baseball

The season runs from April until October.

The Los Angeles Dodgers (National League) are one of the most successful baseball teams and usually they lead the major leagues in attendance. Get tickets as early as possible by calling Dodger Stadium, (213) 224–1500.

The California Angels (American League) play at Anaheim Stadium, 2000 State College Blvd., Anaheim. Call (714) 634–2000.

The San Diego Padres (National League) play at San Diego Jack Murphy Stadium. Call (619) 283–4494 for information.

Basketball

The regular National Basketball Association season runs from October through April, with championship play offs coontinuing until June.

The Los Angeles Lakers are a perennial powerhouse and play their home games at The Forum, 3900 W. Manchester Blvd., Inglewood. Call (213) 674–6000.

The San Diego Clippers play their games at the San Diego Sports Arena, (619) 226–1275.

Hockey

The National Hockey League season runs from October to April.

The Los Angeles Kings play at The Forum in Inglewood.

Football

The National Football League season begins in September and runs through December. There are pre-season games in August and post-season tests in January.

The Los Angeles Rams play their home games at Anaheim Stadium, (714) 585–5400.

The Los Angeles Raiders play at Los Angeles Memorial Coliseum, (213) 322–5901.

The San Diego Chargers play at San Diego Jack Murphy Stadium, (619) 280–2111.

The Los Angeles Express of the new United States Football League also play at the L.A. Coliseum in the spring and summer.

The Rose Bowl is held each January 1 between the best team in the Pac-10 conference and the best team in the Big Ten. The Rose Bowl stadium seats 104,699 people and still difficult to get seats. Perhaps the concierge at your hotel can help you. Each year, 3,500 end-zone seats are sold in a random drawing. Send postcard to Rose Bowl Ticket Drawing, P.O. Box 7122, Pasadena, CA 91109, postmarked between Sept. 15 and Oct. 15. For information, call (213) 793–7193.

Horse Racing

Hollywood Park, 1050 S. Prairie, Inglewood, (213) 678–1181, hosts thoroughbred racing from April to July and harness racing from August to December.

Santa Anita Park, Huntington Drive at Baldwin Avenue, Arcadia, (213) 574–7223, hosts thoroughbred racing from December to April and from October to November.

The Del Mar Track, Via de la Valle, Del Mar, (619) 299–1340, is 30 minutes north of San Diego. Season runs from mid July to early September. Track Closed Tuesdays.

Collegiate Sports

UCLA (University of California at Los Angeles) and USC (University of Southern California) are the two big colleges in Southern California with nationally recognized teams in baseball, basketball, football, swimming, track and field, and many other sports. For UCLA ticket information, call (213) UCLA101. For USC ticket information, call (213) 743–2620. Many smaller schools, such as Pepperdine (in Malibu), California State at Long Beach, and San Diego State University also have good teams in somewhat lower-caliber competition.

Participant Sports

The year-round warm climate makes Southern California an ideal place for outdoor sports. In addition to beaches, golf courses and tennis courts, there are a number of marinas where you can rent or charter a boat for fishing or sightseeing. There are many places in the nearby desert and mountains where you can hike or camp. In the winter, there is skiing less than two hours away from Los Angeles.

Some of the more popular **beaches** are Santa Barbara, Malibu, Santa Monica, Venice, Manhattan Beach, Hermosa Beach, Redondo Beach, Huntington Beach, Laguna Beach, Oceanside,

Solana Beach, La Jolla, Pacific Beach, Mission Beach, Coronado and Imperial Beach.

The best beaches for **surfing** are Malibu, Huntington Beach and San Clemente.

The best beaches for **skin and scuba diving** are Malibu and Laguna Beach.

Boat rentals can be had at Santa Barbara, Ventura, Santa Monica, Marina del Rey, Redondo Beach, San Pedro, Newport Beach and Mission Beach.

Good camping venues include Angeles Forest, Leo Carillo Beach, Saddleback Butte Park and Los Padres National Forest.

Golf courses are plentiful, but the best public courses are Rancho Park Golf Course in West Los Angeles (site of the Los Angeles Open) and Torrey Pines Municipal Golf Course in La Jolla (site of the San Diego Open), and Palm Springs Municipal Golf Course. For the location of a golf course near you, consult the yellow pages; there are more than 200 public golf courses in Southern California.

Tennis courts are too numerous to mention; it seems that there are tennis courts at every school and in every park in Southern California.

One of the better **horseback riding** places is Smoke Tree Stables, 2500 Toledo, Palm Springs. For a breathtaking ride in the foothills above Santa Barbara, horses may be rented at the San Ysidro Stables, 900 San Ysidro Lane, (805) 969–5046; Horse Packing, 1220 Mountainview Rd., El Cajon, (619) 463–2836 (near San Diego); and Azusa Canyon Stables (east of Los Angeles), (213) 334–7000.

There is **skiing** from December through April at Mount Baldy, Big Bear, Snow Summit, Mount Waterman and Kratka Ridge.

Appendix

Accommodations

Downtown (area code 213)

Alexandria Hotel, 501 S. Spring St., 626–7484, (800) 421–8815.
Turn-of-the-century elegance with antique furniture. Restaurant, nightclub. 500 rooms, $39–$45.

The Biltmore Hotel, 515 S. Olive St., 624–1011, (800) 421–0156 nationwide, (800) 252–0175 in California.
Since 1923, the Biltmore has been the king of downtown hotels, hosting foreign dignitaries and presidents. The palatial interiors give a feeling of Old World elegance on a grand scale. Modern guest rooms, meeting rooms, banquet facilities. Fine seafood restaurant (**Bernard's**), plush bar (**The Grand Avenue Bar**), swimming pool, private health club, billiards room, library. Decidedly deluxe. 1,022 rooms, $90 and up.

Best Western Inn Towne Hotel, 925 S. Figueroa St., 628–2222, (800) 421–6662 nationwide, (800) 352–6686 in California.
Near Convention Center and downtown shopping, swimming pool, restaurant and cocktail lounge. 172 rooms, $48–$54.

City Center Motel, 1135 W. 7th St., 628–7141.
One of the best buys downtown: quiet, simple, and inexpensive. Reservations a must. Near downtown shopping. Pool, color TV. 42 rooms, $32.

Figueroa Hotel, 939 S. Figueroa St., 627–8971, (800) 421–9092.
Charming old hotel with pool and Jacuzzi. Free parking, airport bus service. Coffee shop. 280 rooms, $38–$48.

Friendship Inn — Motel De Ville, 1123 W. 7th St., 624–8474.
For the budget-minded; clean and comfortable, close to downtown shopping. Coffee shop, pool, free parking, color TV. 63 rooms $28–$36.

Holiday Inn — Downtown, 750 Garland Ave., 628–5242, (800) 238–8000.
Modern, comfortable, and exceptionally ordinary. Pool, restaurant. 201 rooms, $49–$56.

Hyatt Regency Los Angeles, 711 S. Hope St., 683–1234, (800) 228–9000.
Comfortable and expensive. An agoraphobic's paradise; a virtual city within a city. On the lower levels the Broadway Plaza has 35 shops and restaurants, a major radio station, and the Los Angeles Racquet Club for tennis. Atop the hotel is **Angel's Flight**, a revolving restaurant. Parking is $8 per day. 500 rooms, $95 and up.

Los Angeles Hilton, 930 Wilshire Blvd. 628–4321.
Excellent location; a favorite of foreign travelers. Airport bus service, 24-hour coffee shop, banquet and meeting rooms, babysitting service, wheelchair access, 4 restaurants, pool, multilingual staff. 1,175 rooms, $80–$105.

Mayflower Hotel, 624–1331, (800) 421–8851.
Affordable luxury, near shopping and Music Center. Airport bus service, coffee shop, room service, but no pool. 350 rooms, $60–$80.

The New Otani Hotel & Garden, 120 S. Los Angeles St., 629–1200, (800) 421–8795 nationwide, (800) 252–0197 in California.
This is an ultramodern hotel; walk through the Japanese garden with its mini-waterfall. For those who want more than just a hotel room; rooms have refrigerator, doorbell, alarm clock, bathroom phone, movies. 2 bars, 3 excellent restaurants. Airport bus service. 446 rooms, $95 and up.

Sheraton Grande Hotel, 333 S. Figueroa St., 617–1133, (800) 325–3535.
Elegant design, impeccable service. There's more to do inside this hotel than in the city of Bakersfield. Tennis, swimming, health spa, restaurants, bars, airport bus service, room service, multilingual staff. 550 rooms, $110–$140.

University Hilton, 748–4141.
Adjacent to the USC campus, one of the principal sites of the 1984 Olympics. Pool, Jacuzzi, gourmet dining. Shuttle service to airport and train station. 241 rooms, $70–$95.

The Westin Bonaventure Los Angeles, Fifth and Figueroa Streets, 624–1000, (800) 228–3000.
Space Age design, mirrored glass exterior, lush interior with ponds, fountains, and five levels of shops. Major convention facilities. Pool, tennis, health facilities, restaurants ranging from **Bagel Nosh** to **Beaudry's Gourmet**. Revolving bar on 35th floor. Parking is $8 per day. 1,474 rooms, $85–$126.

Mid-Wilshire (area code 213)

The Ambassador, 3400 Wilshire Blvd., 387–7011, (800) 421–0182 nationwide, (800) 252–0385 in California.
Elegant, sprawling old hotel (built in 1921) with 23 acres of gardens, in the midst of the financial district. Tennis courts, health club, pool, 17 shops, 3 restaurants, convention facilities, airport bus. 500 rooms, $75–$109.

Best Western Executive Motor Inn Mid-Wilshire, 603 S. New Hampshire Ave., 385–4444, (800) 528–1234.
Jacuzzi, Sauna, heated indoor pool, remote color TV, room refrigerators. One block from Wilshire Blvd. 90 rooms, $49–$54.

Cloud Motel, 3400 W. Third St., 385–0061.
Nothing fancy here: a modern motel with pool, coffee shop, and free parking. Ideal for the budget-minded traveler. 116 rooms, $40.

Executive Motor Inn-Mariposa, 457 S. Mariposa Ave., 380–6910. Large rooms, pool, sauna, color TV, and free coffee. 50 rooms, $42–$50.

Hyatt Wilshire Hotel, 3515 Wilshire Blvd., 381–7411, (800) 228–9000.
Recently renovated. Airport bus, pool, room service, banquet facilities. Lounge, disco, restaurant. 397 rooms, $72–$100.

Motel Mariposa, 518 S. Mariposa, 388–1433.
Quiet, clean, near financial district. No pool. Best deal in the area for the budget-minded traveler. 20 rooms, $23.

Sheraton Towne House, 2961 Wilshire Blvd.
Built in the 1920's, a classy old establishment with patio rooms surrounding Olympic-sized pool, 4 tennis courts, coffee shop, gourmet dining room. 300 rooms, $69.

Hollywood (area code 213)

Beverly Sunset Hotel, 8775 Sunset Blvd., 652–0030, (800) 421–3323.
On the Sunset Strip in the nightclub district, a popular music industry hangout. Gourmet dining, pool, free parking. 60 rooms, $85–$120.

Chateau Marmont Hotel, 8221 Sunset Blvd., 656–1010.
Ideal for the traveler who wants a bit of Old World charm and elegance in the midst of the action of the Sunset Strip. Cottages and poolside bungalows available. 62 rooms, $60 and up.

Cine Lodge, see entry under Howards Weekly Apartments.

Franklin Motel, 1824 N. Beachwood Dr., 464–1824.
Kitchen units, 5 minutes to the heart of Hollywood. 24 rooms, $40.

Hallmark House Motor Hotel, 7023 Sunset Blvld., 464–8344.
Central Hollywood location. Pool, nearby coffee shop, free parking. 72 rooms, $37–$43.

Holiday Inn — Hollywood, 1755 N. Highland Ave., 462–7181.
Near Hollywood Bowl. Ten minutes drive to Universal Studios. Perfect location if you have a car. Swimming pool, revolving rooftop restaurant. 445 rooms, $67–$75.

Hollywood Roosevelt Hotel, 7000 Hollywood Blvd., 469–2442.
Across from the footprints of the Chinese Theater, located on the walk of the stars. Kitchen units, suites, and poolside villas available. Olympic-sized pool. The lobby pays homage to the greats of Hollywood. Ideal lodgings for out-of-town cinema buffs. 450 rooms, $41–$53.

Howards Weekly Apartments (Cine Lodge) 1738 N. Whitley, 466–6943.

One block away from the craziness of Hollywood Boulevard. Offers weekly budget rates for kitchenettes. Reservations necessary. 135 units, $85 per week and up.

Ramada Inn-Hollywood, 1160 N. Vermont Ave., 660–1788, (800) 228–2828.

Pool, sauna, Jacuzzi. 130 rooms. $48.

Sunset Marquis Hotel, 1200 Alta Loma Rd., 657–1333, (800) 421–4380.

Near the Sunset Strip and Restaurant Row. Nightclub, Jacuzzi, free parking. 115 rooms, $80–$105.

Sunset Plaza Hotel, 8400 Sunset Blvd., 654–0750, (800) 421–3652 nationwide, (800) 252–0645 in California.

On the Sunset Strip in the heart of the nightclub district. Popular among touring music groups. Modern rooms, pool. 85 rooms, $49.

Beverly Hills/Century City/West Los Angeles (area code 213)

Bel Air Hotel, 701 Stone Canyon Rd., 472–1121.

As elegant and leisurely as a country villa, five minutes from downtown Beverly Hills. You must have a car because the hotel is situated in a residential neighborhood, which translates into block after block of mansions in Bel Air. Heated pool, gourmet dining, beautiful gardens. $100 and up, up, up.

Bel Air Sands Hotel, 11461 Sunset Blvd., 476–6571, (800) 421–6649 nationwide, (800) 352–6680 in California.

Ten minutes from Beverly Hills, ten minutes from the beach. 2 swimming pools, tennis, putting green, gourmet dining, banquet facilities. 162 rooms, $80–$95.

Beverly Hills Hotel, 9641 Sunset Blvd., 276–2251.

This is the hotel most often visited by people staying at *other* hotels. Movie deals are consummated at poolside, foreign dignitaries relax in the poolside bungalows, agents make phone calls from their booths in the Polo Lounge. Twelve acres of tropical gardens. Tennis courts, poolside dining, elegant shops. A Southern California landmark. 325 rooms, $120 and up, up, up.

The Beverly Hilton, 9876 Wilshire Blvd., 274–7777.

Excellent location: close to Beverly Hills shopping, walking distance to Century City, on the bus line to downtown and the ocean. Large and comfortable, with a variety of restaurants and shops. Excellent service. 600 rooms, $84–$120.

Beverly House Hotel, 140 S. Lasky Dr., 271–2145.

Proof that it is possible to find charming quarters in Beverly Hills at reasonable rates. You'll have to do without a pool but the ocean is only 15 minutes away. Small, intimate, close to Century City. 50 rooms, $43–$46.

Beverly Rodeo, 360 N. Rodeo Dr., 273–0300.

Located on the most expensive strip of real estate in California — Rodeo Drive — where window displays are a work of art. Features the outdoor **Cafe Rodeo**, sun deck, free parking. 100 rooms, $70–$82.

Beverly Wilshire, 9500 Wilshire Blvd., 275–4282, (800) 421–4354 nationwide, (800) 282–4804 in California.

European-style hotel with 14 restaurants, including the superb **La Bella Fontana**, 3 bars, beautiful Mediterranean-style swimming pool, sauna. Excellent service. Kitchen units available. Airport bus. 500 rooms, 90 suites, $155 and up, up, up.

Century Plaza Hotel, 2025 Avenue of the Stars, 277–2000, (800) 228–3000.

Amid the futuristic collection of skyscrapers known as Century City. 15 restaurants, swimming pool, jazz nightclub. Adjacent to the large Century City shopping complex and the Schubert Theatre. A favorite of President Reagan's. Color TV and refrigerator in each room. 800 rooms, 77 suites, $118–$138.

Holiday Inn Westwood Plaza Hotel, 10740 Wilshire Blvd., 475–8711, (800) 238–8000.

About the classiest Holiday Inn you'll ever see. 19-story highrise, near UCLA and Westwood Village. Restaurant, pool, bar. $75.

Le Parc Hotel de Luxe, 733 N. West Knoll, West Hollywood, 855–8888, (800) 421–4666 nationwide, (800) 252–2152 in California.

An intimate, European-styled hotel with 152 suites. Each has a fireplace, private balcony, kitchen, and wet bar. Rates include continental breakfast, daily newspaper, parking, and limousine service to nearby locations. $105–$103.

L' Ermitage, 9291 Burton Way, 278–3344, (800) 421–4306.

From the original artwork on the walls, to the step-down living rooms, to the gourmet dining room reserved for hotel guests only, you will immediately sense that you are in an extraordinary hotel. Located within walking distance of Beverly Hills on a quiet residential street. Free limousine service within Beverly Hills. 116 suites, $155–$445.

St. Regis Motor Hotel, 11955 Wilshire Blvd., West Los Angeles, 477–6021.

Near UCLA, 10 minutes to the beach. Pool, free parking, simple but inexpensive. 50 rooms, $26.

Westwood Marquis, 930 Hilgard Ave., 208–8765, (800) 421–2317 nationwide, (800) 352–7454 in California.

Located adjacent to the UCLA campus, this elegant hotel offers the best Sunday brunch in

313

the city. 2 restaurants in the hotel and two dozen more within three blocks. Complimentary limousine service to Beverly Hills. Afternoon "High Tea" in the Westwood Lounge. Beautiful pool. 250 suites, $170–$210.

Airport Area (area code 213)

Airport Century Inn, 5547 W. Century Blvd., 649–4000, (800) 421–2048.
Restaurant, cocktail lounge, pool. 150 rooms, $40–$45.

Amfac Hotel, 8601 Lincoln Blvd., 670–8111, (800) 622–0838.
Two miles north of airport, 24-hour coffee shop, cocktail lounge, pool. 750 rooms, $75–$90.

Best Western Airport Park Hotel, 600 Avenue of Champions, Inglewood, 673–5151, (800) 528–1234.
Adjacent to Hollywood Park race track and the Forum. Four miles from LAX. Restaurant, kitchen units. No pool. 350 rooms, $56–$60.

Hacienda Hotel, 525 N. Sepulveda Blvd., El Segundo, 615–0015, (800) 421–5900 nationwide, (800) 262–1314 in California.
One mile from LAX. Color TV, free movies in room, 24-hour coffee shop, cocktail lounge, 2 swimming pools. 640 rooms, $58–$67.

Holiday Inn-LAX, 9901, S. La Cienega Blvd., 649–5151.
Soundproof rooms, restaurant, lounge with live entertainment, banquet facilities, pool, airport bus. 601 rooms, 15 suites, $82–$90.

Hyatt Hotel-LAX, 6225 W. Century Blvd., 670–9000, (800) 228–9000. Adjacent to airport, soundproof rooms, fine dining, cocktail lounge, banquet facilities, swimming pool, tennis courts. 600 rooms, $68–$83.

Inglewood Airport Travelodge, 3900 W. Century Blvd., Inglewood, 674–7991, (800) 255–3050.
Pool, tennis courts, restaurant, cocktail lounge. Excellent value. 160 rooms, $36.

Los Angeles Marriott, 5855 W. Century Blvd., 641–5700, (800) 228–9290.
Large, elegant, and right next to LAX. Tastefully decorated, artwork in early California motif. Three gourmet restaurants, two cocktail lounges, heated pool. 1,019 rooms, $80–$105.

Manchester House Hotel, 901 W. Manchester, Inglewood, 649–0800. Two miles north of LAX. Heated pool, 46 rooms, $40–$42.

Pacifica Hotel, 6161 Centinela Ave., Culver City, 649–1776, (800) 421–1448.
Four miles north of LAX. Pool, Jacuzzi, two restaurants, three lounges, banquet facilities, free limo service to airport. 375 rooms, $74–$78.

Sheraton Plaza La Reina Hotel, 6101 W. Century Blvd., 642–1111, (800) 325–3535.
Luxurious new 15-story hotel on Airport Row has 3 restaurants, 3 lounges, tennis courts, pool, and free airport shuttle. Its 96 meeting rooms make it ideally suited for conventions. 24-hour coffee shop, 24-hour room service. 48 rooms designed for the handicapped. Sip a brandy in the lobby bar at sunset and you'll never know you're in an airport hotel. 810 rooms, 23 suites, $78–$130.

Travelodge International Hotel, 9750 Airport Blvd., 645–4600, (800) 255–3050.
Half-mile from LAX with free shuttle. Restaurant, cocktail lounges, 24-hour coffee shop, swimming pool. 572 rooms, $70–$80.

Marina del Rey (area code 213)

Marina City Club Hotel, 4333 Admiralty Way, 822–0611.
A sportsman's paradise: 6 tennis courts, 3 swimming pools, Jacuzzi and health club. Charter a yacht and cruise to Catalina or rent a sailboat for a day's relaxation on the Pacific. 5 restaurants, 2 lounges. Superb service in a country club atmosphere. 120 rooms, $90–$165.

Marina del Rey Hotel, 13534 Bali Way, 822–1010, (800) 421–8145.
Waterfront location, charter boats, heated pool. View of the yacht harbor and the Santa Monica Mountains. 154 rooms, $86.

Marina del Rey Marriott, 13480 Maxella Ave., 822–8555, (800) 228–9290.
Located 10 minutes from beach and LAX, near Fox Hills shopping center and MGM studios. Swimming pool, Jacuzzi, restaurant, and lounge. 281 rooms, $86–$101.

Marina International Hotel, 4200 Admiralty Way, 822–1010, (800) 421–8145.
Spacious villas and rooms with patios. Swimming pool, Jacuzzi, access to beach, charter boats. Ten minutes from LAX. 110 rooms, $86.

South Bay Beach Cities (area code 213)

Hyatt Long Beach, 6400 E. Pacific Coast Hwy., 434–8451, (800) 228–9000.
Directly across from Long Beach Harbor. Heated pool and jacuzzi, restaurant and lounge. 249 rooms, $66–$74.

Queen Mary Hotel, Pier 'J,' Long Beach, 435–3511.
First class state rooms aboard the Queen Mary. Don't worry about getting seasick; it stays berthed in the harbor. Restaurants, cocktail lounges, shops, swimming pool. Located 25 minutes south of LAX. Convention facilities. 390 rooms, $64–$84.

Queensway Bay Hilton, 700 Queensway Dr., Long Beach, 435–7676.

Oceanview rooms, pool, restaurant, lounge. 200 rooms, $81–$99.

Sea Sprite Ocean Front Apt. Motel, 1016 Strand, Hermosa Beach, 376–6933.
Charming old motel on the beach is a wonderful bargain for beach lovers. Color TV, heated pool. Five miles from LAX. 50 rooms, $39.

Santa Monica (area code 213)

Breakers Motel, 1501 Ocean Ave., 451–4811.
Moderate priced rooms for beach lovers. Heated pool, color TV. Book in advance. 34 rooms, $32–$75.

Hotel Carmel, 201 Broadway, 395–6195, (800) 421–2048.
Charming old hotel dates back to the 1920s, one block from the beach in downtown Santa Monica. Close to gourmet restaurants, large new shopping mall. 110 rooms, $45.

Holiday Inn-Bayview Plaza, 530 Pico Blvd., 399–9344.
Half-mile from the beach. One of the more elegant Holiday Inns, with gourmet dining, coffee shop, lounge with live entertainment, swimming pool, Jacuzzi, and banquet facilities. 185 rooms, $66–$88.

The Huntley Hotel, 1111 2nd St., 394–5454.
One block from the beach. **Poncho Villa's**, the Mexican restaurant on the 18th floor, has a spectacular view of the ocean, mountains, and entire city. A favorite among flight crews and foreigners. 210 rooms, $66.

Miramar-Sheraton Hotel, 101 Wilshire Blvd., 394–3731.
The most elegant hotel in the area, right across the street from the ocean. 3 restaurants, cocktail lounge with live entertainment, banquet facilities. Beautiful pool area. 276 rooms, $83–$95.

Stardust Motor Hotel, 3202 Wilshire Blvd., 828–4584.
Three miles to beach, UCLA. Probably the best location in the city for the price. On major bus line, near restaurants, shopping. Color TV, pool. 32 rooms, $26.

San Fernando Valley (area code 213)

Burbank Airport Hilton, 2500 Hollywood Way, Burbank, 841–8027.
Across the street from the Burbank Airport, near NBC, Burbank, Universal and Disney studios. Banquet and meeting facilities. Restaurant, lounge, swimming pool. 280 rooms, $66–$90.

Safari Inn, 1911 W. Olive Ave., Burbank, 845–8586.
Used frequently as a film site for TV and

movies. Gourmet French restaurant, lounge, pool, Jacuzzi. 92 rooms, $44–$50.

Sheraton Universal Hotel, 333 Universal Terrace Parkway, Universal City, 980–1212, (800) 325–3535.
Stroll out of your hotel onto the studio lot and take a tour to learn how movies are made. Limo bus to LAX. Restaurant, lounge, rooftop pool, whirlpool, exercise room. 500 rooms, $70–$120.

Sherman Oaks Inn, 12933 Ventura Blvd., Studio City, 788–2200.
Moderately-priced rooms near Universal City, not far from Hollywood. Swimming pool. Kitchen units available. 66 rooms, $40–$45.

Sportsman's Lodge Hotel, 12825 Ventura Blvd., Studio City, 769–4700.
Country-style accommodations, personalized service, Olympic-sized pool, private patios. Beautiful gardens with waterfalls and streams. Near Universal Studios. Gourmet restaurant, lounge. 196 rooms, $60–$72.

Valley Hilton, 15433 Ventura Blvd., Sherman Oaks, 981–5400.
Across from the posh shopping center, the Sherman Oaks Galleria. Near Universal Studios and Magic Mountain. Outside balconies, disco, heated pool. Located near major freeways; you must have a car. Excellent service. Convention facilities. 210 rooms, $64–$76.

San Gabriel Valley (area code 213)

Holiday Inn-Pasadena, 303 E. Cordova St., Pasadena, 449–4000.
One mile from the Rose Bowl. Restaurant, lounge, swimming pool, tennis courts. Sunday Champagne brunch. 312 rooms, $66.

Huntington-Sheraton Hotel, 1401 S. Oak Knoll, Pasadena, 792–0266.
One of Pasadena's oldest landmarks, this beautiful hotel is situated on 23 acres of greenery. Olympic-sized pool, tennis courts, putting green. Poolside cottages available. Gourmet restaurant, lounge. Close to the Rose Bowl, Huntington Library, and major shopping. 525 rooms, $80–$125.

The Pasadena Hilton, 150 S. Los Robles Avenue, Pasadena, 577–1000.
Near Rose Bowl and Civic Center. Penthouse restaurant, coffee shop, 2 lounges, swimming pool. 253 rooms, $79–$95.

Ramada Inn Arcadia, 130 W. Huntington Dr, Arcadia, 446–5211, (800) 228–2828.
Across from Santa Anita Race Track, 10 minutes to Rose Bowl. Restaurant, lounge, pool. 112 rooms, $43.

North of Los Angeles to Morro Bay

Best Western Casa Royale Motor Inn, 251 S. Union Ave., Bakersfield, (805) 327–3333.

Restaurant, entertainment lounge, 24-hour coffee shop, pool, banquet facilities. 120 rooms, $36–$42.

Best Western Shore Cliff Lodge, 2555 Price St., Pismo Beach.
You can taste the saltwater in the late afternoon air. Rooms have refrigerators and patios. Pool, tennis courts. Just south of San Luis Obispo. 100 rooms, moderately priced.

Breakers, 780 Market St., Morro Bay, (805) 772–7317.
Waterfront views, fireplaces in some rooms. Swimming pool. Located just north of San Luis Obispo and a short drive from the Hearst Castle. 25 rooms, moderately priced.

Casa Sirena Marina Hotel, 3605 Peninsula Rd., Oxnard, (805) 985–6311.
Halfway between LA and Santa Barbara, at the Channel Islands Harbor. Tennis, swimming pool, sportfishing, sailing. Restaurant and lounge. 274 rooms, $55–$67.

Holiday Inn-Ventura, 450 E. Harbor Blvd., Ventura, (805) 648–7731.
Highrise resort 60 miles north of Los Angeles. Pool, sauna, revolving restaurant and bar, view of the ocean and mountains. 260 rooms, $55–$80.

Madonna Inn, 100 Madonna Rd., San Luis Obispo, (805) 543–3000.
One of the most talked about hotels in California; each room has a different decor and guests often change rooms each night. Spend one night in a cave, the next in fantasyland. A honeymooner's delight on the way to Hearst Castle. 109 fun rooms, restaurant, coffee shop. Expensive.

Miramar-By-the-Sea, 1555 S. Jamisen Lane, Santa Barbara, (805) 969–2203, (800) 834–9999.
Beautiful resort setting, with private beach, two swimming pools, tennis courts, ping pong, outdoor restaurant, gourmet dining, entertainment lounge. Beautiful grounds, individual cottages, beachfront bungalows. An absolute steal for the price. 200 rooms, $28–$80.

San Ysidro Ranch, 900 San Ysidro Lane, Montecito, (805) 969–5046.
Beauty and serenity on 500 acres of lush countryside in the foothills of the Santa Ynez mountains just north of Santa Barbara. Tennis, swimming, hiking, horseback riding. Gourmet restaurant, lounge. Fireplaces in cottages, no TVs. 38 units, $84–$340.

Shangri-La Hotel, 1301 Ocean Ave., Malibu, (213) 394–2791.
Simple, clean, and staring out at the favorite beach among top Californian surfers. Short stroll to Malibu pier and gourmet dining. Kitchenettes available. 70 rooms. Expensive.

Death Valley

Furnace Creek facilities are open from November through April. They are operated by Fred Harvey, Inc., P.O. Box 187, Death Valley, CA 92328, (619) 786–2345.

Furnace Creek Inn, Tennis, golf, swimming, horseback riding, restaurant, entertainment lounge. Near Mustard Canyon, Harmony Borax Works, and Zabriskie Point. 67 rooms, expensive.

Furnace Creek Ranch, Tennis, golf, swimming, coffee shop, dining, cocktail lounge. 216 rooms, expensive.

Stove Pipe Wells Village facilities are open from November through April. Write: Stovepipe Wells Village, Death Valley, CA 92328. Restaurant, bar. 74 rooms, moderate.

(No other lodging is available within Death Valley.)

Palm Springs (area code 613)

*Prices listed are winter rates which are $10–$40 more than the summer rates.

Americana Canyon Hotel Racquet & Golf Resort, 2850 S. Palm Canyon Dr., 323–5656.
A resort/country club with two championship golf courses, lighted tennis courts, swimming pools, Jacuzzi, gourmet dining, superb service, and acres of grounds situated against the mountains. Banquet and convention facilities. 468 rooms, $95–$165.

Dunes Hotel, 390 S. Indian Ave., 325–1172.
Coffee shop, swimming pool, Jacuzzi, sauna, pets allowed. Excellent location, moderately priced. 108 rooms, $55–$65.

King's Inn, 515 N. Palm Canyon Dr., 325–2591.
Kitchenette available, pool, Jacuzzi. 45 rooms, $35–$50.

Palm Springs Biltmore Hotel Resort, 1000 E. Palm Canyon Dr., 323–1811.
Small and luxurious, gourmet dining, pool, Jacuzzi, 12 acres of plush grounds. Popular Champagne brunch on weekends. Pets allowed. 72 rooms, $85–$200.

Sheraton Plaza, 400 E. Tahquitz-McCallum Way, 320–6868.
Brand new spacious hotel with lovely poolside rooms. Jacuzzi, tennis courts, dining, coffee shop, lounge. One block from the main drag. 263 rooms, expensive.

Westward Ho Seven Seas Hotel, 701 E. Palm Canyon Dr., 327–1531.
Excellent location, pool, Jacuzzi, dining room, 24-hour coffee shop. Luxury at affordable prices. 209 rooms, $40–$57.

Orange County

Anaheim Viking Travelodge, 505 W. Katella Ave., Anaheim, (714) 774–8710, (800) 255–3050.
Close to Disneyland, Anaheim Convention Center. Restaurant, pool. Excellent value. 51 rooms, $38–$47.

Buena Park Quality Inn, 7555 Beach Blvd., Buena Park, (714) 522–7360.
Near Knott's Berry Farm. Pool, jacuzzi. 152 rooms, moderately priced.

Catalina Island Inn, 125 Metropole, Avalon, (213) 510–1623.
Fabulous location half-block from the beach near restaurants and nightlife on Catalina Island. Free shuttle bus from the harbor. Patio overlooking ocean, free coffee. Reservations recommended. $50–$70.

Disneyland Hotel, 1150 W. Cerritos Ave., Anaheim, (714) 635–8600, (800) 854–6165.
If this hotel were in the state of Wyoming, it would be the fifth largest city. Famous for its monorail train that takes guests directly into Disneyland. 14 restaurants and bars, 60 acres of lush grounds. Great fun for families. Swimming, tennis, a complete resort. 1,100 rooms, $84–$108.

Hotel Catalina, 129 Whittley Ave., Avalon, Catalina Island, (231) 510–0027.
Over looking the harbor, all private baths, cottages available. Jacuzzi, sun patio. Expensive.

Hotel Laguna, 425 S. Coast Hwy., Laguna Beach, (714) 494–1151.
Inexpensive, charming old hotel close to beach. Restaurant, entertainment lounge. No pool. Pets allowed. 70 rooms, $36–$52.

Howard Johnson's Motor Lodge, 1380 S. Harbor Blvd., Anaheim, (714) 776–6120, (800) 422–4228.
Free trolley to nearby Disneyland. Two swimming pools, Jacuzzi, 24-hour restaurant, cocktail lounge. 320 rooms, $64.

Marriott Hotel & Tennis Club, 900 Newport Center Dr., Newport Beach, (714) 640–4000.
Complete resort facilities including golfing, tennis, Jacuzzi, boat charters. Two restaurants and entertainment lounge. Banquet facilities. 377 rooms, $84–$110.

Newport Channel Inn, 6030 W. Coast Hwy., Newport Beach, (714) 642–3030.
Inexpensive lodgings on the beach. 30 rooms, $42–$47.

Seacliff Motel, 1661 S. Coast Hwy., Laguna Beach, (714) 494–9717.
Cozy ocean view rooms with sundecks right above the beach. Close to the Laguna artists' community with its many galleries. Swimming pool. 25 rooms, $30–65.

Sea Lark Motel, 2274 Newport Blvd., Costa Mesa, (714) 646–7445.

For the budget-minded, five minutes to beach and the fabulous shopping in South Coast Plaza, 15 minutes to Disneyland. 44 rooms, $24.

San Diego Area

Blue Sea Lodge, 707 Pacific Beach Dr., San Diego, (619) 483–4700, (800) 528–1234.
Ocean-view suites, pool & spa, 1 1/2 miles from Sea World. 48 units, $65–$80.

Circle 8 Motor Inn, 543 Hotel Circle So., (619) 297–8800.
Close to stadium. Refrigerators in all rooms, swimming pool, coffee shop, Jacuzzi, valet services, wheelchair units. 250 rooms, $36–$48.

Del Mar Inn, 720 Camino Del Mar, Del Mar, (619) 755–9765.
Near ocean, Torrey Pines Golf Course, and Del Mar race track. Ocean-view rooms, heated pool, Jacuzzi, laundry, complimentary breakfast. 81 rooms, $56–$74.

Glorietta Bay Inn, 1630 Glorietta Blvd., Coronado, (619) 435–3101, (800) 854–3380 nationwide, (800) 432–7045 in California.
Edwardian mansion built in 1908 situated across the street from beach. Airport bus, bicycle rentals, free coffee, swimming pool, kitchen units. 100 rooms, $66–$195.

Hotel Del Coronado, 1500 Orange Ave., Coronado, (619) 435–6611, (800) 522–1200 in California.
Old World splendor on the ocean. Henry James wrote about his stay here at the turn of the century. Tennis courts, swimming pool, and a museum of local historical artifacts. Gourmet dining, coffee shop, elegant shops. Convention facilities. 700 rooms, $68–$175.

Holiday Inn-Embarcadero, 1355 N. Harbor Dr., San Diego, (619) 232–3861, (800) 238–8000.
Located on San Diego Bay across from Maritime Museum. Gorgeous view of harbor and city. Two miles from airport. Restaurant, lounge, coffee shop, swimming pool. Banquet facilities, foreign currency exchange. 600 rooms, $74–$86.

The Inn at La Jolla, 5540 La Jolla Blvd., La Jolla, (619) 454–6121, (800) 854–3380 nationwide, (800) 432–7045 in California.
Located on bluff overlooking ocean. Pool, Jacuzzi, putting green. Kitchen units, pets allowed. 45 rooms, $44–$58.

Kona Inn, 1901 Shelter Island Dr., San Diego, (619) 222–0421.
Located on Shelter Island in San Diego Bay. Near San Diego Zoo. Suites with balconies overlooking harbor. Restaurant and entertainment lounge. Guests have use of Kona Kai Club which offers tennis, handball, and Jacuzzi. 76 rooms, $65–$68.

La Costa Hotel & Spa, Costa del Mar Road, Carlsbad, (619) 438–9111, (800) 854–6564 nationwide, (800) 542–6200 in California.

Features a world famous spa, superb golf course (site of the Tournament of Champions), 25 tennis courts with professional instructors, movie theater, riding stables, five restaurants, nightclub with dancing. Secluded in the hills 30 miles north of San Diego. 300 rooms, $125–$150.

La Jolla Cove Motel, 1155 Coast Blvd., La Jolla, (619) 459–2621, (800) 647–4783.
Suites and studios overlooking ocean. Private balconies, color TV. Solarium and sundeck, pool. 110 rooms, $38–$123.

Mission Valley Inn, 875 Hotel Circle So., San Diego, (619) 298–8281, (800) 854–2608 nationwide, (800) 542–6082 in California.
Located three miles from San Diego Zoo and Sea World. Three swimming pools, tennis, racquetball, 24-hour coffee shop, entertainment lounge. 210 rooms, $62–$68.

Rancho Bernardo Inn, 17550 Bernardo Oaks Dr., San Diego, (619) 487–1611, (800) 854–1065 nationwide, (800) 542–6096 in California.
Located near Wild Animal Park. Country resort with two golf courses, tennis college, ping pong, and shuffleboard. Gourmet dining, dancing and entertainment. Banquet facilities. 235 rooms, $75–$120.

San Diego Hilton Beach & Tennis Resort, 1775 E. Mission Bay Dr., San Diego, (619) 276–4010.
Located on Mission Bay near Sea World. Swimming, tennis, Jacuzzi, private yacht (owned by the hotel), rental sailboats. Live entertainment nightly. Foreign currency exchange. 355 rooms, $88–$116.

Seapoint Hotel, 4875 N. Harbor Dr., San Diego, (619) 224–3621, (800) 854–2900 nationwide, (800) 532–3737 in California.
Located in Point Loma near sportfishing docks, close to airport. Swimming pool, Jacuzzi, sauna. Coffee shop, complimentary *Wall Street Journal*. 212 rooms, $64–$79.

Sheraton Harbor Island Hotel, 1380 Harbor Island Dr., San Diego, (619) 291–2900, (800) 325–3535.
Located adjacent to airport, near downtown. Balconies have view of San Diego Bay. Lighted tennis courts, private beach, yacht cruises, putting green, exercise room and sauna, convention facilities, foreign currency exchange, rooftop lounge with splendid view of Bay and city. 750 rooms, $100–$120.

Town & Country Hotel, 500 Hotel Circle Dr., San Diego, (619) 219–7131, (800) 854–2608 nationwide, (800) 542–6082 in California.
Gigantic hotel with convention facilities 5 miles from airport. Gift shops, beauty parlor, saunas, shuffleboard, ping pong, Jacuzzi, swimming pool. Guests may work out at the Atlas Health Club. Dining and entertainment. 1000 rooms, $65–$90.

Vacation Village Hotel, 1404 W. Vacation Rd., San Diego, (619) 274–4630, (800) 854–2179

nationwide, (800) 542–6275 in California.
Complete resort facilities on Mission Bay near San Diego Zoo and Sea World. Swimming, tennis, sailing, bicycling, game room, shuffleboard. Kitchen units available. Restaurant, coffee shop, nightly entertainment in lounge. 450 rooms, $68–$98.

Restaurants

Los Angeles Area (are code 213 unless otherwise noted)

The Apple Pan, 10801 W. Pico Blvd., Westwood, 475–3585.
Undiscovered by tourists, but an obsessive haunt for locals. No tables; simply a ring of seats around a counter. People wait behind the seat for their turn at eating, as though this were a gastronomic ride. It is. Basic fare: greasy steakburgers, coffee, apple pie a la mode. Pure Americana, something out of an Edward Hopper painting. Avoid the lunch rush. Very inexpensive.

Canter's, 419 N. Fairfax Ave., Los Angeles, 651–2030.
Movie stars who need to gain 20 pounds in a jiffy tend to hang out at this great deli in the midst of the Jewish district. The waitresses call you "sweetheart," and the ambiance looks like something from a Fifties movie. Go for the *kreplach* soup, *latkes* (potato pancakes), lean corned beef on rye with a pickle, and fattening array of breads and cakes. Open 24 hours, this place is buzzing at four on a Saturday morning. Inexpensive.

Chasen's, 9039 Beverly Blvd., Los Angeles, 271–2168.
This is where locals go to celebrate selling their first screenplay. Try the hobo steak serve. *Continental food*. Very expensive, but definitely worth the experience, even if you can only afford the banana shortcake or the chili.

Dar Maghreb, 7651 Sunset Blvd., Los Angeles, 876–7651.
The best Moroccan restaurant west of Casablanca. Also one of the finest restaurants in Los Angeles. Wash your hands at the table before eating the *couscous* and watching the belly dancers.

El Cid, 4212 Sunset Blvd., Los Angeles, 668–0318.
Have *shrimp Puerta Vallarta* while watching flamenco dancers amidst the decor of a 16th Century Spanish taverna. Mexican food moderately priced, with shows on Thurs. to Sun. at 7:30, 9, and 11.

Gilbert's Restaurant, 2526 Pico Blvd., Santa Monica, 452–9841.
There are a lot of good Mexican restaurants in LA, but this one is the real thing: it's a crowded dive that puts all its attention on the food. Try

the *mole* (moh-lay), or make a meal out of the *albondigas* soup and fresh corn *tortillas*. Decidedly inexpensive.

Gladstone's 4 Fish, 17300 Pacific Coast Highway, Pacific Palisades, GL-4-FISH.
Take an evening drive along the Pacific Coast Highway and watch the sunset from an oceanfront table. The only thing between you and the ocean is 20 feet of sand. Live Maine lobster, excellent chowder. $8–$20 per person.

The Good Earth Restaurants, 17212 Ventura Blvd, Encino, 986–9990; 23397 Mulholand Dr., Woodland Hills, 888–6300; 1002 Westwood Blvd., Westwood, 208–8215; 4730 Lincoln Blvd., Marina del Rey, 822–9033.
Inexpensive gourmet health food; get a soup and half-sandwich on their 10-grain bread with their house blend tea. A chance to observe *health fanaticus*, a species of person prevalent in Southern California.

Harry's Bar and Grill, 2020 Avenue of the Stars, Century City, 277–2333.
An excellent Italian restaurant. This place is always crowded as people eat here before taking in a play at the Schubert Theater. This is where the Hemingway Writing Contest is held.

Lawry's the Prime Rib, 55 N. La Cienega Blvd., Los Angeles, 652–2827.
Here's the most concise menu in the city: one entree. It's roast beef, and they roll it right up to you on a cart so you can specify which cut you want. The salad is prepared at your table in a little production that allows the waiters (often out-of-work actors) a chance to perform.

L' Ermitage, 730 N. La Cienega Blvd., Los Angeles, 652–5840.
The conversation is a tad quiet here because of a mutual respect among patrons who come to appreciate the elegant interior and the creative cuisine. French/continental cuisine. Superb veal and duckling. Expensive.

Ma Maison, 8368 Melrose Ave., Los Angeles, 655–1991.
It's loud, and you feel like you're at a wedding reception underneath a canopy in someone's backyard, but the food is superb, the waiters are highly amusing, and it's a popular hangout among the Hollywood celebrities. Famous for the number of Rolls Royces its parking lot has on any given night. Expensive, but well worth it.

Mario's, 1001 Broxton Ave., Westwood, 208–7077.
One of the best restaurants in Westwood, and it's moderately priced. Italian cuisine; both the minestrone and the cannelloni are fabulous. A big bonus for those people trying to wake up before seeing a film in Westwood Village: the coffee is superb. Reservations a must on weekends.

Mischa's, 7561 Sunset Blvd., Los Angeles, 874–3467.
Russian and Continental cuisine, including *beef Stroganoff, veal Mischa, chicken Czar Alexander, bouillabaisse*, and *shashlick*. Sample a number of exotic vodkas while watching gypsy dancers perform on stage. Closed Monday. $10–$25 per person.

Otto's Pink Pig, 4958 Van Nuys Blvd., Sherman Oaks, 788–9971.
Memorable for its name and for its cherry pie. Basic American food: steak, chicken, beef liver, fish — served in large portions. Special Early Bird dinner from 4 p.m.

The Pantry, 877 S. Figueroa, Los Angeles.
Don't bother calling — they're always open; in fact, the last time they closed the front door was on Christmas in 1924. Basically just a coffee shop, but the steak and eggs are fabulous. Lots of atmosphere because it's always crowded. Don't be surprised if you have to wait for a table — even if it's three in the morning. Inexpensive.

Perino's, 4101 Wilshire Blvd., Los Angeles, 383–1221.
For years, this restaurant has been considered one of the top 10 in the city. Elegant 18th Century decor with lots of fresh flowers. Continental cuisine, featuring veal, fish, and pasta. Expensive.

Phoenicia, 343 N. Central Ave., Glendale, 956–7800.
The menu presents a veritable gastronomical museum — specialties include *La Sole Souffles Cleopatre* (stuffed Dover sole with white wine & truffle sauce), and *L' Evantail de Veau Phoenicia* (sweetbreads, kidneys, chanterelles with Madeira & foie gras). Superb wine list. Not as expensive as it sounds.

Rex Ristorante, 617 So. Olive St., Los Angeles, 627–2300.
Fine dining and dancing in Art Deco surroundings. Features "nuova cucina" — state-of-the-art Italian cuisine made only with fresh ingredients. Expansive wine cellar, very expensive food, home-made ice cream. Closed Sundays.

RJ's the Rib Joint, 252 North Beverly Drive, Beverly Hills, CR-4-RIBS.
The best hickory-smoked beef and pork ribs in the city. Also barbecued chicken and duck, steaks, live Maine lobster, steamed clams, and over 50 brands of beer. Famous for its eclectic salad bar.

Saigon Flavor Restaurant, 1044 S. Fairfax, Los Angeles, 935–1564.
Vietnamese cuisine. *Salted rock crab, crab claws wrapped in shrimp, char-broiled shrimp balls on sugar cane.* Closed Tuesday.

Sarno's Cafe Dell' Opera, 1714 N. Vermont Ave., Los Angeles, 662–3403.

The original opera restaurant — your waiter will serve you food and then bellow out an aria from *Don Giovanni* before getting your capucino. Try the lasagne or trout. And remember to sit away from the front door if you have sensitive ears. $8-$15 per person.

Scandia, 9040 Sunset Blvd., West Hollywood, 278-3555.
The most elegant restaurant on the Sunset Strip, and one of the best in the city. Scandinavian/Continental cuisine featuring *veal Oskar, Gravlaks, Hamlets Dagger,* and a basket of exotic breads on every table. Jackets required for men, closed Monday. More than one big movie deal has been consummated in the Danish Room here. Expensive.

Spago, 8795 Sunset Blvd., West Hollywood, 652-4025.
Owner/chef Wolfgang Puck is the Picasso of gastronomy. No effort is spared to procure the very best — whether it be Santa Barbara shrimp, Sonoma County baby lamb, or California goat cheese. The pizzas are wild — try the one with the homemade duck sausage. Superb pastries and wine list. Better than Disneyland if you've got a few bucks to burn.

Tommy's Burgers, 2575 Beverly at Ramparts, Los Angeles.
If you drive around Los Angeles long enough, you'll see a number of burger dives with similar names: Tom's, Tom's No. 5, and so forth. The idea is to get you confused. Don't fall for it — the original is Tommy's, and the chili dogs and chili burgers are legendary. Root beer, fries. Leave your credit cards at home. Inexpensive.

The Twin Dragon, 8597 W. Pico Blvd., Los Angeles, 655-9805.
In a city with dozens of good Chinese restaurants, this is one of the best. Specialties from Shanghai include *mu-shu pork,* and *spicy chicken.* $6-$12 per person.

Yamashiro, 1999 N. Sycamore Ave., Hollywood, 466-5126.
Located at the top of the first hill north or Hollywood Boulevard, the Sky Room offers the best dining view in the city. Award-winning Japanese and Continental cuisine includes *sushi, Bijoux de la Mer,* and *Tournedos Imperiale.* Expensive.

San Diego Area (area code 619)

Anthony's Star of the Sea Room, Harbor Drive at Ash, San Diego, 232-7408.
Fabulous seafood served with dramatic flair in formal atmosphere. Known for their abalone and salmon, as well as superb chowder. Jackets required, reservations necessary. Located right on the water.

Casa de Pico, 2754 Calhoun St., San Diego, 296-3267.

Located in the Bazaar del Mundo in Old Town. Fine Mexican food, great margaritas. Entertainment nightly. Inexpensive.

Le Ste. Maxime, 1250 Prospect Ave., La Jolla, 454-2434.
Quaint French inn atmosphere a block from the beach. Go for the *tournedos,* or the *coquilles de fruits de mer.* Expensive, but romantic.

Lubach's, 2101 Harbor Dr., San Diego, 232-5129.
Known for having the best steaks in the city. Jackets required. Expensive.

Mister A's, 2550 Fifth Ave., San Diego, 239-1377.
The specialty is rack of lamb. Great panoramic view of Balboa Park and the Bay. Jackets required, reservations recommended. Expensive.

North China, 5043 N. Harbor Dr., San Diego, 224-3568.
Superb Mandarin and Szechuan cuisine. Specialties include *mu shu pork,* and *Hunan beef.* Nightly demonstrations of the ancient art of noodlemaking. Moderately priced.

Old Trieste, 2335 Morena Blvd., San Diego, 276-1841.
For years one of the best Italian restaurants in San Diego. The fish is superb; so is the veal. Closed Sunday and Monday. Expensive.

Reuben E. Lee, 880 E. Harbor Island Dr., San Diego, 291-1974.
Dine aboard a genuine Mississippi steamboat; great view of the surrounding harbor and interesting interior make it more than a dining experience. The kids love it. Moderate-expensive.

Top of the Cove, 1216 Prospect St., La Jolla, 454-7779.
Site of many a perfect romantic evening: great food, extensive wine list, lovely atmosphere — and you can take a moonlit walk on the beach when you're done. Expensive, but memorable.

Orange County and South Beach Cities (area code 714, unless otherwise noted)

Acapulco Mexican Restaurant, 1410 S. Harbor Blvd., Anaheim, 956-7380.
Award-winning Mexican food right across from Disneyland. Go for the *crabmeat enchilada.* Superb margaritas.

Alfredo's, The Westin South Coast Plaza, 666 Anton Blvd., Costa Mesa, 540-1550.
Award-winning menu featuring veal, beef, seafood, and pasta while listening to harpist Nancy Garf. Complete wine list. Moderately priced.

Anthony's World Famous Pier 2, 103 N. Bayside Dr., Newport Beach, 640-5260; also opposite Disneyland at 1640 S. Harbor Blvd., Anaheim, 774-0322.
The claim in the name is the only thing to ques-

tion. The food's a fabulous value. One pound of shrimp for $2.95. Eclectic salad bar with over 60 items. Over 300 types of California wines. Moderately priced, with free oysters and clams during Happy Hour.

Benihana of Tokyo, 2100 E. Ball Road, Anaheim, 774-4940; also 4250 Birch St., Newport Beach, 955-0822.
   Worth it just for the show: Teppanyaki-style cooking (they cook it right at your table) by a fleet of personal chefs who have one thing in common: ultra-quick hands. Specialties include *Teppan Steak*, shrimp, and lobster.

Bob Burns Restaurant, 500 N. Euclid St., Anaheim, 772-2130; also 37 Fashion Island, Newport Beach, 644-2030.
   American/Continental cuisine in a warm Scottish atmosphere. Specialties include *Caesar salad*, steak, and seafood. Moderately priced.

The Cellar Restaurant, 305 N. Harbor Blvd., Fullerton, 525-5682.
   Superb French cuisine, expansive wine cellar. A bit of elegance only 4 miles from Disneyland.

Five Crowns, 3801 East Coast Highway, Corona del Mar, 760-0331.
   Award-winning food served in a beautiful 2-story building patterned after Ye Olde Bell, England's oldest inn. Specialties include prime rib, rack of lamb, and duck. Huge wine cellar. Moderate.

Maxwell's, Huntington Beach Pier, 536-2555.
   Fabulous oceanview dining; *live Maine lobster*, a variety of fresh fish, prime rib. Moderately priced, very romantic.

Ruby Begonia's, 1500 S. Raymond Ave., Fullerton, 635-9000.
   Tiffany stained glass, Victorian furnishings. Try the *Steak Diane*, or other specialities such as *Veal Piccata*, and *Cioppino*. Dancing on Tuesday to Saturday nights. Moderate.

Rusty Scupper, 7887 Center Ave., Huntington Beach, 895-3444.
   Fresh seafood menu features *Shrimp New Orleans*, *Bouillabaisse*, seafood pasta, prime rib, and Australian lobster tail. Happy hour 4-7 p.m. Moderate.

Other Areas

Palm Springs

Banducci's Bit of Italy, 1260 S. Palm Canyon Dr., Palm Springs, (619) 325-2537.
   Steak, lobster, and homemade canelloni prepared to perfection. Open 5 p.m. to 11 p.m. nightly with live entertainment. Moderately priced.

Elmer's Pancake and Steak House, 1030 E. Palm Canyon Dr., Palm Springs, (619) 327-8419.

The most crowded place in town on weekend mornings; it offers 25 varieties of pancakes and waffles including the delicious German pancake that looks like a blonde leather bowl. Dinner menu offers fine steaks and seafood. Inexpensive.

Gaston's, Bank of Palm Springs Center, 777 Tahquitz-McCallum Way, Palm Springs, (619) 320-7750.
   Voted Restaurant of the Year by *Palm Springs Life*. Classical French cuisine in an elegant setting. Piano bar from 8 p.m. nightly, luncheon fashion shows every Tuesday.

Kobe Steak House, Hwy. 111 at Frank Sinatra Drive, Rancho Mirage, (619) 324-1717.
   Hibachi-style steak and chicken in a replica of a 300-year-old Japanese country inn.

Ventura

Andy's Barbecue Heaven & Saloon, 211 E. Santa Clara, Ventura, (805) 648-3011.
   Pig out on barbecue ribs and chicken; also fresh fish and shrimp on a skewer. Great BBQ sandwiches for lunch. Dancing to live music evenings. Moderate.

Santa Barbara

Eleven Twenty-Nine, 1129 State Street, Santa Barbara, (805) 963-7704.
   Crepes, omelettes, quiche, seafood, veal in garden patio setting or indoors with plants hanging all around you. Entertainment nightly. Moderate.

Penelope's, 50 Los Patos Way, Montecito, (805) 969-0307.
   Just a few miles north of Santa Barbara across from the Bird Refuge. "California cuisine," expansive wine list, interior features paintings by contemporary American artists. Entertainment nightly. Moderate.

Nightspots

Comedy/Magic

Comedy Store, 8433 Sunset Blvd., 656-6225.
   King of the comedy clubs, seven or eight comedians per night. Robin Williams occasionally drops by to try out new material here. There are also Comedy Stores in Westwood and La Jolla.

Comedy and Magic Club, 1018 Hermosa Ave., Hermosa Beach, 372-1193.
   On a typical night there will be one magician and two comedians. Full menu for dinner before the show.

The Improv, 8162 Melrose Ave., West Hollywood, 651-2583.
   Major comedy showcase, with successful comics going on to TV and Vegas.

The Laff Shop, 17271 Ventura Blvd., Encino, 501–3737.
A chain of clubs featuring food and comedy.

Funny You Should Ask, 1140 N. Fairfax, Los Angeles, 659–7878.
Wacky improvisational group performs Saturdays.

Ed Wynn Comedy Lounge, 940 S. Figueroa St., downtown LA, 623–9100.

The Deli Smoker, 14513 Ventura Blvd., Sherman Oaks, 990–8650.

The Laugh Factory, 8001 Sunset Blvd., Los Angeles, 656–8860.

Dancing

Chippendale's, 3739 Overland Ave., W. Los Angeles, 838–8411.
Known for their "Women Only" nights, when exotic male dancers take the stage. Also famous for its catalog which features, ahem, above-mentioned male dancers. Tuesdays is for one of LA's sport creations: female mud wrestling. Big dance floor with deejay.

Le Hot Club, 15910 Ventura Bldv., Encino, 986–7034.
Backgammon tables, posh bar and popular disco.

Playboy Club, ABC entertainment Center, 2020 Avenue of the Stars, Century City, 277–2777.
A private club; an entrance key costs $25 and will bring in guests, so go in a group.

The Red Onion is a chain of restaurant/discos with locations in the Valley, Beverly Hills, Marina del Rey, and mid Wilshire.
All are popular dancing spots with full bar and a deejay.

The Speakeasy, 8531 Santa Monica Blvd., W. Hollywood, 657–4777.

Studio One, 652 N. LaPeer Dr., W. Hollywood, 659–047.
Large, predominantly gay disco.

The Tapestry, 10177 Reseda Blvd., Northbridge, 993–7071.
Young crowd, progressive music.

Tennessee Gin and Cotton, 19710 Ventura Blvd., Woodland Hills, 347–4044.
Two dance floors; one has live rock and roll, the other is a disco.

Music

Rock & Pop

At My Place, 1026 Wilshire Blvd., Santa Monica, 451–8596.

Acts range from comedy to jazz to big band music.

Club 88, 11784 Pico Blvd., West Los Angeles, 479–6923.
Features new wave and rock and roll nightly.

Country Club, 18415 Sherman Way, Reseda, 881–5604.
Everything from hard rock to African spiritual music.

Golden Bear, 306 Coast Highway, Huntington Beach, (714) 536–9600.
Has hosted rock, folk, and blues artists.

Madame Wong's, 949 Sun Mun Way, Los Angeles, 624–5346, and **Madame Wong's West**, 2900 Wilshire Blvd., Santa Monica, 829–7361, are ideal places to hear new wave music. Moderately priced, with electronic games.

McCabe's, 3101 Pico Blvd., Santa Monica, 828–4497.
Well-known folk, acoustic rock, and bluegrass artists perform in a room adjacent to the finest guitar shop in the city.

Perkin's Palace, 129 N. Raymond Ave., Pasadena, 796–7001.
Features the more main stream of the new wave acts for a young crowd.

The Troubador, 9081 Santa Monica Blvd., West Hollywood, 276–1158.
Features new wave artists.

Jazz

The Baked Potato, 3787 Cahuenga Blvd., North Hollywood, 980–1615.
Small and funky; they serve, of course, baked potatoes.

Concerts by the Sea, 100 Fisherman's Wharf, Redondo Beach, 379–4998.
Stylish, expensive club with valet parking, three shows nightly.

Donte's, 4269 Lankershim Blvd., North Hollywood, 877–8347.
Dinner and jazz by well-known artists.

The Lighthouse, 30 Pier Ave., Hermosa Beach, 372–6911.

Parisian Room, 4960 W. Washington Blvd., Los Angeles, 936–8704.

Country

Crazy Horse Steakhouse and Saloon, Dyer Road, Santa Ana, (714) 549–1512.

The Palomino, 6907 Lankershim Blvd., North Hollywood, 764–4010.
Hippest country bar you ever saw; loud and

occasionally rowdy. Top notch acts like Jerry Jeff Walker and Lynn Anderson. Sunday barbecue $2.95.

Airlines

Aerolineas Argentinas	(213) 683–1633
Aeromexico	(213) 380–6030
Air Bahia	(800) 532–3933
Air California	(213) 627–5401
Air Canada	(213) 776–7000
Air France	(213) 625–7171
Air New Zealand	(213) 629–5454
American Airlines	(213) 937–6811
Aspen Airways	(800) 525–0256
Avianca Airlines	(800) 327–9899
British Airways	(213) 272–8866
C & M	(714) 377–4442
Capitol	(213) 986–8445
China Airlines	(213) 624–6160
Cochise Airlines	(800) 528–7060
Continental Airlines	(213) 772–6000
CP Air	(213) 625–0131
Delta Air Lines	(213) 386–5510
Eastern Air Lines	(213) 380–2070
Ecuatoriana	(800) 327–1337
El Al Israel Airlines	(800) 223–6700
Finnair	(800) 223–5700
Frontier Airlines	(213) 617–3606
Golden Carriage	(805) 238–0321
Golden Gate	(213) 777–0725
Golden West	(213) 646–3954
Icelandair	(800) 223–5500
Imperial	(800) 542–6158
Inland Empire	(800) 472–1718
Japan Airlines	(213) 620–9580
Jet America	(213) 595–0565
KLM	(213) 776–6300
Korean Airlines	(213) 484–1900
LACSA	(800) 327–7700
Lufthansa	(800) 645–3880
Mexicana	(213) 646–9500
Muse Air	(213) 621–2828
Northwest Orient	(213) 380–1511
Pan American	(213) 679–0171
Premiere Airlines	(213) 772–7137
PSA	(213) 646–9222
Qantas	(800) 622–0850
Republic Airlines	(213) 640–2540
SAS	(213) 652–8600
Singapore Airlines	(213) 620–8581
Southwest Airlines	(213) 880–6022
Sun Aire	(800) 472–4392
Swift Aire	(800) 591–5900
Texas International	(800) 231–0666
Thai Airways	(800) 426–5030
TWA	(213) 483–1100
United Airlines	(213) 772–2121
UTA French Airlines	(213) 625–7171
Varig Brazilian Airlines	(213) 646–2190
Western Airlines	(213) 646–4311
World Airways	(800) 772–2600

Transportation

Bus Charters (Private)

Advanced Bus Charter System, 22949 Ventura Blvd., Woodland Hills, CA 91364, (213) 999–5353.

American Sightseeing Tours, 1902 National Ave., San Diego, CA 92113, (619) 232–7579.

Arrow Charter Lines, Inc., PO Box 880, Huntington Park, CA 90255, (213) 581–6255. Deluxe service at competitive prices.

Associated Charter Bus Co., 5950 St. Andrews Pl., Los Angeles, CA 90047, (213) 873–4171. LA's largest fleet of economy buses.

FunBus Systems, Inc., 304 Katella Way, Anaheim, CA 92802, (714) 635–8360. Offers a narrated ride from San Diego to Anaheim.

Safeway Lines and Tour Company, 1922 E. Gage, Los Angeles, CA 90001, (213) 589–3367. Dependable transportation for over 50 years.

Sundance Stage Lines, 3762 Main St., San Diego, CA 92113, (619) 263–6641.

Limousines and Helicopters

Beta Helicopters, 6129 Baltimore Dr., La Mesa, CA 92041, (619) 292–1252. For a tour of San Diego by air.

The Limousine Connection, 5437 Laurel Canyon Blvd., North Hollywood, CA 91607, (213) 766–4311. Featuring Presidential stretch limousines.

Security Limousines Services, Atlantic Richfield Plaza, Box 71184, Los Angeles, 90071, (213) 641–2744.

V.I.P. Limousine Service, Inc., 8960 Shoreham Drive, Los Angeles, CA 90069, (213) 273–1505. Limos, minibuses, guided tours.

Rent-a-car

Ajax Rent A Car, (800) 262–1776. Anaheim (714) 991–6810. Beverly Hills (213) 278–0601. Burbank (213) 845–2681. Chula Vista (619) 426–3433. El Cajon (619) 440–1156. Fullerton (714) 738–5216. Long Beach (213) 597–8428. Los Angeles (213) 746–1626 or (213) 776–8860. Newport Beach (714) 549–8633. Palm Springs (619) 324–8288. San Diego (619) 232–3191. Santa Barbara (805) 682–1790. Santa Monica (213) 3 2–8315. Studio City (213) 766–4272.

Avis, (800) 331–1212. Los Angeles-downtown (213) 481–2000. Los Angeles International Airport (213) 646–5600. Burbank Airport (213) 985–2302. San Diego (619) 231–7143. Avis has over 50 locations in Southern California; check the phone directory for the location nearest you.

Budget Rent A Car of Century City, (213) 475–9827.

Budget Rent A Car Downtown LA, (800) 527–0700. At the Bonaventure Hotel (213) 624–1000.

Dollar Rent A Car, (800) 421-6868. Anaheim (714) 750–2886. Beverly Hills (213) 652–2600. Buena Park (714) 523–3441. Burbank (213) 846–4471. Claremont (714) 621–9853. Disneyland (714) 776–8460. Hollywood (213) 466–6387. La Jolla (619) 459–9789. Los Angeles (213) 623–2404. LAX (213) 645–9333. Marina del Rey (213) 823–2077. Mission Bay (619) 222–0367. Ontario (714) 986–4541. Palm Springs (619) 325–7333. Santa Barbara (805) 962–8111.

Hertz Rent A Car, (800) 654–3131. Anaheim (714) 772–0425. Beverly Hills (213) 553–8444. Burbank (213) 846–8220. Century City (213) 277–0015. Encino (213) 788–3991. Glendale (213) 244–8654. Hollywood (213) 462–6991. Laguna Beach (714) 499–1616. LAX (213) 646–2851. Los Angeles (213) 626–3225. Marina del Rey (213) 322–6167. Newport Beach (714) 673–4600. Ontario (714) 986–2024. Palm Springs (619) 327–1523. Pasadena (213) 795–8634. Santa Monica (213) 391–1282. Universal City (213) 460–6991. Westwood (213) 478–0473.

National Car Rental, (800) 327–4567. Anaheim-Disneyland (714) 774–6250. Beverly Hills (213) 273–8550. LAX (213) 670–4950. Downtown Los Angeles (213) 626–8550. Long Beach Airport (213) 421–8877. Ontario Airport (714) 988–7444. Orange County Airport (714) 546–1364. Oxnard Airport (805) 985–6100. Palm Springs Airport (714) 327–4100. San Diego Airport (714) 231–7100.

Foreign Missions and Consulates

Argentina
350 S. Figueroa St., 687–8884.

Australia
3550 Wilshire Blvd., 380–0980.

Barbados Board of Tourism
3440 Wilshire Blvd., 380–2198.

Belgium
3921 Wilshire Blvd., 385–8116.

Brazil
5900 Wilshire Blvd., Suite 650, 937–4044.

Canada
510 W. 6th St., 627–9511.

Chile
619 S. Olive St., 624–6357.

Denmark
3440 Wilshire Blvd., 387–4277.

Dominican Republic
548 S. Spring St., 627–3361.

Ecuador
548 S. Spring St., 628–3014.

El Salvador
408 S. Spring St., 680–4343.

Estonia
1053 Vine St., 463–5542.

French Government Tourist Office
9401 Wilshire Blvd., Beverly Hills, 272–2661.

Germany
6435 Wilshire Blvd., 852–0441.

Great Britain
3701 Wilshire Blvd., 385–7381.

Greek National Tourist Organization
611 W. 6th St., 626–6696.

Guyana
2950 Los Feliz Blvd., 666–3243.

Honduras
548 S. Spring St., 623–2301.

Hong Kong Trade Development Council
350 S. Figueroa St., 622–3194.

Iceland
6290 Sunset Blvd., 981–6464.

Indonesia
645 S. Mariposa Ave., 383–5126.

Industrial Development Authority of Ireland
1821 Wilshire Blvd., Santa Monica, 829–0081.

Israel
6380 Wilshire Blvd., 651–5700.

Italian Trade Commissioner
1801 Avenue of the Stars, 879–0950.

Japan
250 E. 1st St., Suites 1401/1507, 624–8305.

Jordan
2049 Century Park East, 557–2243.

Kenya
9100 Wilshire Blvd., Beverly Hills, 274–6635.

Korea
5455 Wilshire Blvd., 931–1331.

Lebanon
1680 Vine St., 462–5384.

Liberia
4757 S. Broadway, 232–2535.

Luxembourg
516 Avondale Ave., 394–2532.

Malaysian Trade Commission
350 S. Figueroa St., 617–1000.

Malta
5428 E. Beverly Blvd., 685–6365.

Mexico
125 Paseo de la Plaza, 624–3261.

Netherlands
3460 Wilshire Blvd., 380–3440.

New Zealand
10960 Wilshire Blvd., Westwood, 477–8241.

Nicaragua
548 S. Spring St., 629–4367.

Norway
350 S. Figueroa St., 626–0338.

Paraguay
4 Alegria St., Irvine, (714) 731–7685.

Peru
1212 Wilshire Blvd., 975–1152.

Philippines
2975 Wilshire Blvd., 387–5321.

Romanian Trade Promotion Office
350 S. Figueroa St., 614–1104.

Singapore Trade Development Board
350 S. Figueroa St., Suite 170, 617–7358.

South Africa
9107 Wilshire Blvd., Beverly Hills, 858–0380

Spain
5455 Wilshire Blvd., 931–1284.

Sweden
10960 Wilshire Blvd., Westwood, 473–0901.

Switzerland
3440 Wilshire Blvd., Suite 817, 388–4127.

Taiwan Trade Information Service
350 S. Figueroa St., 628–8761.

Thailand
3450 Wilshire Blvd., 380–4400.

Venezuela
1052 W. 6th St., 977–0996.

Western Samoa
3422 Madera Ave., 666–2154.

Anaheim Area Visitor and Convention Bureau
800 W. Katella Ave., Anaheim, CA 92802, (714) 999–8999

Beverly Hills Visitors and Convention Bureau
239 S. Beverly Dr., Beverly Hils, CA 90212, (213) 271–8174.

Big Bear Lake Valley Chamber of Commerce
520 Bartlett Rd., PO Box 2860, Big Bear Lake, CA 92315, (714) 866–4601

Buena Park Visitor and Convention Bureau
6696 Beach Blvd., PO Box 5308, Buena Park, CA 90622, (714) 994–1511.

Escondido Visitors and Information Bureau
720 N. Broadway, Escondido, CA 92025, (619) 745–4741

Goleta Valley Chamber of Commerce
5902 Calle Real, Goleta, CA 93017, (805) 967–4618.

Hollywood Chamber of Commerce
6324 Sunset Blvd., Hollywood, CA 90028, (213) 469–8311.

Long Beach Convention and Tourism Bureau
300 E. Ocean Blvd., Long Beach, CA 90802, (213) 436–3645.

Oceanside Economic Development Council
510 Fourth, Oceanside, CA 92054, (619) 722–1534.

Oxnard Convention and Visitors Bureau
325 Esplanade Drive, Oxnard, CA 93030, (805) 485–8833.

Palm Springs Convention and Visitors Bureau
Municipal Airport Terminal, Palm Springs CA 92262, (619) 327–8411.

San Diego Convention and Visitors Bureau
1200 Third Ave., Suite 824, San Diego, CA 92101, (619) 232–3101.

Santa Barbara Chamber of Commerce
1301 Santa Barbara, PO Box 299, Santa Barbara, CA 93102, (805) 965–3021.

Ventura Visitors and Convention Bureau
785 S. Seward Ave., Ventura, CA 93001, (805) 648–2075.

Tourist Centers

Greater Los Angeles Visitors and Convention Bureau
505 S. Flower, Los Angeles, CA 90071, (213) 488–9100.

Further Reading

General

American Automobile Association. *Tour Book: California/Nevada*. 1983.

Barton, Bruce W. *The Tree at the Center of the World*. Santa Barbara: Ross-Erikson, 1980.

California Coastal Commission. *California Coastal Access Guide*. 1982.

Camphouse, Marjorie. *Guide to the Missions of California*. Pasadena; Ward Ritchie, 1974.

Cleberd, Frances. *Hidden Country Villages of California*. San Francisco: Chronicle Books, 1977.

Federal Writers Project. *California: A Guide to the Golden State*. New York: Hastings House, 1939.

Fradkin, Philip L. *California: The Golden Coast*. New York: Viking Press, 1974.

Hale, Dennis, and Jonathan Eisen, editors. *The California Dream*. New York: Collier, 1968.

Johnson, Paul C. *The California Missions*. Menlo Park: Lane, 1964.

Lantis, David W., Rodney Steiner and Arthur E. Karinen. *California: Land of Contrast*. Belmont: 1963.

Leadabrand, Russ. *Exploring California Byways*. Los Angeles: Westernlore Press, 1972.

Leadabrand, Russ. *Guidebook to Rural California*. Pasadena: Ward Ritchie, 1972.

McKinney, John. *California Coastal Trails*.

McWilliams, Carey. *California Country*. Duell, Sloan, Pearce, 1979.

McWilliams, Carey. *Southern California: An Island on the Land*. Santa Barbara: Peregrine Smith, 1946, 1973.

Morgan, Neil. *The California Syndrome*. Englewood Cliffs, N.J.: Prentice-Hall. 1963.

Rapoport, Roger, and Margot Lind. *The California Catalogue*. New York: E.P. Dutton, 1977.

Sunset Travel Guide to Southern California. Menlo Park: Lane, 1970.

Tavenner, Blair. *Seeing California: A Guide to the State*. Boston: Little, Brown and Co., 1948.

Thomas, Earl. *Back Roads of California*. New York: Clarkson N. Potter, 1983.

Wright, Ralph B., editor. *California's Missions*. Arroyo Grande: Hubert A. Lowman, 1978.

Wurman, Richard Saul. *LA/Access*. San Rafael: Presidio Press, 1982.

History

Bass, Charlotta. *Forty Years' Memories From the Pages of a Newspaper*. Los Angeles: Bass, 1960.

Beck and Williams. *California: A History of the Golden State*.

Bauer, Helen. *California: Rancho Days*. New York: Doubleday, 1953.

Cleland, Robert Glass, and Glenn S. Dumke. *From Wilderness to Empire: A History of California*. New York: Alfred Knopf, 1959.

Hart, James. *A Companion to California*. New York: Oxford University Press, 1978.

Johnson, Paul C. *Pictorial History of California*. Bonanza, 1970.

Lavender, David. *California: A Bicentennial History*. New York: W.W. Norton, 1976.

Marinacci, Barbara and Rudy. *California's Spanish Place Names; What They Mean and How They Got There*. San Rafael: Presidio Press, 1980.

Parker, C. and Marilyn. *Indians to Industry*. First American, 1963.

Pitt, Leonard. *The Decline of the Californios*. Los Angeles and Berkeley: University of California Press, 1966.

Rensch, Hero Eugene. *Historic Spots in California*. Palo Alto: Stanford University Press, 1966.

Rintoul, William. *Spudding In: Recollections of Pioneer Days in the California Oil Fields*. California Historial Society, 1976.

Ziebold, Edna B. *Indians of Early Southern California*. Sapsis, 1969.

People

Beasley, Delilah. *Negro Trailblazers of California*. Los Angeles: Beasley, 1919.

Bogle, Donald. *Toms, Coons, Mulattoes, Mammies and Bucks: An Interpretive History of Blacks in American Film*. New York: Viking Press, 1973.

Bullock, Paul. *Watts: The Aftermath*. New York: Grove Press, 1969.

Forbes, Jack D. *Native Americans of California and Nevada*.

Goode, Kenneth G. *California's Black Pioneers*. Santa Barbara: McNally and Loftin, 1976.

Katz, William L. *The Black West*. Anchor, 1973.

Savage, Sherman W. *Blacks in the West*. Greenwood Press, 1976.

Arts

Andree, Herb, and Noel Young. *Santa Barbara Architecture*. Santa Barbara: Capra Press, 1975.

Gebhard and Winter, *A Guide to Architecture in Los Angeles and Southern California*.

Geography and Natural History

Brown, Vinson, and David Hoover. *California Wildlife Map Book*. Naturegraph Publishers, 1967.

Cornett, Jim. *Wildlife of the Southwest Deserts*.

Gentry, Curt. *The Last Days of the Late, Great State of California*. A book for those obsessed with a fear of earthquakes.

Hornbeck, David. *California Patterns: A Geographical and Historical Atlas*. Mayfield, 1983.

Miller, Crane, and Richard Hyslop. *California: The Geography of Diversity*. Mayfield, 1983.

Munz, Philip. *California Desert Wild Flowers*.

Rowntree, Lester. *Hardy Californians*. A classic wildflower text.

Sharp, Dr. Robert P. *Field Guide to Coastal California*. Dubuque, Iowa: Kendall/Hunt.

Sharp, Dr. Robert P. *Field Guide to Southern California*. Dubuque, Iowa: Kendall/Hunt.

Places

Los Angeles

Carr, Harry. *Los Angeles, City of Dreams*. New York: D. Appleton-Century, 1935.

Coughey, John and LaRee. *Los Angeles: Biography of a City*. Los Angeles: University of California Press, 1976.

Chapman, John L. *Incredible Los Angeles*. New York: Harper and Row, 1967.

Gilbert, Richard. *City of the Angels*. London: Seeker and Warburg, 1964.

Morris, Jan. *Destinations*. The essay on Los Angeles in this book captures perfectly the enigmatic feeling of the city.

Robinson, William. *What They Say About the Angels*. Pasadena: Val Trefy Press, 1942.

Weaver, John D. *El Pueblo Grande*. Los Angeles: Ward Ritchie, 1973.

Hollywood

Dunne, John G. *The Studio*.

Fitzgerald, F. Scott. *The Last Tycoon*. In this unfinished masterpiece, Fitzgerald dissected the Hollywood system of the 1930s and the lives of the people in the film industry.

Goldman, William. *Adventures in the Screen Trade*.

Lamparski, Richard. *Lamparski's Hidden Hollywood*.

Schulberg, Budd. *What Makes Sammy Run*.

West, Nathanael. *Day of the Locust*. One of the best novels ever written about Hollywood.

The Deserts

Ainsworth, Katherine. *The McCallum Saga: The Story of the Founding of Palm Springs*.

Fleming, Jack. *Desert Hiking Guide*.

Jaeger, Edmund C. *The California Deserts*. Palo Alto: Stanford University Press, 1965.

Kirk, Ruth. *Exploring Death Valley*. Palo Alto: Stanford University Press, 1978.

Shumway, Nina P. *Your Desert and Mine*.

Stanley, Mildred. *Salton Sea Yesterday and Today*.

Stanford University. *The California Deserts*.

Wynn, Marcia R. *Desert Bonanza*. Glendale: Arthur H. Clark, 1970.

Other Places

Howorth, Peter C. *Channel Islands: The Story Behind the Scenery*. Las Vegas: K.C. Publications, 1982.

Murray, Ken. *The Golden Days of San Simeon*. New York: Doubleday, 1971.

O'Grady, Jack. *Guide to Catalina and the Channel Islands*. 1975.

Continued from page ix

former staff writer for United Press International and *The Los Angeles Times* who once spent 18 months traveling through Europe, North Africa and the Middle East on a 10-speed bicycle. He currently works in television, writing travel documentaries and producing feature segments for *Two on the Town*. **Bob Vivian** ("Palm Springs to the Colorado"), recently appointed to the faculty of California State University, Chico, was for 11 years managing editor of *Palm Springs Life* and other journals published by Desert Publications Inc. He is the author of more than 300 magazine articles, editor of two travel guides and author of a book of satire called *The Good Humor Man*.

The feature section includes essays on aspects of life integral to the Southern California experience.

Ray Loynd ("The Industry") is a staff writer for *Daily Variety*, a prominent entertainment industry trade paper, Formerly the entertainment editor of the *Los Angeles Herald-Examiner* and a reporter and critic for the *Hollywood Reporter*, Loynd — a native of Hollywood — is the author of two books, including *A Million Dollars Down* (Dell, 1979).

Mike McDowell ("The L.A. Sound") is the editor of *Blitz* magazine, a journal devoted to the full gamut of lyrics and melodies from oldies to new wave. And **Mike Tipping** ("The Sporting Lifestyle"), a staff writer for the Santa Monica *Evening Outlook*, is a competitive distance runner, having participated in several marathon and 10-kilometer runs in the L.A. area.

The time-consuming task of compiling the Guide in Brief fell to **Bob Wolff**. Wolff, publisher of a hot-selling book entitled *Lady's Choice: The Most Eligible Bachelors in Los Angeles,* is currently writing a novel.

While the majority of photographs appearing in this book were taken by Lundberg, several other contributors deserve special mention. Foremost among them is **Mireille Vautier** and her Photothèque Vautier-de Nanxe, an important photo library in Paris, France. Vautier and her colleagues traveled extensively through California and the American Southwest for most of 1982, shooting over 1,000 rolls of film along the way. Their vision of California through European eyes lends an important aspect to this book.

Other leading photographic contributors include **Bart Bartholomew**, a Santa Monica-based photojournalist who shoots regularly for *Newsweek* and other magazines; **John Sanford**, instructor of astronomy and photography at Orange Coast Community College; **Gene Russell**, a free-lance photojournalist based in Carlsbad, north of San Diego; and **Bud Lee**, whose unusual work has appeared in such major publications as *Esquire, Life, Rolling Stone, Playboy, Time, Newsweek* and *New West*. His work was previously featured in *Insight Guide: Florida*.

Additional photos were provided by Larry Dunmire, D.J. Hawkins, Jim Hicks, Dennis Lane, Tom Lippert, C. Allan Morgan, Kal Muller, Steve Sakamoto, Chuck Schmid, Joe Viesti and Jan Whiting.

Lundberg's office manager, **Kimberli Ann Campbell**, also contributed several images to this book. A native of Southern California, she was instrumental in coordinating many aspects of this book's production, from organization and communications to gathering photographic material.

Final copy editing in Singapore was handled by expatriate American journalist **Bill Moore**, a former police reporter in Waco, Texas, and Apa assistant editor **Vivien Loo**. Loo also drew the marginal maps, designed to help readers quickly locate destinations cited in the text.

The main selection of color maps was produced by cartographers under the direction of **Günter Nelles** in Munich, West Germany. Additional maps and charts were drawn by **Yong Sock Ming. Anthony Ong** prepared the index. Editorial secretary **June Foong** provided valuable assistance.

Others who helped to make this book possible were Gail Hodge and Shirley Davy of the Catalina Island Chamber of Commerce; David L. Hutchinson of the San Diego Convention and Visitors Bureau; Linda Herman and Jane Olsen of California State University, Fullerton, special collections; the Sherman Library, Corona del Mar; the Newport Beach Chamber of Commerce; Elaine Martín-Cali of the Anaheim Visitor and Convention Bureau; and Bill Roberts of the Bancroft Library, University of California, Berkeley.

When work on a book is completed, the work of getting it to the readers begins. It would be impossible to list all of the thousands of individual bookshop owners, travel agents and special sales representatives whose multiple efforts carry this book into private homes and offices in 30 countries around the world. We wish to acknowledge with thanks their individual and collective contributions. In particular, we wish to thank Michael Hunter, head of the general publishing division of Prentice-Hall Inc., and his team of sales representatives.

— Apa Productions

ART/PHOTO CREDITS

Cover	Steve Sakamoto	50	Bret R. Lundberg	114	Bret R. Lundberg
Cover, corner	Bret R. Lundberg (Sam the Olympic eagle); Vautier de Nanxe (Knotts Berry Farm roller coaster)	51	Bart Bartholomew	115	Lee Foster
		52	Bret R. Lundberg	116	Courtesy of Marineland of the Pacific
		53	Bret R. Lundberg		
End paper, front	Courtesy of Special Collections, California State University, Fullerton	54	Bart Bartholomew	117	Bret R. Lundberg
		55	Bret R. Lundberg	118	Bret R. Lundberg
		56	Bart Bartholomew	119	Bret R. Lundberg
		57	Bret R. Lundberg	120	Bret R. Lundberg
1	Vautier-de Nanxe	58	Bret R. Lundberg	121	Bret R. Lundberg
2-3	Bret R. Lundberg	59	Bret R. Lundberg	122	Courtesy of Tournament of the Roses
4-5	Bret R. Lundberg	61	Vautier-de Nanxe		
6-7	Bret R. Lundberg	62	Bret R. Lundberg	124	G.R. Russell
8-9	Joseph F. Viesti	63	Bret R. Lundberg	125	Joseph F. Viesti
10	Bret R. Lundberg	64	Bret R. Lundberg	126-L	Bret R. Lundberg
12	Bret R. Lundberg	65	Paul Van Riel	126-R	Bret R. Lundberg
14	Bret R. Lundberg	66	Bart Bartholomew	127	Bret R. Lundberg
15-L	Bart Bartholomew	67	Vautier-de Nanxe	128	G.R. Russell
15-R	Bret R. Lundberg	68-69	Bret R. Lundberg	129	Tom Lippert
16	Bret R. Lundberg	70-71	Larry Dunmire	130	Bud Lee
18-19	Bancroft Library, University of California, Berkeley	72	Bret R. Lundberg	132	Courtesy of Special Collections, C.S.U., Fullerton
		76-77	Bret R. Lundberg		
20-21	Bancroft Library	78	Vautier-de Nanxe	133	Courtesy of Special Collections, C.S.U., Fullerton
22	Courtesy of Special Collections, C.S.U. Fullerton	79	Bret R. Lundberg		
		80	Bart Bartholomew	134	Courtesy of Universal Studios
24	Bancroft Library	81-L	Bret R. Lundberg		
25	John Sanford	81-R	Bret R. Lundberg	135-L	Vautier-de Nanxe
26	Vautier-de Nanxe	84	Bart Bartholomew	135-R	Courtesy of NBC Studios
27	Bancroft Library	85	Bret R. Lundberg	136	Bret R. Lundberg
28	Courtesy of Special Collections, C.S.U., Fullerton	87	Bret R. Lundberg	137	Bret R. Lundberg
		88	Vautier-de Nanxe	138	Vautier-de Nanxe
29	From the collection of John Sanford	89	Vautier-de Nanxe	139	Bret R. Lundberg
		90-L	Bret R. Lundberg	140	Bret R. Lundberg
30	Bancroft Library	90-R	Lee Foster	141	Vautier-de Nanxe
31	Courtesy of Sunkist Growers Inc.	91	Van Phillips	142	Bret R. Lundberg
		92	Vautier-de Nanxe	143	Bret R. Lundberg
33	Courtesy of Sherman Foundation Library	94	From the Lundberg family collection	144-145	Vautier-de Nanxe
				146	Bret R. Lundberg
34-35	Courtesy of Sherman Foundation Library	95	Vautier-de Nanxe	147	Bret R. Lundberg
		96	Bud Lee	148	Bret R. Lundberg
36	Courtesy of Sherman Foundation Library	97	Bret R. Lundberg	149	Vautier-de Nanxe
		98	Bret R. Lundberg	150	Bret R. Lundberg
37	From the Lundberg family collection	99	Vautier-de Nanxe	151	Kal Muller
		100-101	Bret R. Lundberg	153	Bret R. Lundberg
39	From the Lundberg family collection	102	Vautier-de Nanxe	154	Bret R. Lundberg
		103	Bret R. Lundberg	155	Courtesy of Buena Park Visitors and Convention Bureau
40-41	Bret R. Lundberg; courtesy of Special Collections, C.S.U. Fullerton	104	Bud Lee		
		105	Vautier-de Nanxe		
		106	Bret R. Lundberg	156-L	Vautier-de Nanxe
42	From the collection of Ken Schessler	107	Bret R. Lundberg	156-R	Bret R. Lundberg
		108-L	Vautier-de Nanxe	157	Bret R. Lundberg
43	Michael Evans, The White House	109-L	Bret R. Lundberg	158-159	Bret R. Lundberg
		109-R	Bret R. Lundberg	160	Bret R. Lundberg
44-45	Bret R. Lundberg	110-111	Bret R. Lundberg	161	Bret R. Lundberg
46	Bret R. Lundberg	112	Bret R. Lundberg	162-L	Bret R. Lundberg
48-49	Bret R. Lundberg	113	Bret R. Lundberg	162-R	Bret R. Lundberg

INDEX

P

pachucos see low-riders
Pacific Amphitheater, 153
Pacific Asia Museum, 125
Pacific Beach, 185, 186, 195
Pacific Coast Highway, 161, 162, 164, 166
Pacific Electric Railway, 37, 124
Pacific Palisades, 106, 108, 273
Pacific Southwest Railway Museum, 201
Pacific Stock Exchange, 87
Pacoima, 54, 131
padres, 25, 135, 201, 215, 225; *also see* Franciscans
Page (George C.) Museum, 99
Pageant of the Masters (Laguna Beach), *164-65,* 165
paintings, 124, 125
Pala, 200
Pala Indian Reservation, 200
Palm Canyon, 256
Palm City, 202
Palmdale, 13, 141, 142
"Palmdale Bulge," 13
Palm Desert, 258
Palm Grove, 261
Palm Springs, 73, *255,* 255-259, *259,* 303
Palm Springs Aerial Tramway, 255, *258,* 303
Palm Springs Airport, 294
Palm Springs Golf Course, 10, *255*
Palm Springs Racquet Club, 257
Palm Springs Spa Hotel, 257
Palomino, Carlos (boxer), 54
Palos Verdes Peninsula, 15, *115,* 115-16
Panama Canal, 37
Panamint Mountains, 245, *246*
Pandora's Box (nightclub), 97
Panorama City, 66
Pantages, Alexander (theater owner), 95
Pantages, The (theater), 95, 305
Paramount Studios, 270, 271
Parker, 263
Parker Dam, 39, 263
Parker, Dorothy (actress), 95
Parkinson, Donald and John (architects), 88
Pasadena, 32, 36, 59, 123-26
Pasadena Museum of Modern Art *see* Simon (Norton) Museum
Paso de Bartolo, 28
passport requirements, 204, 291
Paulhan, Louis, 36
Pearblossom, 142
Pearl Harbor, 41, 65
Pennant, The (restaurant, San Diego), 185, *186*
Performing Arts Center (El Cajon), 201
Perris, *168-69,* 177
Pickfair (mansion, Beverly Hills), 103
Pickford-Fairbanks Studio, 39
Pickford, Mary (actress), 94, 102-03, 104, 197, 228
Pico, Andrés (provisional governor), 57
Pico, Pio (governor), 57, 85
Pico House, 85
piñatas, 85
Pink Lady, The (legendary ghost), 157
Pioneer Museum, 200

Pioneertown, 265
Pioneer Village, 234
Pio Pico Casa State Historic Park, 128
Pismo Beach, 222-224
Pismo Beach State Park, 224
Pixley, 235
Placerita Canyon, 28, 141
Plaza de la Raza *see* Lincoln Park
Plaza Rio Tijuana, 204-05
Point Fermin Park, 117
Point Loma, 184, 192
Point Vicente Lighthouse, 116
Polk, James K. (president), 28
pollution *see* smog
polo *see* sports
Polo Lounge (Beverly Hills Hotel), 103, 106
Pomo weavers, 21
Pomona, 32, 123, 126, 127
Pomona Valley Fair *see* Los Angeles County Fair
poppy, California (state flower), *138,* 142, 292; *also see* flora
population, 40, 42
  Beverly Hills, 103
  Carlsbad, 197
  Chinese, 63, 64
  Chula Vista, 202
  Escondido, 198
  Hollywood, 93
  Imperial Beach, 202
  Indochinese refugees (in Orange County), 147
  Lake Havasu City, 263
  La Mesa, 200
  Long Beach, 120
  Los Angeles, 42, 81, 131
  Oceanside, 197
  Ontario, 176
  Orange County, 146
  Palm Springs, 255
  Riverside, 172
  San Bernardino, 172
  San Diego, 183, 194
  San Fernando Valley, 131
  Twentynine Palms, 26
Porterville, 235
Portman, John (architect), 88
Portolá, Gaspar de, 23-24, 107, 147, 226
Ports o' Call Village, 118
Portuguese, 23, 184
postal services, 297
potatoes, 36
Prentice Park Children's Zoo, 157
Presidio Hill, 183
Presley, Elvis (singer), 105, 108
Progressive Business League, 59
Providence Mountains (state recreation area), 250
publications, 298
Puente Hill, 123
Pyrenees, 234

Q

Quail Botanical Gardens, 197
Queen Anne Cottage and Coach Barn (1885), 124
Queen Mary (ship), 10, *110-11,* 118-19, 120, 301
Quintero, Luis, 59

R

racetracks *see* horse racing
radio, 298

Raging Waters, 127
railroads, 30-31, 37, 47, 59, 63, 64, 80, 123, 131, 172, 173
Rainbow Bar and Grill (restaurant, Hollywood), 96, 97
rainfall, 16
Ramona Bowl, 178
ranches, 10, 26, 27, 28, 131, 135, 140, 171, 174, 220, 222, 227, 250
ranchos
  California, 177
  del Cielo, 221
  La Brea, 15
  Los Alamitos, 120
  Los Cerritos, 120
  Mirage, 258
  Rodeo de las Aguas, 57
  Santa Fe, 197
Rancho Santa Ana Botanical Garden, 124
Rancho Sisquoc Winery, 222
Randall, Tony (actor), 98
Randsburg, 242
Raymond Hotel, 32, 36
Reagan, Ronald (actor-governor-president), 43, *43,* 105, 106, 221, 272
reatas (lariats), 27
Redford, Robert (actor), 93
Redlands, 59, 172, 714
Redlands Bowl, 174
Redondo Beach, 114, *114,* 115
Red Rock Canyon State Recreation Area, *240,* 241
Reeves, Richard (writer), 16
Refugio State Beach, 221
Reid (Hugh) Adobe, 124
Reseda, 131
reservations, Indian, 171; *also see* Indians *and* individual listings of tribes
restaurants, 136, 147, *161,* 166, 174, *176,* 187, 188, 195, 220, 226, 234, 300, 318-21
  continental, 136
  Chinese, 64, 85-87, 136, 300
  Japanese, 87, *148*
  Korean, 66
  Mexican, 85, 165, 300
  Thai, 66
Reyes, Francisco, 57
Reynolds, Burt (actor), 105
Richardson, J.P. "Big Bopper" (singer), 54
Rindge, Frederick H., 109
rhythm-and-blues, 275
Rialto, 173
rickshaws, 64
Ridgecrest, 243
Rio Grande (river), 28
Riverside, 32, 59, 64, 171, 172, *172,* 175, 177
Riverside International Raceway, 175, *175*
Riverside mission, 25
Riverside Municipal Museum, 176
Road Show, The (automobile exhibit), 105
Robinson, Jackie (baseball player), 60
rock 'n' roll, *274,* 275-77, *276*
Rodeo Drive (Beverly Hills), 51, 102, *103,* 104. 136, 300
Rogers Dry Lake, 142
Rogers, Will (humorist), 104, 106
Rogers (Will) State Park, 106, 301
roller skating, 107, *108,* 166